Programed Ear Training   **VOLUME IV: CHORDS,**
Part II

Programed Ear Training
Volume IV: CHORDS, PART 2

Leo Horacek and Gerald Lefkoff
West Virginia University

Under the General Editorship of
Guy Alan Bockmon
University of Tennessee

HARCOURT, BRACE & WORLD, INC.

New York   Chicago   San Francisco   Atlanta

ISBN: 0-15-572018-X

Library of Congress Catalog Number: 70-110129

Printed in the United States of America

Preface to the Instructor

PROGRAMED EAR TRAINING is designed to develop the hearing and notational skills required in the freshman and sophomore music theory courses. It consists of four programed workbooks and accompanying tape recordings that provide a complete course of study in melodic and harmonic dictation, sightsinging, and aural harmonic analysis. The four volumes are:

    I. INTERVALS
   II. MELODY AND RHYTHM
  III. CHORDS, Part I
  IV. CHORDS, Part II

The flexibility of the program makes it suitable for use in any kind of theory program. The volumes may be used singly or as a group, alone or in combination with other text materials. Except for Volume IV, which depends on Volume III, they need not be taken sequentially; experience has shown, in fact, that for some students it is more profitable to work in several volumes concurrently.

Because the course is programed, the student works entirely on his own, at his own pace. Multiple copies of each written lesson are provided, so that he can repeat lessons as often as necessary to improve his skills. As he reaches recommended levels of proficiency, he takes tests, which are provided separately to the instructor and administered under his direction. A guide to the administration and grading of the program is provided in the Instructor's Manual.

PROGRAMED EAR TRAINING was developed at West Virginia University over a seven-year period during which it was in continuous use and was constantly being revised. It has also been used at more than a dozen other colleges and universities across the country; thus it has been thoroughly tested on large and varying groups of students.

The authors would like to express appreciation to Dr. Guy Bockmon, University of Tennessee, for his careful reading of all the materials and his most helpful recommendations; to Dr. Richard E. Duncan, Dean of the Creative Arts Center, West Virginia University, who suggested and supported the project in which these books were developed; to Dr. Frank Lorince, Chairman of the Theory Department, West Virginia University, for his valuable advice and assistance; to the teachers who have used the books and offered suggestions and criticism, and finally to the many students who have worked patiently or otherwise through the program and whose reactions were always useful.

L. H.
G. L.

Contents

INTRODUCTION

This is the last of four volumes designed to help you improve your hearing and notational skills through the technique of programed instruction. This volume is a continuation of Volume III and is devoted to a number of more advanced ear-training skills, including work with non-harmonic tones, modulations, additional seventh chords, and foreign chords. For each lesson in the program, there is a tape recording that provides all the audio material you will need to complete the lesson.

Programed instruction differs from usual instruction in two ways: first, most of the work can be done with little or no help from a teacher; and second, you can progress at your own rate. Where the material is difficult for you, you can move slowly. Where you find it easy, you can move rapidly, saving time and work. A faculty advisor will probably direct and guide your work, but the responsibility for making progress is yours. Through your test scores and your scores for each of the lessons, you will always know how well you are progressing.

The basic idea of programed instruction is as follows. The material to be learned is broken into small units called *frames*. In each frame, a problem is presented and you will be asked to make a response. Immediately after this response, the correct answer is provided so that you will know whether or not your response was correct. Through many confirmations of correct responses and corrections of incorrect responses, complicated and difficult skills and concepts can be learned with ease. With the programed instruction procedures in this book, you will find that you can spend as little or as much time in any one area as you need.

For each lesson a goal has been set for you, to show you whether you are ready to move on to the next lesson. If you complete a lesson with no more than the number of errors indicated in the goal, move on to the next lesson. Otherwise you are to repeat the lesson. For this purpose five copies of every worksheet that requires a written response are provided. If after five tries you have not brought the number of errors down to the limit set in the goal, move on to the next lesson anyway.

When you have done an entire series in this fashion, take the test on that series. You will take the tests on your own, but they will be graded by your instructor. The score you will receive on each test is a *weighted score*, which means that your raw score is multiplied by a factor to compensate for the length, difficulty, and importance of the series.

The evaluation of your work will depend on the total of all your test scores rather than on an average of these scores. Therefore every test you take, even if the score is low, can help raise your grade. If you return to a series for more work in that area, you may retake the test and count the highest grade you make on that test. To help you know how well you are doing, three *achievement levels* are provided for each test.

The *first level* represents a very high degree of learning. Generally, when you have achieved this level you should not plan to return to the material in the series but should spend your time on other material.

The *second level* represents a moderate achievement. The material in the series can be considered to be reasonably well learned, but if time permits or if you wish to raise your grade, it would be practical to return to the series for further work.

The *third level* represents a rather low but nevertheless significant amount of learning. You should at some time return to the series for further work.

Normally it is most advantageous to move on from one series to the next regardless of the test scores, and then at certain points in the course go back and do further work on any series on which your test score was lower than you would like. The most profitable pattern of moving on and working back varies from student to student, and it will be best to seek the advice of your instructor when you are undecided.

The *test record sheet* that appears at the end of this volume indicates for each test the three achievement levels and the maximum possible score and provides a convenient place to keep a record of your scores.

The skills developed through this course of study are extremely valuable in almost any musical activity. Not only are they important in performing music, but they can also help you to understand music you hear, to arrange and write music, and to discuss and learn more about music.

With the method of study used in these volumes, you will find that you can work to develop such skills in a manner best suited to your particular needs and abilities. You can move slowly where you find difficulties, change to a different phase of the course if your progress has slowed down, and work at maximum speed where your competencies are strongest. This modern approach to music theory can enable you to learn these important skills in the most efficient manner possible.

Non-harmonic Tones SERIES D1

The purpose of this series is to develop your ability to identify *non-harmonic tones,* tones that are not members of the prevailing chord. There are several types of classes of non-harmonic tones, determined by the position of the non-harmonic tone in relation to the preceding and following tones in the same voice.

A non-harmonic tone is said to be *approached by step* when the interval between it and the preceding tone is a second. It is said to be *left by step* when the interval between it and the following tone is a second. Two classes of non-harmonic tones are approached and left by step: the *neighboring tone* and the *passing tone.* A *neighboring tone* is one whose preceding and following tones are identical, so that the melodic line turns at this point. A *passing tone* fills the gap between two different tones, so that the melodic line proceeds without changing direction.

A non-harmonic tone is said to be *approached by leap* when the interval between it and the preceding tone is greater than a second. A non-harmonic tone that is approached by leap and left by step is called an *appoggiatura.*

A non-harmonic tone is said to be *left by leap* when the interval between it and the following tone is larger than a second. A non-harmonic tone that is approached by step and left by leap is called an *escape tone.*

A non-harmonic tone that is the same pitch as a preceding chord tone is called a *suspension.* A suspension may be thought of as a tone held over from the preceding chord; when the chord changes the held-over tone becomes non-harmonic. The suspension may be struck when it is introduced at the chord change, repeating the previous pitch, or it may be a continuation of the preceding pitch, either with a tie or with an extended note value. When the suspension is a continuation of the previous chord tone, only the non-harmonic portion of the tone is considered to be the suspension. A suspension is usually left by step, most often downward, although occasionally it is upward.

A non-harmonic tone that is the same pitch as a following chord tone is called an *anticipation.* An anticipation may be thought of as a tone from the following chord that is introduced before the chord itself. An anticipation may be approached by step or by leap.

There are two other kinds of non-harmonic tones, the *free tone* and the *pedal tone,* which are not dealt with in this volume. A free tone, which is relatively rare, is a non-harmonic tone that is approached and left by leap. A pedal tone is a tone sustained through several chords and non-harmonic with some of those chords; thus it is fundamentally very different from the other non-harmonic tones.

The following symbols are used to label non-harmonic tones:

n   neighboring tone
p   passing tone
ap   appoggiatura
e   escape tone
s   suspension
an   anticipation

The following examples contain all the non-harmonic tones dealt with in this volume.

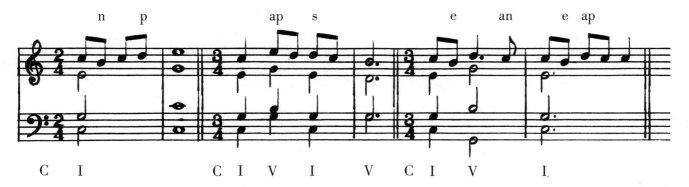

A worksheet and a tape recording are provided for each lesson in this series. In each frame, you will hear a harmonized melody containing non-harmonic tones, which you are to identify. The rhythm of the melody is notated on the printed worksheet. The answer, which consists of the symbols for the non-harmonic tones, is found below the notated rhythm. To do each frame, start by shielding the answer. When you have heard the melody, label each non-harmonic tone with the appropriate symbol; then slide the shield down and check your response. You may stop the tape while answering. Each phrase is heard only once in each frame, but you may rewind the tape for repeated hearings of each frame. In the test for this series, each frame will be heard twice so you should attempt to do each frame in no more than two hearings. Circle each non-harmonic tone that you fail to identify correctly; you may have more than one error in each frame. Your goal is to complete each lesson with no more than fourteen errors. When you have done so, go on to the next lesson. Otherwise repeat the lesson until you reach the goal or until you have done the lesson five times, at which point you should go on to the next lesson regardless of your score.

The melody is in the soprano in lessons D1–1 and D1–2, and in the bass in lesson D1–3. When you have done this series, take Test D1.

D1-1 Identification of non-harmonic tones
(Copy 1)

Shield the answer (the letters below the notes). Listen to the frame and label non-harmonic tones; then uncover the answer and compare your response. Circle tones not correctly identified. Goal: No more than fourteen errors.

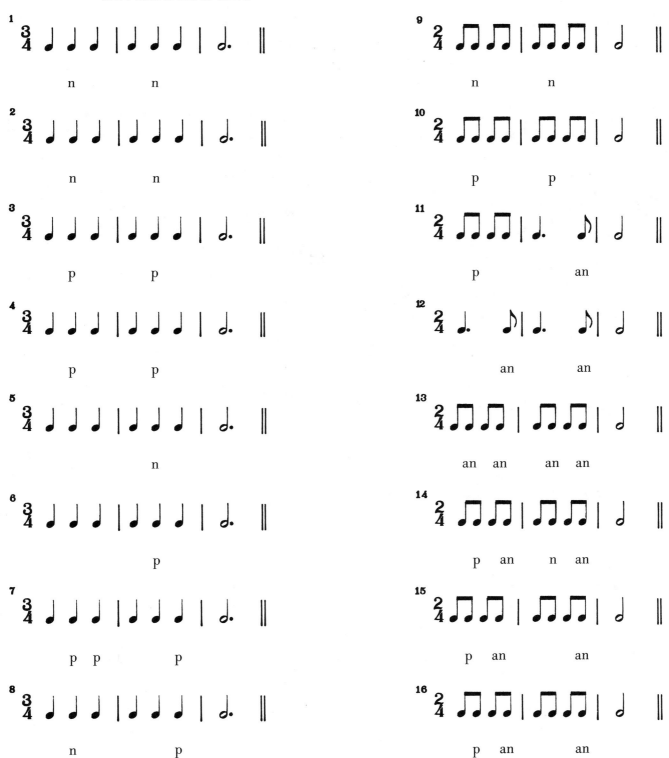

5

17
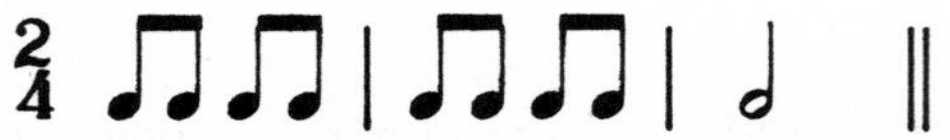

18
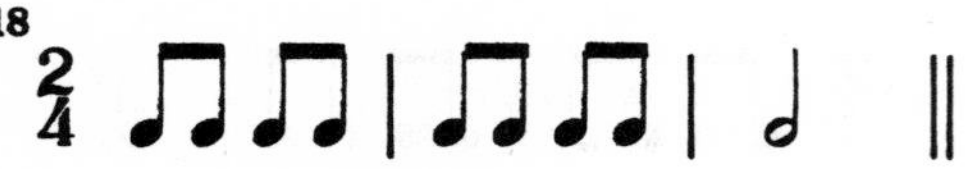

19
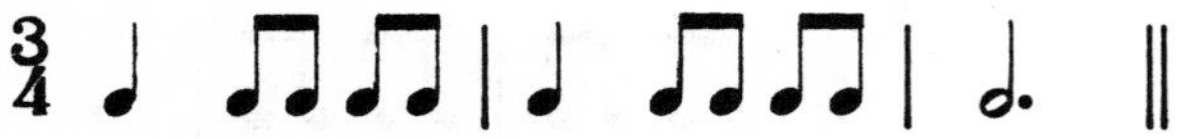

20
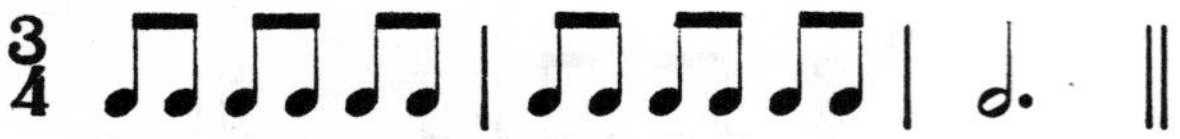

21
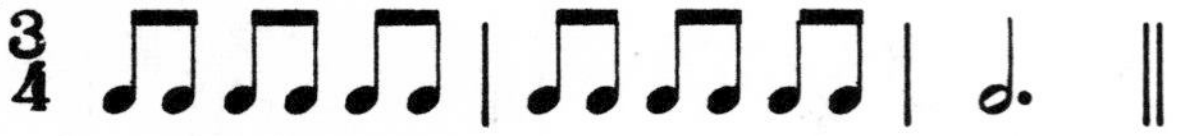

22
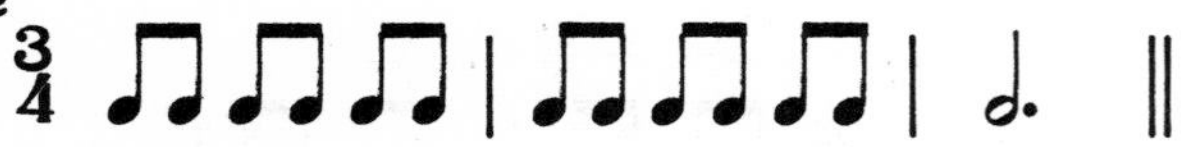

23
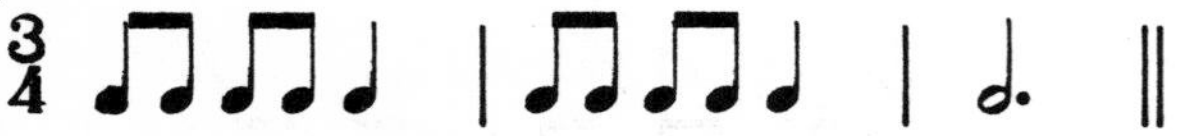

24
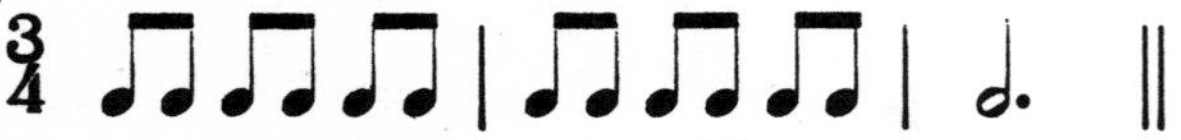

25
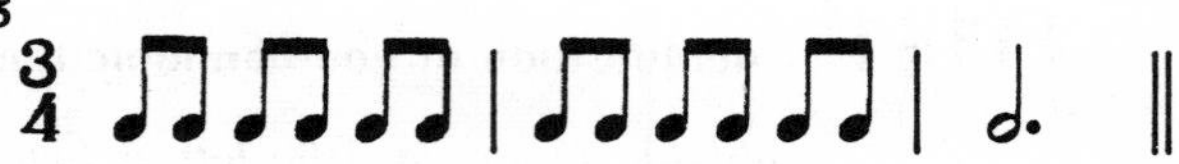

26
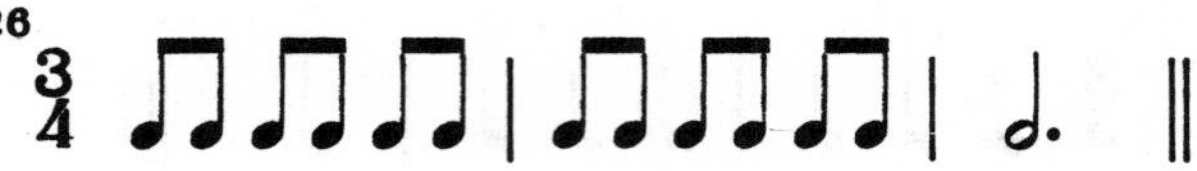

27
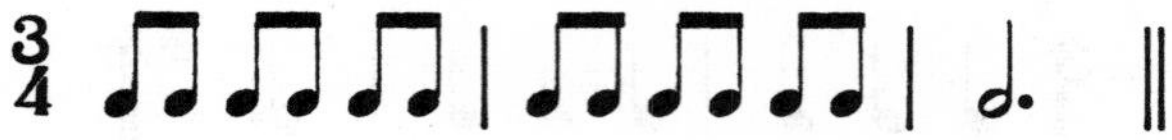

28
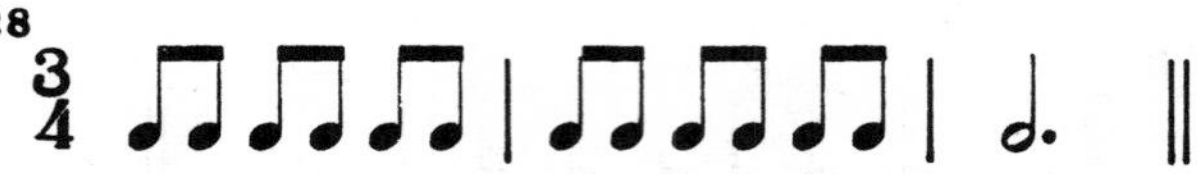

29
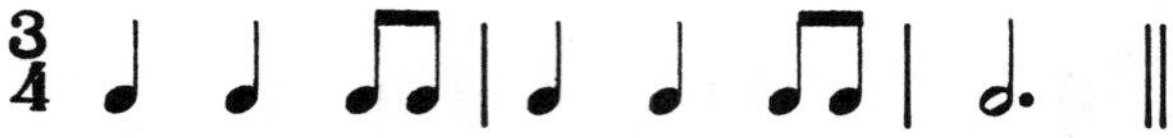

30
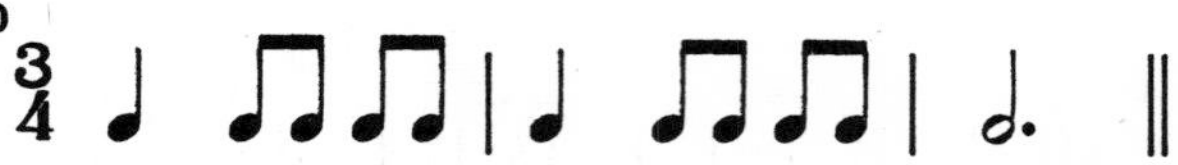

31
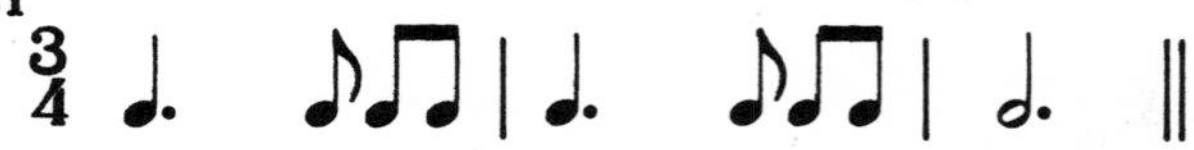

32
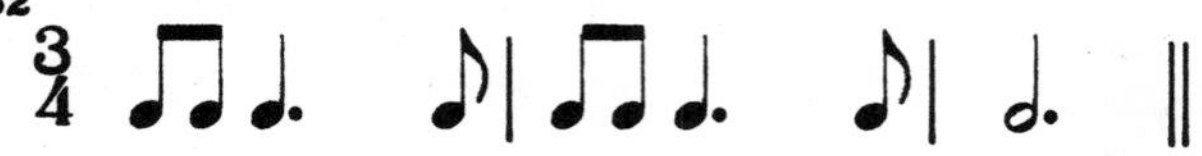

D1-1 Identification of non-harmonic tones
(Copy 2)

Shield the answer (the letters below the notes). Listen to the frame and label non-harmonic tones; then uncover the answer and compare your response. Circle tones not correctly identified. Goal: No more than fourteen errors.

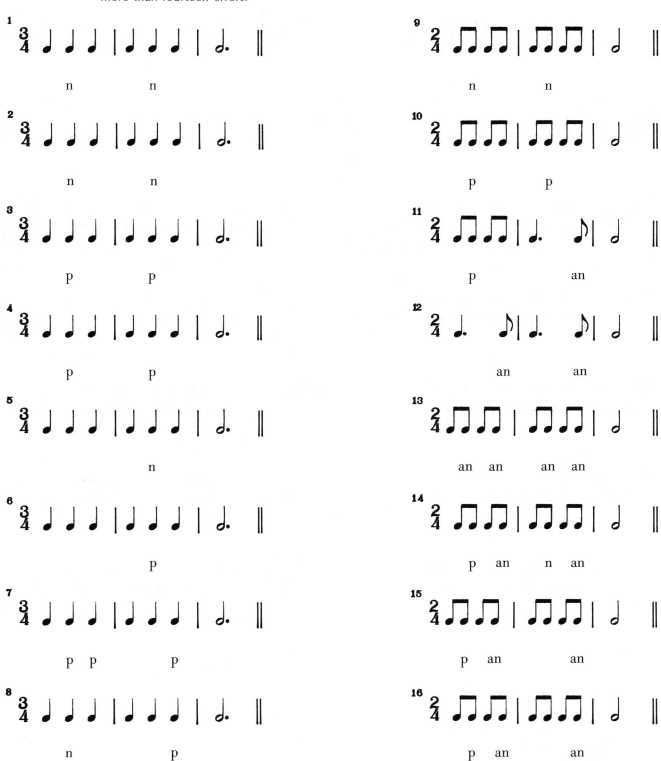

17

an an an

18

p an an

19

p p

20

p p p p

21

p p

22

n n

23

n n n n

24

n p an n p an

25

p p p p

26

p n

27

an p an

28

p p p p

29

e e

30

e e e an

31

e p e an

32

e e e

D1-1 Identification of non-harmonic tones
(Copy 3)

Shield the answer (the letters below the notes). Listen to the frame and label non-harmonic tones; then uncover the answer and compare your response. Circle tones not correctly identified. Goal: No more than fourteen errors.

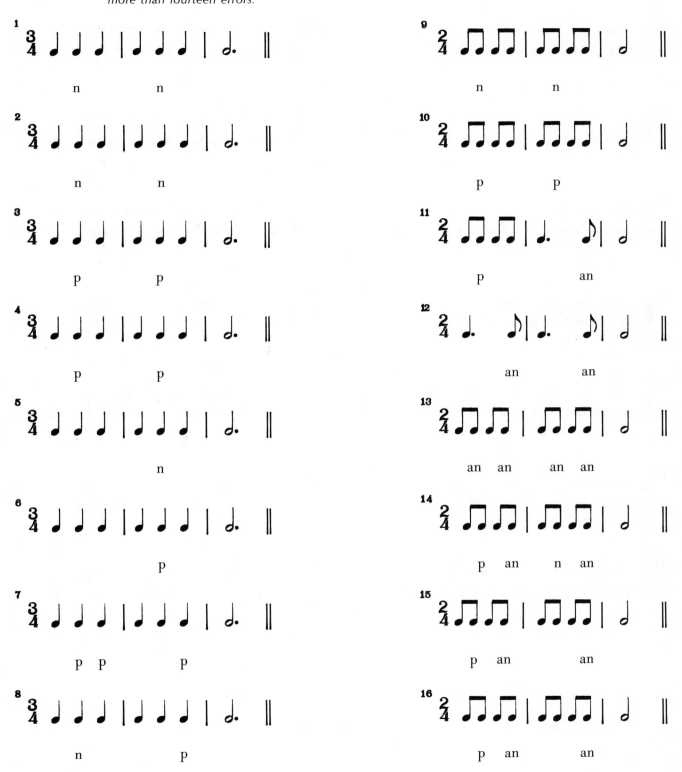

9

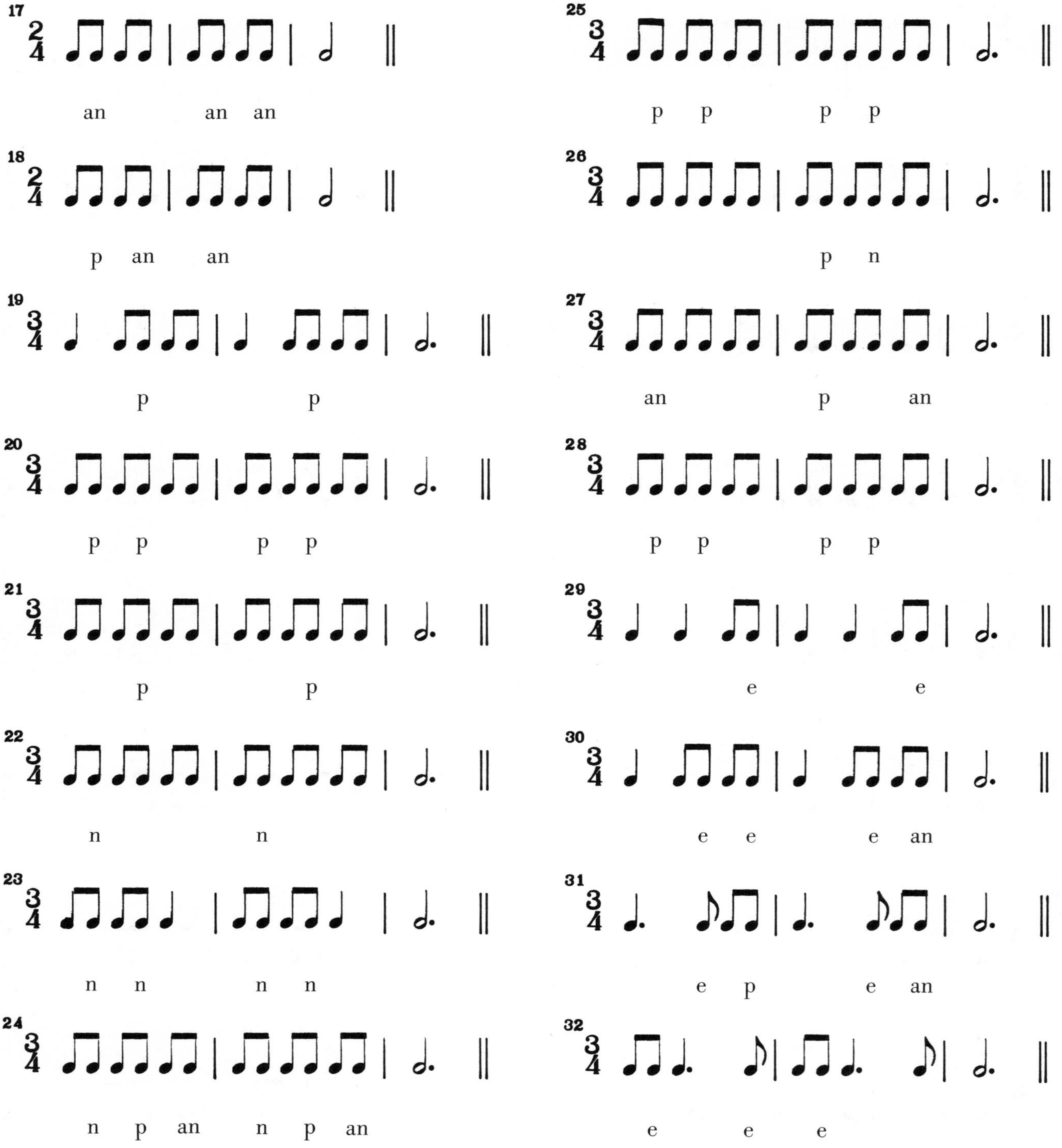
17
an an an
18
p an an
19
p p
20
p p p p
21
p p
22
n n
23
n n n n
24
n p an n p an
25
p p p p
26
p n
27
an p an
28
p p p p
29
e e
30
e e e an
31
e p e an
32
e e e

D1-1 Identification of non-harmonic tones
(Copy 4)

Shield the answer (the letters below the notes). Listen to the frame and label non-harmonic tones; then uncover the answer and compare your response. Circle tones not correctly identified. Goal: No more than fourteen errors.

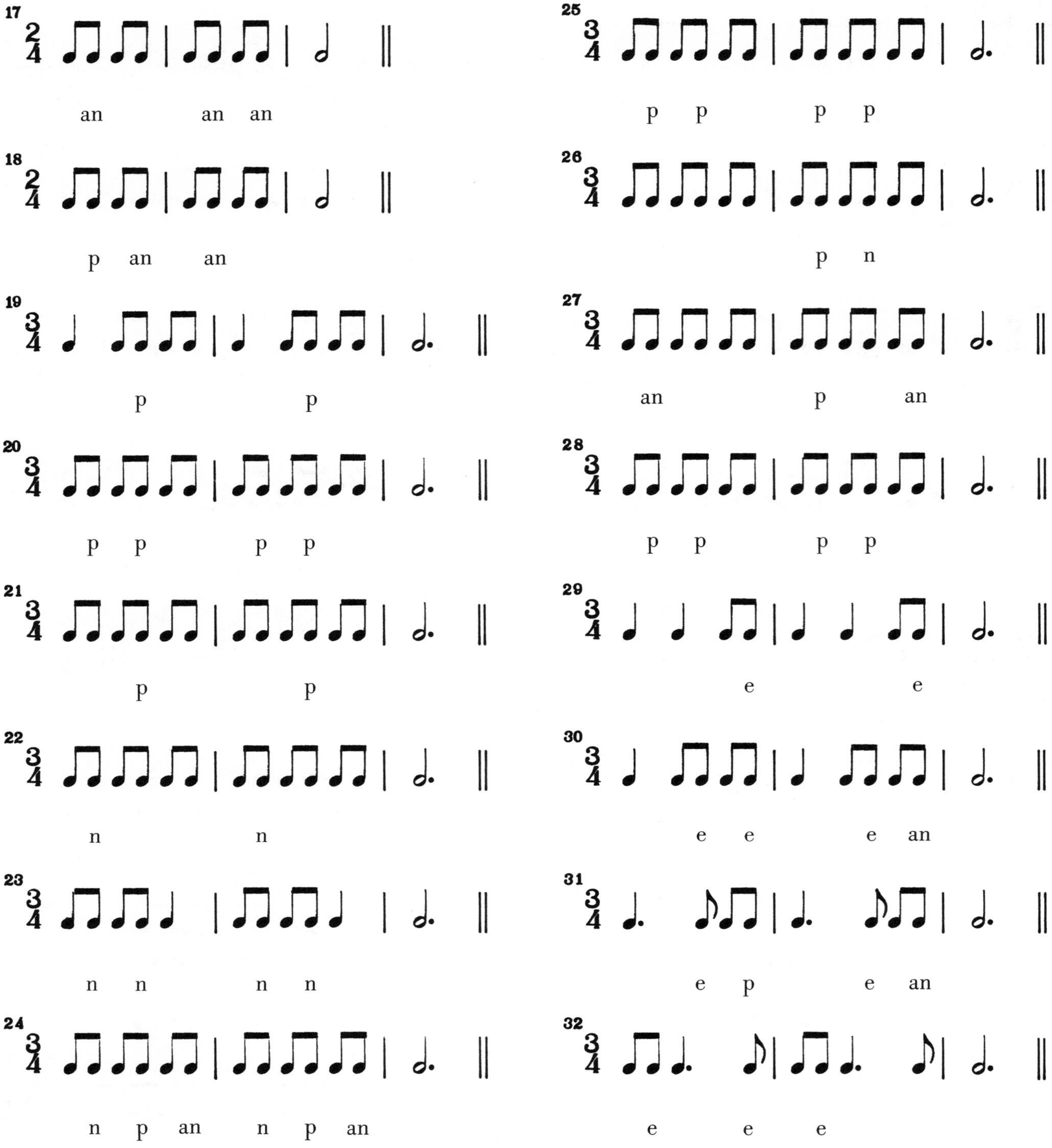
17
2/4
an an an
18
2/4
p an an
19
3/4
p p
20
3/4
p p p p
21
3/4
p p
22
3/4
n n
23
3/4
n n n n
24
3/4
n p an n p an
25
3/4
p p p p
26
3/4
p n
27
3/4
an p an
28
3/4
p p p p
29
3/4
e e
30
3/4
e e e an
31
3/4
e p e an
32
3/4
e e e

D1-1 Identification of non-harmonic tones
(Copy 5)

Shield the answer (the letters below the notes). Listen to the frame and label non-harmonic tones; then uncover the answer and compare your response. Circle tones not correctly identified. Goal: No more than fourteen errors.

13

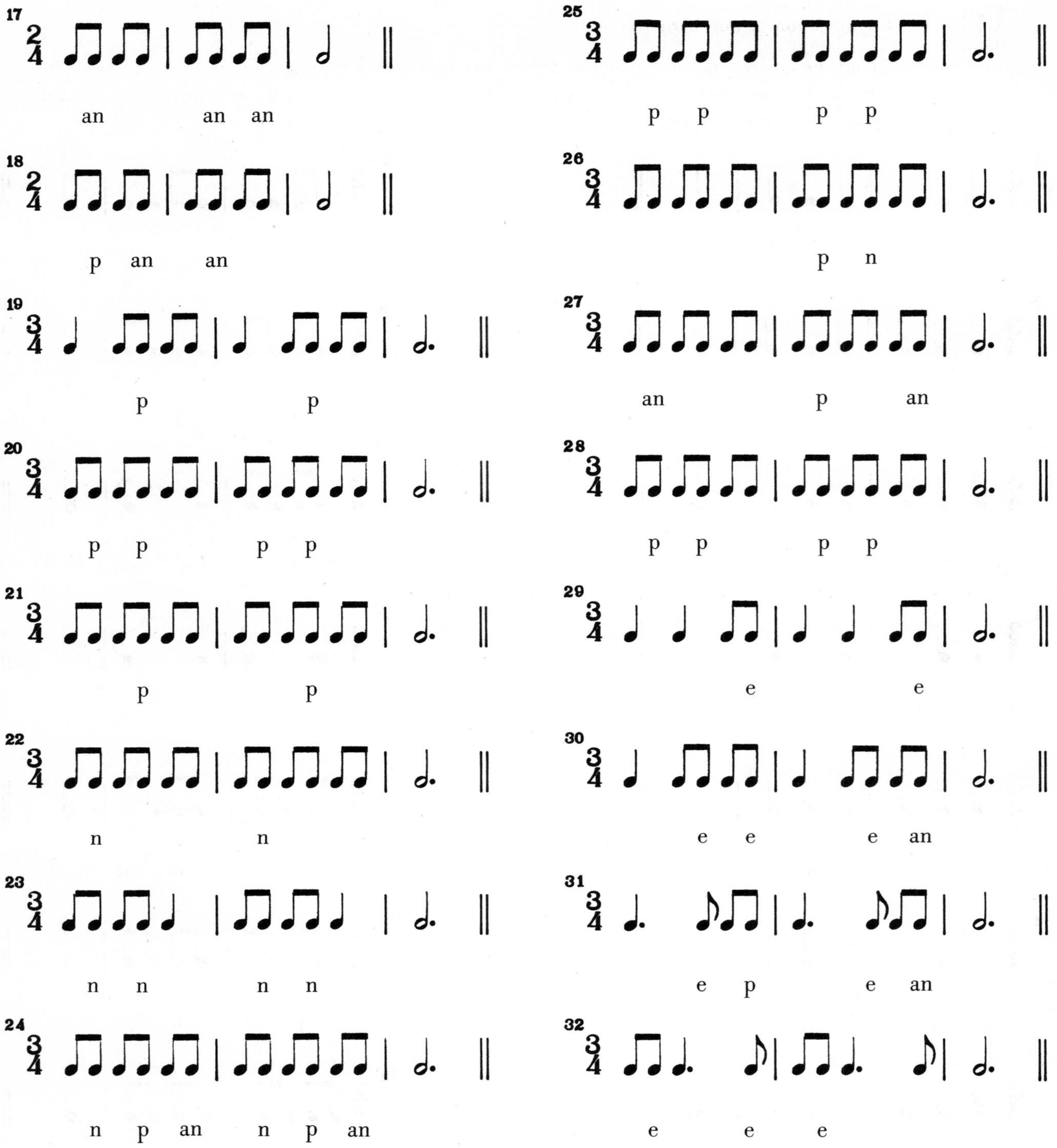
17 2/4
an an an
18 2/4
p an an
19 3/4
p p
20 3/4
p p p p
21 3/4
p p
22 3/4
n n
23 3/4
n n n n
24 3/4
n p an n p an
25 3/4
p p p p
26 3/4
p n
27 3/4
an p an
28 3/4
p p p p
29 3/4
e e
30 3/4
e e e an
31 3/4
e p e an
32 3/4
e e e

D1-2
(Copy 1)

Identification of non-harmonic tones

Shield the answer (the letters below the notes). Listen to the frame and label non-harmonic tones; then uncover the answer and compare your response. Circle tones not correctly identified. Goal: No more than fourteen errors.

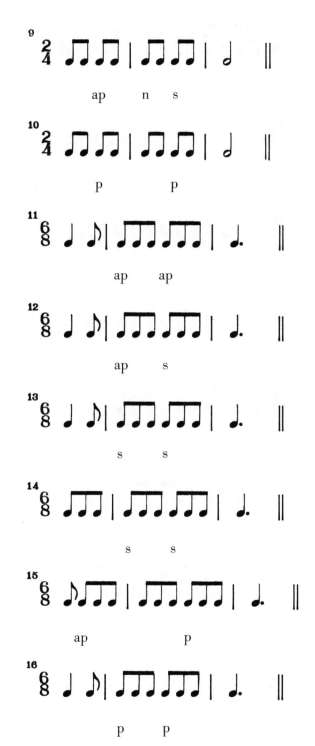

15

17

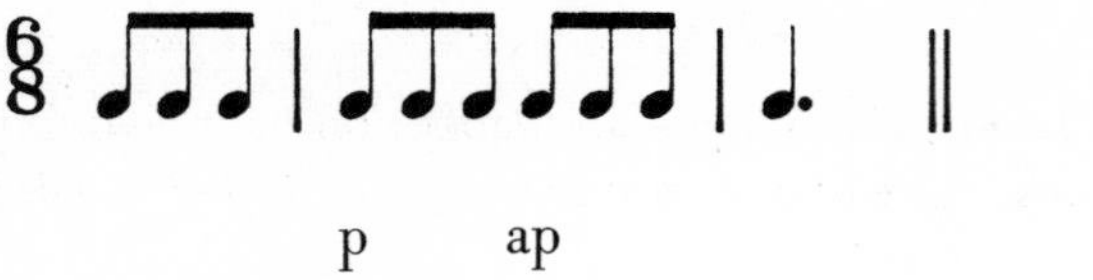

18

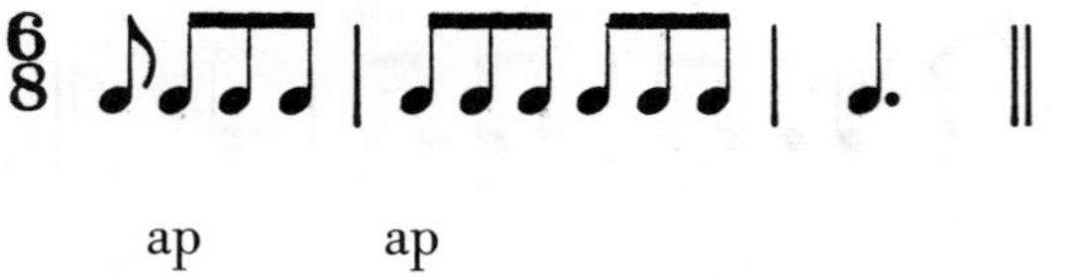

19

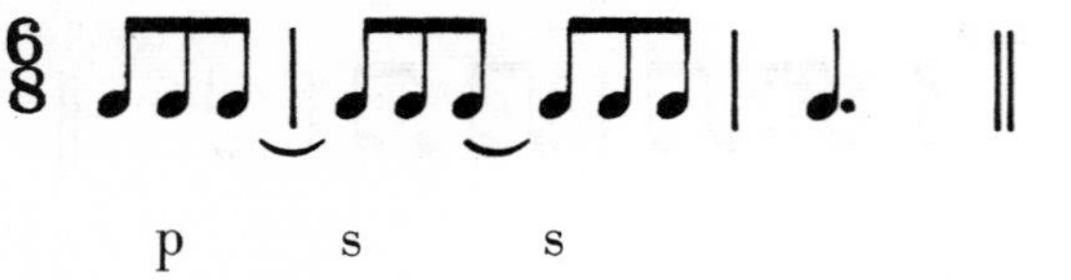

20

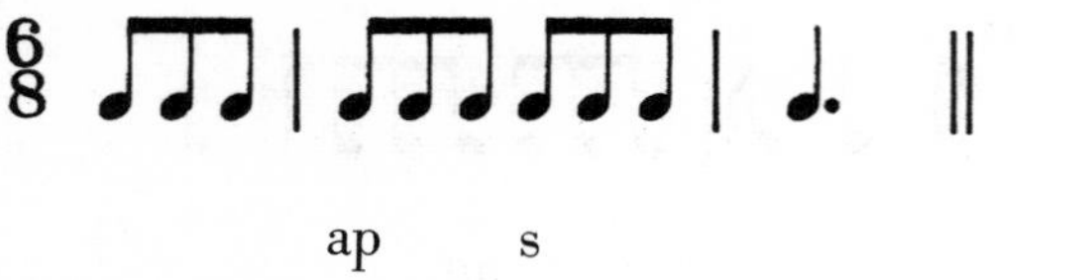

21

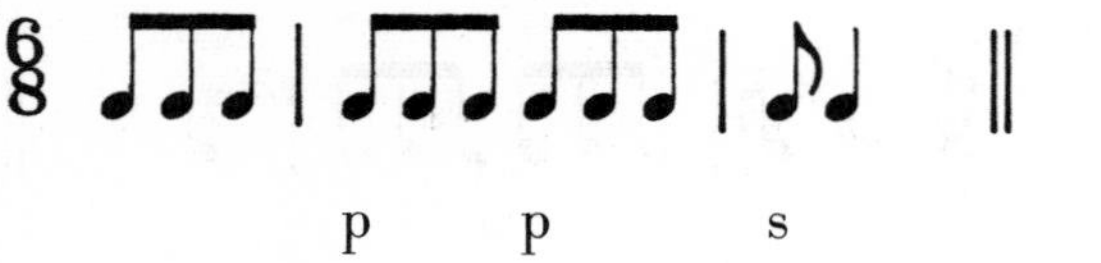

22

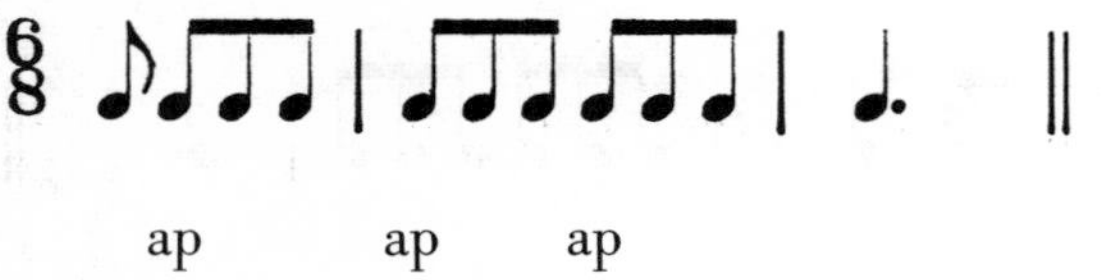

23

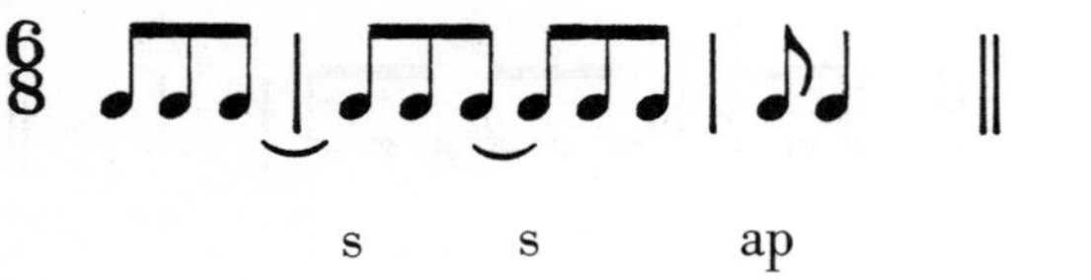

24

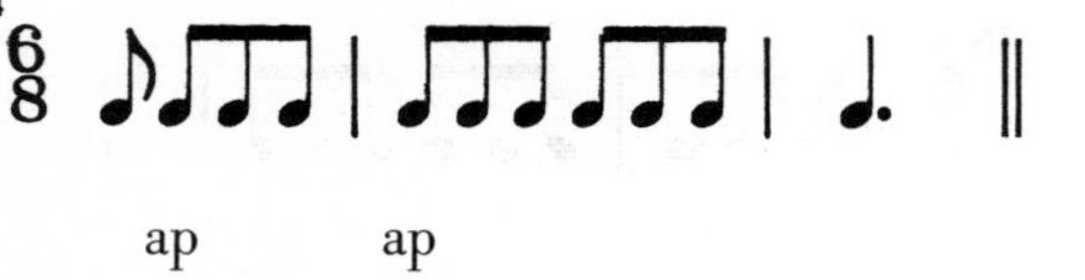

25

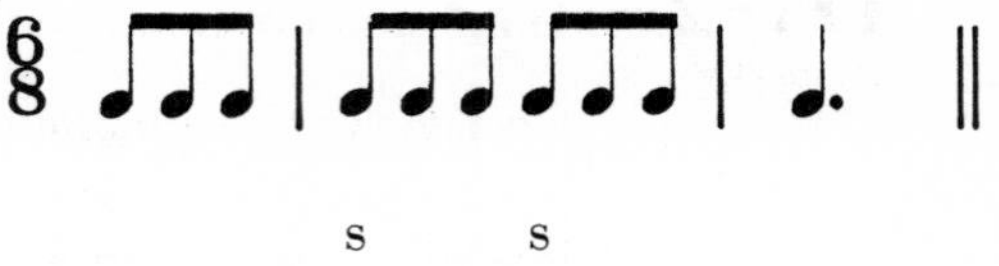

26

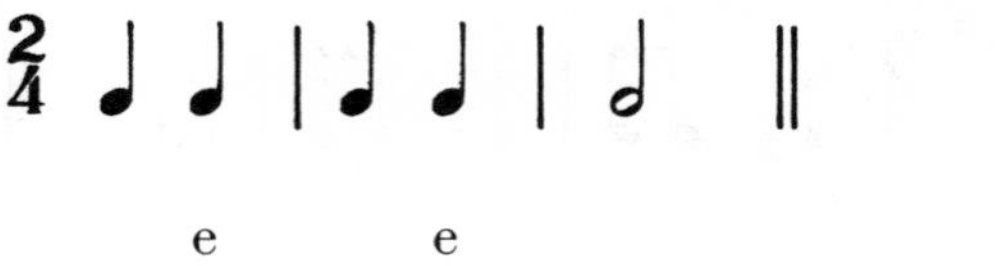

27

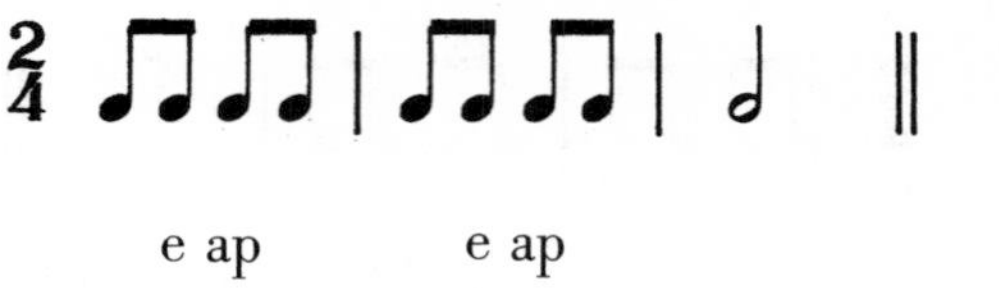

28

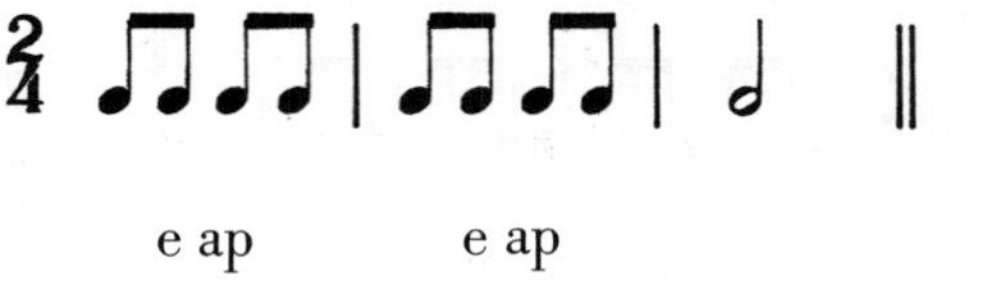

29

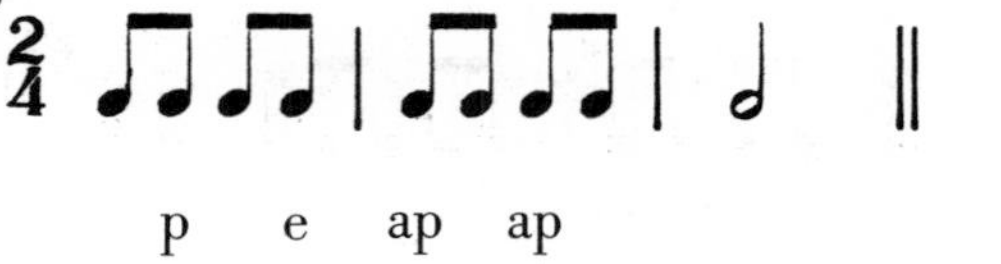

30

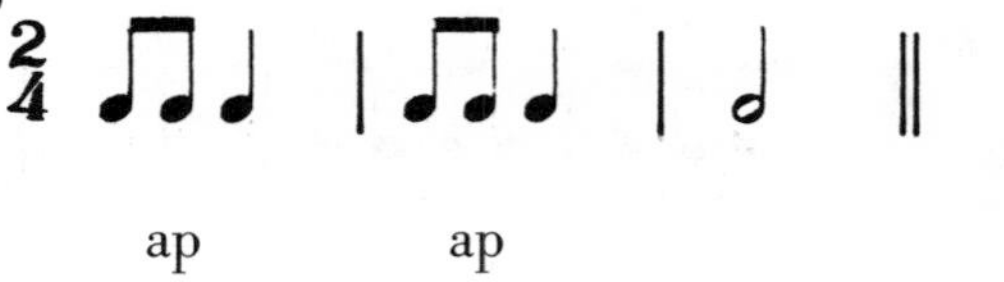

31

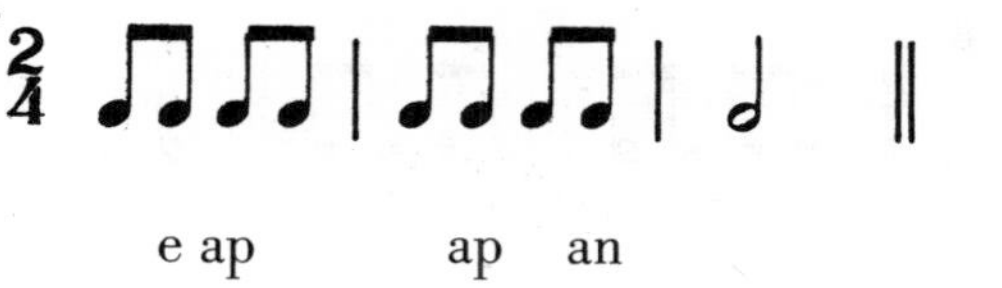

32

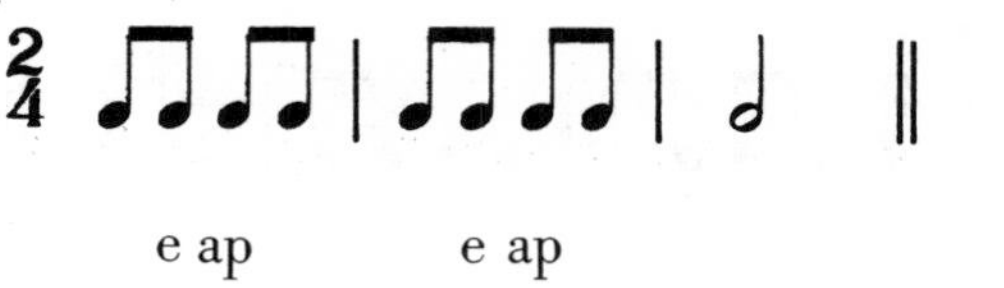

D1-2

Identification of non-harmonic tones

Shield the answer (the letters below the notes). Listen to the frame and label non-harmonic tones; then uncover the answer and compare your response. Circle tones not correctly identified. Goal: No more than fourteen errors.

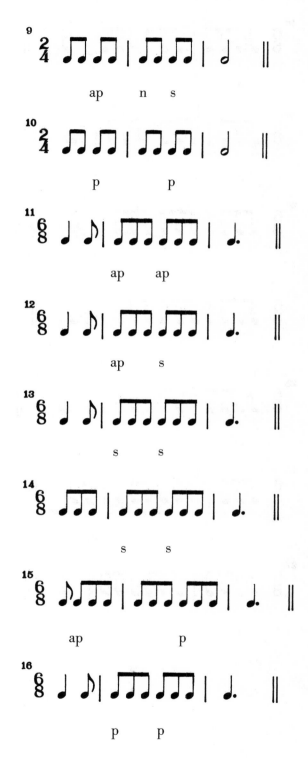

17

17
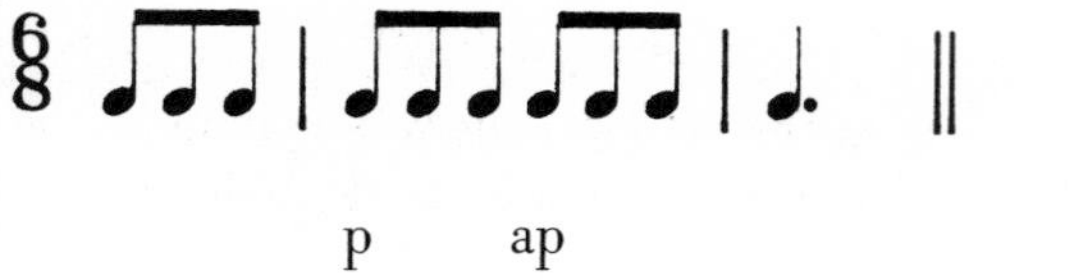

18
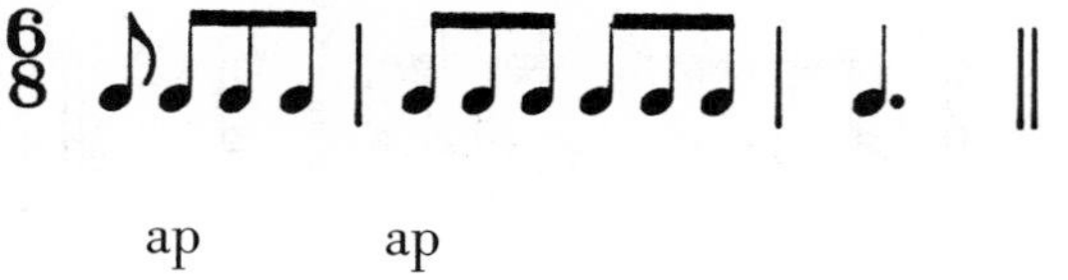

19
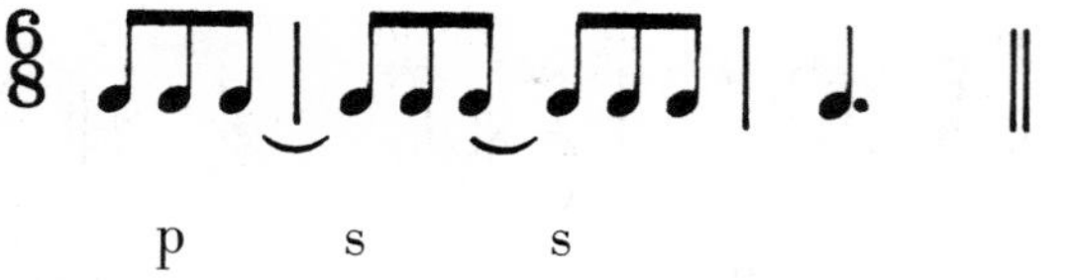

20
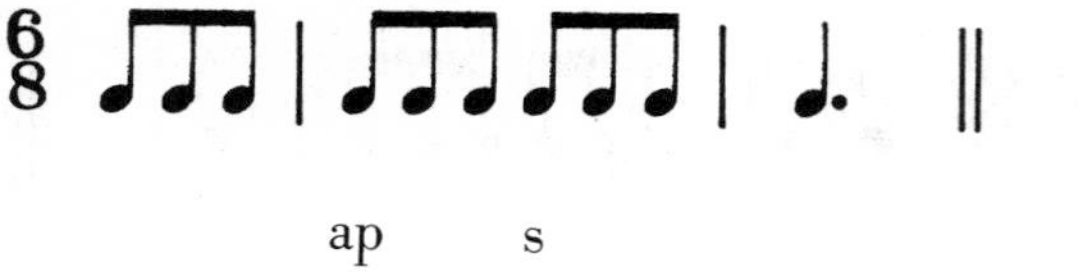

21
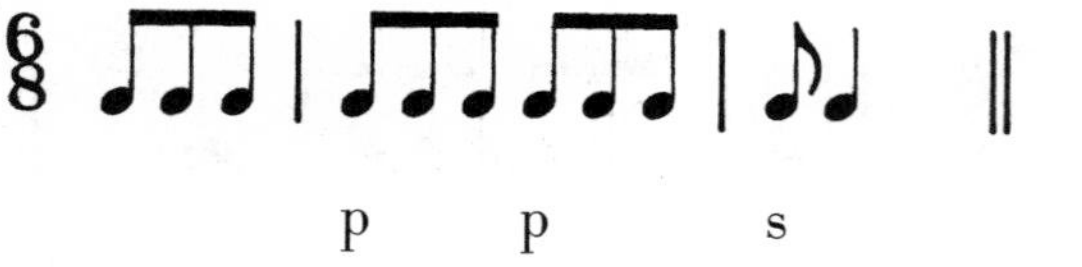

22
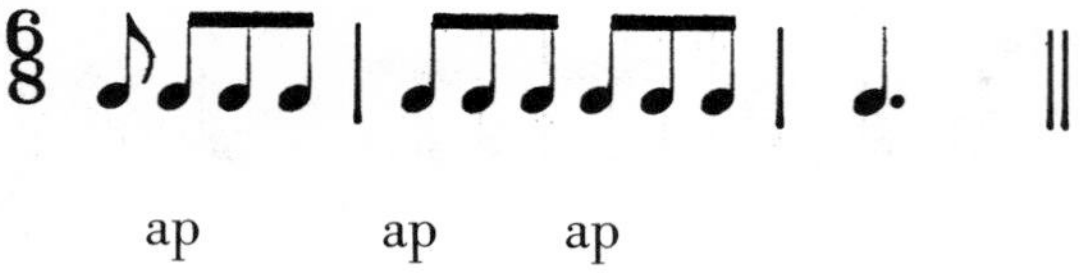

23
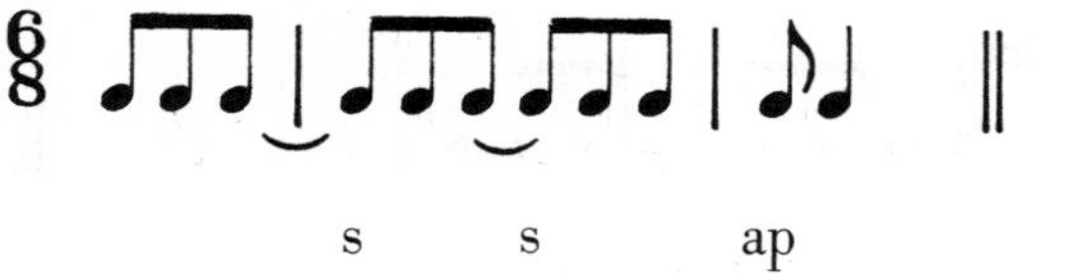

24
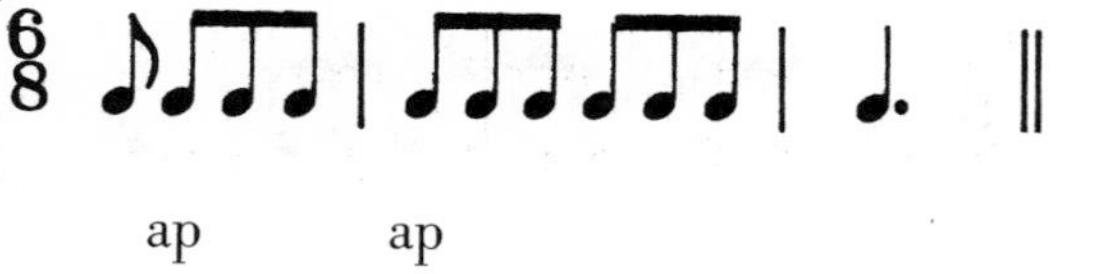

25
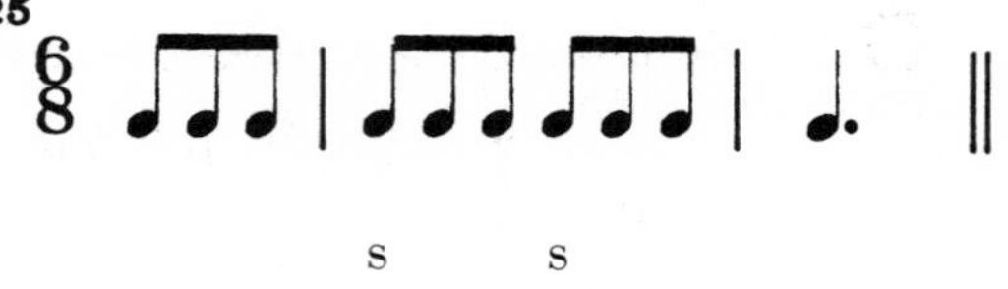

26
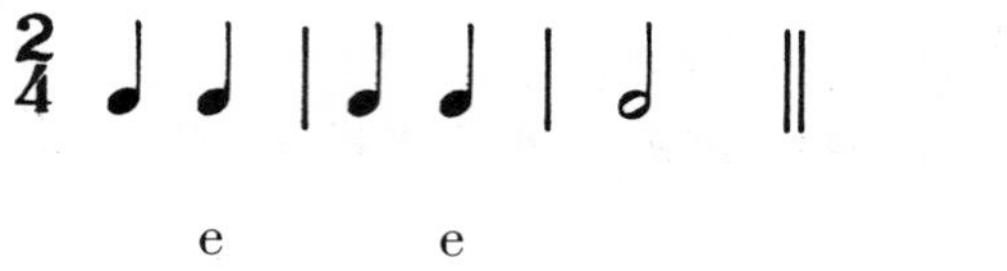

27
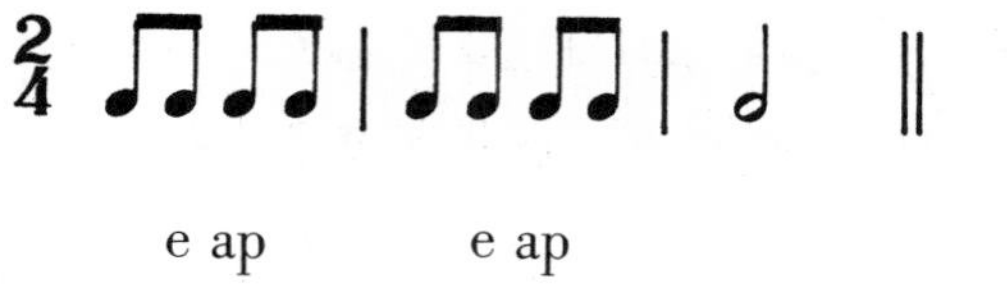

28
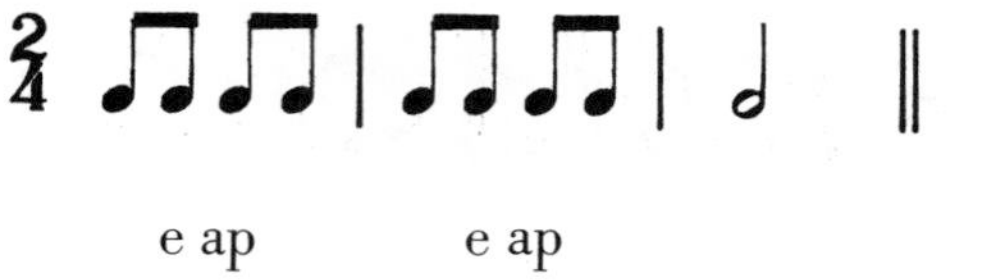

29
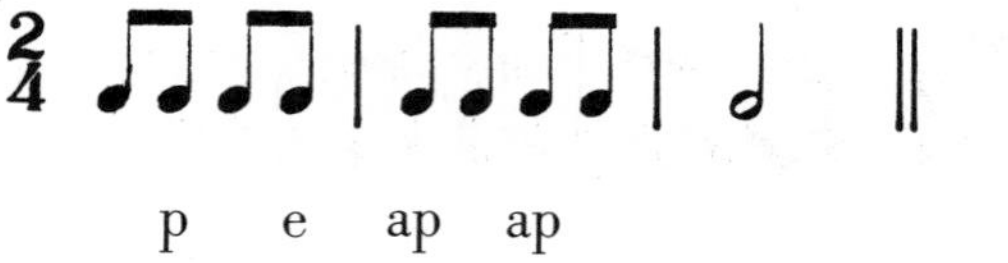

30
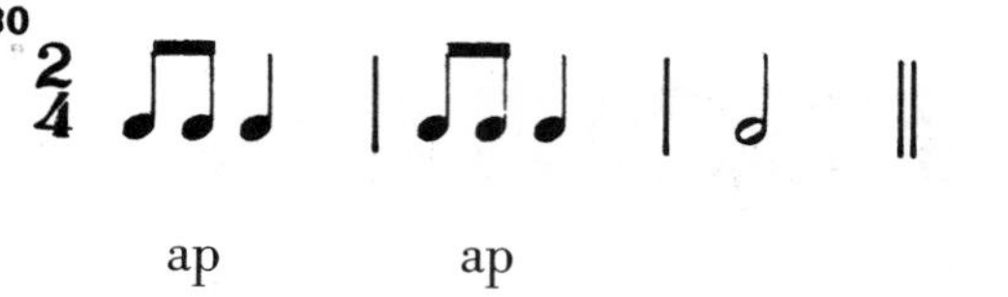

31
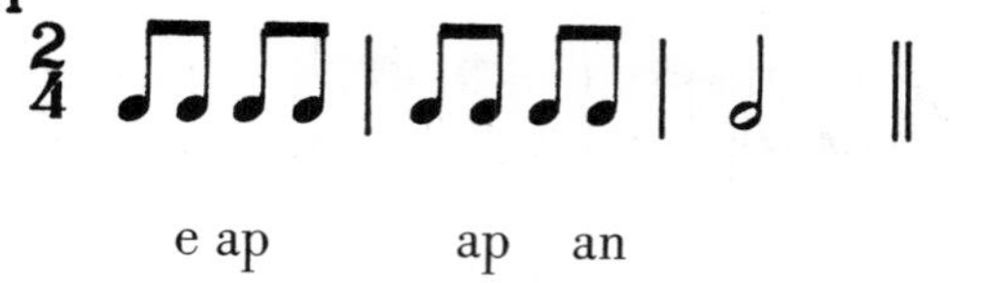

32
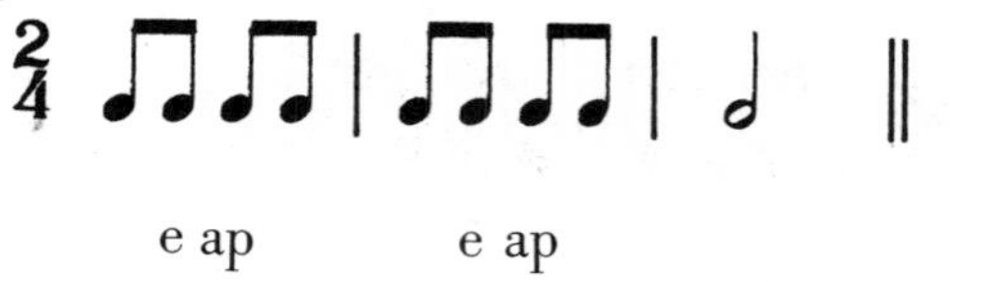

D1-2 Identification of non-harmonic tones
(Copy 3)

Shield the answer (the letters below the notes). Listen to the frame and label non-harmonic tones; then uncover the answer and compare your response. Circle tones not correctly identified. Goal: No more than fourteen errors.

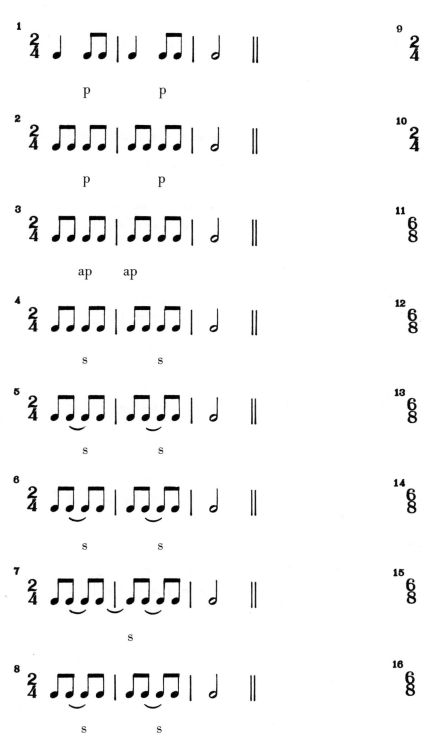

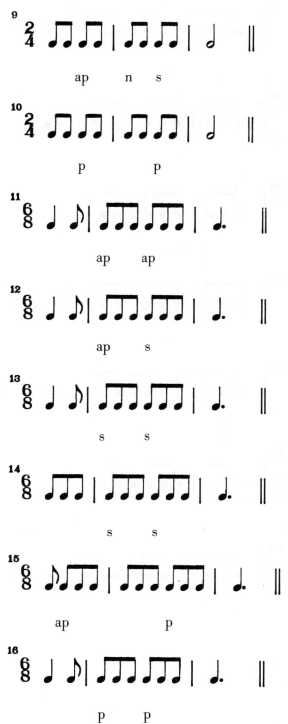

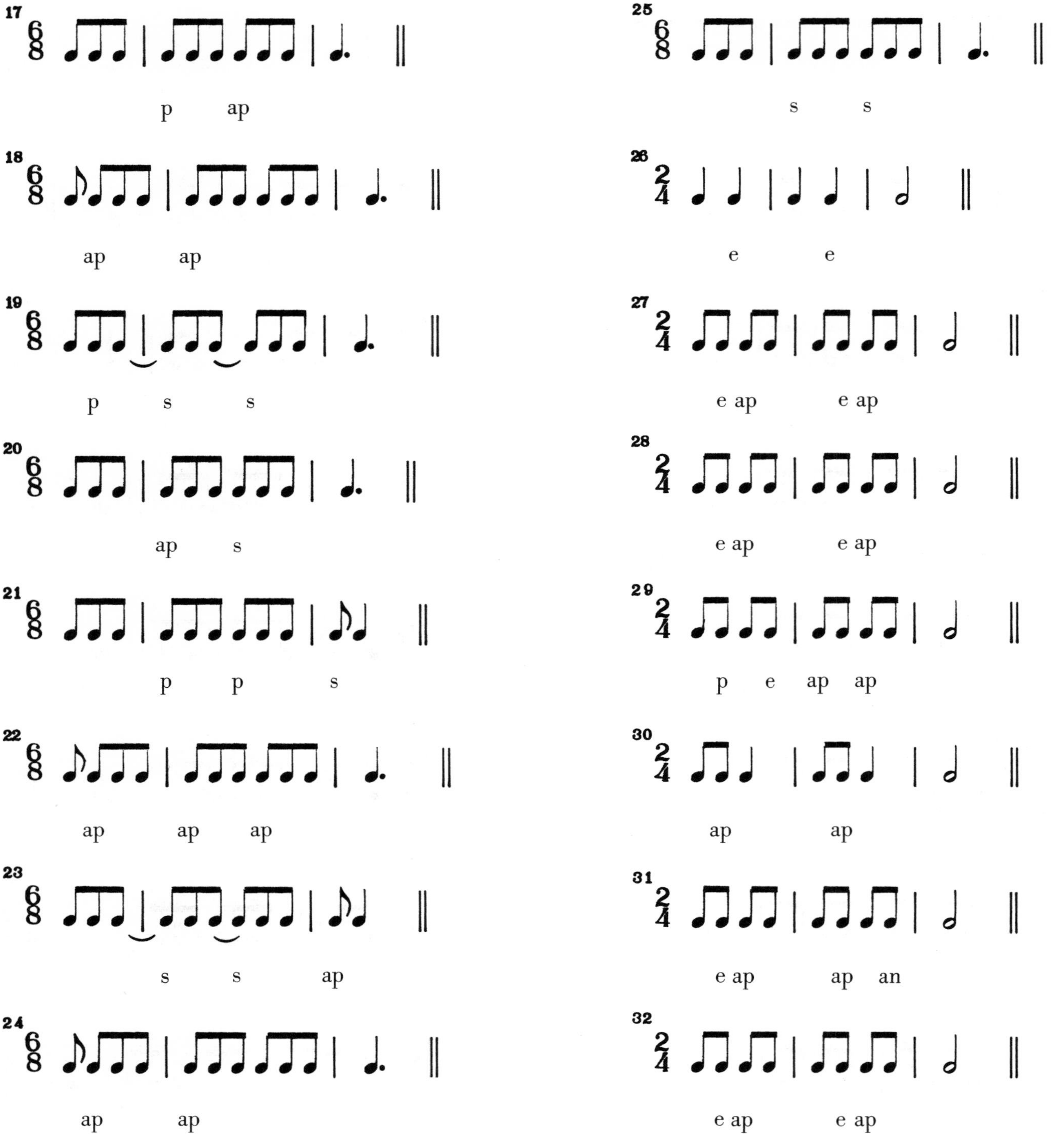
17 6/8
p ap
18 6/8
ap ap
19 6/8
p s s
20 6/8
ap s
21 6/8
p p s
22 6/8
ap ap ap
23 6/8
s s ap
24 6/8
ap ap
25 6/8
s s
26 2/4
e e
27 2/4
e ap e ap
28 2/4
e ap e ap
29 2/4
p e ap ap
30 2/4
ap ap
31 2/4
e ap ap an
32 2/4
e ap e ap

D1-2 Identification of non-harmonic tones
(Copy 4)

Shield the answer (the letters below the notes). Listen to the frame and label non-harmonic tones; then uncover the answer and compare your response. Circle tones not correctly identified. Goal: No more than fourteen errors.

17

p ap

18

ap ap

19

p s s

20

ap s

21

p p s

22

ap ap ap

23

s s ap

24

ap ap

25

s s

26

e e

27

e ap e ap

28

e ap e ap

29

p e ap ap

30

ap ap

31

e ap ap an

32

e ap e ap

D1-2
(Copy 5)

Identification of non-harmonic tones

Shield the answer (the letters below the notes). Listen to the frame and label non-harmonic tones; then uncover the answer and compare your response. Circle tones not correctly identified. Goal: No more than fourteen errors.

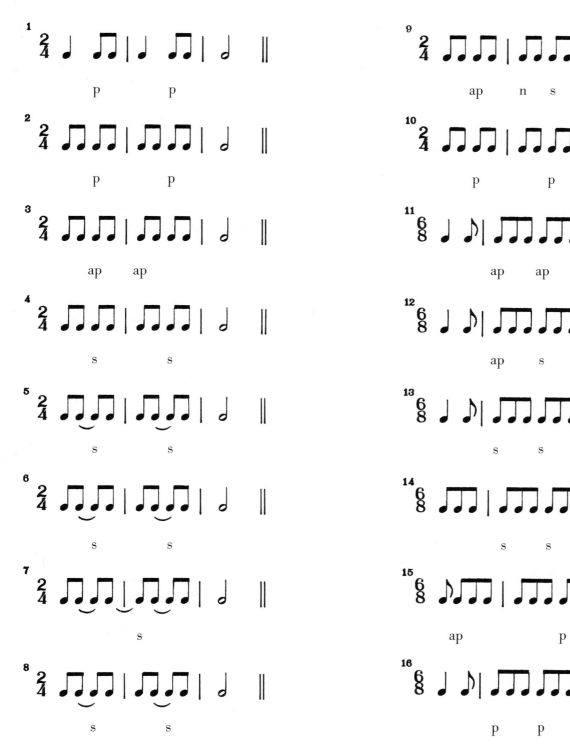

17
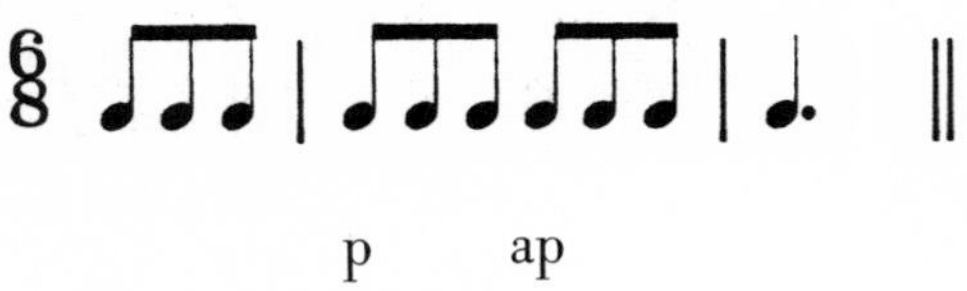

18
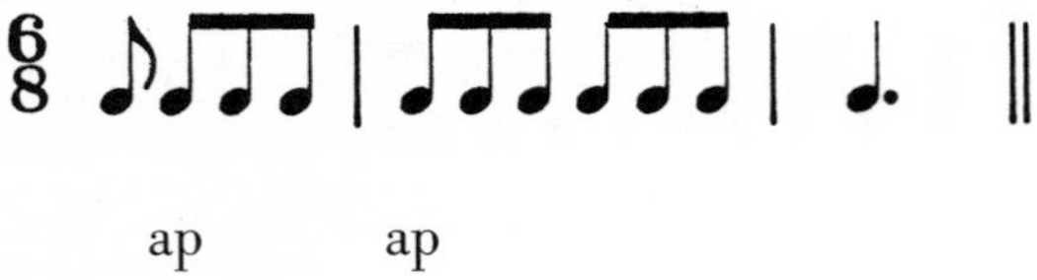

19
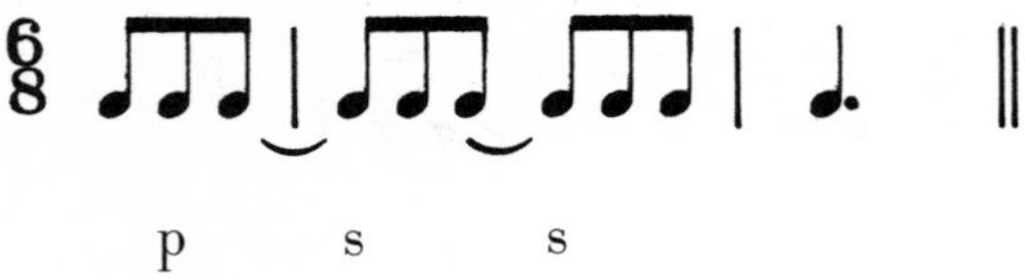

20
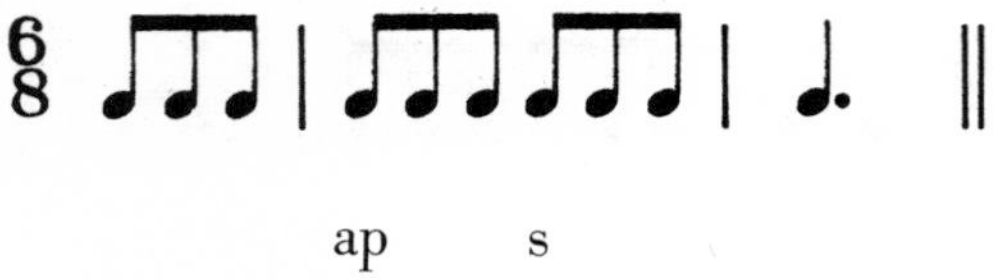

21
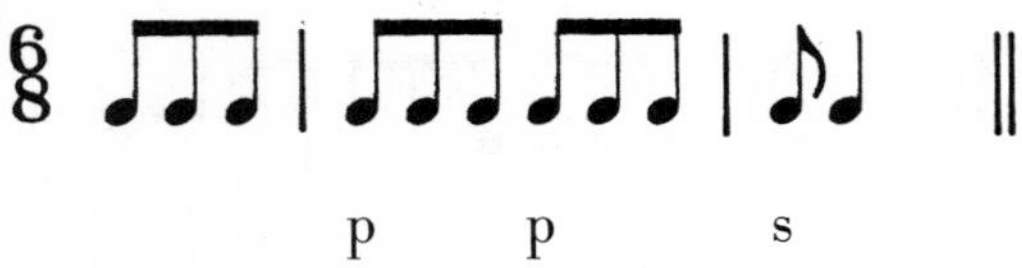

22
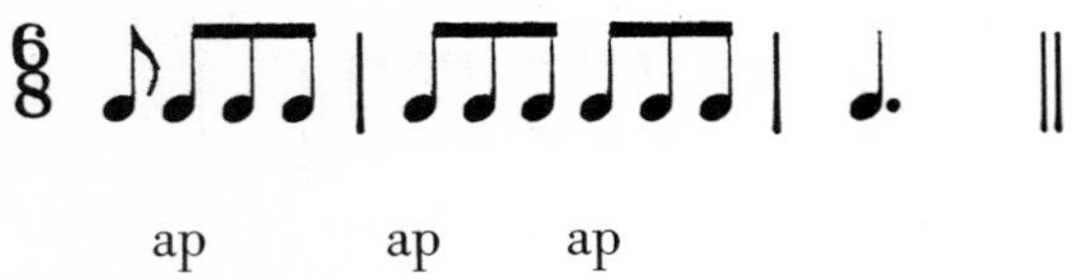

23
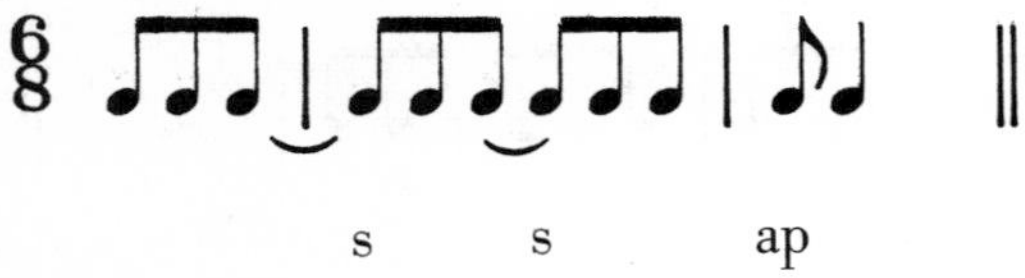

24
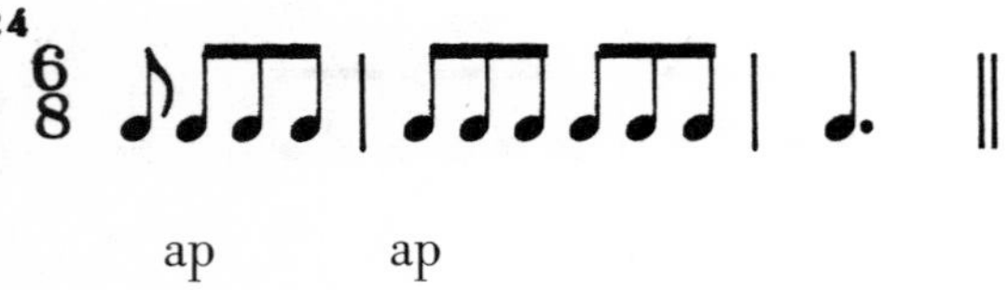

25
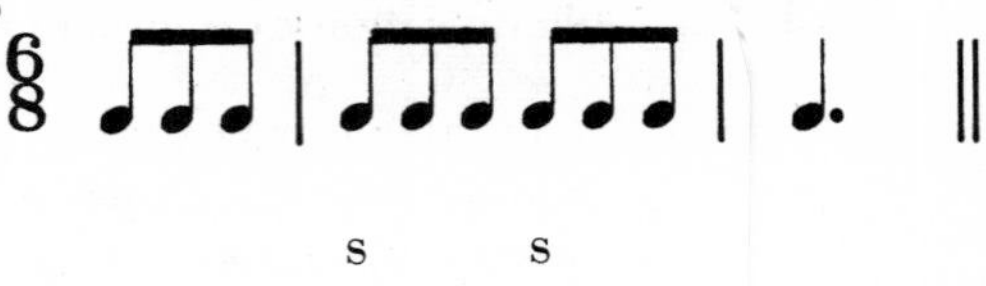

26
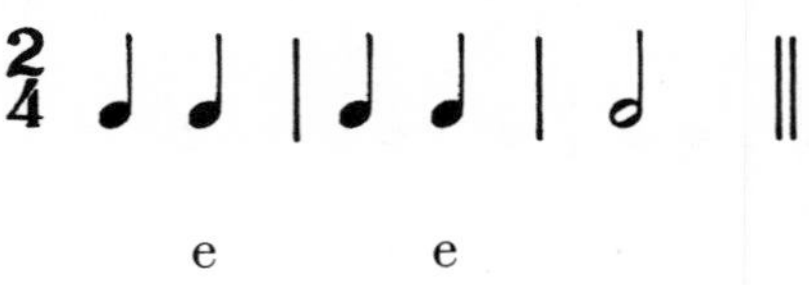

27
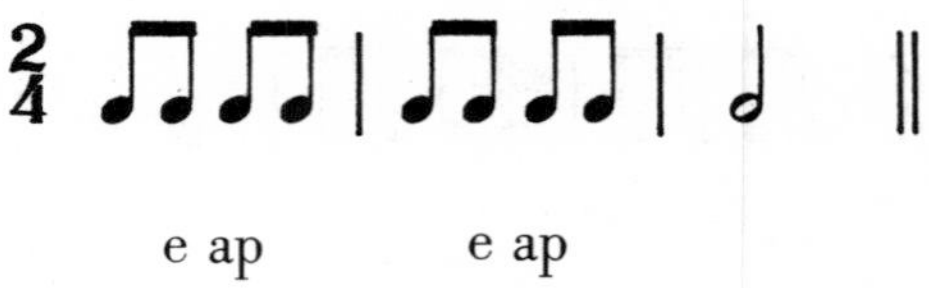

28
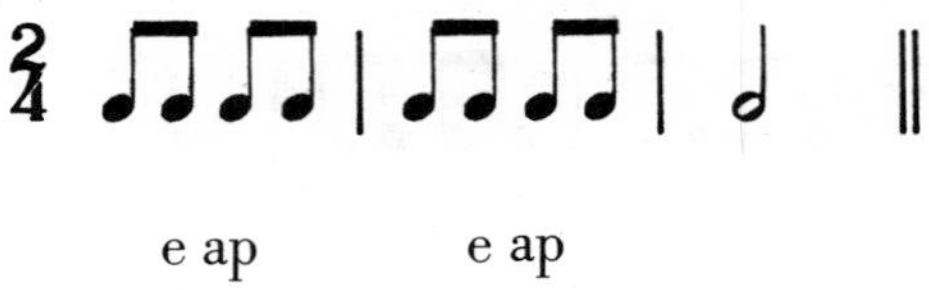

29
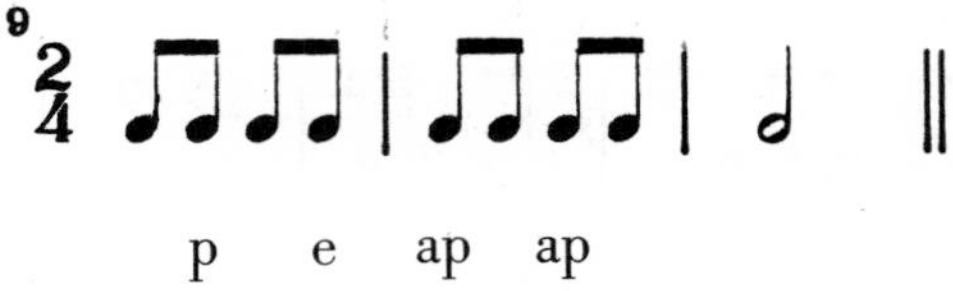

30
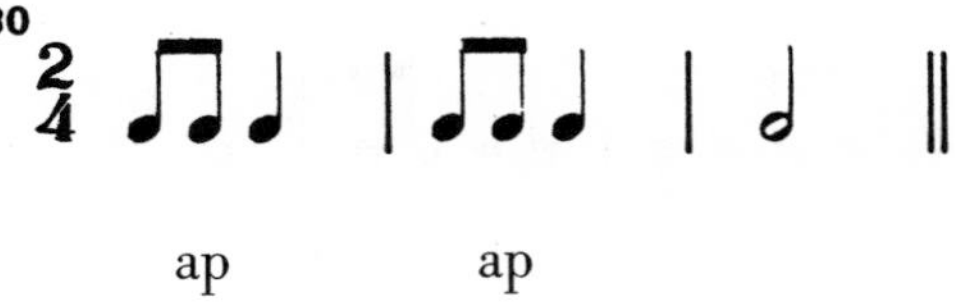

31
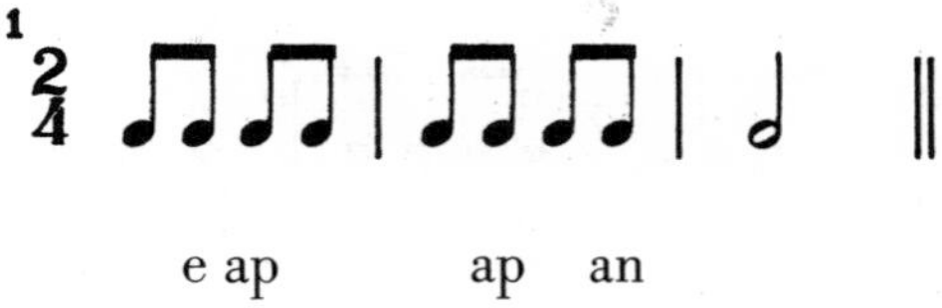

32
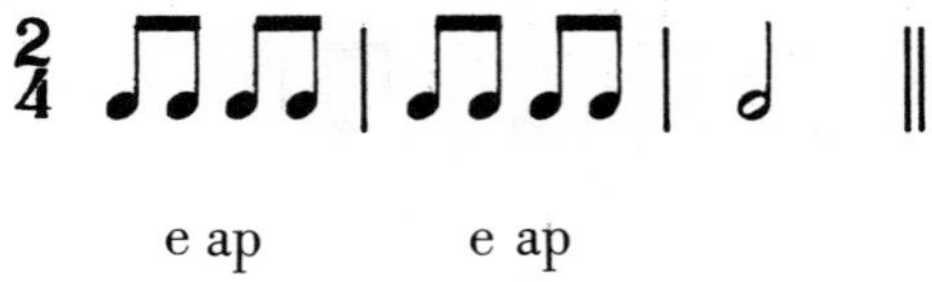

D1-3 Identification of non-harmonic tones
(Copy 1)

Shield the answer. Listen to the frame and label non-harmonic tones; then uncover the answer and compare your response. Circle tones not correctly identified. Goal: No more than fourteen errors. When you have done this lesson, take Test D1.

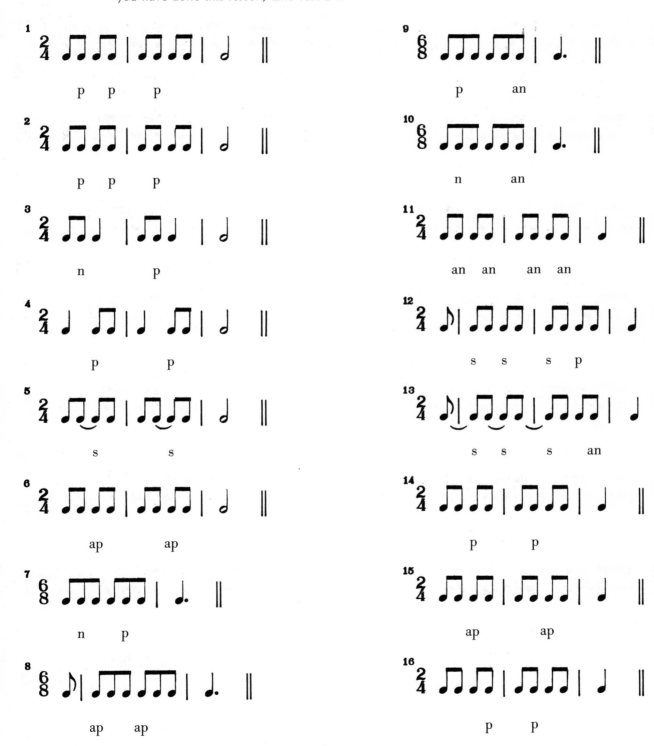

17 2/4
e e
18 2/4
e ap e ap
19 2/4
n p n p p p
20 2/4
p p
21 2/4
p p p an
22 2/4
s s n s
23 2/4
p p p
24 2/4
p an p an
25 2/4
p p p p
26 2/4
p p p p p
27 2/4
p ap ap n
28 2/4
n s p s
29 2/4
s s
30 6/8
e ap e ap
31 6/8
e ap p
32 6/8
p p s p p

D1-3 Identification of non-harmonic tones
(Copy 2)

Shield the answer. Listen to the frame and label non-harmonic tones; then uncover the answer and compare your response. Circle tones not correctly identified. Goal: No more than fourteen errors. When you have done this lesson, take Test D1.

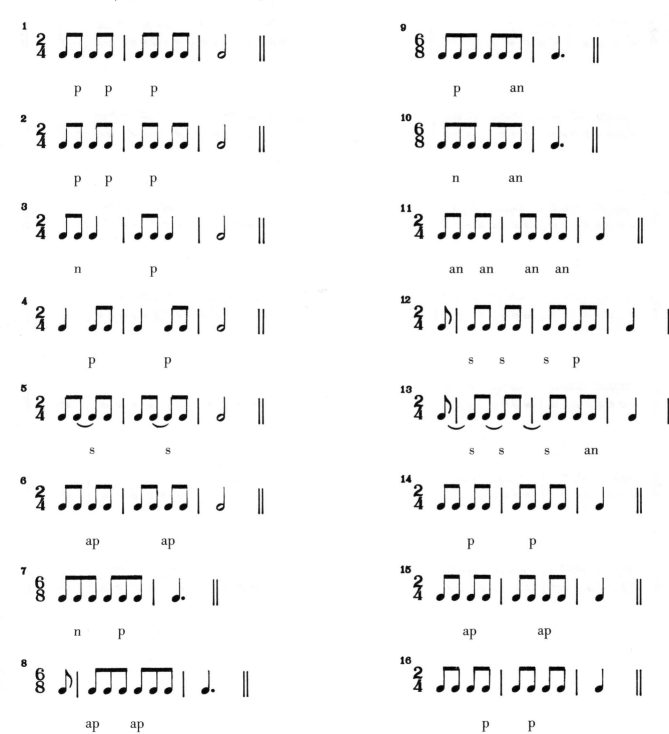

17

e e

18

e ap e ap

19

n p n p p p

20

p p

21

p p p an

22

s s n s

23

p p p

24

p an p an

25

p p p p

26

p p p p p

27

p ap ap n

28

n s p s

29

s s

30

e ap e ap

31

e ap p

32

p p s p p

D1-3

(Copy 3)

Identification of non-harmonic tones

Shield the answer. Listen to the frame and label non-harmonic tones; then uncover the answer and compare your response. Circle tones not correctly identified. Goal: No more than fourteen errors. When you have done this lesson, take Test D1.

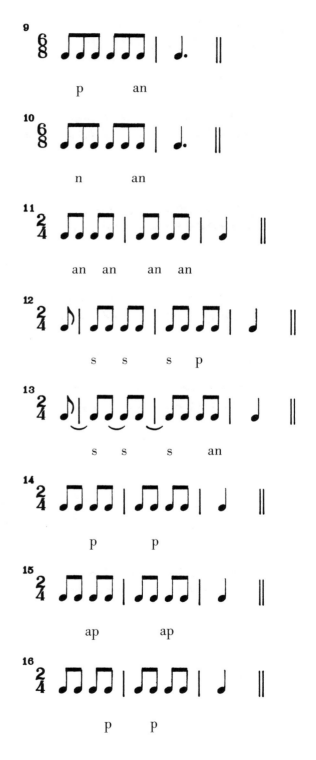

17
e e
18
e ap e ap
19
n p n p p p
20
p p
21
p p p an
22
s s n s
23
p p p
24
p an p an
25
p p p p
26
p p p p p
27
p ap ap n
28
n s p s
29
s s
30
e ap e ap
31
e ap p
32
p p s p p

D1-3 Identification of non-harmonic tones
(Copy 4)

Shield the answer. Listen to the frame and label non-harmonic tones; then uncover the answer and compare your response. Circle tones not correctly identified. Goal: No more than fourteen errors. When you have done this lesson, take Test D1.

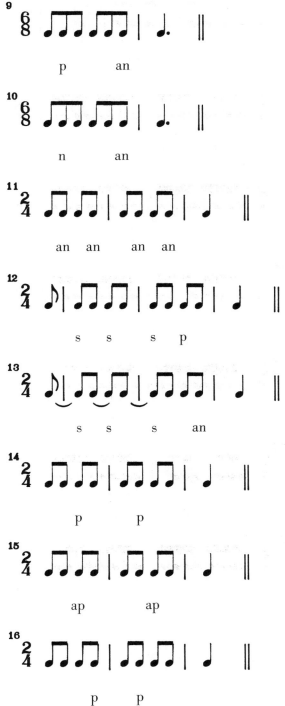

17 2/4
e e
18 2/4
e ap e ap
19 2/4
n p n p p p
20 2/4
p p
21 2/4
p p p an
22 2/4
s s n s
23 2/4
p p p
24 2/4
p an p an
25 2/4
p p p p
26 2/4
p p p p p
27 2/4
p ap ap n
28 2/4
n s p s
29 2/4
s s
30 6/8
e ap e ap
31 6/8
e ap p
32 6/8
p p s p p

D1-3
(Copy 5)

Identification of non-harmonic tones

Shield the answer. Listen to the frame and label non-harmonic tones; then uncover the answer and compare your response. Circle tones not correctly identified. Goal: No more than fourteen errors. When you have done this lesson, take Test D1.

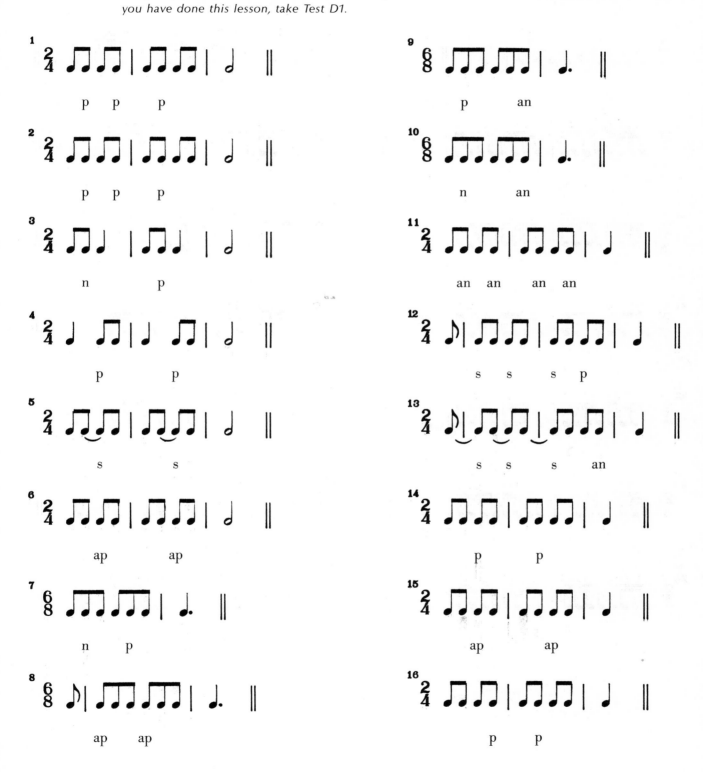

17

e e

18

e ap e ap

19

n p n p p p

20

p p

21

p p p an

22

s s n s

23

p p p

24

p an p an

25

p p p p

26

p p p p p

27

p ap ap n

28

n s p s

29

s s

30

e ap e ap

31

e ap p

32

p p s p p

Key Determination **SERIES D2**

In this series you are asked to determine the key of a group of chords. To indicate the key, you will simply write the composite chord symbols for some of the chords you hear. In lessons involving composite chord symbols in Volume III, the key location of the first chord was usually given as a starting reference. Often, however, it is possible to identify the key location of a chord through its relation to other chords present. For example, when a IV chord and a V chord are heard side by side, a sufficient number of tones are present to establish the key and make apparent the location of these chords in the key.

A printed worksheet and a tape recording are provided for each lesson. Each frame contains a blank in which you will write your response, followed by the correct answer. To do each frame, start by shielding the answer. You will hear a series of five chords in a key. Write the composite chord symbols for the *last three chords* in the series. The printed answer gives the chord symbols for all five chords, but you are required to identify only the last three. (You may include the first two chords in your answer if you wish.) You may stop the tape while you write your answers. When you have responded, slide the shield to the right and check your response. Circle each incorrect composite chord symbol in your response, excluding the first two chords if you chose to give these. Each circled symbol will count as one error. Your goal is to complete each lesson with no more than twenty-four errors. When you have done so, go on to the next lesson. Otherwise repeat the lesson until you reach the goal or until you have done the lesson five times, at which point you should go on to the next lesson regardless of your score.

There are two lessons in this series. When you have done these lessons, take Test D2.

Key determination

Shield the answer. Listen to the series of five chords and write the composite chord symbols for the last three chords; then uncover the answer, which gives all five chords, and compare your response. Circle each incorrect chord symbol. Goal: No more than twenty-four errors.

1 _____ I V^{-7} I IV V

2 _____ IV V I VI⁻ IV

3 _____ VI⁻ IV V^{-7} I IV

4 _____ I⁻ ⁻VI IV⁻ V I⁻

5 _____ ⁻VI IV⁻ V I⁻ ⁻VI

6 _____ V ⁻VI IV⁻ V I⁻

7 _____ I IV I V VI⁻

8 _____ I IV II⁻ V VI⁻

9 _____ I⁻ IV⁻ I⁻ V ⁻VI

10 _____ V I⁻ ⁻VI IV⁻ V

11 _____ IV⁻ V ⁻VI IV⁻ V

12 _____ VI⁻ IV V VI⁻ II⁻

13 _____ VI⁻ II⁻ V^{-7} I IV

14 _____ IV II⁻ V I VI⁻

15 _____ I IV II⁻ V VI⁻

16 _____ IV⁻ I⁻ ⁻VI IV⁻ V

17 _____ V ⁻VI IV⁻ I⁻ V

18 _____ II⁻ V VI⁻ IV I

19 _____ ⁻VI V I⁻ IV⁻ V

20 _____ I VI⁻ V VI⁻ IV

21 _____ II⁻ V I VI⁻ V

22 _____ IV⁻ V I⁻ ⁻VI V

23 _____ IV⁻ I⁻ ⁻VI V I⁻

24 _____ VI⁻ IV II⁻ V VI⁻

25 _____ IV I^6_4 V^{-7} I V

26 _____ ⁻VI IV⁻ I^{-6}_4 V I⁻

27 _____ IV⁻ I⁻ ⁻VI I^{-6}_4 V

28 _____ I III⁻ IV I V

29 _____ I⁻ ⁻III IV⁻ I⁻ V

30 _____ I^{-6}_4 V ⁻VI IV⁻ V

31 _____ VI⁻ IV II⁻ I^6_4 V

32 _____ I⁻ ⁻III IV⁻ I⁻ IV⁻

33 _____ II⁻ I^6_4 V VI⁻ II⁻

34 _____ I IV^6_4 I V VI⁻

35 _____ V I⁻ IV^{-6}_4 I⁻ IV⁻

36 _____ II⁻ V^{-7} I IV^6_4 I

37 _____ V I III⁻ IV I

38 _____ V I IV II⁻ V

39 _____ V ⁻VI IV⁻ I⁻ IV⁻

40 _____ VI⁻ II⁻ V VI⁻ IV

41 _____ ⁻VI IV⁻ I^{-6}_4 V ⁻VI

42 _____ II⁻ I^6_4 V VI⁻ II⁻

43 _____ I III⁻ VI⁻ IV V

44 _____ V I⁻ ⁻III IV⁻ V

45 _____ IV⁻ I^{-6}_4 V I⁻ ⁻III

46 _____ VI⁻ V I IV II⁻

47 _____ IV⁻ I⁻ ⁻VI I^{-6}_4 V

48 _____ IV⁻ I⁻ IV^{-6}_4 I⁻ V

D2-1 Key determination
(Copy 2)

Shield the answer. Listen to the series of five chords and write the composite chord symbols for the last three chords; then uncover the answer, which gives all five chords, and compare your response. Circle each incorrect chord symbol. Goal: No more than twenty-four errors.

1 _____ I V^{-7} I IV V

2 _____ IV V I VI$^-$ IV

3 _____ VI$^-$ IV V^{-7} I IV

4 _____ I$^-$ $^-$VI IV$^-$ V I$^-$

5 _____ $^-$VI IV$^-$ V I$^-$ $^-$VI

6 _____ V $^-$VI IV$^-$ V I$^-$

7 _____ I IV I V VI$^-$

8 _____ I IV II$^-$ V VI$^-$

9 _____ I$^-$ IV$^-$ I$^-$ V $^-$VI

10 _____ V I$^-$ $^-$VI IV$^-$ V

11 _____ IV$^-$ V $^-$VI IV$^-$ V

12 _____ VI$^-$ IV V VI$^-$ II$^-$

13 _____ VI$^-$ II$^-$ V^{-7} I IV

14 _____ IV II$^-$ V I VI$^-$

15 _____ I IV II$^-$ V VI$^-$

16 _____ IV$^-$ I$^-$ $^-$VI IV$^-$ V

17 _____ V $^-$VI IV$^-$ I$^-$ V

18 _____ II$^-$ V VI$^-$ IV I

19 _____ $^-$VI V I$^-$ IV$^-$ V

20 _____ I VI$^-$ V VI$^-$ IV

21 _____ II$^-$ V I VI$^-$ V

22 _____ IV$^-$ V I$^-$ $^-$VI V

23 _____ IV$^-$ I$^-$ $^-$VI V I$^-$

24 _____ VI$^-$ IV II$^-$ V VI$^-$

25 _____ IV I$_4^6$ V^{-7} I V

26 _____ $^-$VI IV$^-$ I$_4^{-6}$ V I$^-$

27 _____ IV$^-$ I$^-$ $^-$VI I$_4^{-6}$ V

28 _____ I III$^-$ IV I V

29 _____ I$^-$ $^-$III IV$^-$ I$^-$ V

30 _____ I$_4^{-6}$ V $^-$VI IV$^-$ V

31 _____ VI$^-$ IV II$^-$ I$_4^6$ V

32 _____ I$^-$ $^-$III IV$^-$ I$^-$ IV$^-$

33 _____ II$^-$ I$_4^6$ V VI$^-$ II$^-$

34 _____ I IV$_4^6$ I V VI$^-$

35 _____ V I$^-$ IV$_4^{-6}$ I$^-$ IV$^-$

36 _____ II$^-$ V^{-7} I IV$_4^6$ I

37 _____ V I III$^-$ IV I

38 _____ V I IV II$^-$ V

39 _____ V $^-$VI IV$^-$ I$^-$ IV$^-$

40 _____ VI$^-$ II$^-$ V VI$^-$ IV

41 _____ $^-$VI IV$^-$ I$_4^{-6}$ V $^-$VI

42 _____ II$^-$ I$_4^6$ V VI$^-$ II$^-$

43 _____ I III$^-$ VI$^-$ IV V

44 _____ V I$^-$ $^-$III IV$^-$ V

45 _____ IV$^-$ I$_4^{-6}$ V I$^-$ $^-$III

46 _____ VI$^-$ V I IV II$^-$

47 _____ IV$^-$ I$^-$ $^-$VI I$_4^{-6}$ V

48 _____ IV$^-$ I$^-$ IV$_4^{-6}$ I$^-$ V

D2-1 Key determination
(Copy 3)

Shield the answer. Listen to the series of five chords and write the composite chord symbols for the last three chords; then uncover the answer, which gives all five chords, and compare your response. Circle each incorrect chord symbol. Goal: No more than twenty-four errors.

1 _____ I V^{-7} I IV V

2 _____ IV V I VI$^-$ IV

3 _____ VI$^-$ IV V^{-7} I IV

4 _____ I$^-$ $^-$VI IV$^-$ V I$^-$

5 _____ $^-$VI IV$^-$ V I$^-$ $^-$VI

6 _____ V $^-$VI IV$^-$ V I$^-$

7 _____ I IV I V VI$^-$

8 _____ I IV II$^-$ V VI$^-$

9 _____ I$^-$ IV$^-$ I$^-$ V $^-$VI

10 _____ V I$^-$ $^-$VI IV$^-$ V

11 _____ IV$^-$ V $^-$VI IV$^-$ V

12 _____ VI$^-$ IV V VI$^-$ II$^-$

13 _____ VI$^-$ II$^-$ V^{-7} I IV

14 _____ IV II$^-$ V I VI$^-$

15 _____ I IV II$^-$ V VI$^-$

16 _____ IV$^-$ I$^-$ $^-$VI IV$^-$ V

17 _____ V $^-$VI IV$^-$ I$^-$ V

18 _____ II$^-$ V VI$^-$ IV I

19 _____ $^-$VI V I$^-$ IV$^-$ V

20 _____ I VI$^-$ V VI$^-$ IV

21 _____ II$^-$ V I VI$^-$ V

22 _____ IV$^-$ V I$^-$ $^-$VI V

23 _____ IV$^-$ I$^-$ $^-$VI V I$^-$

24 _____ VI$^-$ IV II$^-$ V VI$^-$

25 _____ IV I$^6_4$ V^{-7} I V

26 _____ $^-$VI IV$^-$ I$^{-6}_4$ V I$^-$

27 _____ IV$^-$ I$^-$ $^-$VI I$^{-6}_4$ V

28 _____ I III$^-$ IV I V

29 _____ I$^-$ $^-$III IV$^-$ I$^-$ V

30 _____ I$^{-6}_4$ V $^-$VI IV$^-$ V

31 _____ VI$^-$ IV II$^-$ I$^6_4$ V

32 _____ I$^-$ $^-$III IV$^-$ I$^-$ IV$^-$

33 _____ II$^-$ I$^6_4$ V VI$^-$ II$^-$

34 _____ I IV$^6_4$ I V VI$^-$

35 _____ V I$^-$ IV$^{-6}_4$ I$^-$ IV$^-$

36 _____ II$^-$ V^{-7} I IV$^6_4$ I

37 _____ V I III$^-$ IV I

38 _____ V I IV II$^-$ V

39 _____ V $^-$VI IV$^-$ I$^-$ IV$^-$

40 _____ VI$^-$ II$^-$ V VI$^-$ IV

41 _____ $^-$VI IV$^-$ I$^{-6}_4$ V $^-$VI

42 _____ II$^-$ I$^6_4$ V VI$^-$ II$^-$

43 _____ I III$^-$ VI$^-$ IV V

44 _____ V I$^-$ $^-$III IV$^-$ V

45 _____ IV$^-$ I$^{-6}_4$ V I$^-$ $^-$III

46 _____ VI$^-$ V I IV II$^-$

47 _____ IV$^-$ I$^-$ $^-$VI I$^{-6}_4$ V

48 _____ IV$^-$ I$^-$ IV$^{-6}_4$ I$^-$ V

38

D2-1 Key determination
(Copy 4)

Shield the answer. Listen to the series of five chords and write the composite chord symbols for the last three chords; then uncover the answer, which gives all five chords, and compare your response. Circle each incorrect chord symbol. Goal: No more than twenty-four errors.

1. _____ I V^{-7} I IV V
2. _____ IV V I VI$^-$ IV
3. _____ VI$^-$ IV V^{-7} I IV
4. _____ I$^-$ $^-$VI IV$^-$ V I$^-$
5. _____ $^-$VI IV$^-$ V I$^-$ $^-$VI
6. _____ V $^-$VI IV$^-$ V I$^-$
7. _____ I IV I V VI$^-$
8. _____ I IV II$^-$ V VI$^-$
9. _____ I$^-$ IV$^-$ I$^-$ V $^-$VI
10. _____ V I$^-$ $^-$VI IV$^-$ V
11. _____ IV$^-$ V $^-$VI IV$^-$ V
12. _____ VI$^-$ IV V VI$^-$ II$^-$
13. _____ VI$^-$ II$^-$ V^{-7} I IV
14. _____ IV II$^-$ V I VI$^-$
15. _____ I IV II$^-$ V VI$^-$
16. _____ IV$^-$ I$^-$ $^-$VI IV$^-$ V
17. _____ V $^-$VI IV$^-$ I$^-$ V
18. _____ II$^-$ V VI$^-$ IV I
19. _____ $^-$VI V I$^-$ IV$^-$ V
20. _____ I VI$^-$ V VI$^-$ IV
21. _____ II$^-$ V I VI$^-$ V
22. _____ IV$^-$ V I$^-$ $^-$VI V
23. _____ IV$^-$ I$^-$ $^-$VI V I$^-$
24. _____ VI$^-$ IV II$^-$ V VI$^-$

25. _____ IV I$^{6}_{4}$ V^{-7} I V
26. _____ $^-$VI IV$^-$ I$^{-6}_{4}$ V I$^-$
27. _____ IV$^-$ I$^-$ $^-$VI I$^{-6}_{4}$ V
28. _____ I III$^-$ IV I V
29. _____ I$^-$ $^-$III IV$^-$ I$^-$ V
30. _____ I$^{-6}_{4}$ V $^-$VI IV$^-$ V
31. _____ VI$^-$ IV II$^-$ I$^{6}_{4}$ V
32. _____ I$^-$ $^-$III IV$^-$ I$^-$ IV$^-$
33. _____ II$^-$ I$^{6}_{4}$ V VI$^-$ II$^-$
34. _____ I IV$^{6}_{4}$ I V VI$^-$
35. _____ V I$^-$ IV$^{-6}_{4}$ I$^-$ IV$^-$
36. _____ II$^-$ V^{-7} I IV$^{6}_{4}$ I
37. _____ V I III$^-$ IV I
38. _____ V I IV II$^-$ V
39. _____ V $^-$VI IV$^-$ I$^-$ IV$^-$
40. _____ VI$^-$ II$^-$ V VI$^-$ IV
41. _____ $^-$VI IV$^-$ I$^{-6}_{4}$ V $^-$VI
42. _____ II$^-$ I$^{6}_{4}$ V VI$^-$ II$^-$
43. _____ I III$^-$ VI$^-$ IV V
44. _____ V I$^-$ $^-$III IV$^-$ V
45. _____ IV$^-$ I$^{-6}_{4}$ V I$^-$ $^-$III
46. _____ VI$^-$ V I IV II$^-$
47. _____ IV$^-$ I$^-$ $^-$VI I$^{-6}_{4}$ V
48. _____ IV$^-$ I$^-$ IV$^{-6}_{4}$ I$^-$ V

D2–1 Key determination
(Copy 5)

Shield the answer. Listen to the series of five chords and write the composite chord symbols for the last three chords; then uncover the answer, which gives all five chords, and compare your response. Circle each incorrect chord symbol. Goal: No more than twenty-four errors.

1 _____ I V^{-7} I IV V

2 _____ IV V I VI$^-$ IV

3 _____ VI$^-$ IV V^{-7} I IV

4 _____ I$^-$ $^-$VI IV$^-$ V I$^-$

5 _____ $^-$VI IV$^-$ V I$^-$ $^-$VI

6 _____ V $^-$VI IV$^-$ V I$^-$

7 _____ I IV I V VI$^-$

8 _____ I IV II$^-$ V VI$^-$

9 _____ I$^-$ IV$^-$ I$^-$ V $^-$VI

10 _____ V I$^-$ $^-$VI IV$^-$ V

11 _____ IV$^-$ V $^-$VI IV$^-$ V

12 _____ VI$^-$ IV V VI$^-$ II$^-$

13 _____ VI$^-$ II$^-$ V^{-7} I IV

14 _____ IV II$^-$ V I VI$^-$

15 _____ I IV II$^-$ V VI$^-$

16 _____ IV$^-$ I$^-$ $^-$VI IV$^-$ V

17 _____ V $^-$VI IV$^-$ I$^-$ V

18 _____ II$^-$ V VI$^-$ IV I

19 _____ $^-$VI V I$^-$ IV$^-$ V

20 _____ I VI$^-$ V VI$^-$ IV

21 _____ II$^-$ V I VI$^-$ V

22 _____ IV$^-$ V I$^-$ $^-$VI V

23 _____ IV$^-$ I$^-$ $^-$VI V I$^-$

24 _____ VI$^-$ IV II$^-$ V VI$^-$

25 _____ IV I$^6_4$ V^{-7} I V

26 _____ $^-$VI IV$^-$ I$^{-6}_4$ V I$^-$

27 _____ IV$^-$ I$^-$ $^-$VI I$^{-6}_4$ V

28 _____ I III$^-$ IV I V

29 _____ I$^-$ $^-$III IV$^-$ I$^-$ V

30 _____ I$^{-6}_4$ V $^-$VI IV$^-$ V

31 _____ VI$^-$ IV II$^-$ I$^6_4$ V

32 _____ I$^-$ $^-$III IV$^-$ I$^-$ IV$^-$

33 _____ II$^-$ I$^6_4$ V VI$^-$ II$^-$

34 _____ I IV$^6_4$ I V VI$^-$

35 _____ V I$^-$ IV$^{-6}_4$ I$^-$ IV$^-$

36 _____ II$^-$ V^{-7} I IV$^6_4$ I

37 _____ V I III$^-$ IV I

38 _____ V I IV II$^-$ V

39 _____ V $^-$VI IV$^-$ I$^-$ IV$^-$

40 _____ VI$^-$ II$^-$ V VI$^-$ IV

41 _____ $^-$VI IV$^-$ I$^{-6}_4$ V $^-$VI

42 _____ II$^-$ I$^6_4$ V VI$^-$ II$^-$

43 _____ I III$^-$ VI$^-$ IV V

44 _____ V I$^-$ $^-$III IV$^-$ V

45 _____ IV$^-$ I$^{-6}_4$ V I$^-$ $^-$III

46 _____ VI$^-$ V I IV II$^-$

47 _____ IV$^-$ I$^-$ $^-$VI I$^{-6}_4$ V

48 _____ IV$^-$ I$^-$ IV$^{-6}_4$ I$^-$ V

D2-2 Key determination
(Copy 1)

Shield the answer. Listen to the series of five chords and write the composite chord symbols for the last three chords; then uncover the answer, which gives all five chords, and compare your response. Circle each incorrect chord symbol. Goal: No more than twenty-four errors. When you have done this lesson, take Test D2.

1 _____ V^{-7} I I^{-6} IV II$^-$

2 _____ I^{-6} VII$_-^6$ I V^{-6} I

3 _____ I^{-6} IV$^-$ IV^{-6} V $^-$VI

4 _____ $^-$VI II$_-^6$ V IV^6 I$^-$

5 _____ II^6 I$_4^{-6}$ V IV^{-6} IV

6 _____ IV I^{-6} I V^{-6} IV^{-6}

7 _____ I^6 IV$^-$ IV^6 V $^-$VI

8 _____ IV$^-$ I$^-$ I^6 II$_-^6$ V

9 _____ I$^-$ $^-$III IV$^-$ I V^{-6}

10 _____ V^{-6} I IV$_4^6$ I IV^{-6}

11 _____ V I$_4^{-6}$ V $^-$VI IV$^-$

12 _____ IV^{-6} I$_4^6$ IV V VI$^-$

13 _____ IV VII$_-^6$ I^{-6} IV V

14 _____ II$_-^6$ VII$_-^6$ V^{-6} I$^-$ I^6

15 _____ IV^6 II$_-^6$ V $^-$VI IV$^-$

16 _____ I I^{-6} IV IV^{-6} V

17 _____ VI$^-$ IV V IV^{-6} II^6

18 _____ V IV^{-6} V^{-6} I VI$^-$

19 _____ IV^6 I$^-$ VII$_-^6$ V^{-6} I$^-$

20 _____ V IV^{-6} IV I^{-6} VII$_-^6$

21 _____ I$^-$ $^-$III $^-$VI IV$^-$ V

22 _____ V^{-6} I$^-$ I^6 $^-$VI IV$^-$

23 _____ IV^6 V I$^-$ $^-$III IV^6

24 _____ IV I III$^-$ VI$^-$ V^{-6}

25 _____ I^6 IV$^-$ II$_-^6$ V IV^6

26 _____ VI$^-$ V^{-6} I VII$_-^6$ I^{-6}

27 _____ IV$^-$ I^6 V$_4^6$ I$^-$ V^{-6}

28 _____ I^{-6} VI$^-$ II^6 V IV^{-6}

29 _____ I$_4^{-6}$ V IV^6 IV$^-$ I^6

30 _____ IV^{-6} I^{-6} V$_4^6$ I V^{-6}

31 _____ VI$^-$ II^6 II$^-$ V IV^{-6}

32 _____ IV$^-$ IV^6 II$_-^6$ V $^-$VI

33 _____ IV^{-6} II$^-$ V VI$^-$ II^6

34 _____ IV$^-$ I^6 II$_-^6$ V IV^6

35 _____ I$_4^6$ V VI$^-$ IV II$^-$

36 _____ II$^-$ I$_4^6$ V IV^{-6} IV

37 _____ IV^6 I$_4^{-6}$ V V^{-6} I$^-$

38 _____ I$_4^{-6}$ V I$^-$ IV$_4^{-6}$ I$^-$

39 _____ I V^{-6} IV^{-6} I$_4^6$ IV

40 _____ I$^-$ I^6 IV$^-$ IV^6 V

41 _____ VII$_-^6$ I$^-$ V^{-6} I$^-$ $^-$VI

42 _____ V^{-6} I III$^-$ IV I

43 _____ IV I^{-6} VI$^-$ II^6 V

44 _____ I$^-$ $^-$VI IV$^-$ I^6 V

45 _____ I^6 II$_-^6$ VII$_-^6$ I$^-$ IV^6

46 _____ I^{-6} IV I$_4^6$ V VI$^-$

47 _____ IV^6 I$_4^{-6}$ V I$^-$ II$_-^6$

48 _____ IV^{-6} II$^-$ I$_4^6$ V I

41

D2-2 Key determination
(Copy 2)

Shield the answer. Listen to the series of five chords and write the composite chord symbols for the last three chords; then uncover the answer, which gives all five chords, and compare your response. Circle each incorrect chord symbol. Goal: No more than twenty-four errors. When you have done this lesson, take Test D2.

1 _____ V^{-7} I I^{-6} IV II^-

2 _____ I^{-6} $VII^6_{\underline{}}$ I V^{-6} I

3 _____ I^{-6} IV^- IV^{-6} V ^-VI

4 _____ ^-VI $II^6_{\underline{}}$ V IV^6 I^-

5 _____ II^6 I^{-6}_4 V IV^{-6} IV

6 _____ IV I^{-6} I V^{-6} IV^{-6}

7 _____ I^6 IV^- IV^6 V ^-VI

8 _____ IV^- I^- I^6 $II^6_{\underline{}}$ V

9 _____ I^- ^-III IV^- I V^{-6}

10 _____ V^{-6} I IV^6_4 I IV^{-6}

11 _____ V I^{-6}_4 V ^-VI IV^-

12 _____ IV^{-6} I^6_4 IV V VI^-

13 _____ IV $VII^6_{\underline{}}$ I^{-6} IV V

14 _____ $II^6_{\underline{}}$ $VII^6_{\underline{}}$ V^{-6} I^- I^6

15 _____ IV^6 $II^6_{\underline{}}$ V ^-VI IV^-

16 _____ I I^{-6} IV IV^{-6} V

17 _____ VI^- IV V IV^{-6} II^6

18 _____ V IV^{-6} V^{-6} I VI^-

19 _____ IV^6 I^- $VII^6_{\underline{}}$ V^{-6} I^-

20 _____ V IV^{-6} IV I^{-6} $VII^6_{\underline{}}$

21 _____ I^- ^-III ^-VI IV^- V

22 _____ V^{-6} I^- I^6 ^-VI IV^-

23 _____ IV^6 V I^- ^-III IV^6

24 _____ IV I III^- VI^- V^{-6}

25 _____ I^6 IV^- $II^6_{\underline{}}$ V IV^6

26 _____ VI^- V^{-6} I $VII^6_{\underline{}}$ I^{-6}

27 _____ IV^- I^6 V^6_4 I^- V^{-6}

28 _____ I^{-6} VI^- $II^6_{\underline{}}$ V IV^{-6}

29 _____ I^{-6}_4 V IV^6 IV^- I^6

30 _____ IV^{-6} I^{-6} V^6_4 I V^{-6}

31 _____ VI^- $II^6_{\underline{}}$ II^- V IV^{-6}

32 _____ IV^- IV^6 $II^6_{\underline{}}$ V ^-VI

33 _____ IV^{-6} II^- V VI^- $II^6_{\underline{}}$

34 _____ IV^- I^6 $II^6_{\underline{}}$ V IV^6

35 _____ I^6_4 V VI^- IV II^-

36 _____ II^- I^6_4 V IV^{-6} IV

37 _____ IV^6 I^{-6}_4 V V^{-6} I^-

38 _____ I^{-6}_4 V I^- IV^{-6}_4 I^-

39 _____ I V^{-6} IV^{-6} I^6_4 IV

40 _____ I^- I^6 IV^- IV^6 V

41 _____ $VII^6_{\underline{}}$ I^- V^{-6} I^- ^-VI

42 _____ V^{-6} I III^- IV I

43 _____ IV I^{-6} VI^- $II^6_{\underline{}}$ V

44 _____ I^- ^-VI IV^- I^6 V

45 _____ I^6 $II^6_{\underline{}}$ $VII^6_{\underline{}}$ I^- IV^6

46 _____ I^{-6} IV I^6_4 V VI^-

47 _____ IV^6 I^{-6}_4 V I^- $II^6_{\underline{}}$

48 _____ IV^{-6} II^- I^6_4 V I

D2-2 Key determination
(Copy 3)

Shield the answer. Listen to the series of five chords and write the composite chord symbols for the last three chords; then uncover the answer, which gives all five chords, and compare your response. Circle each incorrect chord symbol. Goal: No more than twenty-four errors. When you have done this lesson, take Test D2.

1 _____ V^{-7} I I^{-6} IV II^-

2 _____ I^{-6} VII^6_- I V^{-6} I

3 _____ I^{-6} IV^- IV^{-6} V ^-VI

4 _____ ^-VI II^6_- V IV^6 I^-

5 _____ II^6 I^{-6}_4 V IV^{-6} IV

6 _____ IV I^{-6} I V^{-6} IV^{-6}

7 _____ I^6 IV^- IV^6 V ^-VI

8 _____ IV^- I^- I^6 II^6_- V

9 _____ I^- ^-III IV^- I V^{-6}

10 _____ V^{-6} I IV^6_4 I IV^{-6}

11 _____ V I^{-6}_4 V ^-VI IV^-

12 _____ IV^{-6} I^6_4 IV V VI^-

13 _____ IV VII^6_- I^{-6} IV V

14 _____ II^6_- VII^6_- V^{-6} I^- I^6

15 _____ IV^6 II^6_- V ^-VI IV^-

16 _____ I I^{-6} IV IV^{-6} V

17 _____ VI^- IV V IV^{-6} II^6

18 _____ V IV^{-6} V^{-6} I VI^-

19 _____ IV^6 I^- VII^6_- V^{-6} I^-

20 _____ V IV^{-6} IV I^{-6} VII^6_-

21 _____ I^- ^-III ^-VI IV^- V

22 _____ V^{-6} I^- I^6 ^-VI IV^-

23 _____ IV^6 V I^- ^-III IV^6

24 _____ IV I III^- VI^- V^{-6}

25 _____ I^6 IV^- II^6_- V IV^6

26 _____ VI^- V^{-6} I VII^6_- I^{-6}

27 _____ IV^- I^6 V^6_4 I^- V^{-6}

28 _____ I^{-6} VI^- II^6 V IV^{-6}

29 _____ I^{-6}_4 V IV^6 IV^- I^6

30 _____ IV^{-6} I^{-6} V^6_4 I V^{-6}

31 _____ VI^- II^6 II^- V IV^{-6}

32 _____ IV^- IV^6 II^6_- V ^-VI

33 _____ IV^{-6} II^- V VI^- II^6

34 _____ IV^- I^6 II^6_- V IV^6

35 _____ I^6_4 V VI^- IV II^-

36 _____ II^- I^6_4 V IV^{-6} IV

37 _____ IV^6 I^{-6}_4 V V^{-6} I^-

38 _____ I^{-6}_4 V I^- IV^{-6}_4 I^-

39 _____ I V^{-6} IV^{-6} I^6_4 IV

40 _____ I^- I^6 IV^- IV^6 V

41 _____ VII^6_- I^- V^{-6} I^- ^-VI

42 _____ V^{-6} I III^- IV I

43 _____ IV I^{-6} VI^- II^6 V

44 _____ I^- ^-VI IV^- I^6 V

45 _____ I^6 II^6_- VII^6_- I^- IV^6

46 _____ I^{-6} IV I^6_4 V^-VI

47 _____ IV^6 I^{-6}_4 V I^- II^6_-

48 _____ IV^{-6} II^- I^6_4 V I

D2-2 Key determination
(Copy 4)

Shield the answer. Listen to the series of five chords and write the composite chord symbols for the last three chords; then uncover the answer, which gives all five chords, and compare your response. Circle each incorrect chord symbol. Goal: No more than twenty-four errors. When you have done this lesson, take Test D2.

1. _____ V^{-7} I I^{-6} IV II^-
2. _____ I^{-6} $VII^{\underline{6}}$ I V^{-6} I
3. _____ I^{-6} IV^- IV^{-6} V ^-VI
4. _____ ^-VI $II^{\underline{6}}$ V IV^6 I^-
5. _____ II^6 I^6_4 V IV^{-6} IV
6. _____ IV I^{-6} I V^{-6} IV^{-6}
7. _____ I^6 IV^- IV^6 V ^-VI
8. _____ IV^- I^- I^6 $II^{\underline{6}}$ V
9. _____ I^- ^-III IV^- I V^{-6}
10. _____ V^{-6} I IV^6_4 I IV^{-6}
11. _____ V I^{-6}_4 V ^-VI IV^-
12. _____ IV^{-6} I^6_4 IV V VI^-
13. _____ IV $VII^{\underline{6}}$ I^{-6} IV V
14. _____ $II^{\underline{6}}$ $VII^{\underline{6}}$ V^{-6} I^- I^6
15. _____ IV^6 $II^{\underline{6}}$ V ^-VI IV^-
16. _____ I I^{-6} IV IV^{-6} V
17. _____ VI^- IV V IV^{-6} II^6
18. _____ V IV^{-6} V^{-6} I VI^-
19. _____ IV^6 I^- $VII^{\underline{6}}$ V^{-6} I^-
20. _____ V IV^{-6} IV I^{-6} $VII^{\underline{6}}$
21. _____ I^- ^-III ^-VI IV^- V
22. _____ V^{-6} I^- I^6 ^-VI IV^-
23. _____ IV^6 V I^- ^-III IV^6
24. _____ IV I III^- VI^- V^{-6}

25. _____ I^6 IV^- $II^{\underline{6}}$ V IV^6
26. _____ VI^- V^{-6} I $VII^{\underline{6}}$ I^{-6}
27. _____ IV^- I^6 V^6_4 I^- V^{-6}
28. _____ I^{-6} VI^- II^6 V IV^{-6}
29. _____ I^{-6}_4 V IV^6 IV^- I^6
30. _____ IV^{-6} I^{-6} V^6_4 I V^{-6}
31. _____ VI^- II^6 II^- V IV^{-6}
32. _____ IV^- IV^6 $II^{\underline{6}}$ V ^-VI
33. _____ IV^{-6} II^- V VI^- II^6
34. _____ IV^- I^6 $II^{\underline{6}}$ V IV^6
35. _____ I^6_4 V VI^- IV II^-
36. _____ II^- I^6_4 V IV^{-6} IV
37. _____ IV^6 I^{-6}_4 V V^{-6} I^-
38. _____ I^{-6}_4 V I^- IV^{-6}_4 I^-
39. _____ I V^{-6} IV^{-6} I^6_4 IV
40. _____ I^- I^6 IV^- IV^6 V
41. _____ $VII^{\underline{6}}$ I^- V^{-6} I^- ^-VI
42. _____ V^{-6} I III^- IV I
43. _____ IV I^{-6} VI^- II^6 V
44. _____ I^- ^-VI IV^- I^6 V
45. _____ I^6 $II^{\underline{6}}$ $VII^{\underline{6}}$ I^- IV^6
46. _____ I^{-6} IV I^6_4 V VI^-
47. _____ IV^6 I^{-6}_4 V I^- $II^{\underline{6}}$
48. _____ IV^{-6} II^- I^6_4 V I

D2-2 Key determination
(Copy 5)

Shield the answer. Listen to the series of five chords and write the composite chord symbols for the last three chords; then uncover the answer, which gives all five chords, and compare your response. Circle each incorrect chord symbol. Goal: No more than twenty-four errors. When you have done this lesson, take Test D2.

1. _____ V^{-7} I I^{-6} IV II^-
2. _____ I^{-6} $VII^{\underline{6}}$ I V^{-6} I
3. _____ I^{-6} IV^- IV^{-6} V ^-VI
4. _____ ^-VI $II^{\underline{6}}$ V IV^6 I^-
5. _____ II^6 I^6_4 V IV^{-6} IV
6. _____ IV I^{-6} I V^{-6} IV^{-6}
7. _____ I^6 IV^- IV^6 V ^-VI
8. _____ IV^- I^- I^6 $II^{\underline{6}}$ V
9. _____ I^- ^-III IV^- I V^{-6}
10. _____ V^{-6} I IV^6_4 I IV^{-6}
11. _____ V I^{-6}_4 V ^-VI IV^-
12. _____ IV^{-6} I^6_4 IV V VI^-
13. _____ IV $VII^{\underline{6}}$ I^{-6} IV V
14. _____ $II^{\underline{6}}$ $VII^{\underline{6}}$ V^{-6} I^- I^6
15. _____ IV^6 $II^{\underline{6}}$ V ^-VI IV^-
16. _____ I I^{-6} IV IV^{-6} V
17. _____ VI^- IV V IV^{-6} II^6
18. _____ V IV^{-6} V^{-6} I VI^-
19. _____ IV^6 I^- $VII^{\underline{6}}$ V^{-6} I^-
20. _____ V IV^{-6} IV I^{-6} $VII^{\underline{6}}$
21. _____ I^- ^-III ^-VI IV^- V
22. _____ V^{-6} I^- I^6 ^-VI IV^-
23. _____ IV^6 V I^- ^-III IV^6
24. _____ IV I III^- VI^- V^{-6}

25. _____ I^6 IV^- $II^{\underline{6}}$ V IV^6
26. _____ VI^- V^{-6} I $VII^{\underline{6}}$ I^{-6}
27. _____ IV^- I^6 V^6_4 I^- V^{-6}
28. _____ I^{-6} VI^- II^6 V IV^{-6}
29. _____ I^{-6}_4 V IV^6 IV^- I^6
30. _____ IV^{-6} I^{-6} V^6_4 I V^{-6}
31. _____ VI^- II^6 II^- V IV^{-6}
32. _____ IV^- IV^6 $II^{\underline{6}}$ V ^-VI
33. _____ IV^{-6} II^- V VI^- II^6
34. _____ IV^- I^6 $II^{\underline{6}}$ V IV^6
35. _____ I^6_4 V VI^- IV II^-
36. _____ II^- I^6_4 V IV^{-6} IV
37. _____ IV^6 I^{-6}_4 V V^{-6} I^-
38. _____ I^{-6}_4 V I^- IV^{-6}_4 I^-
39. _____ I V^{-6} IV^{-6} I^6_4 IV
40. _____ I^- I^6 IV^- IV^6 V
41. _____ $VII^{\underline{6}}$ I^- V^{-6} I^- ^-VI
42. _____ V^{-6} I III^- IV I
43. _____ IV I^{-6} VI^- II^6 V
44. _____ I^- ^-VI IV^- I^6 V
45. _____ I^6 $II^{\underline{6}}$ $VII^{\underline{6}}$ I^- IV^6
46. _____ I^{-6} IV I^6_4 V VI^-
47. _____ IV^6 I^{-6}_4 V I^- $II^{\underline{6}}$
48. _____ IV^{-6} II^- I^6_4 V I

Modulations

Modulations, or key changes, may be classified into two types, *common chord modulations* and *direct modulations.*

In *common chord modulations,* the last chord in the initial key is also a member of the final key. In the example below, the fifth chord—an A minor triad—is a member of both the key of C major, the initial key, and the key of G major, the final key. Since the next chord, a D dominant seventh chord, is not a member of the initial key, chord symbols related to the initial key of C major do not apply and can not be used. In the analysis of common chord modulations, chord symbols for both keys are written under the common chord, as shown here.

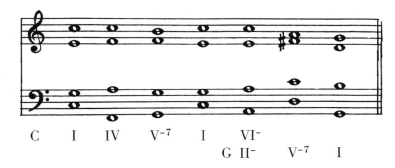

C   I   IV   V⁻⁷   I   VI⁻

G II⁻   V⁻⁷   I

Where a tonic six-four chord is involved in a cadence following a common chord modulation, there is sometimes a problem in determining which chord is the common chord. In the following example, the fifth chord, a G six-four chord, may be considered a I_4^6 chord in G major and a V_4^6 chord in C major. The tonic six-four chord is so often used preceding a dominant chord in a cadence that it is usually heard as a tonic six-four and hence as part of the second key. For this reason, a tonic six-four chord used in this way will not be considered in these exercises to be a common chord. Thus, as in the example below, the chord preceding the cadential six-four chord is considered to be the common chord.

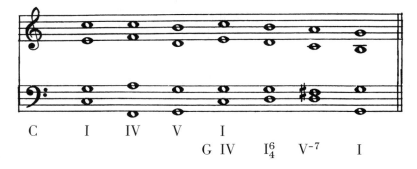

C   I   IV   V   I

G IV I_4^6 V⁻⁷   I

In *direct modulations,* the last chord in the original key is not a member of the key in which the modulation terminates. In the following example the fourth chord—a C major triad—is the last chord in the original key of C major. It is not, however, a member of the next key. The music moves directly into the new key without any common chord. In an analysis of a direct modulation, the new key is indicated before the chord symbol, as in the example.

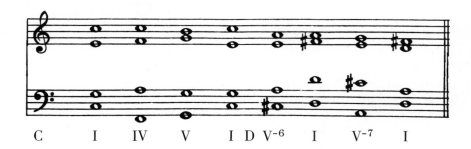

$$C \quad I \quad IV \quad V \quad I \; D \; V^{-6} \quad I \quad V^{-7} \quad I$$

A printed worksheet and a tape recording are provided for each lesson. Each frame on the worksheet contains two staffs. The first staff, on which you are to write your response, contains the bass notes and composite chord symbols for the first three chords. The key in which the phrase begins is indicated with a capital letter for a major key and a lower-case letter for a minor key. The staff directly below contains the correct answer. To do each frame, start by shielding the answer. When you have heard the phrase, write the bass notes and the composite chord symbols and indicate the new key, using the appropriate format; then slide your shield down and check your response. Stop the tape while responding. Each phrase occurs only once on the tape recording, but you may listen to each phrase as often as necessary by rewinding the tape. On Test D3, you will hear each phrase three times, so you should attempt to do each phrase in no more than three hearings. Your goal is to complete each lesson with no more than eight incorrect frames. When you have done so, go on to the next lesson. Otherwise repeat the lesson until you reach the goal or until you have done the lesson five times, at which point you should go on to the next lesson regardless of your score.

There are three lessons in this series. When you have done these lessons, take Test D3.

D3-1

(Copy 1)

Bass dictation and harmonic analysis of modulating phrases

Shield the answer (second staff). Listen to the phrase several times and write the bass notes and composite chord symbols for the chords following the three that are given; then uncover the answer and compare your response. Circle incorrect frames. Goal: No more than eight incorrect frames.

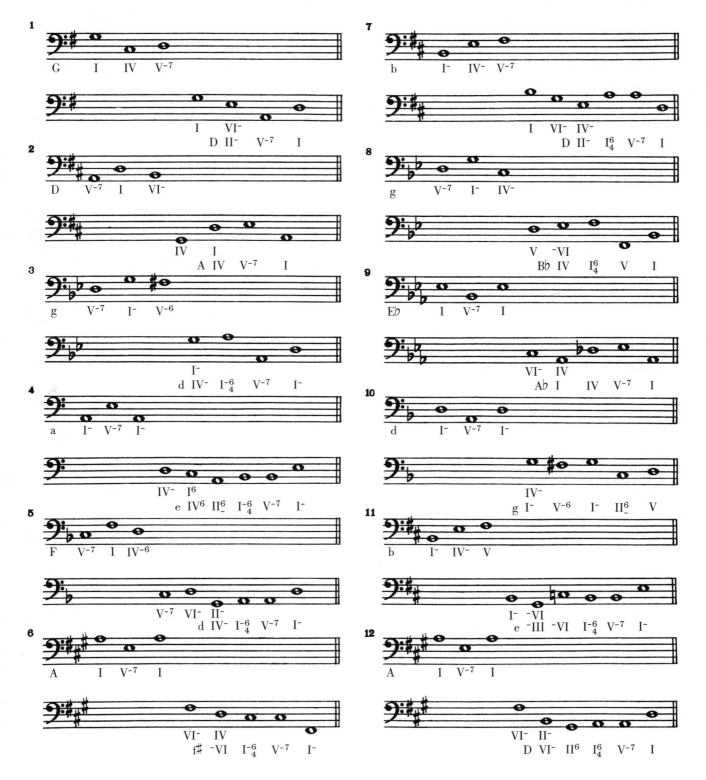

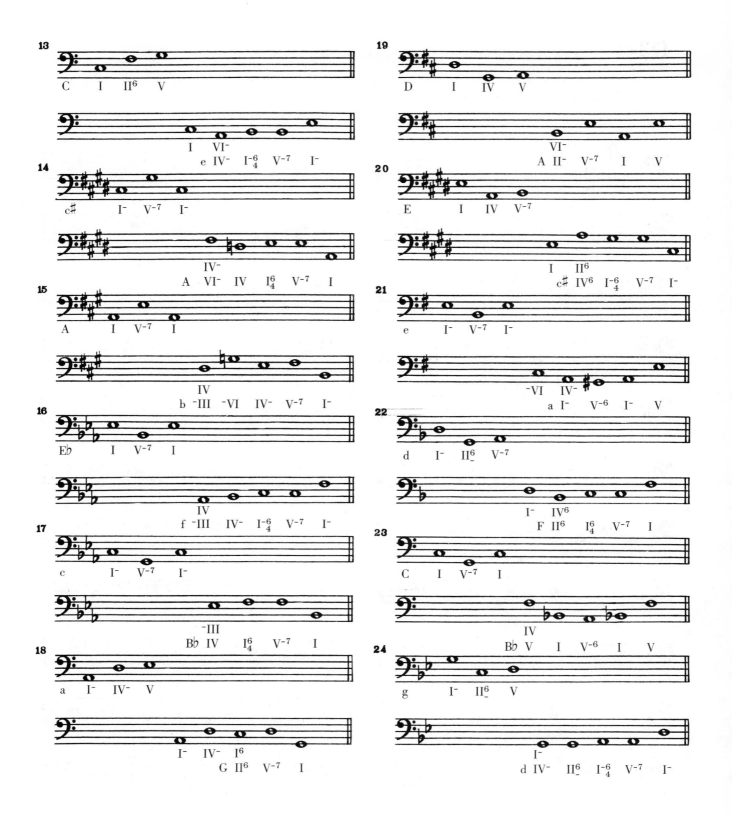

50

D3-1
(Copy 2)

Bass dictation and harmonic analysis of modulating phrases

Shield the answer (second staff). Listen to the phrase several times and write the bass notes and composite chord symbols for the chords following the three that are given; then uncover the answer and compare your response. Circle incorrect frames. Goal: No more than eight incorrect frames.

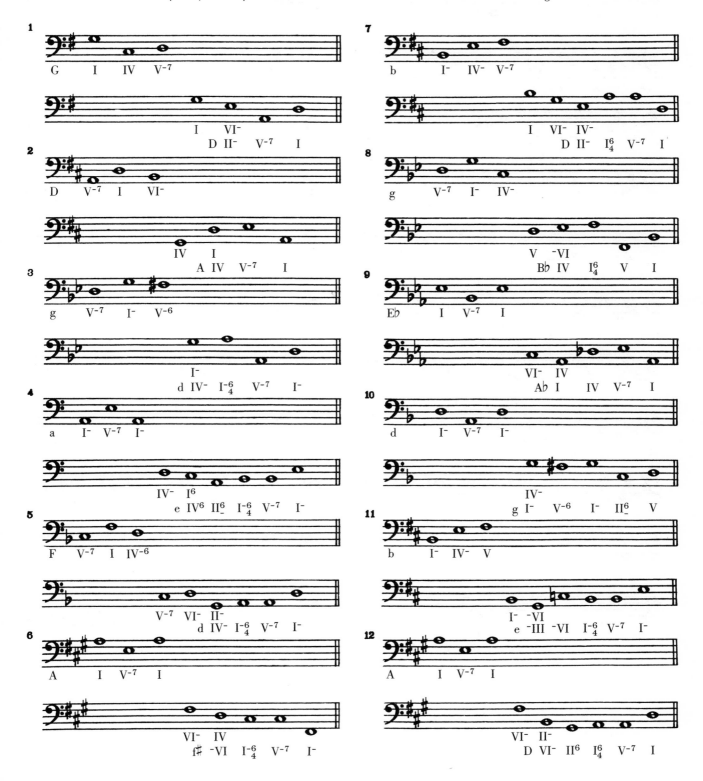

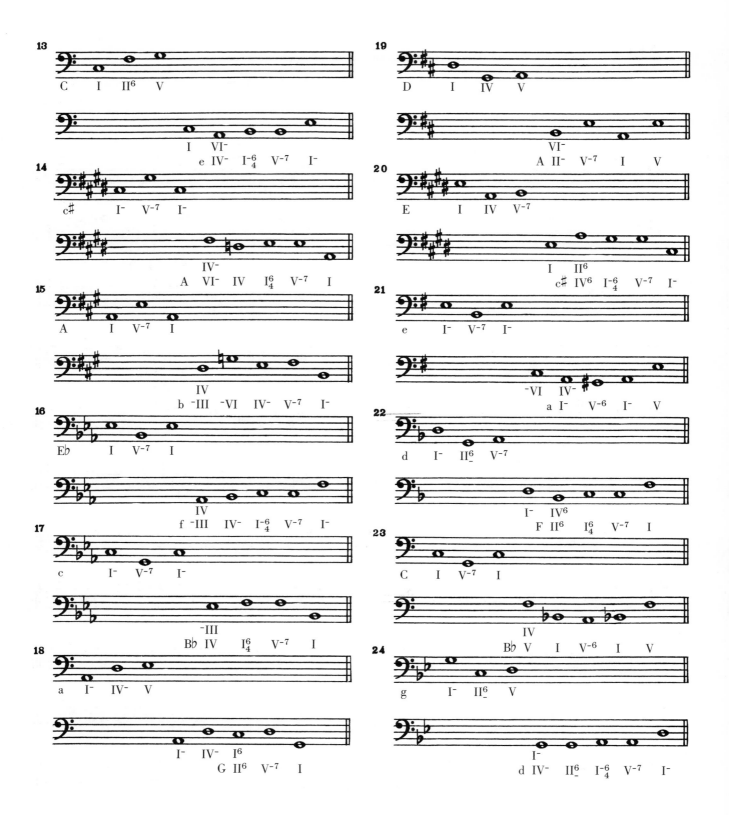

52

D3-1
(Copy 3)

Bass dictation and harmonic analysis of modulating phrases

Shield the answer (second staff). Listen to the phrase several times and write the bass notes and composite chord symbols for the chords following the three that are given; then uncover the answer and compare your response. Circle incorrect frames. Goal: No more than eight incorrect frames.

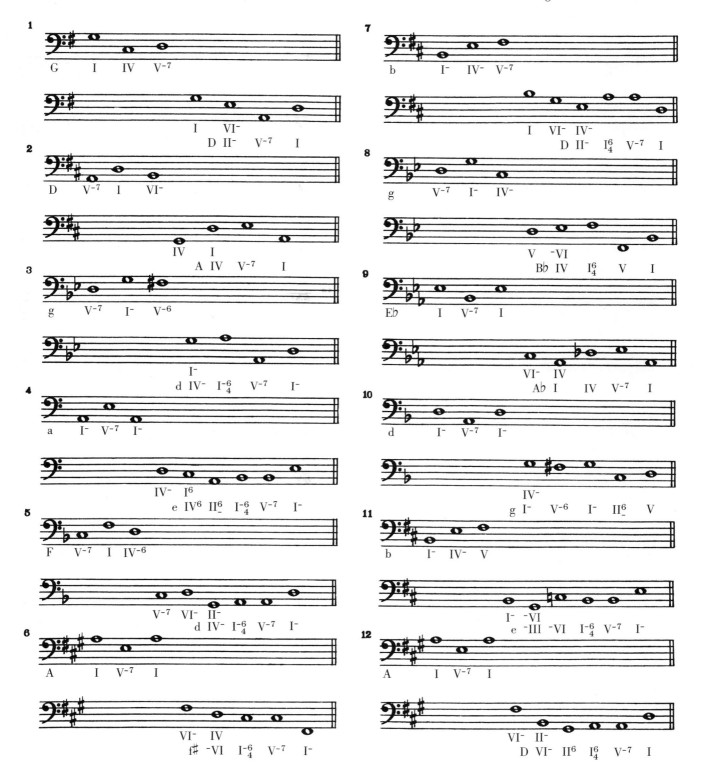

53

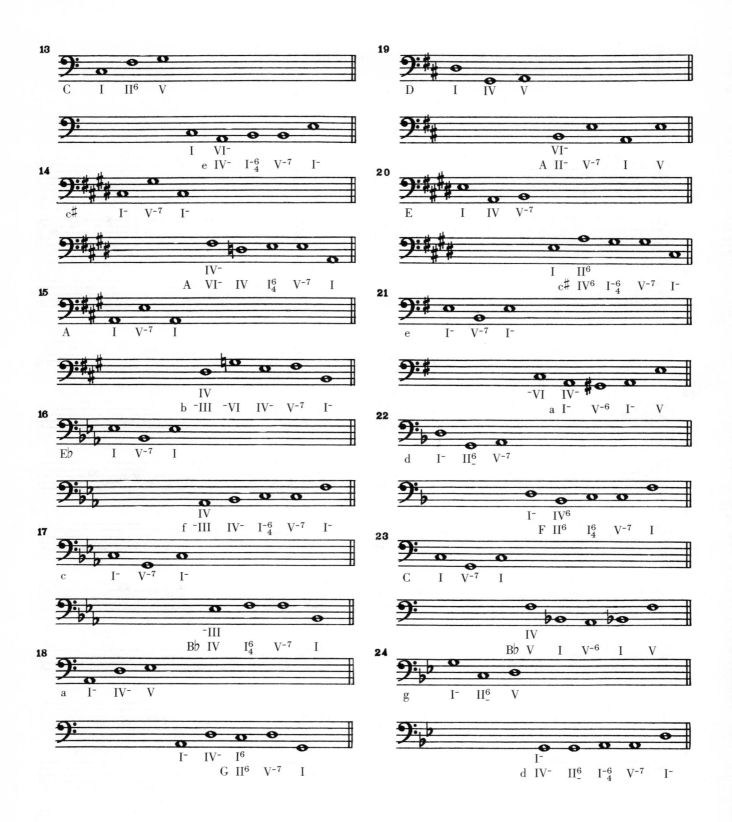

D3-1 Bass dictation and harmonic analysis of modulating phrases

(Copy 4)

Shield the answer (second staff). Listen to the phrase several times and write the bass notes and composite chord symbols for the chords following the three that are given; then uncover the answer and compare your response. Circle incorrect frames. Goal: No more than eight incorrect frames.

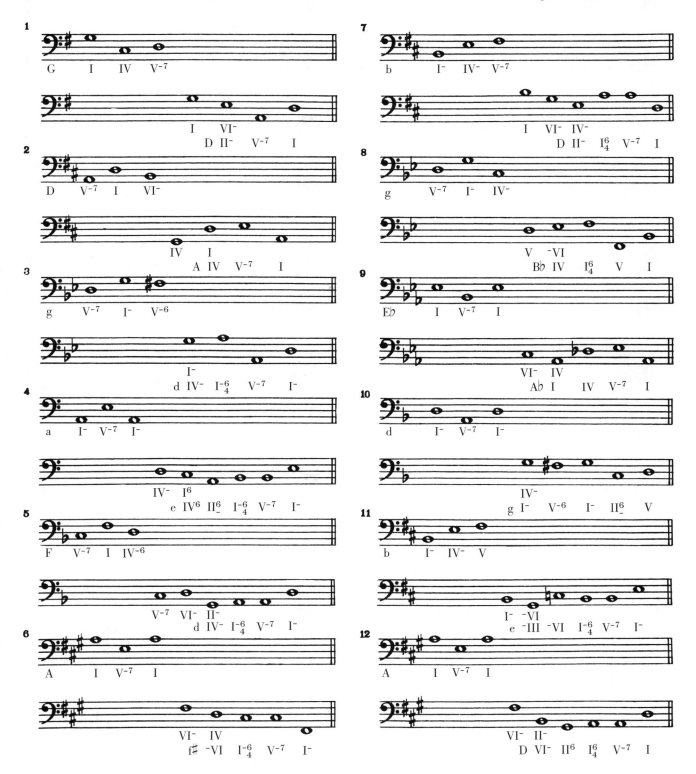

55

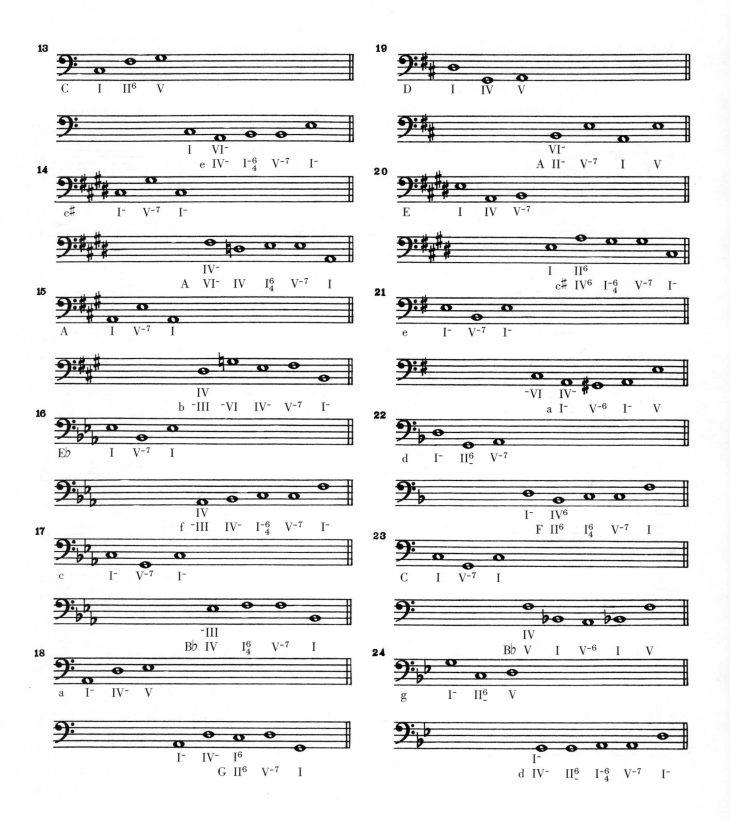

56

D3-1
(Copy 5)

Bass dictation and harmonic analysis of modulating phrases

Shield the answer (second staff). Listen to the phrase several times and write the bass notes and composite chord symbols for the chords following the three that are given; then uncover the answer and compare your response. Circle incorrect frames. Goal: No more than eight incorrect frames.

57

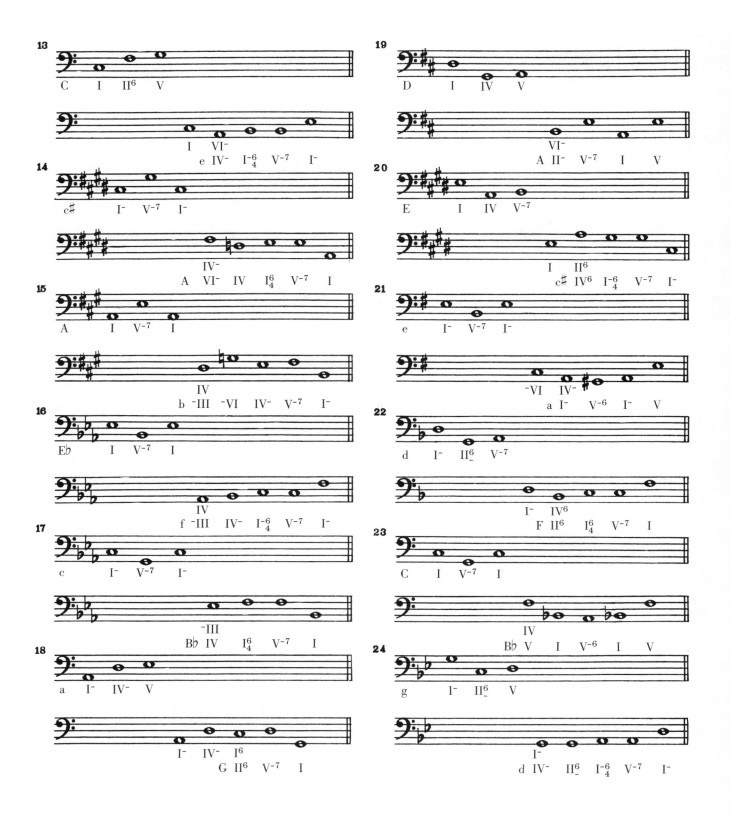

58

D3-2 Bass dictation and harmonic analysis of modulating phrases
(Copy 1)

Shield the answer. Listen to the phrase several times and write the bass notes and composite chord symbols for the chords following the three that are given; then uncover the answer and compare your response. Circle incorrect frames. Goal: No more than eight incorrect frames.

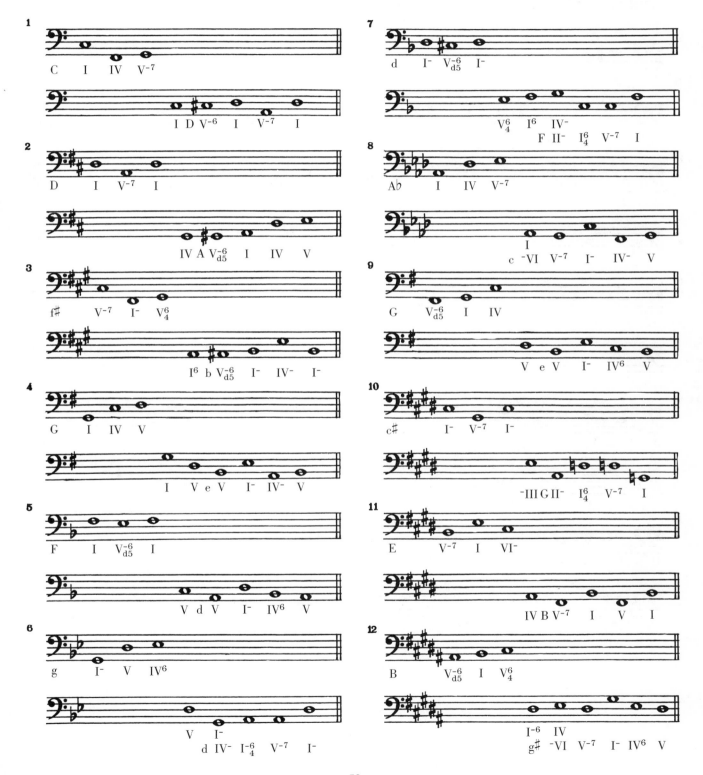

1

C I IV V^{-7}

I D V^{-6} I V^{-7} I

2

D I V^{-7} I

IV A V$^{-6}_{d5}$ I IV V

3

f$\sharp$ V^{-7} I$^-$ V$^6_4$

I^6 b V$^{-6}_{d5}$ I$^-$ IV$^-$ I$^-$

4

G I IV V

I V e V I$^-$ IV$^-$ V

5

F I V$^{-6}_{d5}$ I

V d V I$^-$ IV^6 V

6

g I$^-$ V IV^6

V I$^-$

d IV$^-$ I$^{-6}_4$ V^{-7} I$^-$

7

d I$^-$ V$^{-6}_{d5}$ I$^-$

V$^6_4$ I^6 IV$^-$

F II$^-$ I$^6_4$ V^{-7} I

8

A$\flat$ I IV V^{-7}

I

c -VI V^{-7} I$^-$ IV$^-$ V

9

G V$^{-6}_{d5}$ I IV

V e V I$^-$ IV^6 V

10

c$\sharp$ I$^-$ V^{-7} I$^-$

-III G II$^-$ I$^6_4$ V^{-7} I

11

E V^{-7} I VI$^-$

IV B V^{-7} I V I

12

B V$^{-6}_{d5}$ I V$^6_4$

I^{-6} IV

g$\sharp$ -VI V^{-7} I$^-$ IV^6 V

59

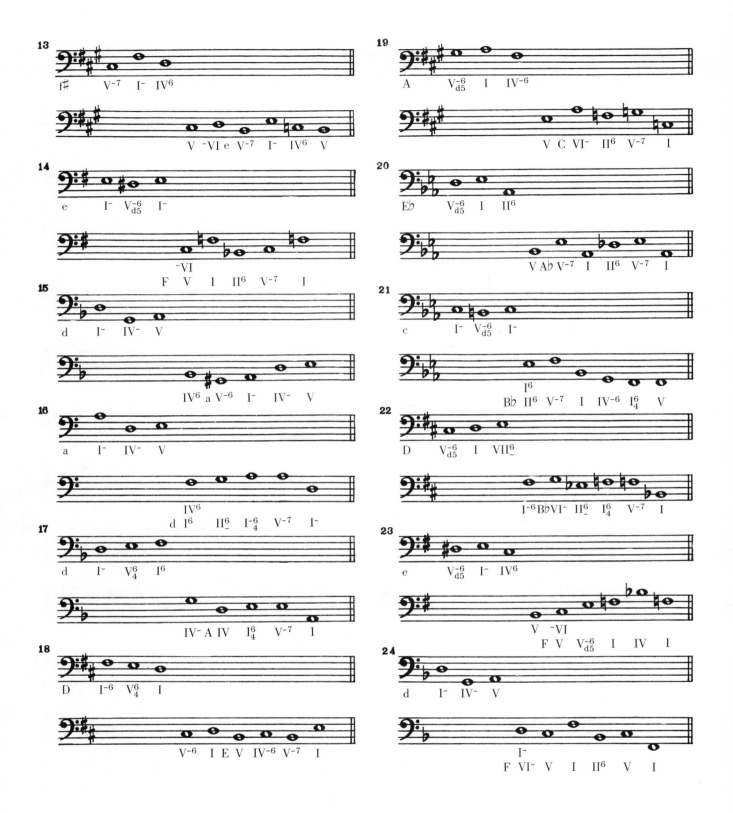

60

Shield the answer. Listen to the phrase several times and write the bass notes and composite chord symbols for the chords following the three that are given; then uncover the answer and compare your response. Circle incorrect frames. Goal: No more than eight incorrect frames.

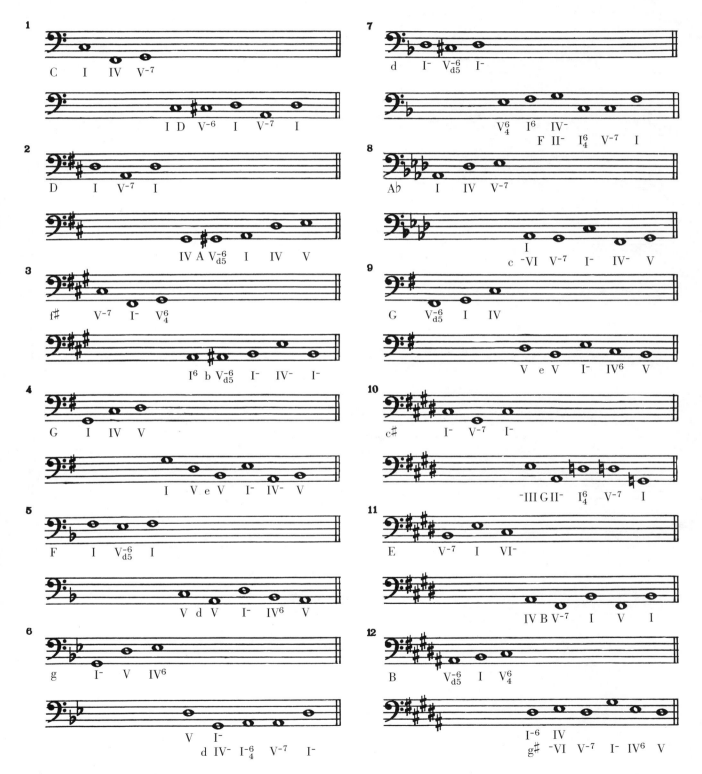

62

D3-2

(Copy 3)

Bass dictation and harmonic analysis of modulating phrases

Shield the answer. Listen to the phrase several times and write the bass notes and composite chord symbols for the chords following the three that are given; then uncover the answer and compare your response. Circle incorrect frames. Goal: No more than eight incorrect frames.

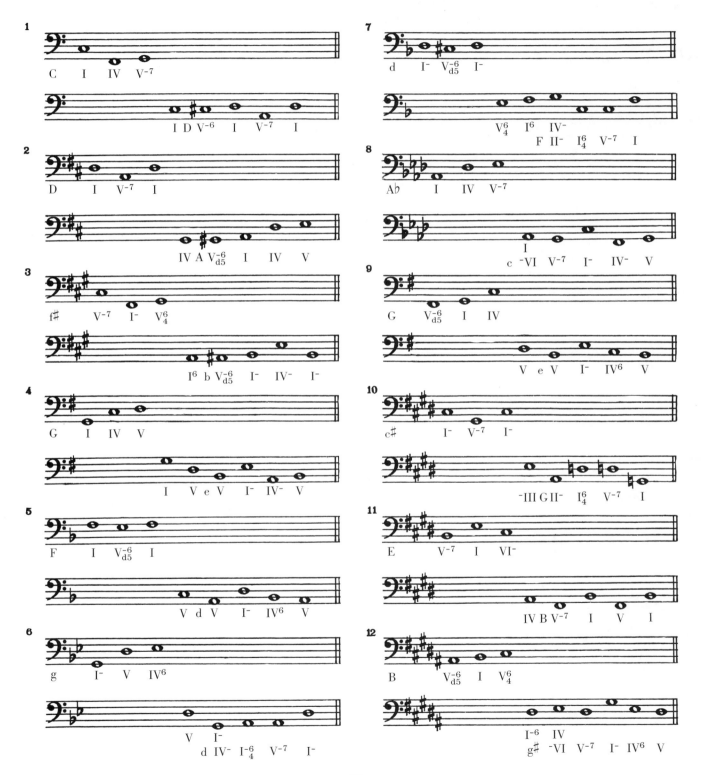

64

D3-2 Bass dictation and harmonic analysis of modulating phrases
(Copy 4)

Shield the answer. Listen to the phrase several times and write the bass notes and composite chord symbols for the chords following the three that are given; then uncover the answer and compare your response. Circle incorrect frames. Goal: No more than eight incorrect frames.

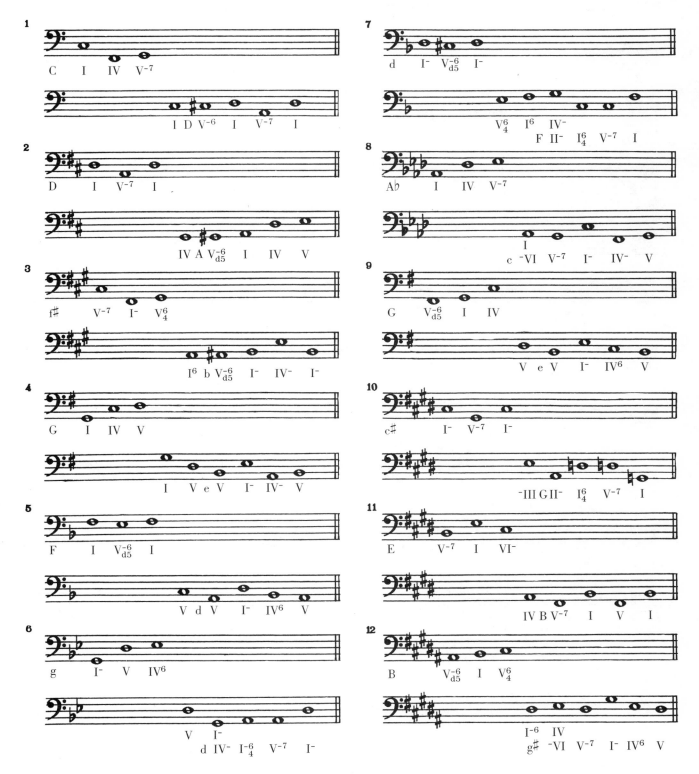

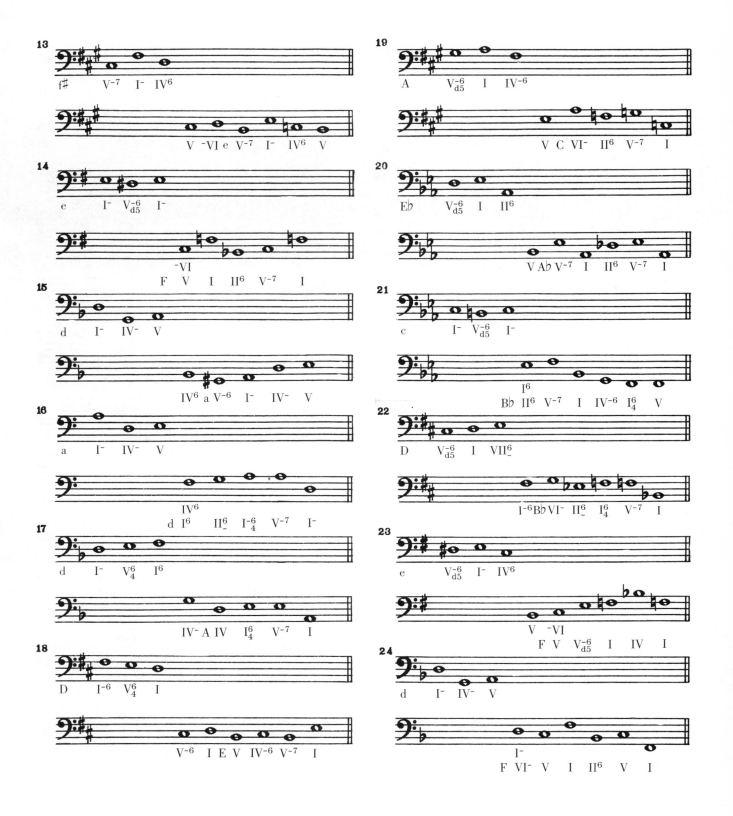

66

Bass dictation and harmonic analysis of modulating phrases

Shield the answer. Listen to the phrase several times and write the bass notes and composite chord symbols for the chords following the three that are given; then uncover the answer and compare your response. Circle incorrect frames. Goal: No more than eight incorrect frames.

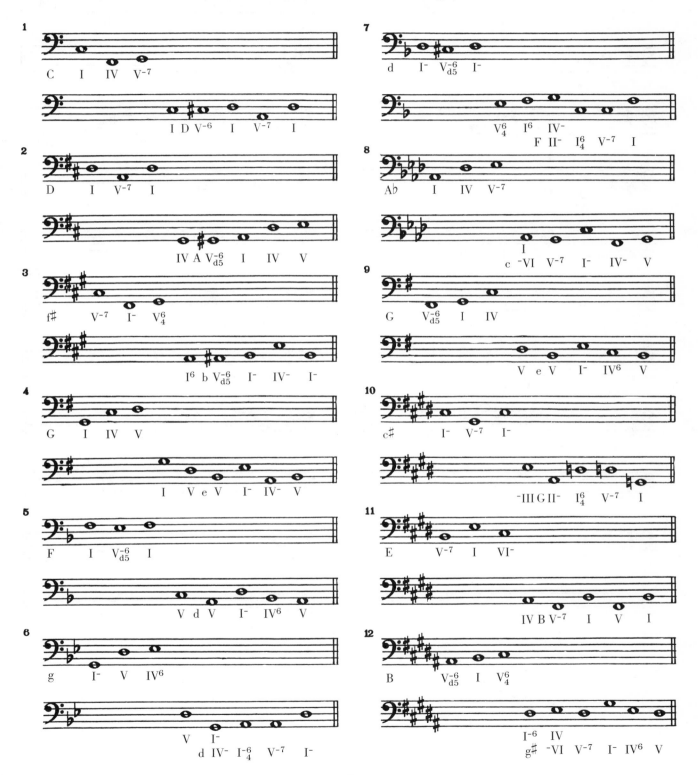

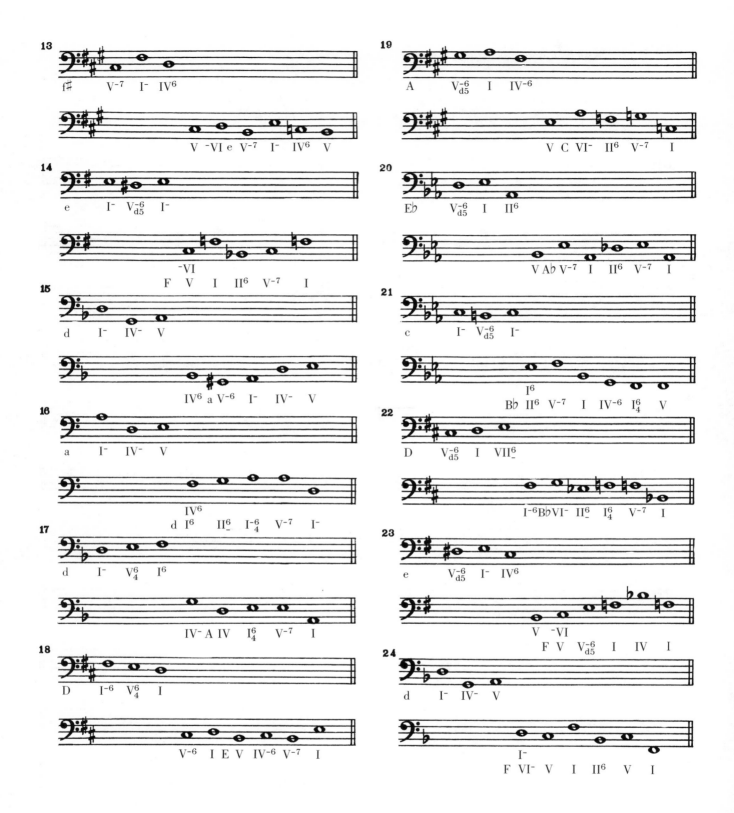

68

D3-3 Bass dictation and harmonic analysis of modulating phrases
(Copy 1)

Shield the answer. Listen to the phrase several times and write the bass notes and composite chord symbols for the chords following the three that are given; then uncover the answer and compare your response. Circle incorrect frames. Goal: No more than eight incorrect frames. When you have done this lesson, take Test D3.

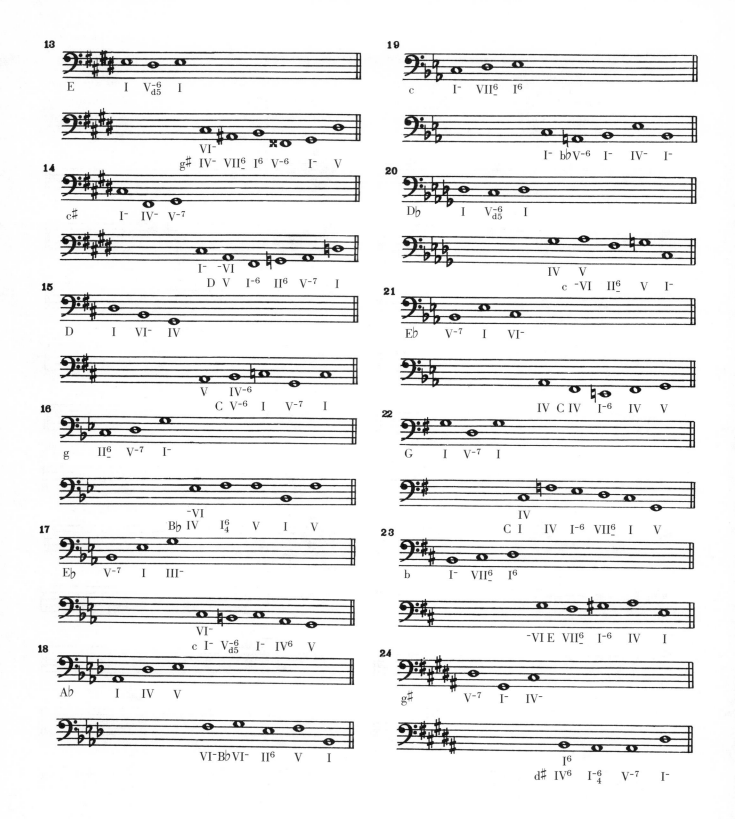

D3-3 Bass dictation and harmonic analysis of modulating phrases
(Copy 2)

Shield the answer. Listen to the phrase several times and write the bass notes and composite chord symbols for the chords following the three that are given; then uncover the answer and compare your response. Circle incorrect frames. Goal: No more than eight incorrect frames. When you have done this lesson, take Test D3.

71

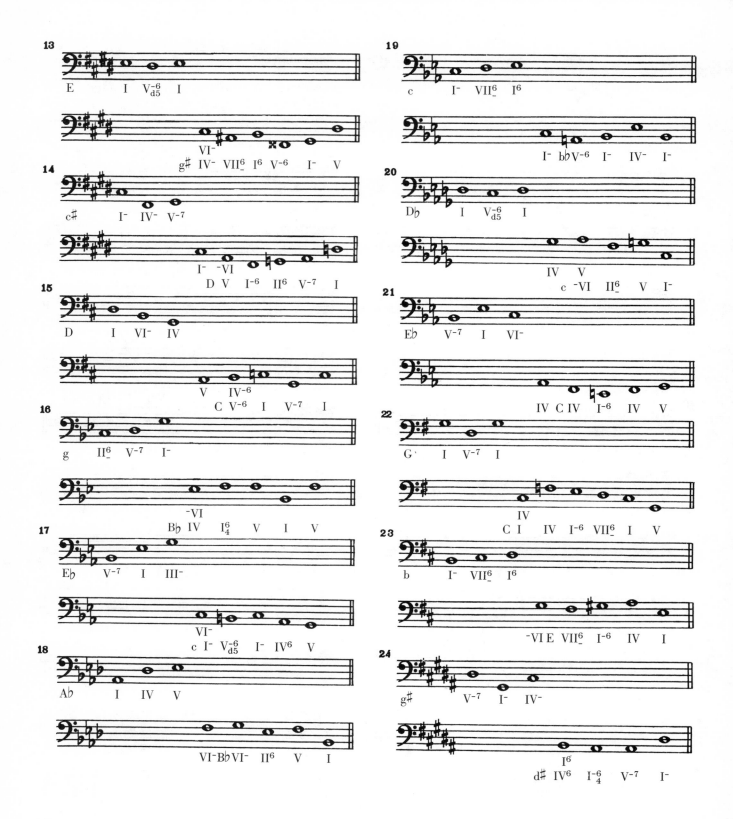

Shield the answer. Listen to the phrase several times and write the bass notes and composite chord symbols for the chords following the three that are given; then uncover the answer and compare your response. Circle incorrect frames. Goal: No more than eight incorrect frames. When you have done this lesson, take Test D3.

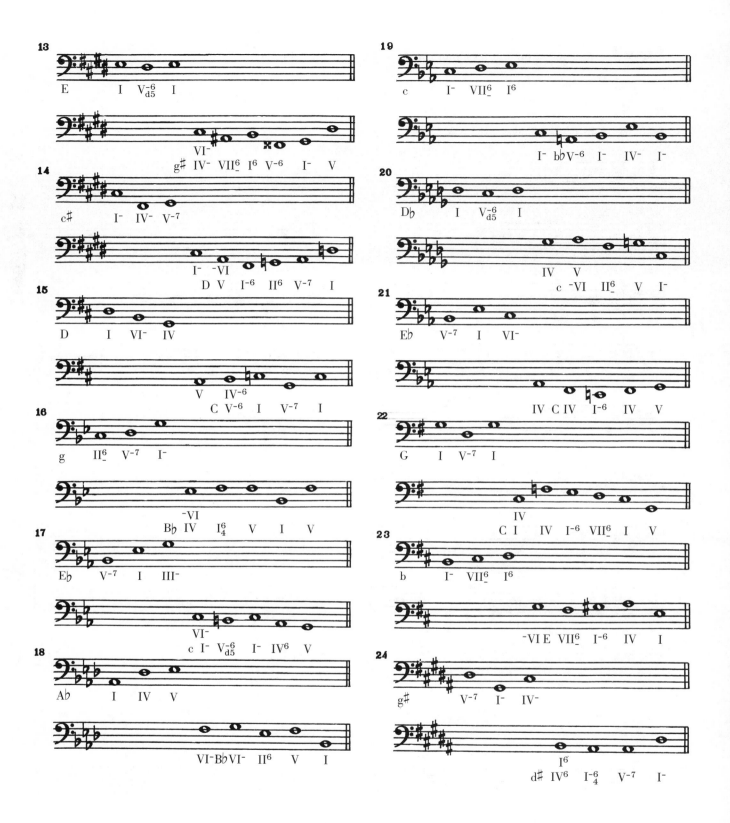

Bass dictation and harmonic analysis of modulating phrases

Shield the answer. Listen to the phrase several times and write the bass notes and composite chord symbols for the chords following the three that are given; then uncover the answer and compare your response. Circle incorrect frames. Goal: No more than eight incorrect frames. When you have done this lesson, take Test D3.

75

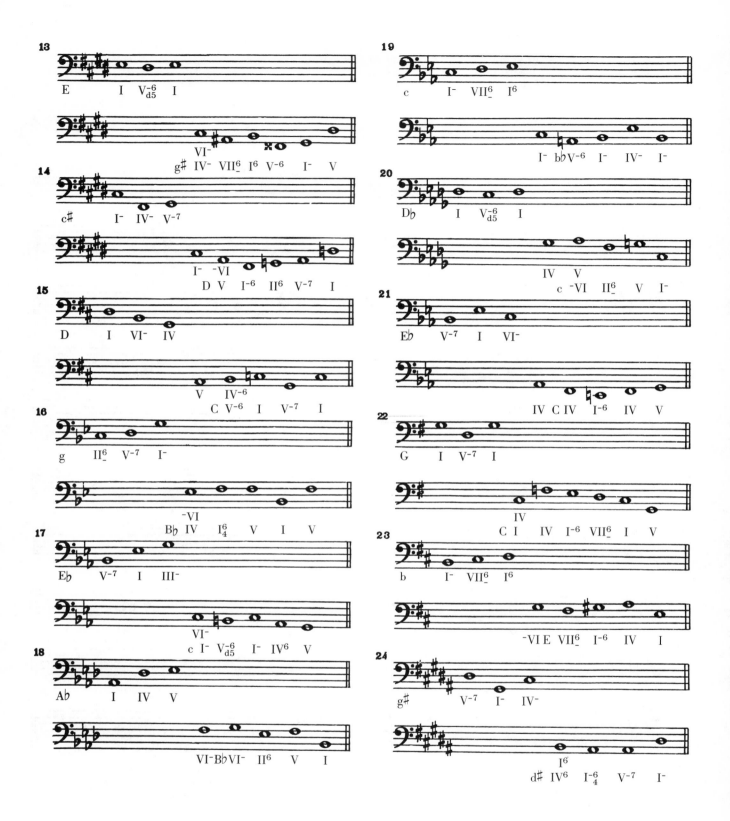

76

D3-3 Bass dictation and harmonic analysis of modulating phrases
(Copy 5)

Shield the answer. Listen to the phrase several times and write the bass notes and composite chord symbols for the chords following the three that are given; then uncover the answer and compare your response. Circle incorrect frames. Goal: No more than eight incorrect frames. When you have done this lesson, take Test D3.

77

78

Major and Minor Seventh Chords in Root Position

The upper tones of the minor seventh chord in root position are at intervals of a minor seventh, a perfect fifth, and a minor third above the base. The upper tones of the major seventh chord in root position are at intervals of a major seventh, a perfect fifth, and a major third above the base.

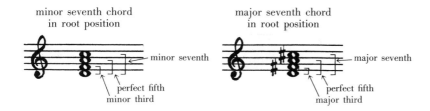

There are four types of lessons in this series: chord dictation, chord identification, figured bass dictation, and chord identification in a key. When you have done this series, take Test D4, which includes sections on each of the four kinds of lessons.

Lesson **D4-1a**

This is a lesson in *chord dictation*. The following instructions apply to all lessons of this type in this volume.

The purpose of the chord dictation lessons is to develop your ability to write chords that you hear. A printed worksheet and a tape recording are provided for each lesson. The frames on the worksheet are separated by bar lines. At the beginning of each frame, you will find a note that corresponds to the lowest tone of the chord that you will hear. The complete chord is shown at the end of the frame. To do each frame, start by shielding the chord at the end of the frame. When you have heard the chord on the tape recording, write the upper notes of the chord above the printed note. Then slide the shield to the right and compare your response with the printed answer. You may stop the tape occasionally if you need more time, but before going on to the next lesson you should be able to complete the lesson without stopping. Circle each frame in which your response is incorrect. Your goal is to complete the lesson with no more than seven errors. When you have done so, go on to the next lesson. If you have made more than seven errors, repeat the lesson until you reach the goal or until you have done the lesson five times, at which point you should go on to the next lesson regardless of your score.

Use tape D4-1 for this lesson. This tape is used for lessons D4-1a and D4-1b. Whenever a tape is used for two lessons the worksheets for those lessons are distinguished by the letters *a* and *b*. These letters do not appear on the label for the tape.

D4-1a Chord dictation

(Copy 1)

Shield the answer. Listen to the chord and write the upper tones above the given note; then uncover the answer and compare your response. Circle incorrect responses. Goal: No more than seven errors.

81

D4-1a Chord dictation

(Copy 2)

Shield the answer. Listen to the chord and write the upper tones above the given note; then uncover the answer and compare your response. Circle incorrect responses. Goal: No more than seven errors.

82

D4–1a Chord dictation

(Copy 3)

Shield the answer. Listen to the chord and write the upper tones above the given note; then uncover the answer and compare your response. Circle incorrect responses. Goal: No more than seven errors.

D4-1a Chord dictation

(Copy 4)

Shield the answer. Listen to the chord and write the upper tones above the given note; then uncover the answer and compare your response. Circle incorrect responses. Goal: No more than seven errors.

84

D4-1a Chord dictation

(Copy 5)

Shield the answer. Listen to the chord and write the upper tones above the given note; then uncover the answer and compare your response. Circle incorrect responses. Goal: No more than seven errors.

Lesson **D4-1b**

In this lesson the figured bass symbols for the minor and major seventh chords in root position are introduced. The intervals between the upper tones and the bass of a minor seventh chord in root position are a minor seventh, a perfect fifth, and a minor third. The complete figured bass symbol is $\begin{smallmatrix} -7 \\ 5 \\ -3 \end{smallmatrix}$, which is abbreviated to -7. In the major seventh chord in root position, the intervals between the upper tones and the bass are a major seventh, a perfect fifth, and a major third. The complete figured bass symbol is $\begin{smallmatrix} 7 \\ 5 \\ 3 \end{smallmatrix}$, abbreviated to 7.

Lesson D4-1b is a lesson in *chord identification*. The following instructions apply to all lessons of this type in this volume.

The purpose of these lessons is to develop your ability to identify types of chords that you hear and to associate them with their figured bass symbols. A printed worksheet and tape recording are provided for each lesson. Each frame contains a blank for your response, followed by the correct answer. To do each frame, start by shielding the answer. When you have heard the chord, write the figured bass symbol for it in the blank; then slide the shield to the right and check your response. Circle each frame in which your response is incorrect. You may stop the tape occasionally if you need more time, but before going on to the next lesson you should be able to complete the lesson without stopping. Your goal is to complete each lesson with no more than seven errors. When you have done so, go on to the next lesson. If you have made more than seven errors, repeat the lesson until you reach the goal or until you have done the lesson five times, at which point you should go on to the next lesson regardless of your score.

D4-1b Chord identification
(Copy 1)

Shield the answer. Listen to the chord and write the figured bass symbol in the blank; then uncover the answer and compare your response. Circle incorrect responses. Goal: No more than seven errors.

1	___	-	___	-7	___	-7	___		___	7	___	-7	___	7
2	___	-7	___	7	___	-7	___	-7	___	7	___	-7	___	-7
3	___		___	7	___		___	7	___	-	___	-7	___	-7
4	___	-7	___	7	___	-7	___	-6	___	-7	___	-7	___	-7
5	___	-	___	-7	___	-	___	-7	___	-6	___	-7	___	-6
6	___	-7	___	7	___	-7	___	6	___	7	___	-7	___	6
7	___	7	___	6	___	7	___	-7	___	-6	___	-7	___	7
8	___	7	___	-7	___	-6	___	-7	___	7	___	-7	___	-7
9	___	-6	___	-7	___	-7	___	7	___	-7	___	6/4	___	7
10	___	-7	___	6/4	___	-7	___	7	___	-6/4	___	-7	___	

D4-1b Chord identification
(Copy 2)

Shield the answer. Listen to the chord and write the figured bass symbol in the blank; then uncover the answer and compare your response. Circle incorrect responses. Goal: No more than seven errors.

1	___	-	___	-7	___	-7	___		___	7	___	-7	___	7
2	___	-7	___	7	___	-7	___	-7	___	7	___	-7	___	-7
3	___		___	7	___		___	7	___	-	___	-7	___	-7
4	___	-7	___	7	___	-7	___	-6	___	-7	___	-7	___	-7
5	___	-	___	-7	___	-	___	-7	___	-6	___	-7	___	-6
6	___	-7	___	7	___	-7	___	6	___	7	___	-7	___	6
7	___	7	___	6	___	7	___	-7	___	-6	___	-7	___	7
8	___	7	___	-7	___	-6	___	-7	___	7	___	-7	___	-7
9	___	-6	___	-7	___	-7	___	7	___	-7	___	6/4	___	7
10	___	-7	___	6/4	___	-7	___	7	___	-6/4	___	-7	___	

D4-1b Chord identification

Shield the answer. Listen to the chord and write the figured bass symbol in the blank; then uncover the answer and compare your response. Circle incorrect responses. Goal: No more than seven errors.

#	1	2	3	4	5	6	7
1	–	–7	–7		7	–7	7
2	–7	7	–7	–7	7	–7	–7
3		7		7	–	–7	–7
4	–7	7	–7	–6	–7	–7	–7
5	–	–7	–	–7	–6	–7	–6
6	–7	7	–7	6	7	–7	6
7	7	6	7	–7	–6	–7	7
8	7	–7	–6	–7	7	–7	–7
9	–6	–7	–7	7	–7	6/4	7
10	–7	6/4	–7	7	–6/4	–7	

D4-1b Chord identification

(Copy 4)

Shield the answer. Listen to the chord and write the figured bass symbol in the blank; then uncover the answer and compare your response. Circle incorrect responses. Goal: No more than seven errors.

#	1	2	3	4	5	6	7
1	–	–7	–7		7	–7	7
2	–7	7	–7	–7	7	–7	–7
3		7		7	–	–7	–7
4	–7	7	–7	–6	–7	–7	–7
5	–	–7	–	–7	–6	–7	–6
6	–7	7	–7	6	7	–7	6
7	7	6	7	–7	–6	–7	7
8	7	–7	–6	–7	7	–7	–7
9	–6	–7	–7	7	–7	6/4	7
10	–7	6/4	–7	7	–6/4	–7	

D4-1b Chord identification
(Copy 5)

Shield the answer. Listen to the chord and write the figured bass symbol in the blank; then uncover the answer and compare your response. Circle incorrect responses. Goal: No more than seven errors.

1 _____ − _____ −7̲ _____ −7̲ _____ _____ 7 _____ −7̲ _____ 7

2 _____ −7̲ _____ 7 _____ −7 _____ −7̲ _____ 7 _____ −7̲ _____ −7̲

3 _____ _____ 7 _____ _____ 7 _____ − _____ −7̲ _____ −7

4 _____ −7 _____ 7 _____ −7 _____ −6 _____ −7̲ _____ −7̲ _____ −7

5 _____ − _____ −7̲ _____ − _____ −7̲ _____ −6 _____ −7̲ _____ −6

6 _____ −7̲ _____ 7 _____ −7̲ _____ 6 _____ 7 _____ −7̲ _____ 6

7 _____ 7 _____ 6 _____ 7 _____ −7 _____ −6 _____ −7̲ _____ 7

8 _____ 7 _____ −7̲ _____ −6 _____ −7̲ _____ 7 _____ −7̲ _____ −7̲

9 _____ −6 _____ −7 _____ −7̲ _____ 7 _____ −7̲ _____ 6/4 _____ 7

10 _____ −7̲ _____ 6/4 _____ −7̲ _____ 7 _____ −6/4 _____ −7 _____

D4-2
(Copy 1) **Chord identification**

Shield the answer. Listen to the chord and write the figured bass symbol in the blank; then uncover the answer and compare your response. Circle incorrect responses. Goal: No more than seven errors.

1	___		___	7	___	7	___	-7	___	-	___	-7	___	-7
2	___		___	7	___	-7	___	6	___	-7	___	7	___	-7
3	___	-6/4	___	-7	___	-	___	7	___		___	-7	___	-7
4	___		___	-7	___	-7	___	-7	___	-	___	7	___	-7
5	___	7	___	-	___	-7	___	6/4	___	7	___	6/4	___	-7
6	___		___	-	___	-7	___		___	7	___	-	___	-7
7	___	-7	___	-7	___	7	___	-7	___	-6	___	-6/4	___	-7
8	___	-	___	-7	___	-7	___	-7	___	6	___	-7	___	7
9	___	-7	___	-6	___	-7	___	-6	___	7	___	7	___	-7
10	___	7	___	-7	___		___	-7	___	7	___	-7	___	7

D4-2
(Copy 2) **Chord identification**

Shield the answer. Listen to the chord and write the figured bass symbol in the blank; then uncover the answer and compare your response. Circle incorrect responses. Goal: No more than seven errors.

1	___		___	7	___	7	___	-7	___	-	___	-7	___	-7
2	___		___	7	___	-7	___	6	___	-7	___	7	___	-7
3	___	-6/4	___	-7	___	-	___	7	___		___	-7	___	-7
4	___		___	-7	___	-7	___	-7	___	-	___	7	___	-7
5	___	7	___	-	___	-7	___	6/4	___	7	___	6/4	___	-7
6	___		___	-	___	-7	___		___	7	___	-	___	-7
7	___	-7	___	-7	___	7	___	-7	___	-6	___	-6/4	___	-7
8	___	-	___	-7	___	-7	___	-7	___	6	___	-7	___	7
9	___	-7	___	-6	___	-7	___	-6	___	7	___	7	___	-7
10	___	7	___	-7	___		___	-7	___	7	___	-7	___	7

D4-2 Chord identification
(Copy 3)

Shield the answer. Listen to the chord and write the figured bass symbol in the blank; then uncover the answer and compare your response. Circle incorrect responses. Goal: No more than seven errors.

#								
1	___	___	7	7	-7	-	-7̲	-7̲
2	___	___	7	-7̲	6	-7	7	-7
3	-6/4	-7	-	7	___	___	-7̲	-7
4	___	___	-7̲	-7̲	-7	-	7	-7
5	7	-	___	-7̲	6/4	7	6/4	-7
6	___	___	-	-7̲	___	7	-	-7̲
7	-7	-7̲	7	-7̲	-6	-6/4	___	-7
8	-	-7̲	-7̲	-7	6	-7	___	7
9	-7	-6	-7̲	-6	7	7	___	-7̲
10	7	-7	___	___	-7̲	7	-7	7

D4-2 Chord identification
(Copy 4)

Shield the answer. Listen to the chord and write the figured bass symbol in the blank; then uncover the answer and compare your response. Circle incorrect responses. Goal: No more than seven errors.

#								
1	___	___	7	7	-7	-	-7̲	-7̲
2	___	___	7	-7̲	6	-7	7	-7
3	-6/4	-7	-	7	___	___	-7̲	-7
4	___	___	-7̲	-7̲	-7	-	7	-7
5	7	-	___	-7̲	6/4	7	6/4	-7
6	___	___	-	-7̲	___	7	-	-7̲
7	-7	-7̲	7	-7̲	-6	-6/4	___	-7
8	-	-7̲	-7̲	-7	6	-7	___	7
9	-7	-6	-7̲	-6	7	7	___	-7̲
10	7	-7	___	___	-7̲	7	-7	7

D4-2 Chord identification
(Copy 5)

Shield the answer. Listen to the chord and write the figured bass symbol in the blank; then uncover the answer and compare your response. Circle incorrect responses. Goal: No more than seven errors.

1 _____   _____ 7   _____ 7   _____ -7   _____ -   _____ -7̲   _____ -7̲

2 _____   _____ 7   _____ -7̲   _____ 6   _____ -7   _____ 7   _____ -7

3 _____ -6/4   _____ -7   _____ -   _____ 7   _____   _____ -7̲   _____ -7

4 _____   _____ -7̲   _____ -7̲   _____ -7   _____ -   _____ 7   _____ -7

5 _____ 7   _____ -   _____ -7̲   _____ 6/4   _____ 7   _____ 6/4   _____ -7

6 _____   _____   _____ -   _____ -7̲   _____   _____ 7   _____ -   _____ -7̲

7 _____ -7   _____ -7̲   _____ 7   _____ -7̲   _____ -6   _____ -6/4   _____ -7

8 _____ -   _____ -7̲   _____ -7̲   _____ -7   _____ 6   _____ -7̲   _____ 7

9 _____ -7   _____ -6   _____ -7̲   _____ -6   _____ 7   _____ 7   _____ -7̲

10 _____ 7   _____ -7   _____   _____ -7̲   _____ 7   _____ -7   _____ 7

92

Lesson **D4-3a**

This is a lesson in *figured bass dictation*. The following instructions apply to all lessons of this type in this volume.

The purpose of figured bass dictation is to develop your ability to determine the bass note of a chord and its chord type. A printed worksheet and a tape recording are provided for each lesson. The frames on the worksheet are separated by bar lines. The first chord on the tape, whose bass note and figured bass symbol are given in the first frame of the worksheet, serves as a starting reference and requires no response. To do each subsequent frame, start by shielding the answer at the end of the frame. When you have heard the chord, write the bass note on the staff and the figured bass symbol below the staff. Then slide the shield to the right and compare your response to the printed answer. Circle each frame in which your response is incorrect. You may stop the tape occasionally if you need more time, but before going on to the next lesson you should be able to complete the lesson without stopping. If you stop the tape, keep the pause short because each chord is a frame of reference for the following chord. Your goal is to complete each lesson with no more than seven errors. When you have done so, go on to the next lesson. If you have made more than seven errors, repeat the lesson until you reach the goal or until you have done the lesson five times, at which point you should go on to the next lesson regardless of your score.

D4-3a Figured bass dictation
(Copy 1)

Shield the answer. Listen to the chord and write the bass note and the figured bass symbol; then uncover the answer and compare your response. Circle incorrect answers. Goal: No more than seven errors. The first frame requires no response.

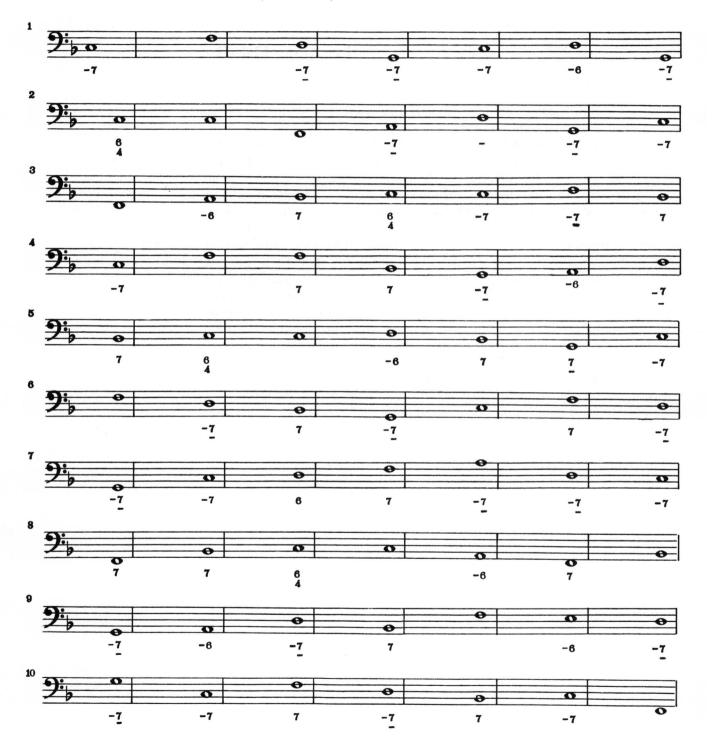

94

D4–3a Figured bass dictation
(Copy 2)

Shield the answer. Listen to the chord and write the bass note and the figured bass symbol; then uncover the answer and compare your response. Circle incorrect answers. Goal: No more than seven errors. The first frame requires no response.

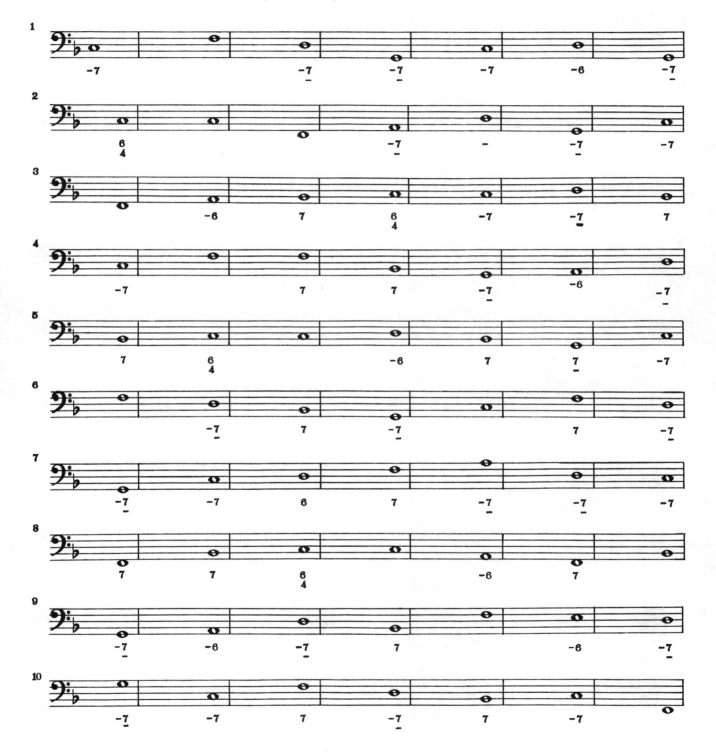

95

D4-3a Figured bass dictation
(Copy 3)

Shield the answer. Listen to the chord and write the bass note and the figured bass symbol; then uncover the answer and compare your response. Circle incorrect answers. Goal: No more than seven errors. The first frame requires no response.

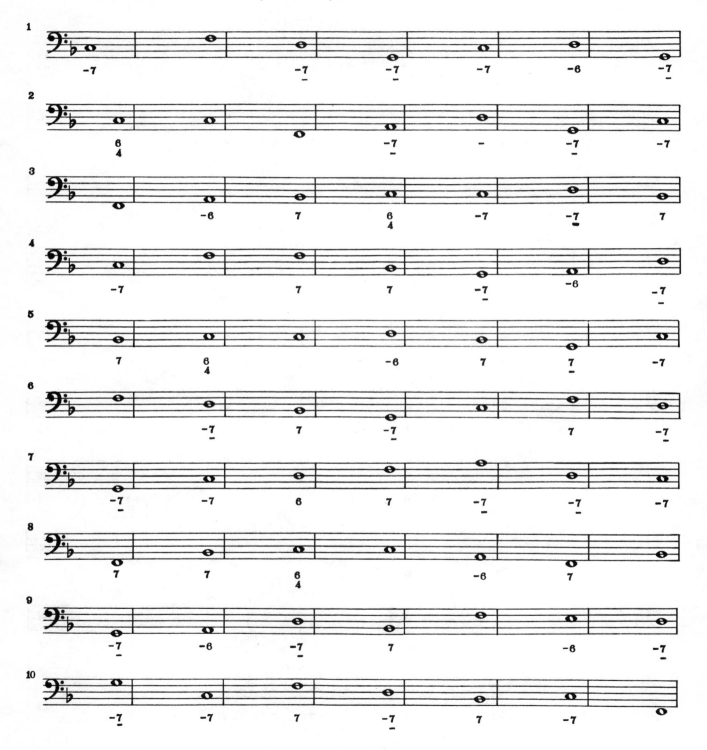

D4-3a Figured bass dictation

(Copy 4)

Shield the answer. Listen to the chord and write the bass note and the figured bass symbol; then uncover the answer and compare your response. Circle incorrect answers. Goal: No more than seven errors. The first frame requires no response.

97

D4–3a Figured bass dictation

(Copy 5)

Shield the answer. Listen to the chord and write the bass note and the figured bass symbol; then uncover the answer and compare your response. Circle incorrect answers. Goal: No more than seven errors. The first frame requires no response.

Lesson **D4–3b**

In this lesson, the following composite chord symbols, which appear in a major key, are introduced: I^7, II^{-7}, III^{-7}, IV^7 and VI^{-7}. In a major key, the seventh chords on the first and fourth degrees are major seventh chords, hence the figured bass portion of the composite chord symbol for these chords is ^{7}. The seventh chords on the second, third and sixth degrees of a major key are minor seventh chords, and the figured bass portion of the composite chord symbol for these chords is therefore $^{-7}$.

Lesson D4–3b is a lesson in *chord identification in a key*. The following instructions apply to all lessons of this type in this volume.

The purpose of these lessons is to develop your ability to identify the type of chords you hear and determine their location in a key. A printed worksheet and a tape recording are provided for each lesson.

The first chord on the tape, whose composite chord symbol is given in the first frame of the worksheet, serves as a starting reference and requires no response. Each subsequent frame contains a blank for your response, followed by the correct answer. To do each frame, start by shielding the answer. When you have heard the chord, write the composite chord symbol for it in the blank; then slide the shield to the right and check your response. You may stop the tape occasionally if you need more time, but before going on to the next lesson you should be able to complete the lesson without stopping. If you stop the tape, keep the pause short, because each chord is a frame of reference for the following chord. Circle each frame in which your response is incorrect. Your goal is to complete each lesson with no more than seven errors. When you have done so, go on to the next lesson. If you have made more than seven errors, repeat the lesson until you reach the goal or until you have done the lesson five times, at which point you should go on to the next lesson regardless of your score.

D4-3b Chord identification in a key
(Copy 1)

Shield the answer. Listen to the chord and write the composite chord symbol in the blank; then uncover the answer and compare your response. Circle incorrect responses. Goal: No more than seven errors. The first frame requires no response.

1   V^{-7} ____ I ____ $VI^{-7}_{\_}$ ____ $II^{-7}_{\_}$ ____ V^{-7} ____ IV^{-6} ____ $II^{-7}_{\_}$

2   ____ I^6_4 ____ V ____ I ____ $III^{-7}_{\_}$ ____ VI^- ____ $II^{-7}_{\_}$ ____ V^{-7}

3   ____ I ____ I^{-6} ____ IV^7 ____ I^6_4 ____ V^{-7} ____ $VI^{-7}_{\_}$ ____ IV^7

4   ____ V^{-7} ____ I ____ I^7 ____ IV^7 ____ $II^{-7}_{\_}$ ____ I^{-6} ____ $VI^{-7}_{\_}$

5   ____ IV^7 ____ I^6_4 ____ V ____ IV^{-6} ____ IV^7 ____ $II^{-7}_{\_}$ ____ V^{-7}

6   ____ I ____ $VI^{-7}_{\_}$ ____ IV^7 ____ $II^{-7}_{\_}$ ____ V ____ I^7 ____ $VI^{-7}_{\_}$

7   ____ $II^{-7}_{\_}$ ____ V^{-7} ____ IV^{-6} ____ I^7 ____ $III^{-7}_{\_}$ ____ $VI^{-7}_{\_}$ ____ V^{-7}

8   ____ I^7 ____ IV^7 ____ I^6_4 ____ V ____ I^{-6} ____ I^7 ____ IV

9   ____ $II^{-7}_{\_}$ ____ I^{-6} ____ $VI^{-7}_{\_}$ ____ IV^7 ____ I ____ V^{-6} ____ $VI^{-7}_{\_}$

10 ____ $II^{-7}_{\_}$ ____ V^{-7} ____ I^7 ____ $VI^{-7}_{\_}$ ____ IV^7 ____ V^{-7} ____ I

D4-3b Chord identification in a key
(Copy 2)

Shield the answer. Listen to the chord and write the composite chord symbol in the blank; then uncover the answer and compare your response. Circle incorrect responses. Goal: No more than seven errors. The first frame requires no response.

1   V^{-7} ____ I ____ $VI^{-7}_{\_}$ ____ $II^{-7}_{\_}$ ____ V^{-7} ____ IV^{-6} ____ $II^{-7}_{\_}$

2   ____ I^6_4 ____ V ____ I ____ $III^{-7}_{\_}$ ____ VI^- ____ $II^{-7}_{\_}$ ____ V^{-7}

3   ____ I ____ I^{-6} ____ IV^7 ____ I^6_4 ____ V^{-7} ____ $VI^{-7}_{\_}$ ____ IV^7

4   ____ V^{-7} ____ I ____ I^7 ____ IV^7 ____ $II^{-7}_{\_}$ ____ I^{-6} ____ $VI^{-7}_{\_}$

5   ____ IV^7 ____ I^6_4 ____ V ____ IV^{-6} ____ IV^7 ____ $II^{-7}_{\_}$ ____ V^{-7}

6   ____ I ____ $VI^{-7}_{\_}$ ____ IV^7 ____ $II^{-7}_{\_}$ ____ V ____ I^7 ____ $VI^{-7}_{\_}$

7   ____ $II^{-7}_{\_}$ ____ V^{-7} ____ IV^{-6} ____ I^7 ____ $III^{-7}_{\_}$ ____ $VI^{-7}_{\_}$ ____ V^{-7}

8   ____ I^7 ____ IV^7 ____ I^6_4 ____ V ____ I^{-6} ____ I^7 ____ IV

9   ____ $II^{-7}_{\_}$ ____ I^{-6} ____ $VI^{-7}_{\_}$ ____ IV^7 ____ I ____ V^{-6} ____ $VI^{-7}_{\_}$

10 ____ $II^{-7}_{\_}$ ____ V^{-7} ____ I^7 ____ $VI^{-7}_{\_}$ ____ IV^7 ____ V^{-7} ____ I

Shield the answer. Listen to the chord and write the composite chord symbol in the blank; then uncover the answer and compare your response. Circle incorrect responses. Goal: No more than seven errors. The first frame requires no response.

1	V^{-7}	___ I	___ $VI^{-\underline{7}}$	___ $II^{-\underline{7}}$	___ V^{-7}	___ IV^{-6} ___ $II^{-\underline{7}}$
2	___ I_4^6	___ V	___ I	___ $III^{-\underline{7}}$	___ VI^-	___ $II^{-\underline{7}}$ ___ V^{-7}
3	___ I	___ I^{-6}	___ IV^7	___ I_4^6	___ V^{-7}	___ $VI^{-\underline{7}}$ ___ IV^7
4	___ V^{-7}	___ I	___ I^7	___ IV^7	___ $II^{-\underline{7}}$	___ I^{-6} ___ $VI^{-\underline{7}}$
5	___ IV^7	___ I_4^6	___ V	___ IV^{-6}	___ IV^7	___ $II^{-\underline{7}}$ ___ V^{-7}
6	___ I	___ VI^{-7}	___ IV^7	___ $II^{-\underline{7}}$	___ V	___ I^7 ___ $VI^{-\underline{7}}$
7	___ $II^{-\underline{7}}$	___ V^{-7}	___ IV^{-6}	___ I^7	___ $III^{-\underline{7}}$	___ VI^{-7} ___ V^{-7}
8	___ I^7	___ IV^7	___ I_4^6	___ V	___ I^{-6}	___ I^7 ___ IV
9	___ $II^{-\underline{7}}$	___ I^{-6}	___ $VI^{-\underline{7}}$	___ IV^7	___ I	___ V^{-6} ___ $VI^{-\underline{7}}$
10	___ $II^{-\underline{7}}$	___ V^{-7}	___ I^7	___ $VI^{-\underline{7}}$	___ IV^7	___ V^{-7} ___ I

D4-3b Chord identification in a key
(Copy 4)

Shield the answer. Listen to the chord and write the composite chord symbol in the blank; then uncover the answer and compare your response. Circle incorrect responses. Goal: No more than seven errors. The first frame requires no response.

1	V^{-7}	___ I	___ $VI^{-\underline{7}}$	___ $II^{-\underline{7}}$	___ V^{-7}	___ IV^{-6} ___ $II^{-\underline{7}}$
2	___ I_4^6	___ V	___ I	___ $III^{-\underline{7}}$	___ VI^-	___ $II^{-\underline{7}}$ ___ V^{-7}
3	___ I	___ I^{-6}	___ IV^7	___ I_4^6	___ V^{-7}	___ $VI^{-\underline{7}}$ ___ IV^7
4	___ V^{-7}	___ I	___ I^7	___ IV^7	___ $II^{-\underline{7}}$	___ I^{-6} ___ $VI^{-\underline{7}}$
5	___ IV^7	___ I_4^6	___ V	___ IV^{-6}	___ IV^7	___ $II^{-\underline{7}}$ ___ V^{-7}
6	___ I	___ $VI^{-\underline{7}}$	___ IV^7	___ $II^{-\underline{7}}$	___ V	___ I^7 ___ $VI^{-\underline{7}}$
7	___ $II^{-\underline{7}}$	___ V^{-7}	___ IV^{-6}	___ I^7	___ $III^{-\underline{7}}$	___ $VI^{-\underline{7}}$ ___ V^{-7}
8	___ I^7	___ IV^7	___ I_4^6	___ V	___ I^{-6}	___ I^7 ___ IV
9	___ $II^{-\underline{7}}$	___ I^{-6}	___ $VI^{-\underline{7}}$	___ IV^7	___ I	___ V^{-6} ___ $VI^{-\underline{7}}$
10	___ $II^{-\underline{7}}$	___ V^{-7}	___ I^7	___ $VI^{-\underline{7}}$	___ IV^7	___ V^{-7} ___ I

D4-3b Chord identification in a key

(Copy 5)

Shield the answer. Listen to the chord and write the composite chord symbol in the blank; then uncover the answer and compare your response. Circle incorrect responses. Goal: No more than seven errors. The first frame requires no response.

1. V^{-7} _____ I _____ VI^{-7} _____ II^{-7} _____ V^{-7} _____ IV^{-6} _____ II^{-7}

2. _____ I_4^6 _____ V _____ I _____ III^{-7} _____ VI^- _____ II^{-7} _____ V^{-7}

3. _____ I _____ I^{-6} _____ IV^7 _____ I_4^6 _____ V^{-7} _____ VI^{-7} _____ IV^7

4. _____ V^{-7} _____ I _____ I^7 _____ IV^7 _____ II^{-7} _____ I^{-6} _____ VI^{-7}

5. _____ IV^7 _____ I_4^6 _____ V _____ IV^{-6} _____ IV^7 _____ II^{-7} _____ V^{-7}

6. _____ I _____ VI^{-7} _____ IV^7 _____ II^{-7} _____ V _____ I^7 _____ VI^{-7}

7. _____ II^{-7} _____ V^{-7} _____ IV^{-6} _____ I^7 _____ III^{-7} _____ VI^{-7} _____ V^{-7}

8. _____ I^7 _____ IV^7 _____ I_4^6 _____ V _____ I^{-6} _____ I^7 _____ IV

9. _____ II^{-7} _____ I^{-6} _____ VI^{-7} _____ IV^7 _____ I _____ V^{-6} _____ VI^{-7}

10. _____ II^{-7} _____ V^{-7} _____ I^7 _____ VI^{-7} _____ IV^7 _____ V^{-7} _____ I

D4–4a Figured bass dictation

(Copy 1)

Shield the answer. Listen to the chord and write the bass note and the figured bass symbol; then uncover the answer and compare your response. Circle incorrect responses. Goal: No more than seven errors. The first frame requires no response.

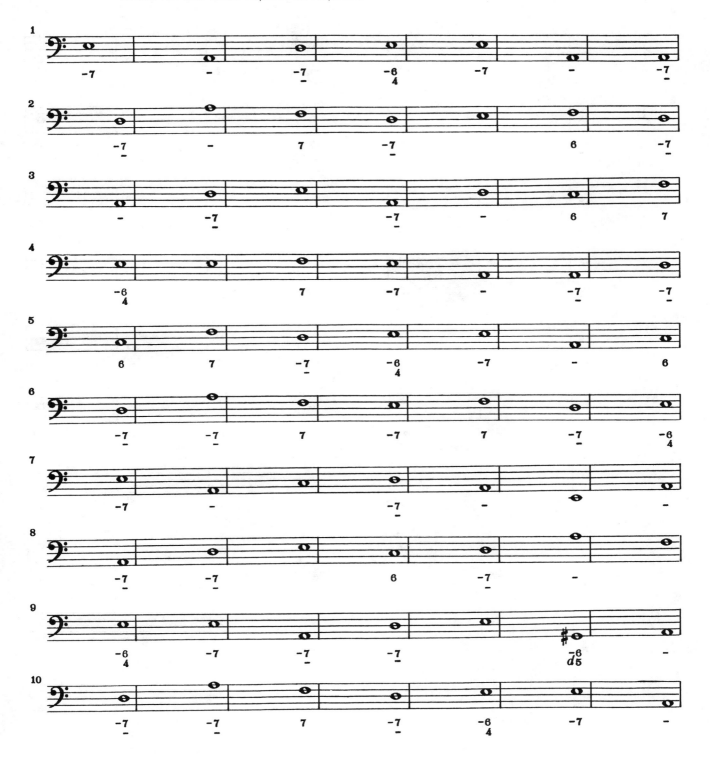

D4–4a Figured bass dictation
(Copy 2)

Shield the answer. Listen to the chord and write the bass note and the figured bass symbol; then uncover the answer and compare your response. Circle incorrect responses. Goal: No more than seven errors. The first frame requires no response.

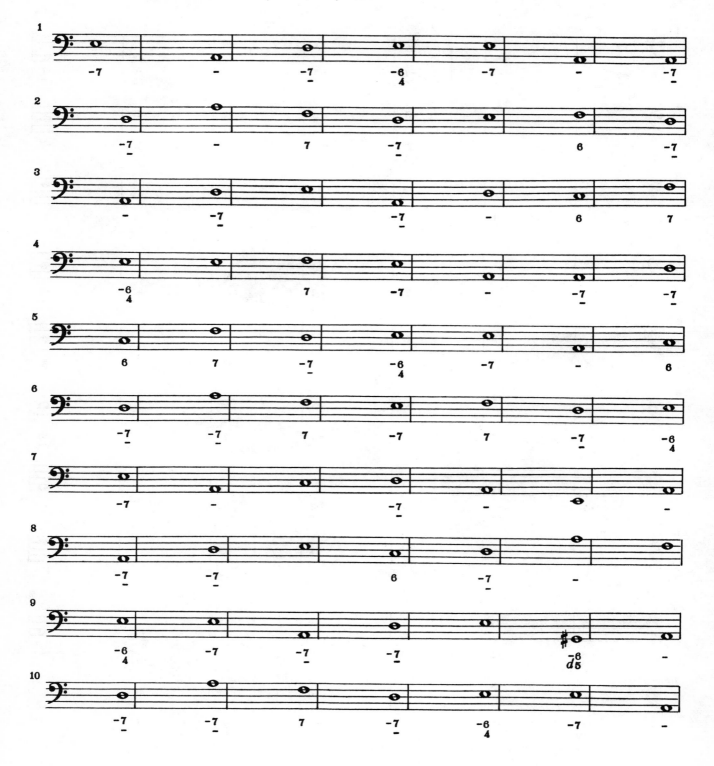

D4-4a Figured bass dictation

(Copy 3)

Shield the answer. Listen to the chord and write the bass note and the figured bass symbol; then uncover the answer and compare your response. Circle incorrect responses. Goal: No more than seven errors. The first frame requires no response.

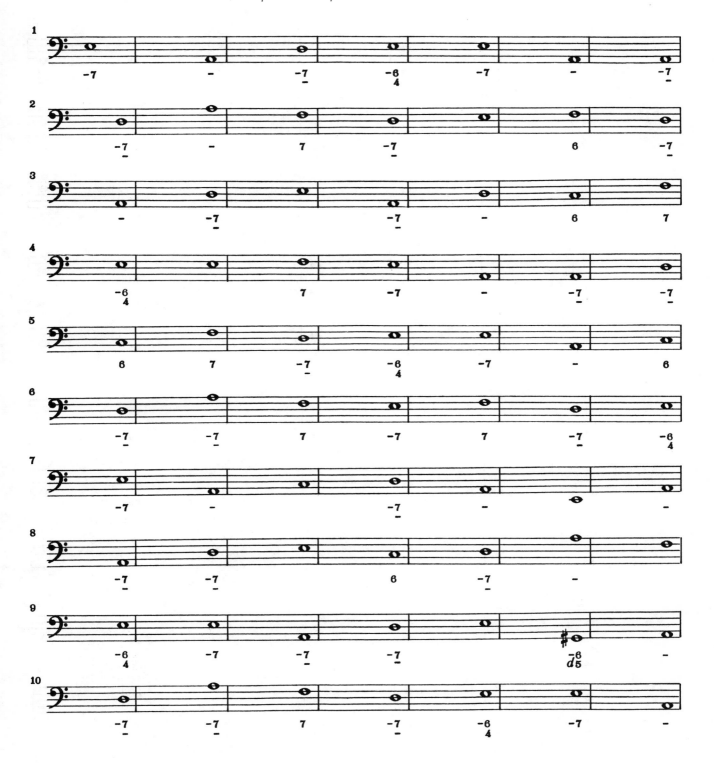

D4-4a Figured bass dictation

(Copy 4)

Shield the answer. Listen to the chord and write the bass note and the figured bass symbol; then uncover the answer and compare your response. Circle incorrect responses. Goal: No more than seven errors. The first frame requires no response.

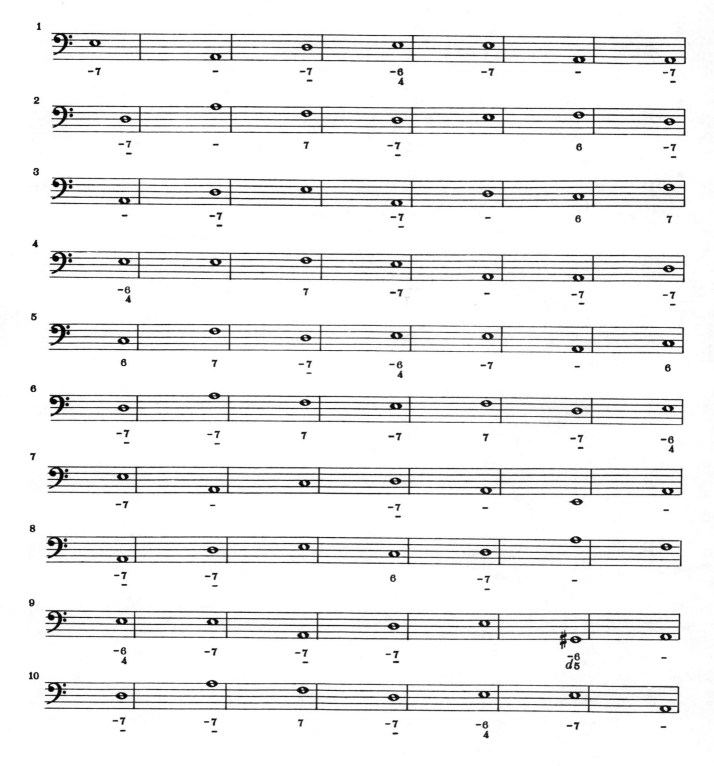

D4-4a Figured bass dictation

(Copy 5)

Shield the answer. Listen to the chord and write the bass note and the figured bass symbol; then uncover the answer and compare your response. Circle incorrect responses. Goal: No more than seven errors. The first frame requires no response.

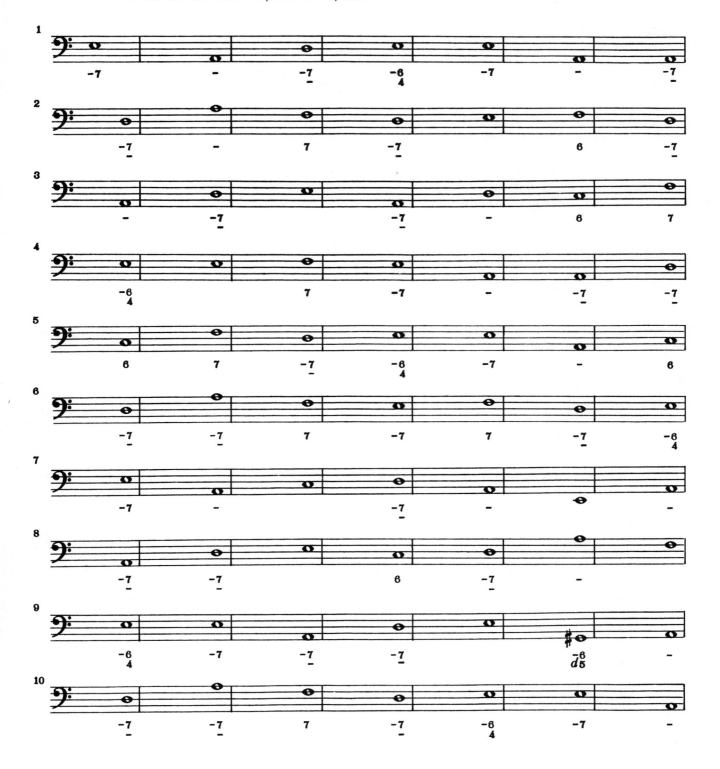

Lesson **D4-4b**

In this lesson the following composite chord symbols, which appear in a minor key, are introduced: $I^{-\underline{7}}$, $^-III^7$, $IV^{-\underline{7}}$ and $^-VI^7$. In a minor key, the seventh chords on the first and fourth degree are minor seventh chords, hence the figured bass portion of the composite chord symbol is $^{-\underline{7}}$. The seventh chords on the third and sixth degrees are major seventh chords, and the figured bass portion of the composite chord symbol is ^{7}.

D4-4b Chord identification in a key
(Copy 1)

Shield the answer. Listen to the chord and write the composite chord symbol in the blank; then uncover the answer and compare your response. Goal: No more than seven errors. The first frame requires no response. After you have done this lesson, take Test D4.

1   V^{-7} ___ I^- ___ $IV^{-\underline{7}}$ ___ I^{-6}_{4} ___ V^{-7} ___ I^- ___ $I^{-\underline{7}}$

2   ___ $IV^{-\underline{7}}$ ___ I^- ___ $^-VI^7$ ___ $IV^{-\underline{7}}$ ___ V ___ IV^6 ___ $IV^{-\underline{7}}$

3   ___ I^- ___ $IV^{-\underline{7}}$ ___ V ___ $I^{-\underline{7}}$ ___ IV^- ___ I^6 ___ $^-VI^7$

4   ___ I^{-6}_{4} ___ V ___ $^-VI^7$ ___ V^{-7} ___ I^- ___ $I^{-\underline{7}}$ ___ $IV^{-\underline{7}}$

5   ___ I^6 ___ $^-VI^7$ ___ $IV^{-\underline{7}}$ ___ I^{-6}_{4} ___ V^{-7} ___ I^- ___ I^6

6   ___ $IV^{-\underline{7}}$ ___ $I^{-\underline{7}}$ ___ $^-VI^7$ ___ V^{-7} ___ $^-VI^7$ ___ $IV^{-\underline{7}}$ ___ I^{-6}_{4}

7   ___ V^{-7} ___ I^- ___ ^-III ___ $IV^{-\underline{7}}$ ___ I^- ___ V ___ I^-

8   ___ $I^{-\underline{7}}$ ___ $IV^{-\underline{7}}$ ___ V ___ I^6 ___ $IV^{-\underline{7}}$ ___ I^- ___ ^-VI

9   ___ I^{-6}_{4} ___ V^{-7} ___ $I^{-\underline{7}}$ ___ $IV^{-\underline{7}}$ ___ V ___ V^{-6}_{d5} ___ I^-

10   ___ $IV^{-\underline{7}}$ ___ $I^{-\underline{7}}$ ___ $^-VI^7$ ___ $IV^{-\underline{7}}$ ___ I^{-6}_{4} ___ V^{-7} ___ I^-

D4-4b Chord identification in a key
(Copy 2)

Shield the answer. Listen to the chord and write the composite chord symbol in the blank; then uncover the answer and compare your response. Goal: No more than seven errors. The first frame requires no response. After you have done this lesson, take Test D4.

1   V^{-7} ___ I^- ___ $\text{IV}^{-\underline{7}}$ ___ I^{-6}_{4} ___ V^{-7} ___ I^- ___ $\text{I}^{-\underline{7}}$

2 ___ $\text{IV}^{-\underline{7}}$ ___ I^- ___ $^-\text{VI}^7$ ___ $\text{IV}^{-\underline{7}}$ ___ V ___ IV^6 ___ $\text{IV}^{-\underline{7}}$

3 ___ I^- ___ $\text{IV}^{-\underline{7}}$ ___ V ___ $\text{I}^{-\underline{7}}$ ___ IV^- ___ I^6 ___ $^-\text{VI}^7$

4 ___ I^{-6}_{4} ___ V ___ $^-\text{VI}^7$ ___ V^{-7} ___ I^- ___ $\text{I}^{-\underline{7}}$ ___ $\text{IV}^{-\underline{7}}$

5 ___ I^6 ___ $^-\text{VI}^7$ ___ $\text{IV}^{-\underline{7}}$ ___ I^{-6}_{4} ___ V^{-7} ___ I^- ___ I^6

6 ___ $\text{IV}^{-\underline{7}}$ ___ $\text{I}^{-\underline{7}}$ ___ $^-\text{VI}^7$ ___ V^{-7} ___ $^-\text{VI}^7$ ___ $\text{IV}^{-\underline{7}}$ ___ I^{-6}_{4}

7 ___ V^{-7} ___ I^- ___ ^-III ___ $\text{IV}^{-\underline{7}}$ ___ I^- ___ V ___ I^-

8 ___ $\text{I}^{-\underline{7}}$ ___ $\text{IV}^{-\underline{7}}$ ___ V ___ I^6 ___ $\text{IV}^{-\underline{7}}$ ___ I^- ___ ^-VI

9 ___ I^{-6}_{4} ___ V^{-7} ___ $\text{I}^{-\underline{7}}$ ___ $\text{IV}^{-\underline{7}}$ ___ V ___ V^{-6}_{d5} ___ I^-

10 ___ $\text{IV}^{-\underline{7}}$ ___ $\text{I}^{-\underline{7}}$ ___ $^-\text{VI}^7$ ___ $\text{IV}^{-\underline{7}}$ ___ I^{-6}_{4} ___ V^{-7} ___ I^-

D4-4b Chord identification in a key
(Copy 3)

Shield the answer. Listen to the chord and write the composite chord symbol in the blank; then uncover the answer and compare your response. Goal: No more than seven errors. The first frame requires no response. After you have done this lesson, take Test D4.

1   V^{-7} ___ I^- ___ $\text{IV}^{-\underline{7}}$ ___ I^{-6}_{4} ___ V^{-7} ___ I^- ___ $\text{I}^{-\underline{7}}$

2 ___ $\text{IV}^{-\underline{7}}$ ___ I^- ___ $^-\text{VI}^7$ ___ $\text{IV}^{-\underline{7}}$ ___ V ___ IV^6 ___ $\text{IV}^{-\underline{7}}$

3 ___ I^- ___ $\text{IV}^{-\underline{7}}$ ___ V ___ $\text{I}^{-\underline{7}}$ ___ IV^- ___ I^6 ___ $^-\text{VI}^7$

4 ___ I^{-6}_{4} ___ V ___ $^-\text{VI}^7$ ___ V^{-7} ___ I^- ___ $\text{I}^{-\underline{7}}$ ___ $\text{IV}^{-\underline{7}}$

5 ___ I^6 ___ $^-\text{VI}^7$ ___ $\text{IV}^{-\underline{7}}$ ___ I^{-6}_{4} ___ V^{-7} ___ I^- ___ I^6

6 ___ $\text{IV}^{-\underline{7}}$ ___ $\text{I}^{-\underline{7}}$ ___ $^-\text{VI}^7$ ___ V^{-7} ___ $^-\text{VI}^7$ ___ $\text{IV}^{-\underline{7}}$ ___ I^{-6}_{4}

7 ___ V^{-7} ___ I^- ___ ^-III ___ $\text{IV}^{-\underline{7}}$ ___ I^- ___ V ___ I^-

8 ___ $\text{I}^{-\underline{7}}$ ___ $\text{IV}^{-\underline{7}}$ ___ V ___ I^6 ___ $\text{IV}^{-\underline{7}}$ ___ I^- ___ ^-VI

9 ___ I^{-6}_{4} ___ V^{-7} ___ $\text{I}^{-\underline{7}}$ ___ $\text{IV}^{-\underline{7}}$ ___ V ___ V^{-6}_{d5} ___ I^-

10 ___ $\text{IV}^{-\underline{7}}$ ___ $\text{I}^{-\underline{7}}$ ___ $^-\text{VI}^7$ ___ $\text{IV}^{-\underline{7}}$ ___ I^{-6}_{4} ___ V^{-7} ___ I^-

D4-4b Chord identification in a key
(Copy 4)

Shield the answer. Listen to the chord and write the composite chord symbol in the blank; then uncover the answer and compare your response. Goal: No more than seven errors. The first frame requires no response. After you have done this lesson, take Test D4.

1. V^{-7} _____ I^- _____ IV^{-7}_- _____ I^{-6}_4 _____ V^{-7} _____ I^- _____ I^{-7}_-

2. _____ IV^{-7}_- _____ I^- _____ $^-VI^7$ _____ IV^{-7}_- _____ V _____ IV^6 _____ IV^{-7}_-

3. _____ I^- _____ IV^{-7}_- _____ V _____ I^{-7}_- _____ IV^- _____ I^6 _____ $^-VI^7$

4. _____ I^{-6}_4 _____ V _____ $^-VI^7$ _____ V^{-7} _____ I^- _____ I^{-7}_- _____ IV^{-7}_-

5. _____ I^6 _____ $^-VI^7$ _____ IV^{-7}_- _____ I^{-6}_4 _____ V^{-7} _____ I^- _____ I^6

6. _____ IV^{-7}_- _____ I^{-7}_- _____ $^-VI^7$ _____ V^{-7} _____ $^-VI^7$ _____ IV^{-7}_- _____ I^{-6}_4

7. _____ V^{-7} _____ I^- _____ ^-III _____ IV^{-7}_- _____ I^- _____ V _____ I^-

8. _____ I^{-7}_- _____ IV^{-7}_- _____ V _____ I^6 _____ IV^{-7}_- _____ I^- _____ ^-VI

9. _____ I^{-6}_4 _____ V^{-7} _____ I^{-7}_- _____ IV^{-7}_- _____ V _____ V^{-6}_{d5} _____ I^-

10. _____ IV^{-7}_- _____ I^{-7}_- _____ $^-VI^7$ _____ IV^{-7}_- _____ I^{-6}_4 _____ V^{-7} _____ I^-

D4-4b Chord identification in a key
(Copy 5)

Shield the answer. Listen to the chord and write the composite chord symbol in the blank; then uncover the answer and compare your response. Goal: No more than seven errors. The first frame requires no response. After you have done this lesson, take Test D4.

1. V^{-7} _____ I^- _____ IV^{-7}_- _____ I^{-6}_4 _____ V^{-7} _____ I^- _____ I^{-7}_-

2. _____ IV^{-7}_- _____ I^- _____ $^-VI^7$ _____ IV^{-7}_- _____ V _____ IV^6 _____ IV^{-7}_-

3. _____ I^- _____ IV^{-7}_- _____ V _____ I^{-7}_- _____ IV^- _____ I^6 _____ $^-VI^7$

4. _____ I^{-6}_4 _____ V _____ $^-VI^7$ _____ V^{-7} _____ I^- _____ I^{-7}_- _____ IV^{-7}_-

5. _____ I^6 _____ $^-VI^7$ _____ IV^{-7}_- _____ I^{-6}_4 _____ V^{-7} _____ I^- _____ I^6

6. _____ IV^{-7}_- _____ I^{-7}_- _____ $^-VI^7$ _____ V^{-7} _____ $^-VI^7$ _____ IV^{-7}_- _____ I^{-6}_4

7. _____ V^{-7} _____ I^- _____ ^-III _____ IV^{-7}_- _____ I^- _____ V _____ I^-

8. _____ I^{-7}_- _____ IV^{-7}_- _____ V _____ I^6 _____ IV^{-7}_- _____ I^- _____ ^-VI

9. _____ I^{-6}_4 _____ V^{-7} _____ I^{-7}_- _____ IV^{-7}_- _____ V _____ V^{-6}_{d5} _____ I^-

10. _____ IV^{-7}_- _____ I^{-7}_- _____ $^-VI^7$ _____ IV^{-7}_- _____ I^{-6}_4 _____ V^{-7} _____ I^-

Four More Seventh Chords   SERIES D5

In this series, four new chords are introduced: the half-diminished seventh chord in root position, the diminished seventh chord, and the dominant seventh chord in second and third inversion. There are four types of lessons: chord dictation, chord identification, figured bass dictation, and chord identification in a key. When you have done this series, take Test D5, which includes sections on each of the four kinds of lessons.

The upper tones of the half-diminished seventh chord in root position are at intervals of a minor seventh, a diminished fifth, and a minor third above the bass.

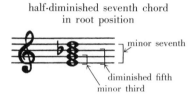

The upper tones of the dominant seventh chord in second inversion are at intervals of a major sixth, a perfect fourth, and a minor third above the bass. In third inversion, the upper tones of the dominant seventh chord are at intervals of a major sixth, an augmented fourth, and a major second above the bass.

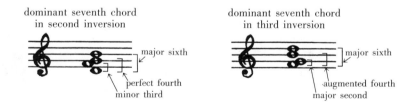

When a diminished seventh chord is notated in root position, the upper tones are at intervals of a diminished seventh, a diminished fifth, and a minor third above the bass.

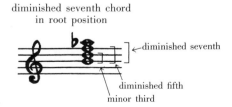

A diminished seventh chord notated as an inversion is enharmonic with one notated in root position (that is, they are notated differently but sound the same). In the following example, the various inversions of the C♯ diminished seventh chord are compared with enharmonic spellings containing a third, fifth and seventh above the lowest tone.

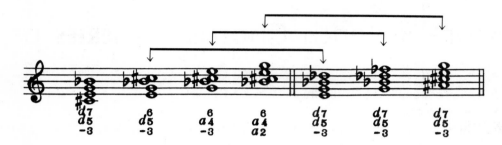

Although the diminished seventh chord can be written in root position and in three inversions, as far as the sound is concerned there is only one form of the chord. In the answers to the chord dictation lessons, the diminished seventh chords are always written in root position. If the notes in your response are enharmonic with the printed answer—that is, if you use different notes to indicate the same pitches, such as D♯ rather than E♭—consider your answer correct.

D5-1a Chord dictation
(Copy 1)

Shield the answer. Listen to the chord and write the upper tones above the given note; then uncover the answer and compare your response. Circle incorrect responses. Goal: No more than seven errors.

113

D5-1a Chord dictation
(Copy 2)

Shield the answer. Listen to the chord and write the upper tones above the given note; then uncover the answer and compare your response. Circle incorrect responses. Goal: No more than seven errors.

114

D5-1a Chord dictation

(Copy 3)

Shield the answer. Listen to the chord and write the upper tones above the given note; then uncover the answer and compare your response. Circle incorrect responses. Goal: No more than seven errors.

D5-1a Chord dictation
(Copy 4)

Shield the answer. Listen to the chord and write the upper tones above the given note; then uncover the answer and compare your response. Circle incorrect responses. Goal: No more than seven errors.

116

D5-1a Chord dictation
(Copy 5)

Shield the answer. Listen to the chord and write the upper tones above the given note; then uncover the answer and compare your response. Circle incorrect responses. Goal: No more than seven errors.

117

Lesson D5-1b

In this lesson, the figured bass symbols for the half-diminished seventh chord in root position and the diminished seventh chord are introduced.

The intervals between the upper tones and the bass of a half-diminished seventh chord in root position are a minor seventh, a diminished fifth, and a minor third. The complete figured bass symbol is $\frac{-7}{d5}{-3}$, which is abbreviated to $\frac{-7}{d5}$.

Because all the notated forms (root position and the three inversions) of the diminished seventh chord are enharmonic (that is, they are notated differently but sound the same), and because they may be spelled in various ways, there is not much value in using different figured bass symbols to distinguish the various inversions. For this reason, you will not be asked to indicate the inversion in the lessons that follow. All diminished seventh chords, regardless of the inversion or spelling, will be identified with the abbreviated figured bass symbol $d7$.

D5-1b Chord identification
(Copy 1)

Shield the answer. Listen to the chord and write the figured bass symbol in the blank; then uncover the answer and compare your response. Circle incorrect responses. Goal: No more than seven errors.

	1	2	3	4	5	6	7
1	-6	$\frac{-6}{-}$	$\frac{-7}{d5}$		d7	$\frac{-6}{d5}$	
2	$\frac{-7}{d5}$	d7	$\frac{-6}{d5}$	-7	−	d7	$\frac{-6}{d5}$
3	$\frac{-7}{d5}$	-7		$\frac{-6}{d5}$	d7	$\frac{-7}{d5}$	
4	-6	$\frac{-6}{-}$	$\frac{-7}{d5}$	$\frac{-6}{-}$		-6	$\frac{-6}{d5}$
5	$\frac{-7}{d5}$		-7	$\frac{-6}{d5}$	$\frac{-7}{d5}$		d7
6	−	$\frac{-7}{d5}$	d7	$\frac{-6}{d5}$	-7	6	$\frac{-7}{d5}$
7	d7	−	$\frac{-7}{d5}$	$\frac{-6}{d5}$	d7	−	-7
8	$\frac{-7}{d5}$	d7	−	$\frac{-6}{d5}$	6	$\frac{-6}{-}$	$\frac{-7}{d5}$
9	d7		$\frac{-6}{d5}$	$\frac{-7}{d5}$		$\frac{-7}{d5}$	
10	d7	−	$\frac{-7}{d5}$	$\frac{-6}{d5}$	−	d7	

D5-1b Chord identification
(Copy 2)

Shield the answer. Listen to the chord and write the figured bass symbol in the blank; then uncover the answer and compare your response. Circle incorrect responses. Goal: No more than seven errors.

#	1	2	3	4	5	6	7
1	-6	-6 / -	-7 / d5		d7	-6 / d5	
2	-7 / d5	d7	-6 / d5	-7	-	d7	-6 / d5
3	-7 / d5	-7		-6 / d5	d7	-7 / d5	
4	-6	-6 / -	-7 / d5	-6 / -		-6	-6 / d5
5	-7 / d5		-7	-6 / d5	-7 / d5		d7
6	-	-7 / d5	d7	-6 / d5	-7	6	-7 / d5
7	d7	-	-7 / d5	-6 / d5	d7	-	-7
8	-7 / d5	d7	-	-6 / d5	6	-6 / -	-7 / d5
9	d7		-6 / d5	-7 / d5		-7 / d5	
10	d7	-	-7 / d5	-6 / d5		d7	

D5-1b Chord identification
(Copy 3)

Shield the answer. Listen to the chord and write the figured bass symbol in the blank; then uncover the answer and compare your response. Circle incorrect responses. Goal: No more than seven errors.

#	1	2	3	4	5	6	7
1	-6	-6 / -	-7 / d5		d7	-6 / d5	
2	-7 / d5	d7	-6 / d5	-7	-	d7	-6 / d5
3	-7 / d5	-7		-6 / d5	d7	-7 / d5	
4	-6	-6 / -	-7 / d5	-6 / -		-6	-6 / d5
5	-7 / d5		-7	-6 / d5	-7 / d5		d7
6	-	-7 / d5	d7	-6 / d5	-7	6	-7 / d5
7	d7	-	-7 / d5	-6 / d5	d7	-	-7
8	-7 / d5	d7	-	-6 / d5	6	-6 / -	-7 / d5
9	d7		-6 / d5	-7 / d5		-7 / d5	
10	d7	-	-7 / d5	-6 / d5		d7	

D5-1b Chord identification

Shield the answer. Listen to the chord and write the figured bass symbol in the blank; then uncover the answer and compare your response. Circle incorrect responses. Goal: No more than seven errors.

1. ____ -6 | ____ -6/- | ____ -7/d5 | ____ | ____ d7 | ____ -6/d5 | ____
2. ____ -7/d5 | ____ d7 | ____ -6/d5 | ____ -7 | ____ - | ____ d7 | ____ -6/d5
3. ____ -7/d5 | ____ -7 | ____ | ____ -6/d5 | ____ d7 | ____ -7/d5
4. ____ -6 | ____ -6/- | ____ -7/d5 | ____ -6/- | ____ -6 | ____ -6/d5
5. ____ -7/d5 | ____ | ____ -7 | ____ -6/d5 | ____ -7/d5 | ____ d7
6. ____ - | ____ -7/d5 | ____ d7 | ____ -6/d5 | ____ -7 | ____ 6 | ____ -7/d5
7. ____ d7 | ____ - | ____ -7/d5 | ____ -6/d5 | ____ d7 | ____ - | ____ -7
8. ____ -7/d5 | ____ d7 | ____ - | ____ -6/d5 | ____ 6 | ____ -6/- | ____ -7/d5
9. ____ d7 | ____ | ____ -6/d5 | ____ -7/d5 | ____ -7/d5
10. ____ d7 | ____ - | ____ -7/d5 | ____ -6/d5 | ____ - | ____ d7

D5-1b Chord identification

Shield the answer. Listen to the chord and write the figured bass symbol in the blank; then uncover the answer and compare your response. Circle incorrect responses. Goal: No more than seven errors.

1. ____ -6 | ____ -6/- | ____ -7/d5 | ____ | ____ d7 | ____ -6/d5 | ____
2. ____ -7/d5 | ____ d7 | ____ -6/d5 | ____ -7 | ____ - | ____ d7 | ____ -6/d5
3. ____ -7/d5 | ____ -7 | ____ | ____ -6/d5 | ____ d7 | ____ -7/d5 | ____
4. ____ -6 | ____ -6/- | ____ -7/d5 | ____ -6/- | ____ -6 | ____ -6/d5
5. ____ -7/d5 | ____ | ____ -7 | ____ -6/d5 | ____ -7/d5 | ____ d7
6. ____ - | ____ -7/d5 | ____ d7 | ____ -6/d5 | ____ -7 | ____ 6 | ____ -7/d5
7. ____ d7 | ____ - | ____ -7/d5 | ____ -6/d5 | ____ d7 | ____ - | ____ -7
8. ____ -7/d5 | ____ d7 | ____ - | ____ -6/d5 | ____ 6 | ____ -6/- | ____ -7/d5
9. ____ d7 | ____ | ____ -6/d5 | ____ -7/d5 | ____ -7/d5
10. ____ d7 | ____ - | ____ -7/d5 | ____ -6/d5 | ____ - | ____ d7 | ____

D5-2 Chord identification
(Copy 1)

Shield the answer. Listen to the chord and write the figured bass symbol in the blank; then uncover the answer and compare your response. Circle incorrect responses. Goal: No more than seven errors.

1	___ -7	___ -6 d5	___ -7 d5	___ d7	___ d7	___ -	___ -7 d5
2	___ d7	___ d7	___ -7	___ -	___ 6 -	___ d7	___ -6 d5
3	___ -7 d5	___ 6	___ d7	___ d7	___ -7	___ -6 d5	___ -7 d5
4	___ d7	___ -	___ -7 d5	___ d7	___ d7	___ -7	___ -
5	___ -	___ -7 d5	___ d7	___ -7	___ -7	___ -7 d5	___ -7
6	___ d7	___ -7	___	___ -7 d5	___ -6 d5	___	___ d7
7	___ d7	___ -7	___ -	___ -7 d5	___ -7	___ 6	___ d7
8	___ d7	___ d7	___ -6 d5	___	___ 6 -	___ -7 d5	___
9	___ 6 -	___ -7 d5	___ -6 d5	___	___ -6 d5	___ d7	___ -7 d5
10	___ -7	___	___ d7	___	___ -7 d5	___ d7	___ -

D5-2 Chord identification
(Copy 2)

Shield the answer. Listen to the chord and write the figured bass symbol in the blank; then uncover the answer and compare your response. Circle incorrect responses. Goal: No more than seven errors.

1	___ -7	___ -6 d5	___ -7 d5	___ d7	___ d7	___ -	___ -7 d5
2	___ d7	___ d7	___ -7	___ -	___ 6 -	___ d7	___ -6 d5
3	___ -7 d5	___ 6	___ d7	___ d7	___ -7	___ -6 d5	___ -7 d5
4	___ d7	___ -	___ -7 d5	___ d7	___ d7	___ -7	___ -
5	___ -	___ -7 d5	___ d7	___ -7	___ -7	___ -7 d5	___ -7
6	___ d7	___ -7	___	___ -7 d5	___ -6 d5	___	___ d7
7	___ d7	___ -7	___ -	___ -7 d5	___ -7	___ 6	___ d7
8	___ d7	___ d7	___ -6 d5	___	___ 6 -	___ -7 d5	___
9	___ 6 -	___ -7 d5	___ -6 d5	___	___ -6 d5	___ d7	___ -7 d5
10	___ -7	___	___ d7	___	___ -7 d5	___ d7	___ -

D5-2 Chord identification
(Copy 3)

Shield the answer. Listen to the chord and write the figured bass symbol in the blank; then uncover the answer and compare your response. Circle incorrect responses. Goal: No more than seven errors.

1	___	-7	___	-6 d5	___	-7 d5	___	d7	___	d7	___	-	___	-7 d5
2	___	d7	___	d7	___	-7	___	-	___	6 -	___	d7	___	-6 d5
3	___	-7 d5	___	6	___	d7	___	d7	___	-7	___	-6 d5	___	-7 d5
4	___	d7	___	-	___	-7 d5	___	d7	___	d7	___	-7	___	-
5	___	-	___	-7 d5	___	d7	___	-7	___	-7	___	-7 d5	___	-7
6	___	d7	___	-7	___		___	-7 d5	___	-6 d5	___		___	d7
7	___	d7	___	-7	___	-	___	-7 d5	___	-7	___	6	___	d7
8	___	d7	___	d7	___	-6 d5	___		___	6 -	___	-7 d5	___	
9	___	6 -	___	-7 d5	___	-6 d5	___		___	-6 d5	___	d7	___	-7 d5
10	___	-7	___		___	d7	___		___	-7 d5	___	d7	___	-

D5-2 Chord identification
(Copy 4)

Shield the answer. Listen to the chord and write the figured bass symbol in the blank; then uncover the answer and compare your response. Circle incorrect responses. Goal: No more than seven errors.

1	___	-7	___	-6 d5	___	-7 d5	___	d7	___	d7	___	-	___	-7 d5
2	___	d7	___	d7	___	-7	___	-	___	6 -	___	d7	___	-6 d5
3	___	-7 d5	___	6	___	d7	___	d7	___	-7	___	-6 d5	___	-7 d5
4	___	d7	___	-	___	-7 d5	___	d7	___	d7	___	-7	___	-
5	___	-	___	-7 d5	___	d7	___	-7	___	-7	___	-7 d5	___	-7
6	___	d7	___	-7	___		___	-7 d5	___	-6 d5	___		___	d7
7	___	d7	___	-7	___	-	___	-7 d5	___	-7	___	6	___	d7
8	___	d7	___	d7	___	-6 d5	___		___	6 -	___	-7 d5	___	
9	___	6 -	___	-7 d5	___	-6 d5	___		___	-6 d5	___	d7	___	-7 d5
10	___	-7	___		___	d7	___		___	-7 d5	___	d7	___	-

D5-2 Chord identification
(Copy 5)

Shield the answer. Listen to the chord and write the figured bass symbol in the blank; then uncover the answer and compare your response. Circle incorrect responses. Goal: No more than seven errors.

1. ____ -7   ____ -6/d5   ____ -7/d5   ____ d7   ____ d7   ____ -   ____ -7/d5

2. ____ d7   ____ d7   ____ -7   ____ -   ____ 6/-   ____ d7   ____ -6/d5

3. ____ -7/d5   ____ 6   ____ d7   ____ d7   ____ -7   ____ -6/d5   ____ -7/d5

4. ____ d7   ____ -   ____ -7/d5   ____ d7   ____ d7   ____ -7   ____ -

5. ____ -   ____ -7/d5   ____ d7   ____ -7   ____ -7   ____ -7/d5   ____ -7

6. ____ d7   ____ -7   ____   ____ -7/d5   ____ -6/d5   ____   ____ d7

7. ____ d7   ____ -7   ____ -   ____ -7/d5   ____ -7   ____ 6   ____ d7

8. ____ d7   ____ d7   ____ -6/d5   ____   ____ 6/-   ____ -7/d5   ____

9. ____ 6/-   ____ -7/d5   ____ -6/d5   ____   ____ -6/d5   ____ d7   ____ -7/d5

10. ____ -7   ____   ____ d7   ____   ____ -7/d5   ____ d7   ____ -

123

D5-3a Chord dictation

(Copy 1)

Shield the answer. Listen to the chord and write the upper tones above the given note; then uncover the answer and compare your response. Circle incorrect responses. Goal: No more than seven errors.

124

D5–3a Chord dictation

(Copy 2)

Shield the answer. Listen to the chord and write the upper tones above the given note; then uncover the answer and compare your response. Circle incorrect responses. Goal: No more than seven errors.

D5-3a Chord dictation

(Copy 3)

Shield the answer. Listen to the chord and write the upper tones above the given note; then uncover the answer and compare your response. Circle incorrect responses. Goal: No more than seven errors.

126

D5-3a Chord dictation

(Copy 4)

Shield the answer. Listen to the chord and write the upper tones above the given note; then uncover the answer and compare your response. Circle incorrect responses. Goal: No more than seven errors.

D5-3a Chord dictation

(Copy 5)

Shield the answer. Listen to the chord and write the upper tones above the given note; then uncover the answer and compare your response. Circle incorrect responses. Goal: No more than seven errors.

128

Lesson D5-3b

In this lesson the figured bass symbols for the dominant seventh chord in second and third inversion are introduced.

The intervals between the upper tones and the bass of a dominant seventh chord in second inversion are a major sixth, perfect fourth, and minor third. The complete figured bass symbol is $^6_4$ (with -3), abbreviated to $^4_-$. The intervals between the upper tones and the bass of a dominant seventh chord in third inversion are a major sixth, an augmented fourth, and a major second. The complete figured bass symbol is $^6_{a4}$ (with 2), abbreviated to $^{a4}_2$.

D5-3b Chord identification

(Copy 1)

Shield the answer. Listen to the chord and write the figured bass symbol in the blank; then uncover the answer and compare your response. Circle incorrect responses. Goal: No more than seven errors.

#														
1	___	−7	___	−6/d5	___	4/−	___	a4/2	___	−6	___	4/−	___	
2	___	−7	___	a4/2	___	4/−	___	−6/d5	___	−7	___	a4/2	___	6
3	___	4/−	___	−	___	a4/2	___	6	___	a4/2	___	6	___	4/−
4	___	−	___	−7/d5	___	4/−	___	d7	___	−	___	a4/2	___	6
5	___	6/−	___	d7	___	−	___	d7	___	4/−	___	a4/2	___	6
6	___	d7	___	4/−	___	−	___	−7	___	a4/2	___	6	___	4/−
7	___	6	___	6/−	___	4/−	___	−	___	−7/d5	___	4/−	___	−
8	___		___	a4/2	___	−6	___	4/−	___		___	−7	___	−7/d5
9	___	4/−	___	a4/2	___	−6/d5	___	d7	___	a4/2	___	d7	___	a4/2
10	___	6	___	6/−	___	4/−	___	−	___	a4/2	___	4/−		

D5-3b Chord identification

(Copy 2)

Shield the answer. Listen to the chord and write the figured bass symbol in the blank; then uncover the answer and compare your response. Circle incorrect responses. Goal: No more than seven errors.

#							
1	___ −7	___ −6/d5	___ 4/−	___ a4/2	___ −6	___ 4/−	___
2	___ −7	___ a4/2	___ 4/−	___ −6/d5	___ −7	___ a4/2	___ 6
3	___ 4/−	___ −	___ a4/2	___ 6	___ a4/2	___ 6	___ 4/−
4	___ −	___ −7/d5	___ 4/−	___ d7	___ −	___ a4/2	___ 6
5	___ 6/−	___ d7	___ −	___ d7	___ 4/−	___ a4/2	___ 6
6	___ d7	___ 4/−	___ −	___ −7	___ a4/2	___ 6	___ 4/−
7	___ 6	___ 6/−	___ 4/−	___ −	___ −7/d5	___ 4/−	___ −
8	___	___ a4/2	___ −6	___ 4/−	___	___ −7	___ −7/d5
9	___ 4/−	___ a4/2	___ −6/d5	___ d7	___ a4/2	___ d7	___ a4/2
10	___ 6	___ 6/−	___ 4/−	___ −	___ a4/2	___ 4/−	

D5-3b Chord identification

(Copy 3)

Shield the answer. Listen to the chord and write the figured bass symbol in the blank; then uncover the answer and compare your response. Circle incorrect responses. Goal: No more than seven errors.

#							
1	___ −7	___ −6/d5	___ 4/−	___ a4/2	___ −6	___ 4/−	___
2	___ −7	___ a4/2	___ 4/−	___ −6/d5	___ −7	___ a4/2	___ 6
3	___ 4/−	___ −	___ a4/2	___ 6	___ a4/2	___ 6	___ 4/−
4	___ −	___ −7/d5	___ 4/−	___ d7	___ −	___ a4/2	___ 6
5	___ 6/−	___ d7	___ −	___ d7	___ 4/−	___ a4/2	___ 6
6	___ d7	___ 4/−	___ −	___ −7	___ a4/2	___ 6	___ 4/−
7	___ 6	___ 6/−	___ 4/−	___ −	___ −7/d5	___ 4/−	___ −
8	___	___ a4/2	___ −6	___ 4/−	___	___ −7	___ −7/d5
9	___ 4/−	___ a4/2	___ −6/d5	___ d7	___ a4/2	___ d7	___ a4/2
10	___ 6	___ 6/−	___ 4/−	___ −	___ a4/2	___ 4/−	

D5-3b Chord identification
(Copy 4)

Shield the answer. Listen to the chord and write the figured bass symbol in the blank; then uncover the answer and compare your response. Circle incorrect responses. Goal: No more than seven errors.

1 ____ -7 ____ -6/d5 ____ 4/- ____ a4/2 ____ -6 ____ 4/- ____

2 ____ -7 ____ a4/2 ____ 4/- ____ -6/d5 ____ -7 ____ a4/2 ____ 6

3 ____ 4/- ____ - ____ a4/2 ____ 6 ____ a4/2 ____ 6 ____ 4/-

4 ____ - ____ -7/d5 ____ 4/- ____ d7 ____ - ____ a4/2 ____ 6

5 ____ 6/- ____ d7 ____ - ____ d7 ____ 4/- ____ a4/2 ____ 6

6 ____ d7 ____ 4/- ____ - ____ -7 ____ a4/2 ____ 6 ____ 4/-

7 ____ 6 ____ 6/- ____ 4/- ____ - ____ -7/d5 ____ 4/- ____ -

8 ____ ____ a4/2 ____ -6 ____ 4/- ____ ____ -7 ____ -7/d5

9 ____ 4/- ____ a4/2 ____ -6/d5 ____ d7 ____ a4/2 ____ d7 ____ a4/2

10 ____ 6 ____ 6/- ____ 4/- ____ - ____ a4/2 ____ 4/- ____

D5-3b Chord identification
(Copy 5)

Shield the answer. Listen to the chord and write the figured bass symbol in the blank; then uncover the answer and compare your response. Circle incorrect responses. Goal: No more than seven errors.

1 ____ -7 ____ -6/d5 ____ 4/- ____ a4/2 ____ -6 ____ 4/- ____

2 ____ -7 ____ a4/2 ____ 4/- ____ -6/d5 ____ -7 ____ a4/2 ____ 6

3 ____ 4/- ____ - ____ a4/2 ____ 6 ____ a4/2 ____ 6 ____ 4/-

4 ____ - ____ -7/d5 ____ 4/- ____ d7 ____ - ____ a4/2 ____ 6

5 ____ 6/- ____ d7 ____ - ____ d7 ____ 4/- ____ a4/2 ____ 6

6 ____ d7 ____ 4/- ____ - ____ -7 ____ a4/2 ____ 6 ____ 4/-

7 ____ 6 ____ 6/- ____ 4/- ____ - ____ -7/d5 ____ 4/- ____ -

8 ____ ____ a4/2 ____ -6 ____ 4/- ____ ____ -7 ____ -7/d5

9 ____ 4/- ____ a4/2 ____ -6/d5 ____ d7 ____ a4/2 ____ d7 ____ a4/2

10 ____ 6 ____ 6/- ____ 4/- ____ - ____ a4/2 ____ 4/- ____

Shield the answer. Listen to the chord and write the figured bass symbol in the blank; then uncover the answer and compare your response. Circle incorrect responses. Goal: No more than seven errors.

1. ____ -7   ____ a4/2   ____ 4/-   ____ -6/d5   ____   ____ a4/2   ____ -6

2. ____ 4/-   ____   ____ -6/d5   ____ -7   ____   ____ d7   ____ -6/d5

3. ____ 4/-   ____   ____ a4/2   ____ 6   ____ -7/d5   ____ 4/-   ____ -

4. ____ a4/2   ____ 6   ____ -   ____ -7/d5   ____ -6/d5   ____   ____ d7

5. ____ d7   ____ -6/d5   ____   ____ a4/2   ____ -6   ____ 4/-   ____

6. ____ a4/2   ____ 6   ____ 6/-   ____ 4/-   ____ -   ____ d7   ____ -6/d5

7. ____ -   ____ -7/d5   ____ 4/-   ____ -   ____ -7   ____   ____ 6/-

8. ____ -6   ____ 4/-   ____   ____ a4/2   ____ -6   ____ 4/-   ____

9. ____ -7   ____ -7   ____ d7   ____ -7   ____ a4/2   ____ -6   ____ 6/4

10. ____   ____ 6/4   ____ -6   ____ 4/-   ____   ____ -6/d5   ____

D5–4 Chord identification
(Copy 2)

Shield the answer. Listen to the chord and write the figured bass symbol in the blank; then uncover the answer and compare your response. Circle incorrect responses. Goal: No more than seven errors.

1. ____ -7   ____ a4/2   ____ 4/-   ____ -6/d5   ____   ____ a4/2   ____ -6

2. ____ 4/-   ____   ____ -6/d5   ____ -7   ____   ____ d7   ____ -6/d5

3. ____ 4/-   ____   ____ a4/2   ____ 6   ____ -7/d5   ____ 4/-   ____ -

4. ____ a4/2   ____ 6   ____ -   ____ -7/d5   ____ -6/d5   ____   ____ d7

5. ____ d7   ____ -6/d5   ____   ____ a4/2   ____ -6   ____ 4/-   ____

6. ____ a4/2   ____ 6   ____ 6/-   ____ 4/-   ____ -   ____ d7   ____ -6/d5

7. ____ -   ____ -7/d5   ____ 4/-   ____ -   ____ -7   ____   ____ 6/-

8. ____ -6   ____ 4/-   ____   ____ a4/2   ____ -6   ____ 4/-   ____

9. ____ -7   ____ -7   ____ d7   ____ -7   ____ a4/2   ____ -6   ____ 6/4

10. ____   ____ 6/4   ____ -6   ____ 4/-   ____   ____ -6/d5   ____

D5-4
(Copy 3)

Chord identification

Shield the answer. Listen to the chord and write the figured bass symbol in the blank; then uncover the answer and compare your response. Circle incorrect responses. Goal: No more than seven errors.

#							
1	____ -7	____ $\frac{a4}{2}$	____ $\frac{4}{-}$	____ $\frac{-6}{d5}$	____	____ $\frac{a4}{2}$	____ -6
2	____ $\frac{4}{-}$	____	____ $\frac{-6}{d5}$	____ -7	____	____ d7	____ $\frac{-6}{d5}$
3	____ $\frac{4}{-}$	____	____ $\frac{a4}{2}$	____ 6	____ $\frac{-7}{d5}$	____ $\frac{4}{-}$	____ -
4	____ $\frac{a4}{2}$	____ 6	____ -	____ $\frac{-7}{d5}$	____ $\frac{-6}{d5}$	____	____ d7
5	____ d7	____ $\frac{-6}{d5}$	____	____ $\frac{a4}{2}$	____ -6	____ $\frac{4}{-}$	____
6	____ $\frac{a4}{2}$	____ 6	____ $\frac{6}{-}$	____ $\frac{4}{-}$	____ -	____ d7	____ $\frac{-6}{d5}$
7	____ -	____ $\frac{-7}{d5}$	____ $\frac{4}{-}$	____ -	____ -7	____	____ $\frac{6}{-}$
8	____ -6	____ $\frac{4}{-}$	____	____ $\frac{a4}{2}$	____ -6	____ $\frac{4}{-}$	____
9	____ -7	____ -7	____ d7	____ -7	____ $\frac{a4}{2}$	____ -6	____ $\frac{6}{4}$
10	____	____ $\frac{6}{4}$	____ -6	____ $\frac{4}{-}$	____	____ $\frac{-6}{d5}$	____

D5-4
(Copy 4)

Chord identification

Shield the answer. Listen to the chord and write the figured bass symbol in the blank; then uncover the answer and compare your response. Circle incorrect responses. Goal: No more than seven errors.

#							
1	____ -7	____ $\frac{a4}{2}$	____ $\frac{4}{-}$	____ $\frac{-6}{d5}$	____	____ $\frac{a4}{2}$	____ -6
2	____ $\frac{4}{-}$	____	____ $\frac{-6}{d5}$	____ -7	____	____ d7	____ $\frac{-6}{d5}$
3	____ $\frac{4}{-}$	____	____ $\frac{a4}{2}$	____ 6	____ $\frac{-7}{d5}$	____ $\frac{4}{-}$	____ -
4	____ $\frac{a4}{2}$	____ 6	____ -	____ $\frac{-7}{d5}$	____ $\frac{-6}{d5}$	____	____ d7
5	____ d7	____ $\frac{-6}{d5}$	____	____ $\frac{a4}{2}$	____ -6	____ $\frac{4}{-}$	____
6	____ $\frac{a4}{2}$	____ 6	____ $\frac{6}{-}$	____ $\frac{4}{-}$	____ -	____ d7	____ $\frac{-6}{d5}$
7	____ -	____ $\frac{-7}{d5}$	____ $\frac{4}{-}$	____ -	____ -7	____	____ $\frac{6}{-}$
8	____ -6	____ $\frac{4}{-}$	____	____ $\frac{a4}{2}$	____ -6	____ $\frac{4}{-}$	____
9	____ -7	____ -7	____ d7	____ -7	____ $\frac{a4}{2}$	____ -6	____ $\frac{6}{4}$
10	____	____ $\frac{6}{4}$	____ -6	____ $\frac{4}{-}$	____	____ $\frac{-6}{d5}$	____

D5-4
Chord identification

Shield the answer. Listen to the chord and write the figured bass symbol in the blank; then uncover the answer and compare your response. Circle incorrect responses. Goal: No more than seven errors.

1. ____ -7   ____ a4/2   ____ 4/-   ____ -6/d5   ____   ____ a4/2   ____ -6

2. ____ 4/-   ____   ____ -6/d5   ____ -7   ____   ____ d7   ____ -6/d5

3. ____ 4/-   ____   ____ a4/2   ____ 6   ____ -7/d5   ____ 4/-   ____ -

4. ____ a4/2   ____ 6   ____ -   ____ -7/d5   ____ -6/d5   ____   ____ d7

5. ____ d7   ____ -6/d5   ____   ____ a4/2   ____ -6   ____ 4/-   ____

6. ____ a4/2   ____ 6   ____ 6/-   ____ 4/-   ____ -   ____ d7   ____ -6/d5

7. ____ -   ____ -7/d5   ____ 4/-   ____ -   ____ -7   ____   ____ 6/-

8. ____ -6   ____ 4/-   ____   ____ a4/2   ____ -6   ____ 4/-   ____

9. ____ -7   ____ -7   ____ d7   ____ -7   ____ a4/2   ____ -6   ____ 6/4

10. ____   ____ 6/4   ____ -6   ____ 4/-   ____   ____ -6/d5   ____

D5-5a Figured bass dictation
(Copy 1)

Shield the answer. Listen to the chord and write the bass note and the figured bass symbol; then uncover the answer and compare your response. Circle incorrect responses. Goal: No more than seven errors. The first frame requires no response.

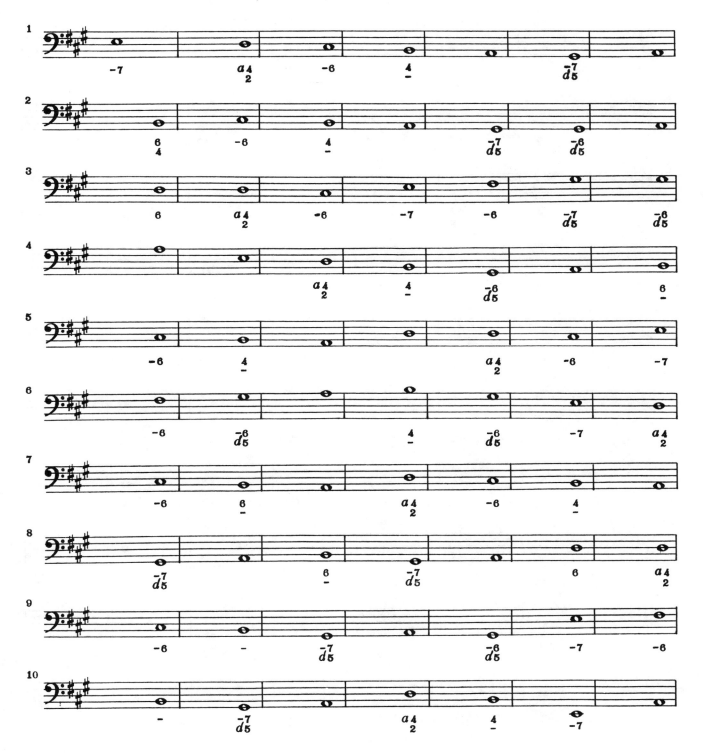

Shield the answer. Listen to the chord and write the bass note and the figured bass symbol; then uncover the answer and compare your response. Circle incorrect responses. Goal: No more than seven errors. The first frame requires no response.

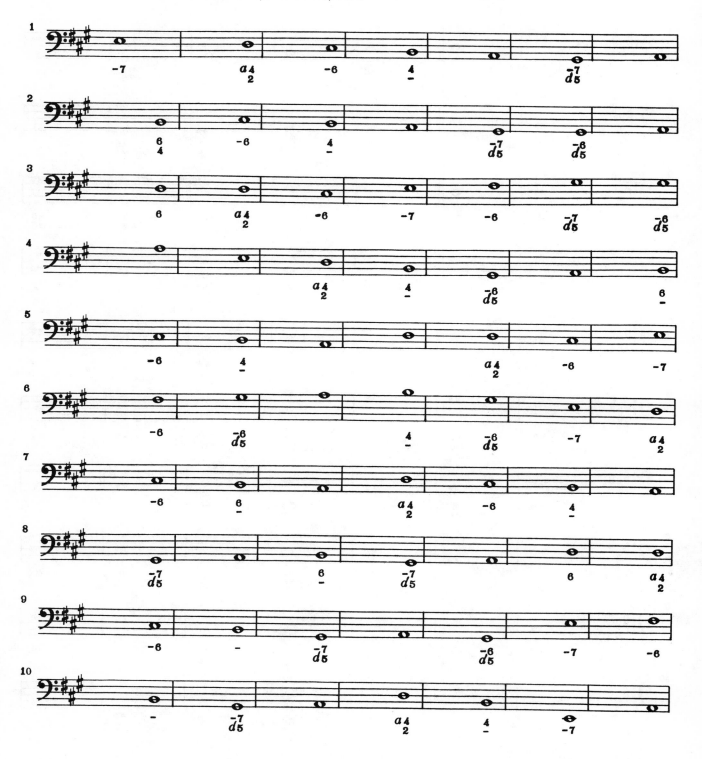

D5-5a Figured bass dictation

(Copy 3)

Shield the answer. Listen to the chord and write the bass note and the figured bass symbol; then uncover the answer and compare your response. Circle incorrect responses. Goal: No more than seven errors. The first frame requires no response.

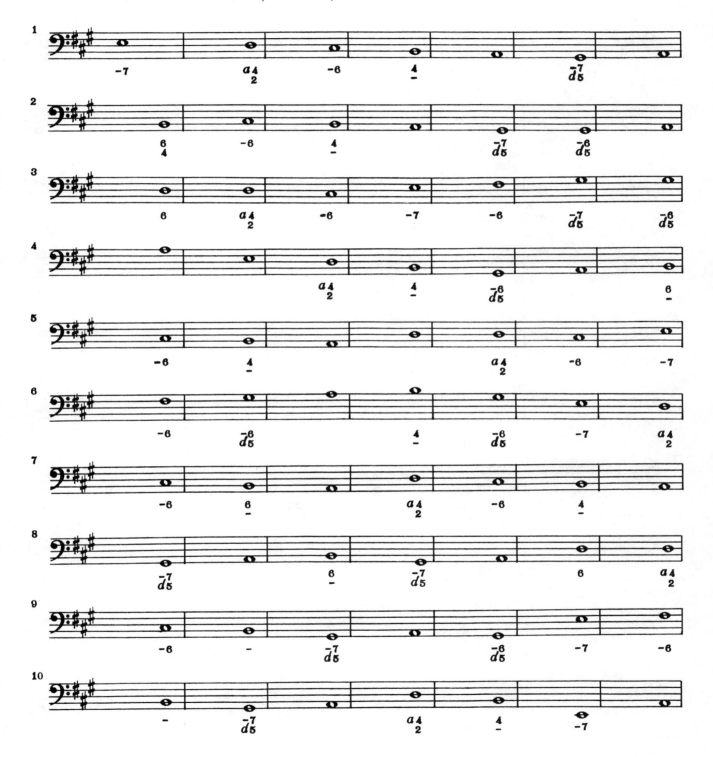

D5–5a Figured bass dictation

(Copy 4)

Shield the answer. Listen to the chord and write the bass note and the figured bass symbol; then uncover the answer and compare your response. Circle incorrect responses. Goal: No more than seven errors. The first frame requires no response.

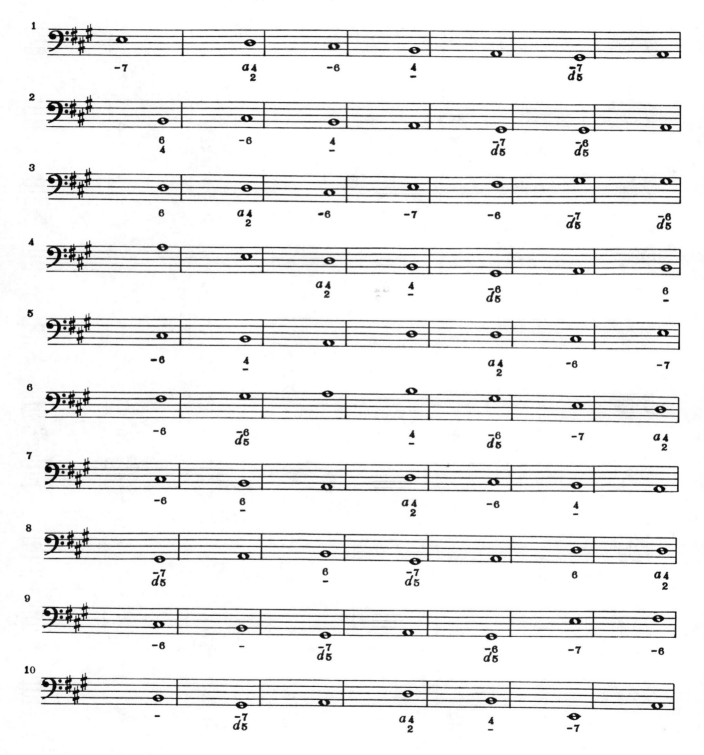

D5-5a Figured bass dictation

(Copy 5)

Shield the answer. Listen to the chord and write the bass note and the figured bass symbol; then uncover the answer and compare your response. Circle incorrect responses. Goal: No more than seven errors. The first frame requires no response.

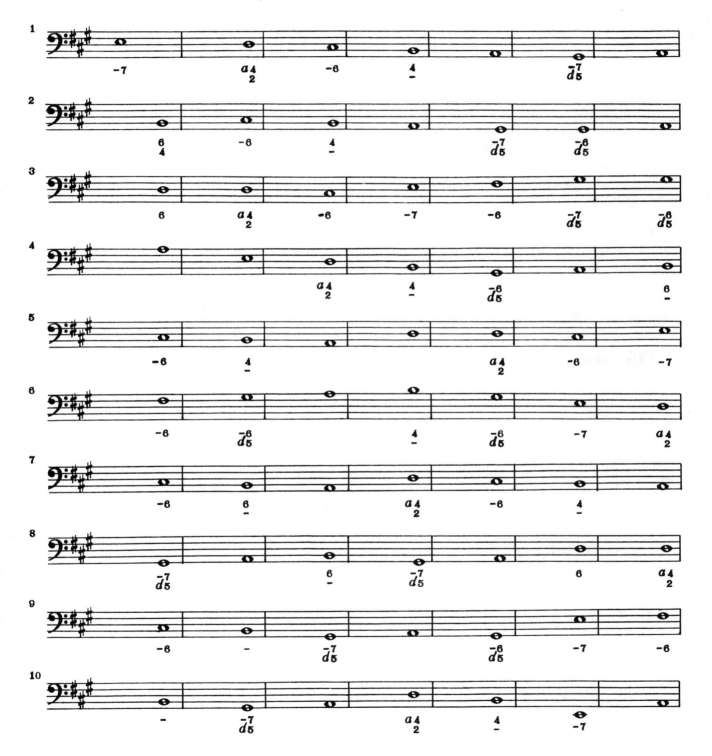

Lesson D5-5b

In this lesson the following composite chord symbols, which appear in a major key, are introduced: V^4_-, V^{a4}_2 and VII^{-7}_{d5}.

The seventh chord on the seventh degree of a major key is a half-diminished seventh chord. The figured bass portion of the composite chord symbol for this chord in root position is $^{-7}_{d5}$, and the composite chord symbol is VII^{-7}_{d5}.

The seventh chord on the fifth degree of both major and minor keys is a dominant seventh chord. The figured bass portion of the composite chord symbol for this chord in second inversion is $^4_-$ and in third inversion is $^{a4}_2$. The composite chord symbols are V^4_- and V^{a4}_2.

In a second inversion of a seventh chord, the fifth of the chord appears in the bass. In the V^4_- chord, therefore, the second degree of the key, which is the fifth of the chord, appears in the bass.

In a seventh chord in third inversion, the seventh of the chord appears in the bass. Therefore in the V^{a4}_2 chord, the fourth degree of the key is in the bass because that degree is the seventh of the chord.

D5-5b Chord identification in a key
(Copy 1)

Shield the answer. Listen to the chord and write the composite chord symbol in the blank; then uncover the answer and compare your response. Circle incorrect responses. Goal: No more than seven errors. The first frame requires no response.

#							
1	V^{-7}	___ V^{a4}_2	___ I^{-6}	___ V^4_-	___ I	___ VII^{-7}_{d5}	___ I
2	___ V^6_4	___ I^{-6}	___ V^4_-	___ I	___ VII^{-7}_{d5}	___ V^{-6}_{d5}	___ I
3	___ II^6	___ V^{a4}_2	___ I^{-6}	___ V^{-7}	___ IV^{-6}	___ VII^{-7}_{d5}	___ V^{-6}_{d5}
4	___ I	___ V	___ V^{a4}_2	___ V^4_-	___ V^{-6}_{d5}	___ I	___ VII^6_-
5	___ I^{-6}	___ V^4_-	___ I	___ IV	___ V^{a4}_2	___ I^{-6}	___ V^{-7}
6	___ IV^{-6}	___ V^{-6}_{d5}	___ I	___ V^4_-	___ V^{-6}_{d5}	___ V^{-7}	___ V^{a4}_2
7	___ I^{-6}	___ VII^6_-	___ I	___ V^{a4}_2	___ I^{-6}	___ V^4_-	___
8	___ VII^{-7}_{d5}	___ I	___ VII^6_-	___ VII^{-7}_{d5}	___ I	___ II^6	___ V^{a4}_2
9	___ I^{-6}	___ II^-	___ VII^{-7}_{d5}	___	___ V^{-6}_{d5}	___ V^{-7}	___ IV^{-6}
10	___ II^-	___ VII^{-7}_{d5}	___ I	___ V^{a4}_2	___ V^4_-	___ V^{-7}	___ I

D5-5b Chord identification in a key
(Copy 2)

Shield the answer. Listen to the chord and write the composite chord symbol in the blank; then uncover the answer and compare your response. Circle incorrect responses. Goal: No more than seven errors. The first frame requires no response.

1. V^{-7} ____ V^{a4}_2 ____ I^{-6} ____ V^4_- ____ I ____ VII^{-7}_{d5} ____ I

2. ____ V^6_4 ____ I^{-6} ____ V^4_- ____ I ____ VII^{-7}_{d5} ____ V^{-6}_{d5} ____ I

3. ____ II^6 ____ V^{a4}_2 ____ I^{-6} ____ V^{-7} ____ IV^{-6} ____ VII^{-7}_{d5} ____ V^{-6}_{d5}

4. ____ I ____ V ____ V^{a4}_2 ____ V^4_- ____ V^{-6}_{d5} ____ I ____ VII^6_-

5. ____ I^{-6} ____ V^4_- ____ I ____ IV ____ V^{a4}_2 ____ I^{-6} ____ V^{-7}

6. ____ IV^{-6} ____ V^{-6}_{d5} ____ I ____ V^4_- ____ V^{-6}_{d5} ____ V^{-7} ____ V^{a4}_2

7. ____ I^{-6} ____ VII^6_- ____ I ____ V^{a4}_2 ____ I^{-6} ____ V^4_- ____

8. ____ VII^{-7}_{d5} ____ I ____ VII^6_- ____ VII^{-7}_{d5} ____ I ____ II^6 ____ V^{a4}_2

9. ____ I^{-6} ____ II^- ____ VII^{-7}_{d5} ____ ____ V^{-6}_{d5} ____ V^{-7} ____ IV^{-6}

10. ____ II^- ____ VII^{-7}_{d5} ____ I ____ V^{a4}_2 ____ V^4_- ____ V^{-7} ____ I

D5-5b Chord identification in a key
(Copy 3)

Shield the answer. Listen to the chord and write the composite chord symbol in the blank; then uncover the answer and compare your response. Circle incorrect responses. Goal: No more than seven errors. The first frame requires no response.

1. V^{-7} ____ V^{a4}_2 ____ I^{-6} ____ V^4_- ____ I ____ VII^{-7}_{d5} ____ I

2. ____ V^6_4 ____ I^{-6} ____ V^4_- ____ I ____ VII^{-7}_{d5} ____ V^{-6}_{d5} ____ I

3. ____ II^6 ____ V^{a4}_2 ____ I^{-6} ____ V^{-7} ____ IV^{-6} ____ VII^{-7}_{d5} ____ V^{-6}_{d5}

4. ____ I ____ V ____ V^{a4}_2 ____ V^4_- ____ V^{-6}_{d5} ____ I ____ VII^6_-

5. ____ I^{-6} ____ V^4_- ____ I ____ IV ____ V^{a4}_2 ____ I^{-6} ____ V^{-7}

6. ____ IV^{-6} ____ V^{-6}_{d5} ____ I ____ V^4_- ____ V^{-6}_{d5} ____ V^{-7} ____ V^{a4}_2

7. ____ I^{-6} ____ VII^6_- ____ I ____ V^{a4}_2 ____ I^{-6} ____ V^4_- ____

8. ____ VII^{-7}_{d5} ____ I ____ VII^6_- ____ VII^{-7}_{d5} ____ I ____ II^6 ____ V^{a4}_2

9. ____ I^{-6} ____ II^- ____ VII^{-7}_{d5} ____ ____ V^{-6}_{d5} ____ V^{-7} ____ IV^{-6}

10. ____ II^- ____ VII^{-7}_{d5} ____ I ____ V^{a4}_2 ____ V^4_- ____ V^{-7} ____ I

D5–5b Chord identification in a key
(Copy 4)

Shield the answer. Listen to the chord and write the composite chord symbol in the blank; then uncover the answer and compare your response. Circle incorrect responses. Goal: No more than seven errors. The first frame requires no response.

1 V^{-7} ___ V^{a4}_{2} ___ I^{-6} ___ V^{4}_{-} ___ I ___ VII^{-7}_{d5} ___ I

2 ___ V^{6}_{4} ___ I^{-6} ___ V^{4}_{-} ___ I ___ VII^{-7}_{d5} ___ V^{-6}_{d5} ___ I

3 ___ II^{6} ___ V^{a4}_{2} ___ I^{-6} ___ V^{-7} ___ IV^{-6} ___ VII^{-7}_{d5} ___ V^{-6}_{d5}

4 ___ I ___ V ___ V^{a4}_{2} ___ V^{4}_{-} ___ V^{-6}_{d5} ___ I ___ VII^{6}_{-}

5 ___ I^{-6} ___ V^{4}_{-} ___ I ___ IV ___ V^{a4}_{2} ___ I^{-6} ___ V^{-7}

6 ___ IV^{-6} ___ V^{-6}_{d5} ___ I ___ V^{4}_{-} ___ V^{-6}_{d5} ___ V^{-7} ___ V^{a4}_{2}

7 ___ I^{-6} ___ VII^{6}_{-} ___ I ___ V^{a4}_{2} ___ I^{-6} ___ V^{4}_{-} ___

8 ___ VII^{-7}_{d5} ___ I ___ VII^{6}_{-} ___ VII^{-7}_{d5} ___ I ___ II^{6} ___ V^{a4}_{2}

9 ___ I^{-6} ___ II^{-} ___ VII^{-7}_{d5} ___ ___ V^{-6}_{d5} ___ V^{-7} ___ IV^{-6}

10 ___ II^{-} ___ VII^{-7}_{d5} ___ I ___ V^{a4}_{2} ___ V^{4}_{-} ___ V^{-7} ___ I

D5–5b Chord identification in a key
(Copy 5)

Shield the answer. Listen to the chord and write the composite chord symbol in the blank; then uncover the answer and compare your response. Circle incorrect responses. Goal: No more than seven errors. The first frame requires no response.

1 V^{-7} ___ V^{a4}_{2} ___ I^{-6} ___ V^{4}_{-} ___ I ___ VII^{-7}_{d5} ___ I

2 ___ V^{6}_{4} ___ I^{-6} ___ V^{4}_{-} ___ I ___ VII^{-7}_{d5} ___ V^{-6}_{d5} ___ I

3 ___ II^{6} ___ V^{a4}_{2} ___ I^{-6} ___ V^{-7} ___ IV^{-6} ___ VII^{-7}_{d5} ___ V^{-6}_{d5}

4 ___ I ___ V ___ V^{a4}_{2} ___ V^{4}_{-} ___ V^{-6}_{d5} ___ I ___ VII^{6}_{-}

5 ___ I^{-6} ___ V^{4}_{-} ___ I ___ IV ___ V^{a4}_{2} ___ I^{-6} ___ V^{-7}

6 ___ IV^{-6} ___ V^{-6}_{d5} ___ I ___ V^{4}_{-} ___ V^{-6}_{d5} ___ V^{-7} ___ V^{a4}_{2}

7 ___ I^{-6} ___ VII^{6}_{-} ___ I ___ V^{a4}_{2} ___ I^{-6} ___ V^{4}_{-} ___

8 ___ VII^{-7}_{d5} ___ I ___ VII^{6}_{-} ___ VII^{-7}_{d5} ___ I ___ II^{6} ___ V^{a4}_{2}

9 ___ I^{-6} ___ II^{-} ___ VII^{-7}_{d5} ___ ___ V^{-6}_{d5} ___ V^{-7} ___ IV^{-6}

10 ___ II^{-} ___ VII^{-7}_{d5} ___ I ___ V^{a4}_{2} ___ V^{4}_{-} ___ V^{-7} ___ I

D5-6a Figured bass dictation
(Copy 1)

Shield the answer. Listen to the chord and write the bass note and figured bass symbol; then uncover the answer and compare your response. Circle incorrect answers. Goal: No more than seven errors. The first frame requires no response.

D5-6a Figured bass dictation
(Copy 2)

Shield the answer. Listen to the chord and write the bass note and figured bass symbol; then uncover the answer and compare your response. Circle incorrect answers. Goal: No more than seven errors. The first frame requires no response.

D5-6a Figured bass dictation

(Copy 3)

Shield the answer. Listen to the chord and write the bass note and figured bass symbol; then uncover the answer and compare your response. Circle incorrect answers. Goal: No more than seven errors. The first frame requires no response.

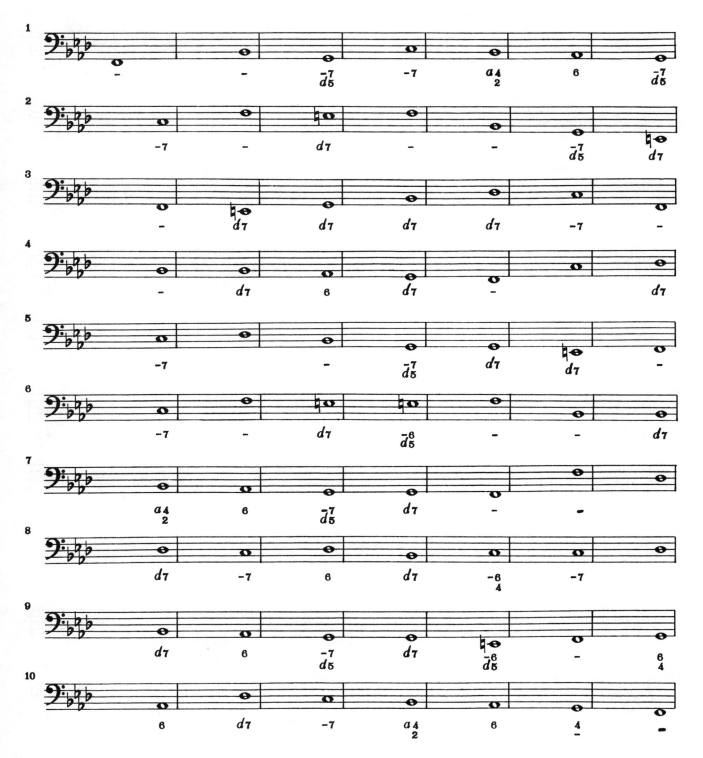

D5-6a Figured bass dictation
(Copy 4)

Shield the answer. Listen to the chord and write the bass note and figured bass symbol; then uncover the answer and compare your response. Circle incorrect answers. Goal: No more than seven errors. The first frame requires no response.

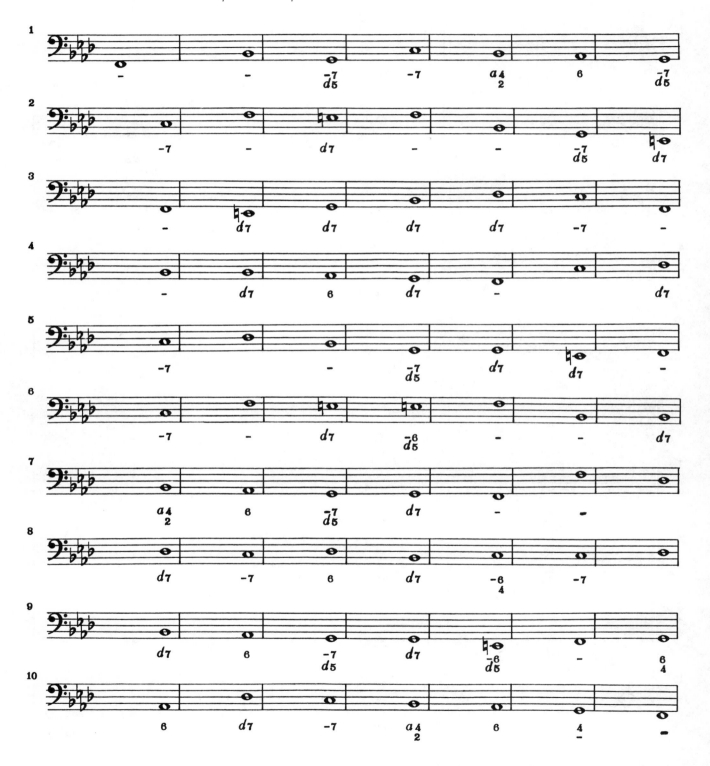

D5-6a Figured bass dictation

(Copy 5)

Shield the answer. Listen to the chord and write the bass note and figured bass symbol; then uncover the answer and compare your response. Circle incorrect answers. Goal: No more than seven errors. The first frame requires no response.

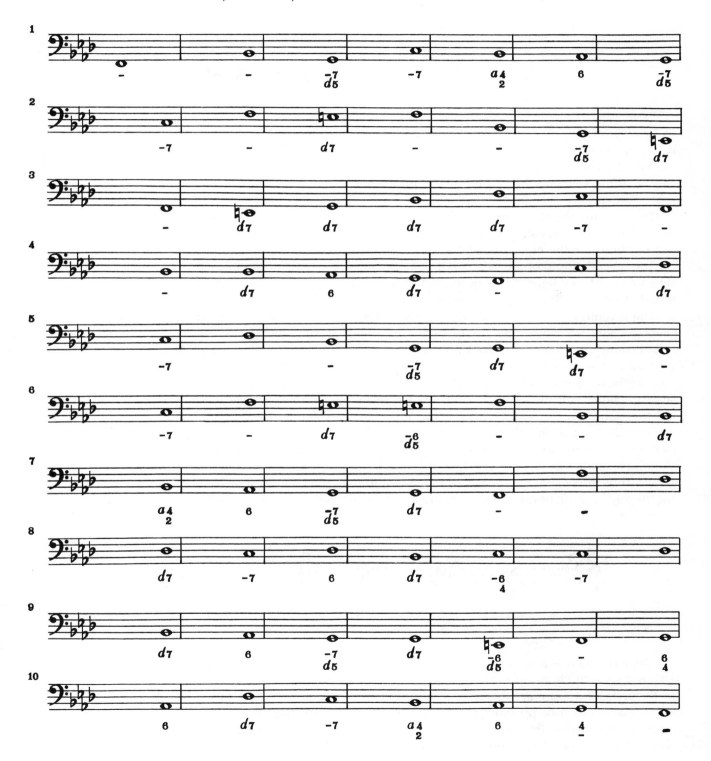

Lesson **D5–6b**

In this lesson the composite chord symbols for the following seventh chords in a minor key are introduced: the seventh chord in second and third inversion on the fifth degree of the key, the seventh chord in root position on the second degree of the key, and the seventh chord on the seventh degree of the key in root position and in all inversions.

The seventh chord on the fifth degree of a minor key is the same as in a major key. The composite chord symbols for the second and third inversions of this chord are therefore V^4_3 and V^{a4}_2, as in the major key.

The seventh chord on the second degree of a minor key is a half-diminished seventh chord. The figured bass portion of the composite chord symbol for that chord in root position is $^{-7}_{d5}$. The composite chord symbol is II^{-7}_{d5}.

The seventh chord on the seventh degree of the minor key is a diminished seventh chord. Remember that because the inversions of the diminished seventh chord sound the same as the root position, all diminished seventh chords, regardless of the inversion or spelling, are identified with the abbreviated figured bass symbol ^{d7}. Since no reference will be made to the inversion of a diminished seventh chord with the figured bass symbol, a special procedure for indicating key location must be used. Ordinarily, the key location is indicated with reference to the root of the chord. Since we do not distinguish among inversions of diminished seventh chords, we do not identify the root. Instead, we will adopt the much simpler procedure of referring to the key location of the *bass* of the chord. Thus the position in the key of the lowest tone of the chord will be used for the key location portion of the composite chord symbol, as in the following examples.

$$\text{c} \qquad VII^{d7} \qquad II^{d7} \qquad IV^{d7} \qquad -VI^{d7}$$

There is only one place in a key where a diminished seventh chord is found. This is a seventh chord on the seventh degree, or leading tone, of a minor key. In the following example, the seventh chord on the leading tone of a minor key is shown in root position and in all inversions. Notice that the Roman numeral refers to the lowest tone, not to the root (which would always be VII), and that the figured bass symbol is always ^{d7}.

148

the leading tone seventh chord

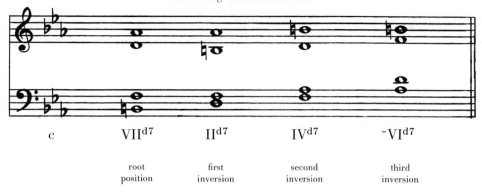

c	VII^{d7}	II^{d7}	IV^{d7}	⁻VI^{d7}
	root position	first inversion	second inversion	third inversion

D5-6b Chord identification in a key

(Copy 1)

Shield the answer. Listen to the chord and write the composite chord symbol in the blank; then uncover the answer and compare your response. Circle incorrect responses. Goal: No more than seven errors. The first frame requires no response. After you have done this lesson, take Test D5.

1. I^- ___ IV^- ___ II^{-7}_{d5} ___ V^{-7} ___ V^{a4}_2 ___ I^6 ___ II^{-7}_{d5}

2.   ___ V^{-7} ___ I^- ___ VII^{d7} ___ I^- ___ IV^- ___ II^{-7}_{d5} ___ VII^{d7}

3.   ___ I^- ___ VII^{d7} ___ II^{d7} ___ IV^{d7} ___ $^-VI^{d7}$ ___ V^{-7} ___ I^-

4.   ___ IV^- ___ IV^{d7} ___ I^6 ___ II^{d7} ___ I^- ___ V ___ $^-VI^{d7}$

5.   ___ V^{-7} ___ ^-VI ___ IV^- ___ II^{-7}_{d5} ___ II^{d7} ___ VII^{d7} ___ I^-

6.   ___ V^{-7} ___ I^- ___ VII^{d7} ___ V^{-6}_{d5} ___ I^- ___ IV^- ___ IV^{d7}

7.   ___ V^{a4}_2 ___ I^6 ___ II^{-7}_{d5} ___ II^{d7} ___ I^- ___ I^- ___ ^-VI

8.   ___ $^-VI^{d7}$ ___ V^{-7} ___ IV^6 ___ IV^{d7} ___ I^{-6}_4 ___ V^{-7} ___ ^-VI

9.   ___ IV^{d7} ___ I^6 ___ II^{-7}_{d5} ___ II^{d7} ___ V^{-6}_{d5} ___ I^- ___ V^6_4

10.   ___ I^6 ___ $^-VI^{d7}$ ___ V^{-7} ___ V^{a4}_2 ___ I^6 ___ V^4_- ___ $-$

D5-6b Chord identification in a key

(Copy 2)

Shield the answer. Listen to the chord and write the composite chord symbol in the blank; then uncover the answer and compare your response. Circle incorrect responses. Goal: No more than seven errors. The first frame requires no response. After you have done this lesson, take Test D5.

1. I^- ___ IV^- ___ II^{-7}_{d5} ___ V^{-7} ___ V^{a4}_2 ___ I^6 ___ II^{-7}_{d5}

2.   ___ V^{-7} ___ I^- ___ VII^{d7} ___ I^- ___ IV^- ___ II^{-7}_{d5} ___ VII^{d7}

3.   ___ I^- ___ VII^{d7} ___ II^{d7} ___ IV^{d7} ___ $^-VI^{d7}$ ___ V^{-7} ___ I^-

4.   ___ IV^- ___ IV^{d7} ___ I^6 ___ II^{d7} ___ I^- ___ V ___ $^-VI^{d7}$

5.   ___ V^{-7} ___ ^-VI ___ IV^- ___ II^{-7}_{d5} ___ II^{d7} ___ VII^{d7} ___ I^-

6.   ___ V^{-7} ___ I^- ___ VII^{d7} ___ V^{-6}_{d5} ___ I^- ___ IV^- ___ IV^{d7}

7.   ___ V^{a4}_2 ___ I^6 ___ II^{-7}_{d5} ___ II^{d7} ___ I^- ___ I^- ___ ^-VI

8.   ___ $^-VI^{d7}$ ___ V^{-7} ___ IV^6 ___ IV^{d7} ___ I^{-6}_4 ___ V^{-7} ___ ^-VI

9.   ___ IV^{d7} ___ I^6 ___ II^{-7}_{d5} ___ II^{d7} ___ V^{-6}_{d5} ___ I^- ___ V^6_4

10.   ___ I^6 ___ $^-VI^{d7}$ ___ V^{-7} ___ V^{a4}_2 ___ I^6 ___ V^4_- ___ $-$

D5–6b Chord identification in a key
(Copy 3)

Shield the answer. Listen to the chord and write the composite chord symbol in the blank; then uncover the answer and compare your response. Circle incorrect responses. Goal: No more than seven errors. The first frame requires no response. After you have done this lesson, take Test D5.

1. I^- ___ IV^- ___ II^{-7}_{d5} ___ V^{-7} ___ V^{a4}_{2} ___ I^{6} ___ II^{-7}_{d5}

2. ___ V^{-7} ___ I^- ___ VII^{d7} ___ I^- ___ IV^- ___ II^{-7}_{d5} ___ VII^{d7}

3. ___ I^- ___ VII^{d7} ___ II^{d7} ___ IV^{d7} ___ $^-\text{VI}^{d7}$ ___ V^{-7} ___ I^-

4. ___ IV^- ___ IV^{d7} ___ I^{6} ___ II^{d7} ___ I^- ___ V ___ $^-\text{VI}^{d7}$

5. ___ V^{-7} ___ ^-VI ___ IV^- ___ II^{-7}_{d5} ___ II^{d7} ___ VII^{d7} ___ I^-

6. ___ V^{-7} ___ I^- ___ VII^{d7} ___ V^{-6}_{d5} ___ I^- ___ IV^- ___ IV^{d7}

7. ___ V^{a4}_{2} ___ I^{6} ___ II^{-7}_{d5} ___ II^{d7} ___ I^- ___ I^- ___ ^-VI

8. ___ $^-\text{VI}^{d7}$ ___ V^{-7} ___ IV^{6} ___ IV^{d7} ___ I^{-6}_{4} ___ V^{-7} ___ ^-VI

9. ___ IV^{d7} ___ I^{6} ___ II^{-7}_{d5} ___ II^{d7} ___ V^{-6}_{d5} ___ I^- ___ V^{6}_{4}

10. ___ I^{6} ___ $^-\text{VI}^{d7}$ ___ V^{-7} ___ V^{a4}_{2} ___ I^{6} ___ V^{4}_{-} ___ $-$

D5–6b Chord identification in a key
(Copy 4)

Shield the answer. Listen to the chord and write the composite chord symbol in the blank; then uncover the answer and compare your response. Circle incorrect responses. Goal: No more than seven errors. The first frame requires no response. After you have done this lesson, take Test D5.

1. I^- ___ IV^- ___ II^{-7}_{d5} ___ V^{-7} ___ V^{a4}_{2} ___ I^{6} ___ II^{-7}_{d5}

2. ___ V^{-7} ___ I^- ___ VII^{d7} ___ I^- ___ IV^- ___ II^{-7}_{d5} ___ VII^{d7}

3. ___ I^- ___ VII^{d7} ___ II^{d7} ___ IV^{d7} ___ $^-\text{VI}^{d7}$ ___ V^{-7} ___ I^-

4. ___ IV^- ___ IV^{d7} ___ I^{6} ___ II^{d7} ___ I^- ___ V ___ $^-\text{VI}^{d7}$

5. ___ V^{-7} ___ ^-VI ___ IV^- ___ II^{-7}_{d5} ___ II^{d7} ___ VII^{d7} ___ I^-

6. ___ V^{-7} ___ I^- ___ VII^{d7} ___ V^{-6}_{d5} ___ I^- ___ IV^- ___ IV^{d7}

7. ___ V^{a4}_{2} ___ I^{6} ___ II^{-7}_{d5} ___ II^{d7} ___ I^- ___ I^- ___ ^-VI

8. ___ $^-\text{VI}^{d7}$ ___ V^{-7} ___ IV^{6} ___ IV^{d7} ___ I^{-6}_{4} ___ V^{-7} ___ ^-VI

9. ___ IV^{d7} ___ I^{6} ___ II^{-7}_{d5} ___ II^{d7} ___ V^{-6}_{d5} ___ I^- ___ V^{6}_{4}

10. ___ I^{6} ___ $^-\text{VI}^{d7}$ ___ V^{-7} ___ V^{a4}_{2} ___ I^{6} ___ V^{4}_{-} ___ $-$

D5–6b Chord identification in a key

(Copy 5)

Shield the answer. Listen to the chord and write the composite chord symbol in the blank; then uncover the answer and compare your response. Circle incorrect responses. Goal: No more than seven errors. The first frame requires no response. After you have done this lesson, take Test D5.

1. I^- ____ IV^- ____ II^{-7}_{d5} ____ V^{-7} ____ V^{a4}_{2} ____ I^6 ____ II^{-7}_{d5}

2. ____ V^{-7} ____ I^- ____ VII^{d7} ____ I^- ____ IV^- ____ II^{-7}_{d5} ____ VII^{d7}

3. ____ I^- ____ VII^{d7} ____ II^{d7} ____ IV^{d7} ____ $^-VI^{d7}$ ____ V^{-7} ____ I^-

4. ____ IV^- ____ IV^{d7} ____ I^6 ____ II^{d7} ____ I^- ____ V ____ $^-VI^{d7}$

5. ____ V^{-7} ____ ^-VI ____ IV^- ____ II^{-7}_{d5} ____ II^{d7} ____ VII^{d7} ____ I^-

6. ____ V^{-7} ____ I^- ____ VII^{d7} ____ V^{-6}_{d5} ____ I^- ____ IV^- ____ IV^{d7}

7. ____ V^{a4}_{2} ____ I^6 ____ II^{-7}_{d5} ____ II^{d7} ____ I^- ____ I^- ____ ^-VI

8. ____ $^-VI^{d7}$ ____ V^{-7} ____ IV^6 ____ IV^{d7} ____ I^{-6}_{4} ____ V^{-7} ____ ^-VI

9. ____ IV^{d7} ____ I^6 ____ II^{-7}_{d5} ____ II^{d7} ____ V^{-6}_{d5} ____ I^- ____ V^6_4

10. ____ I^6 ____ $^-VI^{d7}$ ____ V^{-7} ____ V^{a4}_{2} ____ I^6 ____ V^4_- ____ $^-$

Minor and Half-Diminished Seventh Chords in First Inversion

The upper tones of the minor seventh chord in first inversion are at intervals of a major sixth, a perfect fifth, and a major third above the bass.

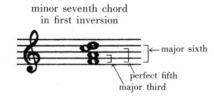

The upper tones of the half-diminished seventh chord in first inversion are at intervals of a major sixth, a perfect fifth, and a minor third above the bass.

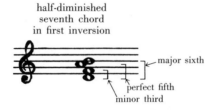

There are four types of lessons in this series: chord dictation, chord identification, figured bass dictation, and chord identification in a key. When you have done this series, take Test D6 which includes sections on each of the four kinds of lessons.

D6-1a Chord dictation
(Copy 1)

Shield the answer. Listen to the chord and write the upper tones above the given note; then uncover the answer and compare your response. Circle incorrect responses. Goal: No more than seven errors.

D6-1a Chord dictation

(Copy 2)

Shield the answer. Listen to the chord and write the upper tones above the given note; then uncover the answer and compare your response. Circle incorrect responses. Goal: No more than seven errors.

155

D6-1a Chord dictation

(Copy 3)

Shield the answer. Listen to the chord and write the upper tones above the given note; then uncover the answer and compare your response. Circle incorrect responses. Goal: No more than seven errors.

D6-1a Chord dictation
(Copy 4)

Shield the answer. Listen to the chord and write the upper tones above the given note; then uncover the answer and compare your response. Circle incorrect responses. Goal: No more than seven errors.

157

D6-1a Chord dictation

(Copy 5)

Shield the answer. Listen to the chord and write the upper tones above the given note; then uncover the answer and compare your response. Circle incorrect responses. Goal: No more than seven errors.

158

Lesson **D6-1b**

In this lesson the figured bass symbols for minor and half-diminished seventh chords in first inversion are introduced.

    The intervals between the upper tones and the bass of a minor seventh chord in first inversion are a major sixth, a perfect fifth, and a major third. The complete figured bass symbol is $\frac{6}{5}$, abbreviated to $\frac{6}{5}$.

    The intervals between the upper tones and the bass of a half-diminished seventh chord in first inversion are a major sixth, a perfect fifth, and a minor third. The complete figured bass symbol is $\frac{6}{5}$, abbreviated to $\frac{6}{5}$.

D6-1b Chord identification
(Copy 1)

Shield the answer. Listen to the chord and write the figured bass symbol in the blank; then uncover the answer and compare your response. Circle incorrect responses. Goal: No more than seven errors.

#							
1	–	-7	6/5		6/5	-7	6/5
2	-7/d5	6/5	6/–	6/5	-7/d5		6/5
3	-7	6	6/5	-6/d5	6	d7	-7/d5
4	6/5		6/5	6/5	-7/d5	d7	-6/d5
5	–	6	6/5	6	6	6/5	d7
6	-7	-6/d5		6/5	-7	6/5	-7
7	d7		-6	6	6/5	-6	6/5
8	-7/d5	6/5	-6/d5	-7	-6	6	6/5
9	-7/d5	–	6/5		6/5	-7	-6
10	6/5	6/5	-7	6/5	-7/d5	-6/d5	–

D6–1b Chord identification
(Copy 2)

Shield the answer. Listen to the chord and write the figured bass symbol in the blank; then uncover the answer and compare your response. Circle incorrect responses. Goal: No more than seven errors.

#							
1	–	-7/-	6/5		6/5	-7/-	6/5
2	-7/d5	6/5	6/-	6/5	-7/d5		6/5
3	-7/-	6	6/-	-6/d5	6	d7	-7/d5
4	6/5		6/5	6/5	-7/d5	d7	-6/d5
5	–	6	6/5	6	6/-	6/5	d7
6	-7	-6/d5		6/5	-7/-	6/5	-7/-
7	d7		-6	6/-	6/5	-6	6/5
8	-7/d5	6/5	-6/d5	-7	-6	6/-	6/5
9	-7/d5	–	6/5		6/5	-7	-6
10	6/5	6/5	-7/-	6/5	-7/d5	-6/d5	–

D6–1b Chord identification
(Copy 3)

Shield the answer. Listen to the chord and write the figured bass symbol in the blank; then uncover the answer and compare your response. Circle incorrect responses. Goal: No more than seven errors.

#							
1	–	-7/-	6/5		6/5	-7/-	6/5
2	-7/d5	6/5	6/-	6/5	-7/d5		6/5
3	-7/-	6	6/5	-6/d5	6	d7	-7/d5
4	6/5		6/5	6/5	-7/d5	d7	-6/d5
5	–	6	6/5	6	6/-	6/5	d7
6	-7	-6/d5		6/5	-7/-	6/5	-7/-
7	d7		-6	6/-	6/5	-6	6/5
8	-7/d5	6/5	-6/d5	-7	-6	6/-	6/5
9	-7/d5	–	6/5		6/5	-7	-6
10	6/5	6/5	-7/-	6/5	-7/d5	-6/d5	–

D6-1b Chord identification

(Copy 4)

Shield the answer. Listen to the chord and write the figured bass symbol in the blank; then uncover the answer and compare your response. Circle incorrect responses. Goal: No more than seven errors.

#							
1	—	-7/-	6/5	—	6/5	-7/-	6/5
2	-7/d5	6/5	6/-	6/5	-7/d5	—	6/5
3	-7/-	6/-	6/5	-6/d5	6	d7	-7/d5
4	6/5	—	6/5	6/5	-7/d5	d7	-6/d5
5	-	6/-	6/5	6	6/-	6/5	d7
6	-7	-6/d5	—	6/5	-7/-	6/5	-7/-
7	d7	—	-6	6/-	6/5	-6	6/5
8	-7/d5	6/5	-6/d5	-7	-6	6/-	6/5
9	-7/d5	-	6/5	—	6/5	-7	-6
10	6/5	6/5	-7/-	6/5	-7/d5	-6/d5	-

D6-1b Chord identification

(Copy 5)

Shield the answer. Listen to the chord and write the figured bass symbol in the blank; then uncover the answer and compare your response. Circle incorrect responses. Goal: No more than seven errors.

#							
1	—	-7/-	6/5	—	6/5	-7/-	6/5
2	-7/d5	6/5	6/-	6/5	-7/d5	—	6/5
3	-7/-	6/-	6/5	-6/d5	6	d7	-7/d5
4	6/5	—	6/5	6/5	-7/d5	d7	-6/d5
5	-	6/-	6/5	6	6/-	6/5	d7
6	-7	-6/d5	—	6/5	-7/-	6/5	-7/-
7	d7	—	-6	6/-	6/5	-6	6/5
8	-7/d5	6/5	-6/d5	-7	-6	6/-	6/5
9	-7/d5	-	6/5	—	6/5	-7	-6
10	6/5	6/5	-7/-	6/5	-7/d5	-6/d5	-

D6–2 Chord identification
(Copy 1)

Shield the answer. Listen to the chord and write the figured bass symbol in the answer blank; then uncover the answer and compare your response. Circle incorrect responses. Goal: No more than seven errors.

#													
1	___	–	___	-7/–	___	6/5	___	-7/–	___	6/5	___	-7	___
2	___		___	6/5	___	-7/–	___	-7/d5	___	6/5	___		___ -7/–
3	___	6/5	___	-7	___	–	___	-7/–	___	6/5	___	6/5	___ -7/d5
4	___		___	6/5	___	-6/d5	___	–	___	-7/d5	___	d7	___ -6/d5
5	___	–	___	6/5	___	-7/d5	___	d7	___	d7	___	-6/d5	___ –
6	___	-7/–	___	6/5	___	6/5	___	-7/d5	___	-6/d5	___		___ -7/–
7	___	-7/d5	___	d7	___	-6/d5	___		___	-7/d5	___	6/5	___ d7
8	___	6	___	–	___	6/5	___	d7	___	-7	___	–	___ 6/5
9	___	d7	___	6	___	6/5	___	-7/–	___	6/5	___	-7/d5	___ d7
10	___	-6/d5	___		___	6/5	___	6/5	___	-7/d5	___	d7	___ –

D6–2 Chord identification
(Copy 2)

Shield the answer. Listen to the chord and write the figured bass symbol in the answer blank; then uncover the answer and compare your response. Circle incorrect responses. Goal: No more than seven errors.

#													
1	___	–	___	-7/–	___	6/5	___	-7/–	___	6/5	___	-7	___
2	___		___	6/5	___	-7/–	___	-7/d5	___	6/5	___		___ -7/–
3	___	6/5	___	-7	___	–	___	-7/–	___	6/5	___	6/5	___ -7/d5
4	___		___	6/5	___	-6/d5	___	–	___	-7/d5	___	d7	___ -6/d5
5	___	–	___	6/5	___	-7/d5	___	d7	___	d7	___	-6/d5	___ –
6	___	-7/–	___	6/5	___	6/5	___	-7/d5	___	-6/d5	___		___ -7/–
7	___	-7/d5	___	d7	___	-6/d5	___		___	-7/d5	___	6/5	___ d7
8	___	6	___	–	___	6/5	___	d7	___	-7	___	–	___ 6/5
9	___	d7	___	6	___	6/5	___	-7/–	___	6/5	___	-7/d5	___ d7
10	___	-6/d5	___		___	6/5	___	6/5	___	-7/d5	___	d7	___ –

D6-2 Chord identification

(Copy 3)

Shield the answer. Listen to the chord and write the figured bass symbol in the answer blank; then uncover the answer and compare your response. Circle incorrect responses. Goal: No more than seven errors.

#							
1	___ -	___ -7/-	___ 6/5	___ -7/-	___ 6/5	___ -7	___
2	___	___ 6/5	___ -7/-	___ -7/d5	___ 6/5	___	___ -7/-
3	___ 6/5	___ -7	___ -	___ -7/-	___ 6/5	___ 6/5	___ -7/d5
4	___ -	___ 6/5	___ -6/d5	___ -	___ -7/d5	___ d7	___ -6/d5
5	___ -	___ 6/5	___ -7/d5	___ d7	___ d7	___ -6/d5	___ -
6	___ -7/-	___ 6/5	___ 6/5	___ -7/d5	___ -6/d5	___	___ -7/-
7	___ -7/d5	___ d7	___ -6/d5	___	___ -7/d5	___ 6/5	___ d7
8	___ 6	___ -	___ 6/5	___ d7	___ -7	___ -	___ 6/5
9	___ d7	___ 6	___ 6/5	___ -7/-	___ 6/5	___ -7/d5	___ d7
10	___ -6/d5	___	___ 6/5	___ 6/5	___ -7/d5	___ d7	___ -

D6-2 Chord identification

(Copy 4)

Shield the answer. Listen to the chord and write the figured bass symbol in the answer blank; then uncover the answer and compare your response. Circle incorrect responses. Goal: No more than seven errors.

#							
1	___ -	___ -7/-	___ 6/5	___ -7/-	___ 6/5	___ -7	___
2	___	___ 6/5	___ -7/-	___ -7/d5	___ 6/5	___	___ -7/-
3	___ 6/5	___ -7	___ -	___ -7/-	___ 6/5	___ 6/5	___ -7/d5
4	___ -	___ 6/5	___ -6/d5	___ -	___ -7/d5	___ d7	___ -6/d5
5	___ -	___ 6/5	___ -7/d5	___ d7	___ d7	___ -6/d5	___ -
6	___ -7/-	___ 6/5	___ 6/5	___ -7/d5	___ -6/d5	___	___ -7/-
7	___ -7/d5	___ d7	___ -6/d5	___	___ -7/d5	___ 6/5	___ d7
8	___ 6	___ -	___ 6/5	___ d7	___ -7	___ -	___ 6/5
9	___ d7	___ 6	___ 6/5	___ -7/-	___ 6/5	___ -7/d5	___ d7
10	___ -6/d5	___	___ 6/5	___ 6/5	___ -7/d5	___ d7	___ -

D6–2 Chord identification

(Copy 5)

Shield the answer. Listen to the chord and write the figured bass symbol in the answer blank; then uncover the answer and compare your response. Circle incorrect responses. Goal: No more than seven errors.

1. ____ – ____ $\frac{-7}{-}$ ____ $\frac{6}{5}$ ____ $\frac{-7}{-}$ ____ $\frac{6}{5}$ ____ –7 ____

2. ____ ____ $\frac{6}{5}$ ____ $\frac{-7}{-}$ ____ $\frac{-7}{d5}$ ____ $\frac{6}{5}$ ____ ____ $\frac{-7}{-}$

3. ____ $\frac{6}{5}$ ____ –7 ____ – ____ $\frac{-7}{-}$ ____ $\frac{6}{5}$ ____ $\frac{6}{5}$ ____ $\frac{-7}{d5}$

4. ____ ____ $\frac{6}{5}$ ____ $\frac{-6}{d5}$ ____ – ____ $\frac{-7}{d5}$ ____ d7 ____ $\frac{-6}{d5}$

5. ____ – ____ $\frac{6}{5}$ ____ $\frac{-7}{d5}$ ____ d7 ____ d7 ____ $\frac{-6}{d5}$ ____ –

6. ____ $\frac{-7}{-}$ ____ $\frac{6}{5}$ ____ $\frac{6}{5}$ ____ $\frac{-7}{d5}$ ____ $\frac{-6}{d5}$ ____ $\frac{-7}{-}$

7. ____ $\frac{-7}{d5}$ ____ d7 ____ $\frac{-6}{d5}$ ____ ____ $\frac{-7}{d5}$ ____ $\frac{6}{5}$ ____ d7

8. ____ 6 ____ – ____ $\frac{6}{5}$ ____ d7 ____ –7 ____ – ____ $\frac{6}{5}$

9. ____ d7 ____ 6 ____ $\frac{6}{5}$ ____ $\frac{-7}{-}$ ____ $\frac{6}{5}$ ____ $\frac{-7}{d5}$ ____ d7

10. ____ $\frac{-6}{d5}$ ____ ____ $\frac{6}{5}$ ____ $\frac{6}{5}$ ____ $\frac{-7}{d5}$ ____ d7 ____ –

Shield the answer. Listen to the chord and write the bass note and the figured bass symbol; then uncover the answer and compare your response. Circle incorrect responses. Goal: No more than seven errors. The first frame requires no response.

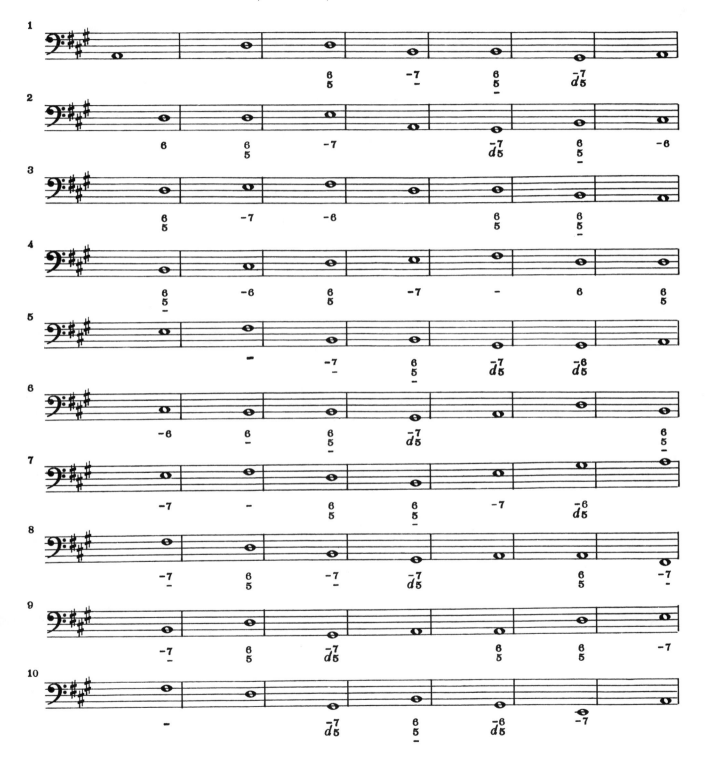

D6-3a Figured bass dictation

(Copy 2)

Shield the answer. Listen to the chord and write the bass note and the figured bass symbol; then uncover the answer and compare your response. Circle incorrect responses. Goal: No more than seven errors. The first frame requires no response.

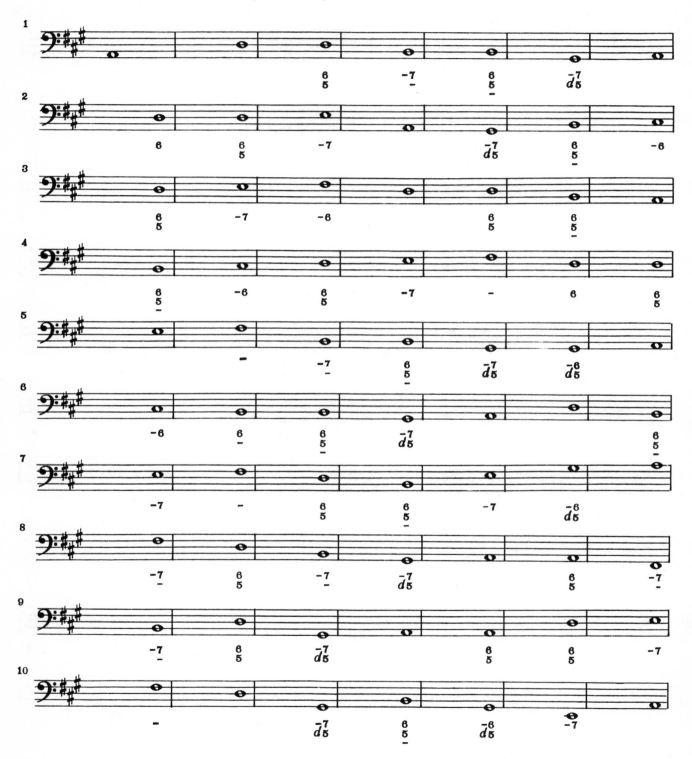

D6-3a Figured bass dictation
(Copy 3)

Shield the answer. Listen to the chord and write the bass note and the figured bass symbol; then uncover the answer and compare your response. Circle incorrect responses. Goal: No more than seven errors. The first frame requires no response.

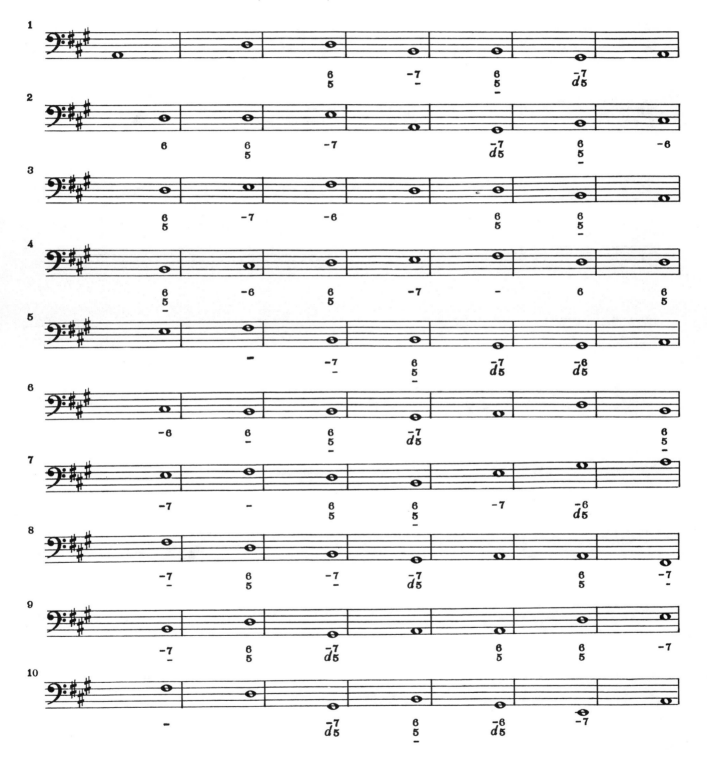

D6-3a Figured bass dictation

(Copy 4)

Shield the answer. Listen to the chord and write the bass note and the figured bass symbol; then uncover the answer and compare your response. Circle incorrect responses. Goal: No more than seven errors. The first frame requires no response.

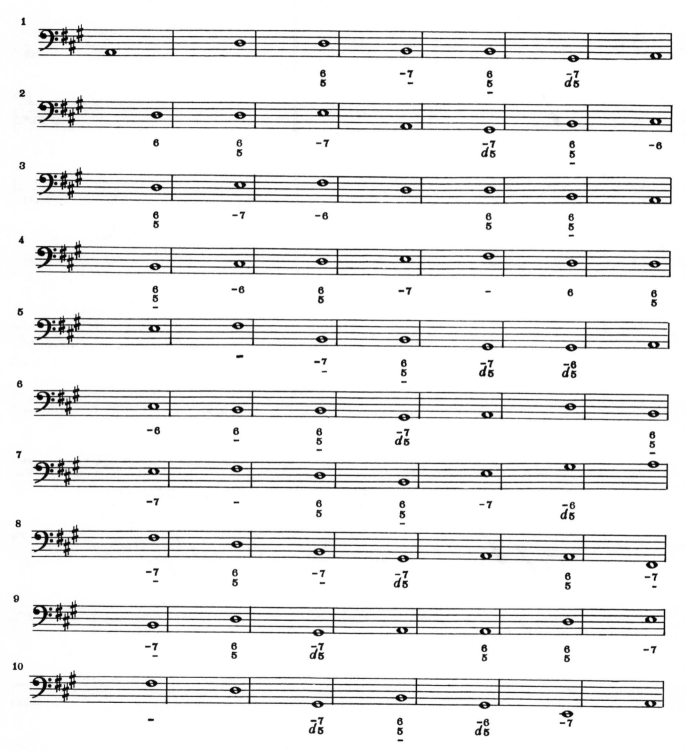

D6–3a Figured bass dictation

(Copy 5)

Shield the answer. Listen to the chord and write the bass note and the figured bass symbol; then uncover the answer and compare your response. Circle incorrect responses. Goal: No more than seven errors. The first frame requires no response.

Lesson D6-3b

In this lesson, the following composite chord symbols, which occur in a major key, are introduced: II^6_5 and VII^6_5.

The seventh chord on the second degree of the major key is a minor seventh chord. The figured bass portion of the composite chord symbol for this chord when it appears in first inversion is $^6_5$. The third of this chord, which appears in the bass, is the fourth degree of the key.

The seventh chord on the seventh degree of a major key is a half-diminished seventh chord. The figured bass portion of the composite chord symbol for this chord when it appears in first inversion is $^6_5$. The third of this chord, which appears in the bass, is the second degree of the key.

D6-3b Chord identification in a key
(Copy 1)

Shield the answer. Listen to the chord and write the composite chord symbol in the blank; then uncover the answer and compare your response. Circle incorrect responses. Goal: No more than seven errors. First frame requires no response.

1	I	IV	II^6_5	II^{-7}	VII^6_5	VII^{-7}_{d5}	I
2	II^6	II^6_5	V^{-7}	I	VII^{-7}_{d5}	VII^6_5	I^{-6}
3	II^6_5	V^{-7}	IV^{-6}	IV	II^6_5	VII^6_5	I
4	VII^6_5	I^{-6}	II^6_5	V^{-7}	VI^-	II^6	II^6_5
5	V	VI^-	II^{-7}	VII^6_5	VII^{-7}_{d5}	V^{-6}_{d5}	I
6	I^{-6}	VII^6	VII^6_5	VII^{-7}_{d5}	I	IV	VII^6_5
7	V^{-7}	VI^-	II^6_5	VII^6_5	V^{-7}	V^{-6}_{d5}	I
8	VI^{-7}	II^6_5	II^{-7}	VII^{-7}_{d5}	I	VI^6_5	VI^{-7}
9	II^{-7}	II^6_5	VII^{-7}_{d5}	I	VI^6_5	II^6_5	V^{-7}
10	VI^-	IV	VII^{-7}_{d5}	VII^6_5	V^{-6}_{d5}	V^{-7}	I

D6-3b Chord identification in a key
(Copy 2)

Shield the answer. Listen to the chord and write the composite chord symbol in the blank; then uncover the answer and compare your response. Circle incorrect responses. Goal: No more than seven errors. First frame requires no response.

1. I ____ IV ____ II_{5}^{6} ____ $\text{II}_{\text{–}}^{-7}$ ____ $\text{VII}_{\underline{5}}^{6}$ ____ VII_{d5}^{-7} ____ I

2. ____ II^{6} ____ II_{5}^{6} ____ V^{-7} ____ I ____ VII_{d5}^{-7} ____ $\text{VII}_{\underline{5}}^{6}$ ____ I^{-6}

3. ____ II_{5}^{6} ____ V^{-7} ____ IV^{-6} ____ IV ____ II_{5}^{6} ____ $\text{VII}_{\underline{5}}^{6}$ ____ I

4. ____ $\text{VII}_{\underline{5}}^{6}$ ____ I^{-6} ____ II_{5}^{6} ____ V^{-7} ____ VI^{-} ____ II^{6} ____ II_{5}^{6}

5. ____ V ____ VI^{-} ____ $\text{II}_{\text{–}}^{-7}$ ____ $\text{VII}_{\underline{5}}^{6}$ ____ VII_{d5}^{-7} ____ V_{d5}^{-6} ____ I

6. ____ I^{-6} ____ $\text{VII}_{\text{–}}^{6}$ ____ $\text{VII}_{\underline{5}}^{6}$ ____ VII_{d5}^{-7} ____ I ____ IV ____ $\text{VII}_{\underline{5}}^{6}$

7. ____ V^{-7} ____ VI^{-} ____ II_{5}^{6} ____ $\text{VII}_{\underline{5}}^{6}$ ____ V^{-7} ____ V_{d5}^{-6} ____ I

8. ____ $\text{VI}_{\text{–}}^{-7}$ ____ II_{5}^{6} ____ $\text{II}_{\text{–}}^{-7}$ ____ VII_{d5}^{-7} ____ I ____ VI_{5}^{6} ____ $\text{VI}_{\text{–}}^{-7}$

9. ____ $\text{II}_{\text{–}}^{-7}$ ____ II_{5}^{6} ____ VII_{d5}^{-7} ____ I ____ VI_{5}^{6} ____ II_{5}^{6} ____ V^{-7}

10. ____ VI^{-} ____ IV ____ VII_{d5}^{-7} ____ $\text{VII}_{\underline{5}}^{6}$ ____ V_{d5}^{-6} ____ V^{-7} ____ I

D6-3b Chord identification in a key
(Copy 3)

Shield the answer. Listen to the chord and write the composite chord symbol in the blank; then uncover the answer and compare your response. Circle incorrect responses. Goal: No more than seven errors. First frame requires no response.

1. I ____ IV ____ II_{5}^{6} ____ $\text{II}_{\text{–}}^{-7}$ ____ $\text{VII}_{\underline{5}}^{6}$ ____ VII_{d5}^{-7} ____ I

2. ____ II^{6} ____ II_{5}^{6} ____ V^{-7} ____ I ____ VII_{d5}^{-7} ____ $\text{VII}_{\underline{5}}^{6}$ ____ I^{-6}

3. ____ II_{5}^{6} ____ V^{-7} ____ IV^{-6} ____ IV ____ II_{5}^{6} ____ $\text{VII}_{\underline{5}}^{6}$ ____ I

4. ____ $\text{VII}_{\underline{5}}^{6}$ ____ I^{-6} ____ II_{5}^{6} ____ V^{-7} ____ VI^{-} ____ II^{6} ____ II_{5}^{6}

5. ____ V ____ VI^{-} ____ $\text{II}_{\text{–}}^{-7}$ ____ $\text{VII}_{\underline{5}}^{6}$ ____ VII_{d5}^{-7} ____ V_{d5}^{-6} ____ I

6. ____ I^{-6} ____ $\text{VII}_{\text{–}}^{6}$ ____ $\text{VII}_{\underline{5}}^{6}$ ____ VII_{d5}^{-7} ____ I ____ IV ____ $\text{VII}_{\underline{5}}^{6}$

7. ____ V^{-7} ____ VI^{-} ____ II_{5}^{6} ____ $\text{VII}_{\underline{5}}^{6}$ ____ V^{-7} ____ V_{d5}^{-6} ____ I

8. ____ $\text{VI}_{\text{–}}^{-7}$ ____ II_{5}^{6} ____ $\text{II}_{\text{–}}^{-7}$ ____ VII_{d5}^{-7} ____ I ____ VI_{5}^{6} ____ $\text{VI}_{\text{–}}^{-7}$

9. ____ $\text{II}_{\text{–}}^{-7}$ ____ II_{5}^{6} ____ VII_{d5}^{-7} ____ I ____ VI_{5}^{6} ____ II_{5}^{6} ____ V^{-7}

10. ____ VI^{-} ____ IV ____ VII_{d5}^{-7} ____ $\text{VII}_{\underline{5}}^{6}$ ____ V_{d5}^{-6} ____ V^{-7} ____ I

D6-3b Chord identification in a key
(Copy 4)

Shield the answer. Listen to the chord and write the composite chord symbol in the blank; then uncover the answer and compare your response. Circle incorrect responses. Goal: No more than seven errors. First frame requires no response.

1. I —— IV —— II^6_5 —— II^{-7} —— VII^6_5 —— VII^{-7}_{d5} —— I

2. —— II^6 —— II^6_5 —— V^{-7} —— I —— VII^{-7}_{d5} —— VII^6_5 —— I^{-6}

3. —— II^6_5 —— V^{-7} —— IV^{-6} —— IV —— II^6_5 —— VII^6_5 —— I

4. —— VII^6_5 —— I^{-6} —— II^6_5 —— V^{-7} —— VI^- —— II^6 —— II^6_5

5. —— V —— VI^- —— II^{-7} —— VII^6_5 —— VII^{-7}_{d5} —— V^{-6}_{d5} —— I

6. —— I^{-6} —— VII^6 —— VII^6_5 —— VII^{-7}_{d5} —— I —— IV —— VII^6_5

7. —— V^{-7} —— VI^- —— II^6_5 —— VII^6_5 —— V^{-7} —— V^{-6}_{d5} —— I

8. —— VI^{-7} —— II^6_5 —— II^{-7} —— VII^{-7}_{d5} —— I —— VI^6_5 —— VI^{-7}

9. —— II^{-7} —— II^6_5 —— VII^{-7}_{d5} —— I —— VI^6_5 —— II^6_5 —— V^{-7}

10. —— VI^- —— IV —— VII^{-7}_{d5} —— VII^6_5 —— V^{-6}_{d5} —— V^{-7} —— I

D6-3b Chord identification in a key
(Copy 5)

Shield the answer. Listen to the chord and write the composite chord symbol in the blank; then uncover the answer and compare your response. Circle incorrect responses. Goal: No more than seven errors. First frame requires no response.

1. I —— IV —— II^6_5 —— II^{-7} —— VII^6_5 —— VII^{-7}_{d5} —— I

2. —— II^6 —— II^6_5 —— V^{-7} —— I —— VII^{-7}_{d5} —— VII^6_5 —— I^{-6}

3. —— II^6_5 —— V^{-7} —— IV^{-6} —— IV —— II^6_5 —— VII^6_5 —— I

4. —— VII^6_5 —— I^{-6} —— II^6_5 —— V^{-7} —— VI^- —— II^6 —— II^6_5

5. —— V —— VI^- —— II^{-7} —— VII^6_5 —— VII^{-7}_{d5} —— V^{-6}_{d5} —— I

6. —— I^{-6} —— VII^6 —— VII^6_5 —— VII^{-7}_{d5} —— I —— IV —— VII^6_5

7. —— V^{-7} —— VI^- —— II^6_5 —— VII^6_5 —— V^{-7} —— V^{-6}_{d5} —— I

8. —— VI^{-7} —— II^6_5 —— II^{-7} —— VII^{-7}_{d5} —— I —— VI^6_5 —— VI^{-7}

9. —— II^{-7} —— II^6_5 —— VII^{-7}_{d5} —— I —— VI^6_5 —— II^6_5 —— V^{-7}

10. —— VI^- —— IV —— VII^{-7}_{d5} —— VII^6_5 —— V^{-6}_{d5} —— V^{-7} —— I

172

D6-4a Figured bass dictation

(Copy 1)

Shield the answer. Listen to the chord and write the bass note and the figured bass symbol; then uncover the answer and compare your response. Circle incorrect responses. Goal: No more than seven errors. The first frame requires no response.

173

D6-4a Figured bass dictation
(Copy 2)

Shield the answer. Listen to the chord and write the bass note and the figured bass symbol; then uncover the answer and compare your response. Circle incorrect responses. Goal: No more than seven errors. The first frame requires no response.

D6-4a Figured bass dictation

(Copy 3)

Shield the answer. Listen to the chord and write the bass note and the figured bass symbol; then uncover the answer and compare your response. Circle incorrect responses. Goal: No more than seven errors. The first frame requires no response.

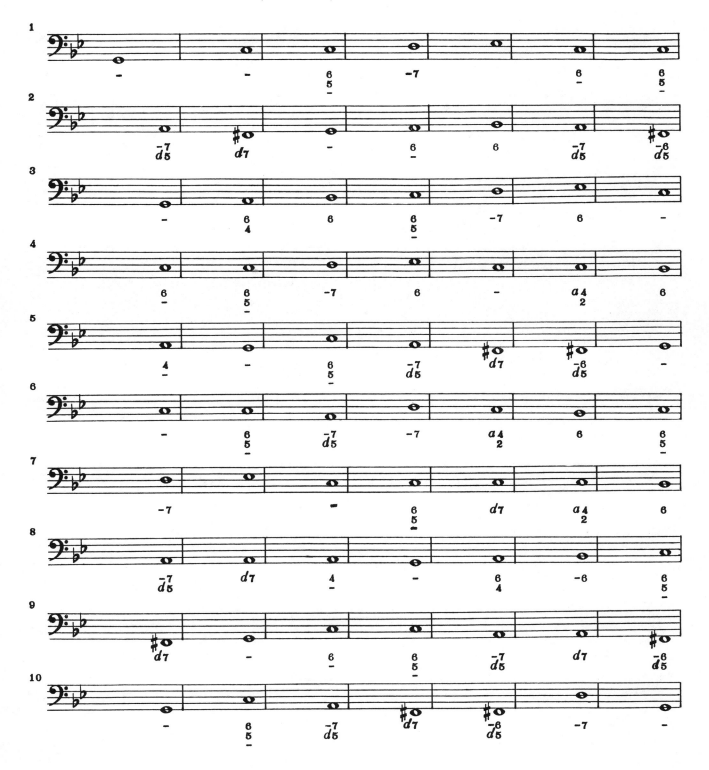

D6-4a Figured bass dictation
(Copy 4)

Shield the answer. Listen to the chord and write the bass note and the figured bass symbol; then uncover the answer and compare your response. Circle incorrect responses. Goal: No more than seven errors. The first frame requires no response.

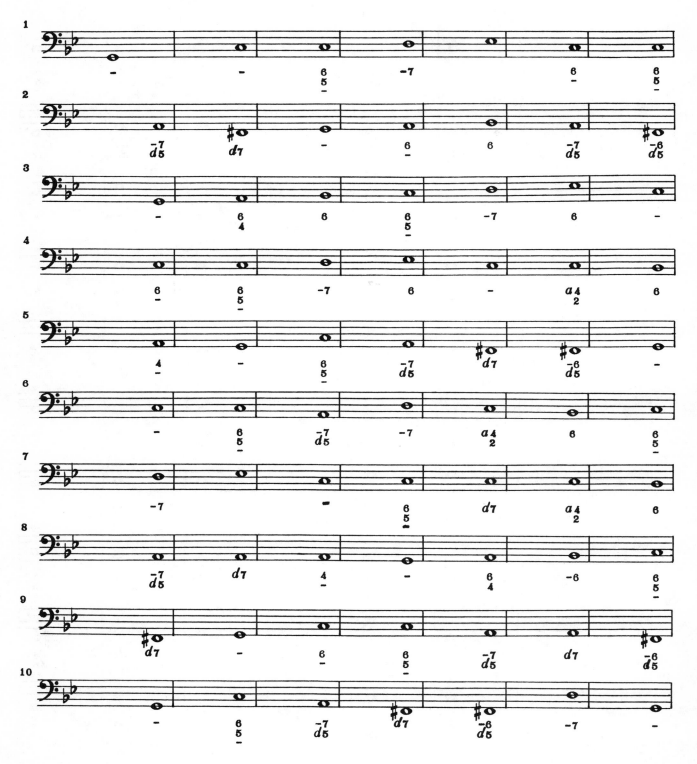

D6-4a Figured bass dictation
(Copy 5)

Shield the answer. Listen to the chord and write the bass note and the figured bass symbol; then uncover the answer and compare your response. Circle incorrect responses. Goal: No more than seven errors. The first frame requires no response.

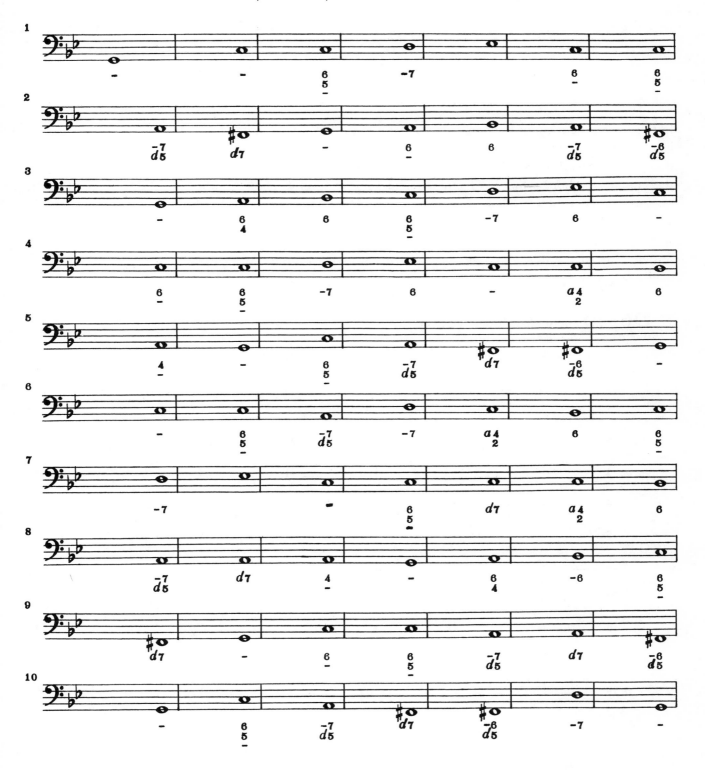

Lesson **D6-4b**

In this lesson the composite chord symbol is introduced for the seventh chord in first inversion on the second degree of a minor key. This chord is a half-diminished seventh chord. In first inversion the figured bass symbol is $^6_5$, and the composite chord symbol is II^{6}_{5}. In a major key the seventh chord on the second degree of the scale is a minor seventh chord, and the composite chord symbol for this chord in first inversion is II^{6}_{5}. Thus, in a major key we have the symbol II^{6}_{5}, and in a minor key we have the symbol $\underline{\text{II}}^{6}_{5}$.

The third of the $\underline{\text{II}}^{6}_{5}$ chord, which appears in the bass, is the fourth degree of the key.

D6-4b Chord identification in a key

(Copy 1)   *Shield the answer. Listen to the chord and write the composite chord symbol in the blank; then uncover the answer and compare your response. Circle incorrect responses. Goal: No more than seven errors. The first frame requires no response. After you have done this lesson, take Test D6.*

1	I^{-}	___ IV^{-}	___ II^{6}_{5}	___ V^{-7}	___ ^{-}VI	___ $\underline{\text{II}}^{6}$	___ $\underline{\text{II}}^{6}_{5}$
2	___ II^{-7}_{d5}	___ VII^{d7}	___ I^{-}	___ $\underline{\text{VII}}^{6}$	___ I^{6}	___ II^{-7}_{d5}	___ V^{-6}_{d5}
3	___ I^{-}	___ V^{6}_{4}	___ I^{6}	___ $\underline{\text{II}}^{6}_{5}$	___ V^{-7}	___ IV^{6}	___ IV^{-}
4	___ $\underline{\text{II}}^{6}$	___ $\underline{\text{II}}^{6}_{5}$	___ V^{-7}	___ IV^{6}	___ IV^{-}	___ V^{a4}_{2}	___ I^{6}
5	___ $\underline{\text{V}}^{4}$	___ I^{-}	___ $\underline{\text{II}}^{6}_{5}$	___ II^{-7}_{d5}	___ VII^{d7}	___ V^{-6}_{d5}	___ I^{-}
6	___ IV^{-}	___ $\underline{\text{II}}^{6}_{5}$	___ II^{-7}_{d5}	___ V^{-7}	___ V^{a4}_{2}	___ I^{6}	___ $\underline{\text{II}}^{6}_{5}$
7	___ V^{-7}	___ ^{-}VI	___ IV^{-}	___ $\underline{\text{IV}}^{6}_{5}$	___ IV^{d7}	___ V^{a4}_{2}	___ I^{6}
8	___ II^{-7}_{d5}	___ II^{d7}	___ $\underline{\text{V}}^{4}$	___ I^{-}	___ V^{6}_{4}	___ I^{6}	___ $\underline{\text{II}}^{6}_{5}$
9	___ VII^{d7}	___ I^{-}	___ $\underline{\text{II}}^{6}$	___ $\underline{\text{II}}^{6}_{5}$	___ II^{-7}_{d5}	___ II^{d7}	___ V^{-6}_{d5}
10	___ I^{-}	___ $\underline{\text{II}}^{6}_{5}$	___ II^{-7}_{d5}	___ VII^{d7}	___ V^{-6}_{d5}	___ V^{-7}	___ I^{-}

D6–4b Chord identification in a key

(Copy 2)

Shield the answer. Listen to the chord and write the composite chord symbol in the blank; then uncover the answer and compare your response. Circle incorrect responses. Goal: No more than seven errors. The first frame requires no response. After you have done this lesson, take Test D6.

1. I$^-$ ___ IV$^-$ ___ II$^6_5$ ___ V^{-7} ___ $^-$VI ___ II$^6_-$ ___ II$^6_5$
2. ___ II$^{-7}_{d5}$ ___ VII^{d7} ___ I$^-$ ___ VII$^6_-$ ___ I^6 ___ II$^{-7}_{d5}$ ___ V$^{-6}_{d5}$
3. ___ I$^-$ ___ V$^6_4$ ___ I^6 ___ II$^6_5$ ___ V^{-7} ___ IV^6 ___ IV$^-$
4. ___ II$^6_-$ ___ II$^6_5$ ___ V^{-7} ___ IV^6 ___ IV$^-$ ___ V$^{a4}_2$ ___ I^6
5. ___ V$^4_-$ ___ I$^-$ ___ II$^6_5$ ___ II$^{-7}_{d5}$ ___ VII^{d7} ___ V$^{-6}_{d5}$ ___ I$^-$
6. ___ IV$^-$ ___ II$^6_5$ ___ II$^{-7}_{d5}$ ___ V^{-7} ___ V$^{a4}_2$ ___ I^6 ___ II$^6_5$
7. ___ V^{-7} ___ $^-$VI ___ IV$^-$ ___ IV$^6_5$ ___ IV^{d7} ___ V$^{a4}_2$ ___ I^6
8. ___ II$^{-7}_{d5}$ ___ II^{d7} ___ V$^4_-$ ___ I$^-$ ___ V$^6_4$ ___ I^6 ___ II$^6_5$
9. ___ VII^{d7} ___ I$^-$ ___ II$^6_-$ ___ II$^6_5$ ___ II$^{-7}_{d5}$ ___ II^{d7} ___ V$^{-6}_{d5}$
10. ___ I$^-$ ___ II$^6_5$ ___ II$^{-7}_{d5}$ ___ VII^{d7} ___ V$^{-6}_{d5}$ ___ V^{-7} ___ I$^-$

D6–4b Chord identification in a key

(Copy 3)

Shield the answer. Listen to the chord and write the composite chord symbol in the blank; then uncover the answer and compare your response. Circle incorrect responses. Goal: No more than seven errors. The first frame requires no response. After you have done this lesson, take Test D6.

1. I$^-$ ___ IV$^-$ ___ II$^6_5$ ___ V^{-7} ___ $^-$VI ___ II$^6_-$ ___ II$^6_5$
2. ___ II$^{-7}_{d5}$ ___ VII^{d7} ___ I$^-$ ___ VII$^6_-$ ___ I^6 ___ II$^{-7}_{d5}$ ___ V$^{-6}_{d5}$
3. ___ I$^-$ ___ V$^6_4$ ___ I^6 ___ II$^6_5$ ___ V^{-7} ___ IV^6 ___ IV$^-$
4. ___ II$^6_-$ ___ II$^6_5$ ___ V^{-7} ___ IV^6 ___ IV$^-$ ___ V$^{a4}_2$ ___ I^6
5. ___ V$^4_-$ ___ I$^-$ ___ II$^6_5$ ___ II$^{-7}_{d5}$ ___ VII^{d7} ___ V$^{-6}_{d5}$ ___ I$^-$
6. ___ IV$^-$ ___ II$^6_5$ ___ II$^{-7}_{d5}$ ___ V^{-7} ___ V$^{a4}_2$ ___ I^6 ___ II$^6_5$
7. ___ V^{-7} ___ $^-$VI ___ IV$^-$ ___ IV$^6_5$ ___ IV^{d7} ___ V$^{a4}_2$ ___ I^6
8. ___ II$^{-7}_{d5}$ ___ II^{d7} ___ V$^4_-$ ___ I$^-$ ___ V$^6_4$ ___ I^6 ___ II$^6_5$
9. ___ VII^{d7} ___ I$^-$ ___ II$^6_-$ ___ II$^6_5$ ___ II$^{-7}_{d5}$ ___ II^{d7} ___ V$^{-6}_{d5}$
10. ___ I$^-$ ___ II$^6_5$ ___ II$^{-7}_{d5}$ ___ VII^{d7} ___ V$^{-6}_{d5}$ ___ V^{-7} ___ I$^-$

D6-4b Chord identification in a key

(Copy 4)   *Shield the answer. Listen to the chord and write the composite chord symbol in the blank; then uncover the answer and compare your response. Circle incorrect responses. Goal: No more than seven errors. The first frame requires no response. After you have done this lesson, take Test D6.*

1	I^-	___ IV^-	___ II^6_5	___ V^{-7}	___ ^-VI	___ II_-^6	___ II^6_5
2	___ II^{-7}_{d5}	___ VII^{d7}	___ I^-	___ VII_-^6	___ I^6	___ II^{-7}_{d5}	___ V^{-6}_{d5}
3	___ I^-	___ V^6_4	___ I^6	___ II^6_5	___ V^{-7}	___ IV^6	___ IV^-
4	___ II_-^6	___ II^6_5	___ V^{-7}	___ IV^6	___ IV^-	___ V^{a4}_2	___ I^6
5	___ V^4_-	___ I^-	___ II^6_5	___ II^{-7}_{d5}	___ VII^{d7}	___ V^{-6}_{d5}	___ I^-
6	___ IV^-	___ II^6_5	___ II^{-7}_{d5}	___ V^{-7}	___ V^{a4}_2	___ I^6	___ II^6_5
7	___ V^{-7}	___ ^-VI	___ IV^-	___ IV^6_5	___ IV^{d7}	___ V^{a4}_2	___ I^6
8	___ II^{-7}_{d5}	___ II^{d7}	___ V^4_-	___ I^-	___ V^6_4	___ I^6	___ II^6_5
9	___ VII^{d7}	___ I^-	___ II_-^6	___ II^6_5	___ II^{-7}_{d5}	___ II^{d7}	___ V^{-6}_{d5}
10	___ I^-	___ II^6_5	___ II^{-7}_{d5}	___ VII^{d7}	___ V^{-6}_{d5}	___ V^{-7}	___ I^-

D6-4b Chord identification in a key

(Copy 5)   *Shield the answer. Listen to the chord and write the composite chord symbol in the blank; then uncover the answer and compare your response. Circle incorrect responses. Goal: No more than seven errors. The first frame requires no response. After you have done this lesson, take Test D6.*

1	I^-	___ IV^-	___ II^6_5	___ V^{-7}	___ ^-VI	___ II_-^6	___ II^6_5
2	___ II^{-7}_{d5}	___ VII^{d7}	___ I^-	___ VII_-^6	___ I^6	___ II^{-7}_{d5}	___ V^{-6}_{d5}
3	___ I^-	___ V^6_4	___ I^6	___ II^6_5	___ V^{-7}	___ IV^6	___ IV^-
4	___ II_-^6	___ II^6_5	___ V^{-7}	___ IV^6	___ IV^-	___ V^{a4}_2	___ I^6
5	___ V^4_-	___ I^-	___ II^6_5	___ II^{-7}_{d5}	___ VII^{d7}	___ V^{-6}_{d5}	___ I^-
6	___ IV^-	___ II^6_5	___ II^{-7}_{d5}	___ V^{-7}	___ V^{a4}_2	___ I^6	___ II^6_5
7	___ V^{-7}	___ ^-VI	___ IV^-	___ IV^6_5	___ IV^{d7}	___ V^{a4}_2	___ I^6
8	___ II^{-7}_{d5}	___ II^{d7}	___ V^4_-	___ I^-	___ V^6_4	___ I^6	___ II^6_5
9	___ VII^{d7}	___ I^-	___ II_-^6	___ II^6_5	___ II^{-7}_{d5}	___ II^{d7}	___ V^{-6}_{d5}
10	___ I^-	___ II^6_5	___ II^{-7}_{d5}	___ VII^{d7}	___ V^{-6}_{d5}	___ V^{-7}	___ I^-

All Seventh Chords Previously Studied   **SERIES D7**

This series is designed as a summary in which each of the skills that have been developed in Series D4, D5, and D6 is applied to all seventh chords studied so far. In the tests for this series, the skills of chord dictation, chord identification, figured bass dictation, and chord identification in a key are tested separately rather than together, as in the earlier series. If you wish to improve your score on any of these tests, you may find it helpful to review earlier lessons on that particular skill.

Test D7a is a test in chord dictation and should be taken after you have done lesson D7–1. The lessons that may be reviewed for this test are D4–1a, D5–1a, D5–3a, and D6–1a.

Test D7b is a test in chord identification and should be taken after you have done lesson D7–2. The lessons that may be reviewed for this test are D4–2, D5–2, D5–4, and D6–2.

Test D7c is a test in figured bass dictation and should be taken after you have done lessons D7–3a and D7–4a. The lessons that may be reviewed for this test are D4–3a, D4–4a, D5–5a, D5–6a, D6–3a, and D6–4a.

Test D7d is a test in chord identification in a key and should be taken after you have done lessons D7–3b and D7–4b. The lessons that may be reviewed for this test are D4–3b, D4–4b, D5–5b, D5–6b, D6–3b, and D6–4b.

D7-1 Chord dictation
(Copy 1)

Shield the answer. Listen to the chord and write the upper tones above the given note; then uncover the answer and compare your response. Circle incorrect responses. Goal: No more than seven errors. When you have done this lesson, take Test D7a.

182

D7-1 Chord dictation

(Copy 2)

Shield the answer. Listen to the chord and write the upper tones above the given note; then uncover the answer and compare your response. Circle incorrect responses. Goal: No more than seven errors. When you have done this lesson, take Test D7a.

D7-1 Chord dictation

(Copy 3)

Shield the answer. Listen to the chord and write the upper tones above the given note; then uncover the answer and compare your response. Circle incorrect responses. Goal: No more than seven errors. When you have done this lesson, take Test D7a.

184

D7–1 Chord dictation

(Copy 4)

Shield the answer. Listen to the chord and write the upper tones above the given note; then uncover the answer and compare your response. Circle incorrect responses. Goal: No more than seven errors. When you have done this lesson, take Test D7a.

D7-1 Chord dictation

(Copy 5)

Shield the answer. Listen to the chord and write the upper tones above the given note; then uncover the answer and compare your response. Circle incorrect responses. Goal: No more than seven errors. When you have done this lesson, take Test D7a.

D7-2 Chord identification
(Copy 1)

Shield the answer. Listen to the chord and write the figured bass symbol in the blank; then uncover the answer and compare your response. Circle incorrect responses. Goal: No more than seven errors. When you have done this lesson, take Test D7b.

#							
1	___ −7/−	___ 6/5	___ −7	___ a4/2	___ −6	___ 6/5	___ −7/d5
2	___ −6/d5	___	___ −7/−	___ 6/5	___ −7/−	___ −7	___ a4/2
3	___ −6	___ −6/d5	___ −7/d5	___ d7	___ −	___ −7/−	___ 6/5
4	___ −7	___ d7	___ d7	___	___ 7	___ 7	___ 6/5
5	___ −7/−	___ −7/d5	___ −7	___ −7/−	___ 7	___ a4/2	___ −6
6	___ −6/d5	___ −	___ d7	___ d7	___ 6	___ −7/d5	___ −7
7	___ a4/2	___ 6	___ 4/−	___ −	___ −7/−	___ 6/5/−	___ −7
8	___ 7	___ 6/5/−	___ d7	___ d7	___ −6/d5	___ −	___ 7
9	___ 7	___ −6/d5	___	___ −7/−	___ 6/5	___ 6/4	___ d7
10	___ −7	___	___ 7	___ 6/5	___ −7/d5	___ d7	

D7-2 Chord identification
(Copy 2)

Shield the answer. Listen to the chord and write the figured bass symbol in the blank; then uncover the answer and compare your response. Circle incorrect responses. Goal: No more than seven errors. When you have done this lesson, take Test D7b.

#							
1	___ −7/−	___ 6/5	___ −7	___ a4/2	___ −6	___ 6/5	___ −7/d5
2	___ −6/d5	___	___ −7/−	___ 6/5	___ −7/−	___ −7	___ a4/2
3	___ −6	___ −6/d5	___ −7/d5	___ d7	___ −	___ −7/−	___ 6/5
4	___ −7	___ d7	___ d7	___	___ 7	___ 7	___ 6/5
5	___ −7/−	___ −7/d5	___ −7	___ −7/−	___ 7	___ a4/2	___ −6
6	___ −6/d5	___ −	___ d7	___ d7	___ 6	___ −7/d5	___ −7
7	___ a4/2	___ 6	___ 4/−	___ −	___ −7/−	___ 6/5/−	___ −7
8	___ 7	___ 6/5/−	___ d7	___ d7	___ −6/d5	___ −	___ 7
9	___ 7	___ −6/d5	___	___ −7/−	___ 6/5	___ 6/4	___ d7
10	___ −7	___	___ 7	___ 6/5	___ −7/d5	___ d7	

D7-2 Chord identification
(Copy 3)

Shield the answer. Listen to the chord and write the figured bass symbol in the blank; then uncover the answer and compare your response. Circle incorrect responses. Goal: No more than seven errors. When you have done this lesson, take Test D7b.

1. ___ -7/-   ___ 6/5   ___ -7   ___ a4/2   ___ -6   ___ 6/5   ___ -7/d5

2. ___ -6/d5   ___   ___ -7/-   ___ 6/5   ___ -7/-   ___ -7   ___ a4/2

3. ___ -6   ___ -6/d5   ___ -7/d5   ___ d7   ___   ___ -7/-   ___ 6/5

4. ___ -7   ___ d7   ___ d7   ___   ___ 7   ___ 7   ___ 6/5

5. ___ -7/-   ___ -7/d5   ___ -7   ___ -7/-   ___ 7   ___ a4/2   ___ -6

6. ___ -6/d5   ___ -   ___ d7   ___ d7   ___ 6   ___ -7/d5   ___ -7

7. ___ a4/2   ___ 6   ___ 4/-   ___ -   ___ -7/-   ___ 6/5   ___ -7

8. ___ 7   ___ 6/5   ___ d7   ___ d7   ___ -6/d5   ___ -   ___ 7

9. ___ 7   ___ -6/d5   ___   ___ -7/-   ___ 6/5   ___ 6/4   ___ d7

10. ___ -7   ___   ___ 7   ___ 6/5   ___ -7/d5   ___ d7   ___

D7-2 Chord identification
(Copy 4)

Shield the answer. Listen to the chord and write the figured bass symbol in the blank; then uncover the answer and compare your response. Circle incorrect responses. Goal: No more than seven errors. When you have done this lesson, take Test D7b.

1. ___ -7/-   ___ 6/5   ___ -7   ___ a4/2   ___ -6   ___ 6/5   ___ -7/d5

2. ___ -6/d5   ___   ___ -7/-   ___ 6/5   ___ -7/-   ___ -7   ___ a4/2

3. ___ -6   ___ -6/d5   ___ -7/d5   ___ d7   ___ -   ___ -7/-   ___ 6/5

4. ___ -7   ___ d7   ___ d7   ___   ___ 7   ___ 7   ___ 6/5

5. ___ -7/-   ___ -7/d5   ___ -7   ___ -7/-   ___ 7   ___ a4/2   ___ -6

6. ___ -6/d5   ___ -   ___ d7   ___ d7   ___ 6   ___ -7/d5   ___ -7

7. ___ a4/2   ___ 6   ___ 4/-   ___ -   ___ -7/-   ___ 6/5   ___ -7

8. ___ 7   ___ 6/5   ___ d7   ___ d7   ___ -6/d5   ___ -   ___ 7

9. ___ 7   ___ -6/d5   ___   ___ -7/-   ___ 6/5   ___ 6/4   ___ d7

10. ___ -7   ___   ___ 7   ___ 6/5   ___ -7/d5   ___ d7   ___

Chord identification

Shield the answer. Listen to the chord and write the figured bass symbol in the blank; then uncover the answer and compare your response. Circle incorrect responses. Goal: No more than seven errors. When you have done this lesson, take Test D7b.

#							
1	$\dfrac{-7}{-}$	$\dfrac{6}{5}$	-7	$\dfrac{a4}{2}$	-6	$\dfrac{6}{\underline{5}}$	$\dfrac{-7}{d5}$
2	$\dfrac{-6}{d5}$		$\dfrac{-7}{-}$	$\dfrac{6}{5}$	$\dfrac{-7}{-}$	-7	$\dfrac{a4}{2}$
3	-6	$\dfrac{-6}{d5}$	$\dfrac{-7}{d5}$	$d7$	$-$	$\dfrac{-7}{-}$	$\dfrac{6}{5}$
4	-7	$d7$	$d7$		7	7	$\dfrac{6}{5}$
5	$\dfrac{-7}{-}$	$\dfrac{-7}{d5}$	-7	$\dfrac{-7}{-}$	7	$\dfrac{a4}{2}$	-6
6	$\dfrac{-6}{d5}$	$-$	$d7$	$d7$	6	$\dfrac{-7}{d5}$	-7
7	$\dfrac{a4}{2}$	6	$\dfrac{4}{-}$	$-$	$\dfrac{-7}{-}$	$\dfrac{6}{\underline{5}}$	-7
8	7	$\dfrac{6}{\underline{5}}$	$d7$	$d7$	$\dfrac{-6}{d5}$	$-$	7
9	7	$\dfrac{-6}{d5}$		$\dfrac{-7}{-}$	$\dfrac{6}{5}$	$\dfrac{6}{4}$	$d7$
10	-7		7	$\dfrac{6}{5}$	$\dfrac{-7}{d5}$	$d7$	

D7-3a Figured bass dictation
(Copy 1)

Shield the answer. Listen to the chord and write the bass note and figured bass symbol; then uncover the answer and compare your response. Circle incorrect answers. Goal: No more than seven errors. The first frame requires no response.

D7-3a Figured bass dictation

(Copy 2)

Shield the answer. Listen to the chord and write the bass note and figured bass symbol; then uncover the answer and compare your response. Circle incorrect answers. Goal: No more than seven errors. The first frame requires no response.

D7-3a Figured bass dictation
(Copy 3)

Shield the answer. Listen to the chord and write the bass note and figured bass symbol; then uncover the answer and compare your response. Circle incorrect answers. Goal: No more than seven errors. The first frame requires no response.

D7-3a Figured bass dictation

(Copy 4)

Shield the answer. Listen to the chord and write the bass note and figured bass symbol; then uncover the answer and compare your response. Circle incorrect answers. Goal: No more than seven errors. The first frame requires no response.

D7-3a Figured bass dictation
(Copy 5)

Shield the answer. Listen to the chord and write the bass note and figured bass symbol; then uncover the answer and compare your response. Circle incorrect answers. Goal: No more than seven errors. The first frame requires no response.

194

D7-3b Chord identification in a key
(Copy 1)

Shield the answer. Listen to the chord and write the composite chord symbol in the blank; then uncover the answer and compare your response. Circle incorrect responses. Goal: No more than seven errors. First frame requires no response.

1 I ___ II^{6}_{5} ___ V^{a4}_{2} ___ I^{-6} ___ $\text{V}^{4}_{\_}$ ___ I ___ VII^{6}_{5}

2 ___ VII^{-7}_{d5} ___ I ___ IV^{7} ___ $\text{II}^{-7}_{\_}$ ___ VII^{6}_{5} ___ I ___ $\text{VI}^{-7}_{\_}$

3 ___ IV^{7} ___ $\text{II}^{-7}_{\_}$ ___ V^{-7} ___ V^{a4}_{2} ___ $\text{V}^{4}_{\_}$ ___ I ___ IV^{7}

4 ___ II^{6}_{5} ___ V^{-7} ___ V^{-6}_{d5} ___ I ___ $\text{III}^{-7}_{\_}$ ___ $\text{VI}^{-7}_{\_}$ ___ $\text{II}^{-7}_{\_}$

5 ___ VII^{-7}_{d5} ___ V^{-6}_{d5} ___ I ___ $\text{VI}^{-7}_{\_}$ ___ II^{6}_{5} ___ $\text{II}^{-7}_{\_}$ ___ VII^{6}_{5}

6 ___ VII^{-7}_{d5} ___ V^{-6}_{d5} ___ I ___ I^{7} ___ IV^{7} ___ V^{-7} ___ V^{a4}_{2}

7 ___ I^{-6} ___ $\text{V}^{4}_{\_}$ ___ I ___ II^{6}_{5} ___ I^{6}_{4} ___ V^{-7} ___ I

8 ___ $\text{VI}^{-7}_{\_}$ ___ VII^{-7}_{d5} ___ V^{-6}_{d5} ___ I ___ $\text{III}^{-7}_{\_}$ ___ $\text{VI}^{-7}_{\_}$ ___ $\text{II}^{-7}_{\_}$

9 ___ VII^{-7}_{d5} ___ V^{-7} ___ IV^{-6} ___ II^{6}_{5} ___ $\text{II}^{-7}_{\_}$ ___ V^{-7} ___ V^{a4}_{2}

10 ___ I^{-6} ___ $\text{V}^{4}_{\_}$ ___ I ___ VII^{-7}_{d5} ___ V^{-6}_{d5} ___ V^{-7} ___ I

D7-3b Chord identification in a key
(Copy 2)

Shield the answer. Listen to the chord and write the composite chord symbol in the blank; then uncover the answer and compare your response. Circle incorrect responses. Goal: No more than seven errors. First frame requires no response.

1 I ___ II^{6}_{5} ___ V^{a4}_{2} ___ I^{-6} ___ $\text{V}^{4}_{\_}$ ___ I ___ VII^{6}_{5}

2 ___ VII^{-7}_{d5} ___ I ___ IV^{7} ___ $\text{II}^{-7}_{\_}$ ___ VII^{6}_{5} ___ I ___ $\text{VI}^{-7}_{\_}$

3 ___ IV^{7} ___ $\text{II}^{-7}_{\_}$ ___ V^{-7} ___ V^{a4}_{2} ___ $\text{V}^{4}_{\_}$ ___ I ___ IV^{7}

4 ___ II^{6}_{5} ___ V^{-7} ___ V^{-6}_{d5} ___ I ___ $\text{III}^{-7}_{\_}$ ___ $\text{VI}^{-7}_{\_}$ ___ $\text{II}^{-7}_{\_}$

5 ___ VII^{-7}_{d5} ___ V^{-6}_{d5} ___ I ___ $\text{VI}^{-7}_{\_}$ ___ II^{6}_{5} ___ $\text{II}^{-7}_{\_}$ ___ VII^{6}_{5}

6 ___ VII^{-7}_{d5} ___ V^{-6}_{d5} ___ I ___ I^{7} ___ IV^{7} ___ V^{-7} ___ V^{a4}_{2}

7 ___ I^{-6} ___ $\text{V}^{4}_{\_}$ ___ I ___ II^{6}_{5} ___ I^{6}_{4} ___ V^{-7} ___ I

8 ___ $\text{VI}^{-7}_{\_}$ ___ VII^{-7}_{d5} ___ V^{-6}_{d5} ___ I ___ $\text{III}^{-7}_{\_}$ ___ $\text{VI}^{-7}_{\_}$ ___ $\text{II}^{-7}_{\_}$

9 ___ VII^{-7}_{d5} ___ V^{-7} ___ IV^{-6} ___ II^{6}_{5} ___ $\text{II}^{-7}_{\_}$ ___ V^{-7} ___ V^{a4}_{2}

10 ___ I^{-6} ___ $\text{V}^{4}_{\_}$ ___ I ___ VII^{-7}_{d5} ___ V^{-6}_{d5} ___ V^{-7} ___ I

D7-3b Chord identification in a key
(Copy 3)

Shield the answer. Listen to the chord and write the composite chord symbol in the blank; then uncover the answer and compare your response. Circle incorrect responses. Goal: No more than seven errors. First frame requires no response.

1. I   ____ II_5^6 ____ V_2^{a4} ____ I^{-6} ____ V_-^4 ____ I   ____ VII_5^6

2. ____ VII_{d5}^{-7} ____ I   ____ IV^7 ____ II_-^{-7} ____ VII_5^6 ____ I   ____ VI_-^{-7}

3. ____ IV^7 ____ II_-^{-7} ____ V^{-7} ____ V_2^{a4} ____ V_-^4 ____ I   ____ IV^7

4. ____ II_5^6 ____ V^{-7} ____ V_{d5}^{-6} ____ I   ____ III_-^{-7} ____ VI_-^{-7} ____ II_-^{-7}

5. ____ VII_{d5}^{-7} ____ V_{d5}^{-6} ____ I   ____ VI_-^{-7} ____ II_5^6 ____ II_-^{-7} ____ VII_5^6

6. ____ VII_{d5}^{-7} ____ V_{d5}^{-6} ____ I   ____ I^7 ____ IV^7 ____ V^{-7} ____ V_2^{a4}

7. ____ I^{-6} ____ V_-^4 ____ I   ____ II_5^6 ____ I_4^6 ____ V^{-7} ____ I

8. ____ VI_-^{-7} ____ VII_{d5}^{-7} ____ V_{d5}^{-6} ____ I   ____ III_-^{-7} ____ VI_-^{-7} ____ II_-^{-7}

9. ____ VII_{d5}^{-7} ____ V^{-7} ____ IV^{-6} ____ II_5^6 ____ II_-^{-7} ____ V^{-7} ____ V_2^{a4}

10. ____ I^{-6} ____ V_-^4 ____ I   ____ VII_{d5}^{-7} ____ V_{d5}^{-6} ____ V^{-7} ____ I

D7-3b Chord identification in a key
(Copy 4)

Shield the answer. Listen to the chord and write the composite chord symbol in the blank; then uncover the answer and compare your response. Circle incorrect responses. Goal: No more than seven errors. First frame requires no response.

1. I   ____ II_5^6 ____ V_2^{a4} ____ I^{-6} ____ V_-^4 ____ I   ____ VII_5^6

2. ____ VII_{d5}^{-7} ____ I   ____ IV^7 ____ II_-^{-7} ____ VII_5^6 ____ I   ____ VI_-^{-7}

3. ____ IV^7 ____ II_-^{-7} ____ V^{-7} ____ V_2^{a4} ____ V_-^4 ____ I   ____ IV^7

4. ____ II_5^6 ____ V^{-7} ____ V_{d5}^{-6} ____ I   ____ III_-^{-7} ____ VI_-^{-7} ____ II_-^{-7}

5. ____ VII_{d5}^{-7} ____ V_{d5}^{-6} ____ I   ____ VI_-^{-7} ____ II_5^6 ____ II_-^{-7} ____ VII_5^6

6. ____ VII_{d5}^{-7} ____ V_{d5}^{-6} ____ I   ____ I^7 ____ IV^7 ____ V^{-7} ____ V_2^{a4}

7. ____ I^{-6} ____ V_-^4 ____ I   ____ II_5^6 ____ I_4^6 ____ V^{-7} ____ I

8. ____ VI_-^{-7} ____ VII_{d5}^{-7} ____ V_{d5}^{-6} ____ I   ____ III_-^{-7} ____ VI_-^{-7} ____ II_-^{-7}

9. ____ VII_{d5}^{-7} ____ V^{-7} ____ IV^{-6} ____ II_5^6 ____ II_-^{-7} ____ V^{-7} ____ V_2^{a4}

10. ____ I^{-6} ____ V_-^4 ____ I   ____ VII_{d5}^{-7} ____ V_{d5}^{-6} ____ V^{-7} ____ I

D7-3b Chord identification in a key
(Copy 5)

Shield the answer. Listen to the chord and write the composite chord symbol in the blank; then uncover the answer and compare your response. Circle incorrect responses. Goal: No more than seven errors. First frame requires no response.

1 I   ____ II_5^6 ____ V_2^{a4} ____ I^{-6} ____ V_-^4 ____ I   ____ $VII_{\underline{5}}^6$

2 ____ VII_{d5}^{-7} ____ I   ____ IV^7 ____ II_-^7 ____ $VII_{\underline{5}}^6$ ____ I   ____ VI_-^7

3 ____ IV^7 ____ II_-^7 ____ V^{-7} ____ V_2^{a4} ____ V_-^4 ____ I   ____ IV^7

4 ____ II_5^6 ____ V^{-7} ____ V_{d5}^{-6} ____ I   ____ III_-^7 ____ VI_-^7 ____ II_-^7

5 ____ VII_{d5}^{-7} ____ V_{d5}^{-6} ____ I   ____ VI_-^7 ____ II_5^6 ____ II_-^7 ____ $VII_{\underline{5}}^6$

6 ____ VII_{d5}^{-7} ____ V_{d5}^{-6} ____ I   ____ I^7 ____ IV^7 ____ V^{-7} ____ V_2^{a4}

7 ____ I^{-6} ____ V_-^4 ____ I   ____ II_5^6 ____ I_4^6 ____ V^{-7} ____ I

8 ____ VI_-^7 ____ VII_{d5}^{-7} ____ V_{d5}^{-6} ____ I   ____ III_-^7 ____ VI_-^7 ____ II_-^7

9 ____ VII_{d5}^{-7} ____ V^{-7} ____ IV^{-6} ____ II_5^6 ____ II_-^7 ____ V^{-7} ____ V_2^{a4}

10 ____ I^{-6} ____ V_-^4 ____ I   ____ VII_{d5}^{-7} ____ V_{d5}^{-6} ____ V^{-7} ____ I

D7-4a Figured bass dictation
(Copy 1)

Shield the answer. Listen to the chord and write the bass note and the figured bass symbol; then uncover the answer and compare your response. Circle incorrect answers. Goal: No more than seven errors. The first frame requires no response. When you have done this lesson, take Test D7c.

D7-4a Figured bass dictation
(Copy 2)

Shield the answer. Listen to the chord and write the bass note and the figured bass symbol; then uncover the answer and compare your response. Circle incorrect answers. Goal: No more than seven errors. The first frame requires no response. When you have done this lesson, take Test D7c.

D7-4a Figured bass dictation
(Copy 3)

Shield the answer. Listen to the chord and write the bass note and the figured bass symbol; then uncover the answer and compare your response. Circle incorrect answers. Goal: No more than seven errors. The first frame requires no response. When you have done this lesson, take Test D7c.

200

D7-4a Figured bass dictation
(Copy 4)

Shield the answer. Listen to the chord and write the bass note and the figured bass symbol; then uncover the answer and compare your response. Circle incorrect answers. Goal: No more than seven errors. The first frame requires no response. When you have done this lesson, take Test D7c.

D7-4a Figured bass dictation
(Copy 5)

Shield the answer. Listen to the chord and write the bass note and the figured bass symbol; then uncover the answer and compare your response. Circle incorrect answers. Goal: No more than seven errors. The first frame requires no response. When you have done this lesson, take Test D7c.

D7-4b Chord identification in a key
(Copy 1)

Shield the answer. Listen to the chord and write the composite chord symbol in the blank; then uncover the answer and compare your response. Circle incorrect responses. Goal: No more than seven errors. The first frame requires no response. When you have done this lesson, take Test D7d.

1   I^- ____ II^6_5 ____ V^{-7} ____ V^{a4}_2 ____ I^6 ____ II^{d7} ____ I^-

2   ____ VII^{d7} ____ $^-VI^{d7}$ ____ V^{-7} ____ I^- ____ $^-VI^7$ ____ IV^{-7} ____ II^6_5

3   ____ II^{-7}_{d5} ____ II^{d7} ____ I^- ____ IV^{-7} ____ II^{-7}_{d5} ____ V^4 ____ I^-

4   ____ $^-VI^{d7}$ ____ V^{-7} ____ IV^6 ____ II^6_5 ____ II^{d7} ____ I^- ____ II^6

5   ____ II^6_5 ____ II^{-7}_{d5} ____ II^{d7} ____ V^{-6}_{d5} ____ I^- ____ I^{-7} ____ IV^{-7}

6   ____ V^{-7} ____ I^- ____ $^-VI^7$ ____ IV^{-7} ____ II^6_5 ____ V^{a4}_2 ____ I^6

7   ____ II^{d7} ____ IV^{d7} ____ $^-VI^{d7}$ ____ V^{-7} ____ V^{-6}_{d5} ____ I^- ____ II^6_5

8   ____ I^{-6}_4 ____ V^{-7} ____ $^-VI^{d7}$ ____ IV^{d7} ____ II^{d7} ____ VII^{d7} ____ I^-

9   ____ ^-III ____ $^-VI^7$ ____ $^-VI^{d7}$ ____ V^{-7} ____ IV^6 ____ II^6_5 ____ II^{-7}_{d5}

10 ____ VII^{d7} ____ I^- ____ $^-VI^7$ ____ IV^{-7} ____ II^{-7}_{d5} ____ VII^{d7} ____ I^-

D7-4b Chord identification in a key
(Copy 2)

Shield the answer. Listen to the chord and write the composite chord symbol in the blank; then uncover the answer and compare your response. Circle incorrect responses. Goal: No more than seven errors. The first frame requires no response. When you have done this lesson, take Test D7d.

1   I^- ____ II^6_5 ____ V^{-7} ____ V^{a4}_2 ____ I^6 ____ II^{d7} ____ I^-

2   ____ VII^{d7} ____ $^-VI^{d7}$ ____ V^{-7} ____ I^- ____ $^-VI^7$ ____ IV^{-7} ____ II^6_5

3   ____ II^{-7}_{d5} ____ II^{d7} ____ I^- ____ IV^{-7} ____ II^{-7}_{d5} ____ V^4 ____ I^-

4   ____ $^-VI^{d7}$ ____ V^{-7} ____ IV^6 ____ II^6_5 ____ II^{d7} ____ I^- ____ II^6

5   ____ II^6_5 ____ II^{-7}_{d5} ____ II^{d7} ____ V^{-6}_{d5} ____ I^- ____ I^{-7} ____ IV^{-7}

6   ____ V^{-7} ____ I^- ____ $^-VI^7$ ____ IV^{-7} ____ II^6_5 ____ V^{a4}_2 ____ I^6

7   ____ II^{d7} ____ IV^{d7} ____ $^-VI^{d7}$ ____ V^{-7} ____ V^{-6}_{d5} ____ I^- ____ II^6_5

8   ____ I^{-6}_4 ____ V^{-7} ____ $^-VI^{d7}$ ____ IV^{d7} ____ II^{d7} ____ VII^{d7} ____ I^-

9   ____ ^-III ____ $^-VI^7$ ____ $^-VI^{d7}$ ____ V^{-7} ____ IV^6 ____ II^6_5 ____ II^{-7}_{d5}

10 ____ VII^{d7} ____ I^- ____ $^-VI^7$ ____ IV^{-7} ____ II^{-7}_{d5} ____ VII^{d7} ____ I^-

D7–4b Chord identification in a key
(Copy 3)

Shield the answer. Listen to the chord and write the composite chord symbol in the blank; then uncover the answer and compare your response. Circle incorrect responses. Goal: No more than seven errors. The first frame requires no response. When you have done this lesson, take Test D7d.

1   I^- ___ II^6_5 ___ V^{-7} ___ V^{a4}_2 ___ I^6 ___ II^{d7} ___ I^-

2 ___ VII^{d7} ___ $^-VI^{d7}$ ___ V^{-7} ___ I^- ___ $^-VI^7$ ___ IV^{-7} ___ II^6_5

3 ___ II^{-7}_{d5} ___ II^{d7} ___ I^- ___ IV^{-7} ___ II^{-7}_{d5} ___ V^4 ___ I^-

4 ___ $^-VI^{d7}$ ___ V^{-7} ___ IV^6 ___ II^6_5 ___ II^{d7} ___ I^- ___ II^6

5 ___ II^6_5 ___ II^{-7}_{d5} ___ II^{d7} ___ V^{-6}_{d5} ___ I^- ___ I^{-7} ___ IV^{-7}

6 ___ V^{-7} ___ I^- ___ $^-VI^7$ ___ IV^{-7} ___ II^6_5 ___ V^{a4}_2 ___ I^6

7 ___ II^{d7} ___ IV^{d7} ___ $^-VI^{d7}$ ___ V^{-7} ___ V^{-6}_{d5} ___ I^- ___ II^6_5

8 ___ I^{-6}_4 ___ V^{-7} ___ $^-VI^{d7}$ ___ IV^{d7} ___ II^{d7} ___ VII^{d7} ___ I^-

9 ___ ^-III ___ $^-VI^7$ ___ $^-VI^{d7}$ ___ V^{-7} ___ IV^6 ___ II^6_5 ___ II^{-7}_{d5}

10 ___ VII^{d7} ___ I^- ___ $^-VI^7$ ___ IV^{-7} ___ II^{-7}_{d5} ___ VII^{d7} ___ I^-

D7–4b Chord identification in a key
(Copy 4)

Shield the answer. Listen to the chord and write the composite chord symbol in the blank; then uncover the answer and compare your response. Circle incorrect responses. Goal: No more than seven errors. The first frame requires no response. When you have done this lesson, take Test D7d.

1   I^- ___ II^6_5 ___ V^{-7} ___ V^{a4}_2 ___ I^6 ___ II^{d7} ___ I^-

2 ___ VII^{d7} ___ $^-VI^{d7}$ ___ V^{-7} ___ I^- ___ $^-VI^7$ ___ IV^{-7} ___ II^6_5

3 ___ II^{-7}_{d5} ___ II^{d7} ___ I^- ___ IV^{-7} ___ II^{-7}_{d5} ___ V^4 ___ I^-

4 ___ $^-VI^{d7}$ ___ V^{-7} ___ IV^6 ___ II^6_5 ___ II^{d7} ___ I^- ___ II^6

5 ___ II^6_5 ___ II^{-7}_{d5} ___ II^{d7} ___ V^{-6}_{d5} ___ I^- ___ I^{-7} ___ IV^{-7}

6 ___ V^{-7} ___ I^- ___ $^-VI^7$ ___ IV^{-7} ___ II^6_5 ___ V^{a4}_2 ___ I^6

7 ___ II^{d7} ___ IV^{d7} ___ $^-VI^{d7}$ ___ V^{-7} ___ V^{-6}_{d5} ___ I^- ___ II^6_5

8 ___ I^{-6}_4 ___ V^{-7} ___ $^-VI^{d7}$ ___ IV^{d7} ___ II^{d7} ___ VII^{d7} ___ I^-

9 ___ ^-III ___ $^-VI^7$ ___ $^-VI^{d7}$ ___ V^{-7} ___ IV^6 ___ II^6_5 ___ II^{-7}_{d5}

10 ___ VII^{d7} ___ I^- ___ $^-VI^7$ ___ IV^{-7} ___ II^{-7}_{d5} ___ VII^{d7} ___ I^-

D7–4b Chord identification in a key
(Copy 5)

Shield the answer. Listen to the chord and write the composite chord symbol in the blank; then uncover the answer and compare your response. Circle incorrect responses. Goal: No more than seven errors. The first frame requires no response. When you have done this lesson, take Test D7d.

1 I^- ____ II^6_5 ____ V^{-7} ____ V^{a4}_2 ____ I^6 ____ II^{d7} ____ I^-

2 ____ VII^{d7} ____ $^-VI^{d7}$ ____ V^{-7} ____ I^- ____ $^-VI^7$ ____ IV^{-7} ____ II^6_5

3 ____ II^{-7}_{d5} ____ II^{d7} ____ I^- ____ IV^{-7} ____ II^{-7}_{d5} ____ V^4 ____ I^-

4 ____ $^-VI^{d7}$ ____ V^{-7} ____ IV^6 ____ II^6_5 ____ II^{d7} ____ I^- ____ II^6

5 ____ II^6_5 ____ II^{-7}_{d5} ____ II^{d7} ____ V^{-6}_{d5} ____ I^- ____ I^{-7} ____ IV^{-7}

6 ____ V^{-7} ____ I^- ____ $^-VI^7$ ____ IV^{-7} ____ II^6_5 ____ V^{a4}_2 ____ I^6

7 ____ II^{d7} ____ IV^{d7} ____ $^-VI^{d7}$ ____ V^{-7} ____ V^{-6}_{d5} ____ I^- ____ II^6_5

8 ____ I^{-6}_4 ____ V^{-7} ____ $^-VI^{d7}$ ____ IV^{d7} ____ II^{d7} ____ VII^{d7} ____ I^-

9 ____ ^-III ____ $^-VI^7$ ____ $^-VI^{d7}$ ____ V^{-7} ____ IV^6 ____ II^6_5 ____ II^{-7}_{d5}

10 ____ VII^{d7} ____ I^- ____ $^-VI^7$ ____ IV^{-7} ____ II^{-7}_{d5} ____ VII^{d7} ____ I^-

Arpeggio Singing of Seventh Chords

This series involves all seventh chords previously studied and some triads. There are two kinds of lessons: arpeggio singing from figured bass symbols and arpeggio singing from composite chord symbols. This kind of experience will help you to mentally hear chords and chord progressions.

When you have done this series, take Test D8. The test does not include arpeggio singing from figured bass symbols. While your achievement in this skill is not tested, it will help you with arpeggio singing from composite chord symbols, which is tested.

Lessons **D8-1** and **D8-2**

These are lessons in arpeggio singing from figured bass symbols. The purpose of these lessons is to develop your ability to hear mentally various types of seventh chords and to sing their pitches in arpeggio fashion. The format for each frame on the tape is as follows: you will hear the starting tone, followed by four clicks on the metronome. Sing the arpeggio in time with the clicks. Immediately after the clicks you will hear an arpeggio giving the pitches you should have sung. You can then judge if you sang the arpeggio correctly.

Sing the seventh chords in the following fashion:

Depending on the range of your voice, you may find it necessary to sing in a different octave from that of the tones you hear on the tape recording. You may also find it necessary to change octaves in the course of the lesson. Sing in the most comfortable part of your vocal range at all times.

Whenever you have sung a frame incorrectly, make a tally mark on a piece of paper. Your goal is to complete each lesson with no more than five incorrect frames. When you have done so, go on to the next lesson. If you have more than five incorrect frames, repeat the lesson until you reach the goal or until you have done the lesson five times, at which point you should go on to the next lesson regardless of your score.

D8-1 Arpeggio singing from figured bass symbols

Listen to the starting tone, then sing the arpeggio in time with the metronome. Compare your response with the arpeggio you then hear and tally your errors. Goal: No more than five incorrect frames.

1	-7 –	-7 –	-7 –	7	7	-7 –	-7 –	7	-7 d5	d7
2	-7 –	-7 d5	d7	-7 –	7	-7	7	-7 d5	d7	7
3	7	-7	-7 –	-7 d5	d7	d7	-7 d5	-7 –	-7	7
4	-7	d7	7	-7 d5	-7 –	-7 –	d7	-7	7	-7 d5
5	-7 –	7	-7 d5	d7	-7 –	-7	7	-7 d5	d7	7

D8-2 Arpeggio singing from figured bass symbols

Listen to the starting tone, then sing the arpeggio in time with the metronome. Compare your response with the arpeggio you then hear and tally your errors. Goal: No more than five incorrect frames.

1	7	6 5	-7 –	-7 –	6 5	7	-7 d5	6 5 –	-7 –	6 5 –
2	-7 –	6 5 –	6 5	7	-7	-6 d5	4 –	a4 2	4 –	a4 2
3	-7	-6 d5	4 –	a4 2	6 5 –	6 5	4 –	a4 2	7	6 5
4	6 5 –	4 –	a4 2	6 5 –	d7	-7 d5	-6 d5	6 5	a4 2	6 5 –
5	4 –	d7	a4 2	-7 d5	-7 –	6 5	-6 d5	4 –	a4 2	6 5

Lessons **D8-3, D8-4, D8-5,** and **D8-6**

These are lessons in arpeggio singing from composite chord symbols. The purpose of these lessons is to develop your ability to hear chord progressions mentally and to sing the pitches in arpeggio fashion. Each frame on the worksheet contains one composite chord symbol. You will be given the starting pitch for the first frame only. In subsequent frames, you must sing each new arpeggio using the preceding arpeggio as a reference. In each frame you will hear four clicks along with which you should sing the arpeggio in the same fashion as in the lessons in arpeggio singing on a given pitch. Immediately after the clicks, you will hear an arpeggio which will tell you the pitches you should have sung. Then sing the next arpeggio with the following clicks. Your goal is to complete each lesson with no more than five incorrect frames. When you have done so, go on to the next lesson. If you have more than five incorrect frames, repeat the lesson until you reach the goal or until you have done the lesson five times, at which point you should go on to the next lesson regardless of your score.

In this lesson you will sing triads as well as seventh chords in arpeggios. The arpeggio for a seventh should be sung in the same rhythm as in the lessons in arpeggio singing on a given tone. Sing the triads in the following fashion: arpeggio for a seventh chord should be sung in the same rhythm as in the lessons in arpeggio singing on a given tone. Sing the triads in the following fashion:

The first tone which you sing should be the bass which is appropriate for the given chord symbol. For example, if the given chord symbol is V^{-7}, the first tone you sing should be the fifth degree of the key because the chord is in root position. If the given chord symbol is V^{-6}_{d5}, you should start with the seventh degree of the scale because that degree is the third of the chord and the chord is in first inversion.

D8-3 Arpeggio singing from composite chord symbols

Sing the arpeggio in time with the metronome. Compare your response with the arpeggio you then hear and tally your errors. The starting tone is given for the first frame only. Goal: No more than five incorrect frames.

1   I VI^{-7} V^{-7} VI^{-7} IV^{7} II^{-7} V^{-7} I IV^{7} II^{-7} VII^{-7}_{d5} V^{-7}

2   VI^{-7} II^{-7} V^{-7} VI^{-7} IV^{7} I^{7} III^{-7} VI^{-7} II^{-7} V^{-7} I VII^{-7}_{d5}

3   I VII^{-7}_{d5} V^{-7} VI^{-7} IV^{7} I^{7} IV^{7} II^{-7} V^{-7} VI^{-7} VII^{-7}_{d5} I

4   III^{-7} IV II^{-7} VII^{-7}_{d5} V^{-7} VI^{-7} II^{-7} V^{-7} VII^{-7}_{d5} I^{7} VI^{-7} VII^{-7}_{d5}

5   I^{7} III^{-7} VI^{-7} II^{-7} V^{-7} I^{7} IV^{7} II^{-7} VII^{-7}_{d5} V^{-7} VII^{-7}_{d5} I

D8-4 Arpeggio singing from composite chord symbols

Sing the arpeggio in time with the metronome. Compare your response with the arpeggio you then hear and tally your errors. The starting tone is given for the first time only. Goal: No more than five incorrect frames.

1   I^{-} IV^{-7} II^{-7}_{d5} VII^{d7} I^{-} $^{-}VI^{7}$ IV^{-7} V^{-7} VII^{d7} I^{-} II^{-7}_{d5} V^{-7}

2   $^{-}VI^{7}$ IV^{-7} II^{-7}_{d5} VII^{d7} V^{-7} I^{-} $^{-}III^{7}$ $^{-}VI^{7}$ IV^{-7} VII^{d7} I^{-} IV^{-7}

3   II^{-7}_{d5} VII^{d7} I^{-} IV^{-7} VII^{d7} V^{-7} $^{-}VI^{7}$ IV^{-7} II^{-7}_{d5} V^{-7} I^{-} VII^{d7}

4   V^{-7} $^{-}VI^{7}$ IV^{-7} II^{-7}_{d5} VII^{d7} I^{-} II^{-7}_{d5} V^{-7} $^{-}VI^{7}$ IV^{-7} VII^{d7} V^{-7}

5   I^{-} $^{-}III^{7}$ $^{-}VI^{7}$ IV^{-7} II^{-7}_{d5} VII^{d7} I^{-} $^{-}VI^{7}$ IV^{-7} II^{-7}_{d5} VII^{d7} I^{-}

D8-5 Arpeggio singing from composite chord symbols

Sing the arpeggio in time with the metronome. Compare your response with the arpeggio you then hear and tally your errors. The starting tone is given for the first frame only. Goal: No more than five incorrect frames.

1 I V_{d5}^{-6} $V_{\_}^{4}$ V_{2}^{a4} I^{-6} $V_{\_}^{4}$ I VII_{d5}^{-7} VII_{5}^{6} I VII_{5}^{6} I^{-6}

2 IV II_{5}^{6} V^{-7} $VI_{\_}^{-7}$ II_{5}^{6} V^{-7} V_{2}^{a4} I^{-6} V_{4}^{6} $V_{\_}^{4}$ I VII_{d5}^{-7}

3 I VII_{5}^{6} I^{-6} II_{5}^{6} V^{-7} IV^{-6} II_{5}^{6} $II_{\_}^{-7}$ VII_{5}^{6} $V_{\_}^{4}$ I VII_{d5}^{-7}

4 V^{-7} I II_{5}^{6} V^{-7} $VI_{\_}^{-7}$ $II_{\_}^{-7}$ VII_{5}^{6} VII_{d5}^{-7} V_{d5}^{-6} I II_{5}^{6} V^{-7}

5 V_{2}^{a4} I^{-6} II_{5}^{6} V_{2}^{a4} I^{-6} $V_{\_}^{4}$ I II_{5}^{6} VII_{5}^{6} VII_{d5}^{-7} V_{d5}^{-6} I

D8-6 Arpeggio singing from composite chord symbols

Sing the arpeggio in time with the metronome. Compare your response with the arpeggio you then hear and tally your errors. The starting tone is given for the first frame only. Goal: No more than five incorrect frames. When you have done this lesson, take Test D8.

1 I^- $IV_{\_}^{-7}$ II_{5}^{6} V^{-7} I^- VII^{d7} II^{d7} I^- IV^- II_{5}^{6} IV^{d7} I_{4}^{-6}

2 V^{-7} $^-VI^{d7}$ V^{-7} V_{2}^{a4} I^6 $V_{\_}^{4}$ I^- II_{5}^{6} V^{-7} $^-VI^{d7}$ V^{-7} IV^6

3 II_{5}^{6} V^{-7} V_{2}^{a4} I^6 II^{d7} I^- VII^{d7} I^- IV^{-7} II_{d5}^{-7} II^{d7} I^-

4 $^-VI^7$ V^{-7} $^-VI^{d7}$ V^{-7} $^-VI^7$ II_{5}^{6} $II_{\_}^{-7}$ VII^{d7} I^- ^-VI II_{5}^{6} IV^{d7}

5 I^6 II^{d7} I^- II_{5}^{6} V^{-7} $^-VI^{d7}$ V^{-7} IV^6 IV^{-7} II_{5}^{6} V^{-7} I^-

Soprano and Bass Dictation with Harmonic Analysis

This series combines the skills of dictation and *aural harmonic analysis,* which includes the determination of key, identification of chords in a key, and identification of non-harmonic tones. The phrases in these lessons contain non-harmonic tones, triads and seventh chords, and modulations. Each phrase appears only once on the tape recording, but you may listen to each one as often as necessary by rewinding the tape. On Test D9 you will hear each phrase six times so you should attempt to complete each phrase in no more than six hearings.

For each phrase, you will find initial material followed by the answer, which is the complete phrase. You will need your own manuscript paper for these lessons. To do each frame, start by copying the initial material on your manuscript paper. Then listen to the phrase as many times as you need to write the soprano line, the bass line, the key, and the composite chord symbols, and to label the non-harmonic tones. You may find it useful to concentrate in successive hearings on the soprano line alone, the bass line alone, the composite chord symbols alone, and the non-harmonic tones alone. When you have completed your response for each phrase, compare it with the printed answer. Each lesson in the series should be done only once in preparation for Test D9. The test itself will serve to measure your achievement. Then if you wish to raise your test score, do each of the lessons once more and take the test again.

D9-1 Soprano and bass dictation with harmonic analysis

For each frame, copy the initial material on manuscript paper. Listen to the phrase several times. Write the soprano, the bass, the key, the composite chord symbols, and the non-harmonic tone labels. Do this lesson only once.

5

b   I⁻   I⁶ V⁴₋   I⁻   IV⁶   I⁶

b I^- I^6 V^4_- I^- IV^6 I^6

                        f♯ IV^6 I^{-6}_4 V^{-7} I^-

6

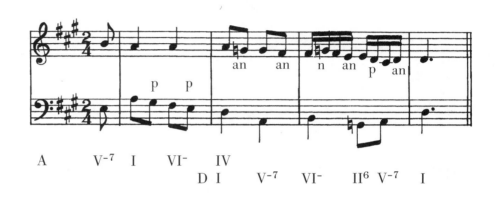

A V^{-7} I VI^- IV

                   D I V^{-7} VI^- II^6 V^{-7} I

7

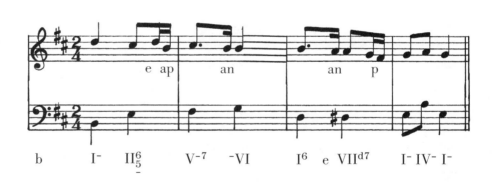

b I^- II^6_5 V^{-7} ^-VI I^6 e VII^{d7} I^- IV^- I^-

8

a I^- IV^- II^{d7} I^6 d V^{-6}_{d5} I^- II^6_5 V I^-

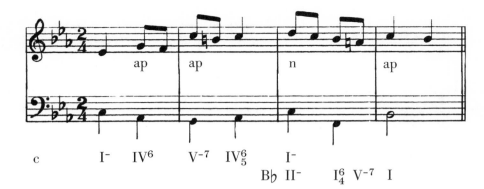

c   I⁻   IV⁶   V⁻⁷ IV$_5^6$ I⁻

B♭ II⁻   I$_4^6$ V⁻⁷   I

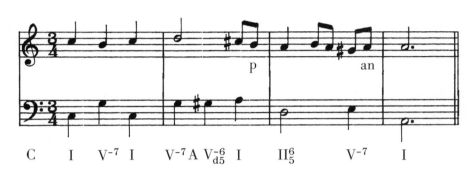

C   I   V⁻⁷ I   V⁻⁷ A V$_{d5}^{-6}$ I   II$_5^6$ V⁻⁷   I

e   I⁻   V⁻⁷   I⁻ f♯ VII^{d7} I⁻   IV⁶   II$_5^6$ V⁻⁷ I⁻

g   I⁻   V   I⁻ B♭ V   I IV V⁻⁷   I

F   I   VI^{-7} IV^7 II^{-7} I$^6_4$ V^{-7} I g VII^{d7} V^{-7} I$^-$

D   I^{-6} V$^4_-$ I   VII$^{-7}_{d5}$ V$^{-6}_{d5}$ I   III$^-$
                      E II$^-$ I$^6_4$ V^{-7} I

f♯   I$^-$ V^{-7} I$^-$ $^-$VI IV$^-$ e$^-$VI   I$^{-6}_4$ V^{-7} I$^-$ V

F   I III$^-$ IV   I V^{-7} VI$^-$ d I$^-$ V I$^{-6}_4$ V   I$^-$

D9-2 Soprano and bass dictation with harmonic analysis

For each frame, copy the initial material on manuscript paper. Listen to the phrase several times. Write the soprano, the bass, the key, the composite chord symbols, and the non-harmonic tone labels. When you have done this lesson once, take Test D9.

221

222

223

Transient Dominant and Transient Leading Tone Chords

The transient dominant and transient leading tone chords are *foreign chords*. A triad or seventh chord containing one or more tones that are not regular members of the prevailing key is said to be a foreign chord. A chord in which all tones are regular members of the prevailing key will be referred to as a regular chord.

A transient dominant chord is a foreign chord of the same type as a regular chord found on the fifth degree of the key—that is, a major triad or dominant seventh chord—but it is on some degree of the key other than the dominant. It precedes another chord in the key in a progression resembling that of an authentic or deceptive cadence and therefore appears to be a dominant of a new key. The chords that follow, however, make clear that there is no new key and that the music is continuing in the original key. A transient dominant chord can be seen in the example below, in which the A dominant seventh chord leads to the D minor triad in a progression that sounds and looks like an authentic cadence in the key of D minor. The prevailing key, however, is C major, and except for the one foreign chord, all the chords are in this key.

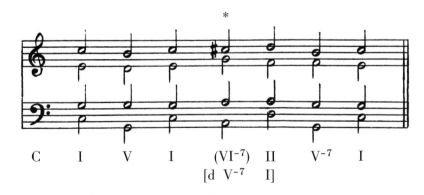

In the next examples, we see other transient dominants (marked with an *), each leading to another chord in a fashion typical of progressions involving dominant chords.

D   I   VI⁻   IV   (II$_{d5}^{-6}$)   V   I   F   I   IV   (II^{-7})   I^{-6} V^{-7} I

[A   V$_{d5}^{-6}$ I]   [C   V^{-7} IV^{-6}]

    Other commonly used names for the transient dominant chord are *secondary dominant, applied dominant,* and *dominant embellishment.*

    A transient leading tone chord is of the same type as a regular chord on the seventh degree of the key—that is, a diminished triad or half-diminished or diminished seventh chord—but is on some degree other than the leading tone of the key, and precedes another chord in the key in a progression resembling an authentic or deceptive cadence. A transient leading tone chord (marked with an *) can be seen in the example below, in which the F♯ seventh chord leads to the G major triad in a pattern like that of an authentic cadence in the key of G major.

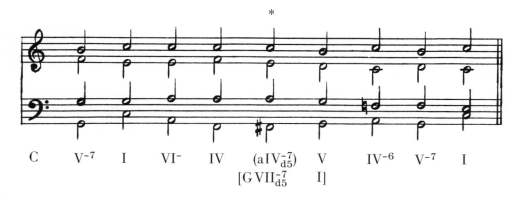

C   V^{-7} I   VI⁻   IV   (aIV$_{d5}^{-7}$)   V   IV^{-6} V^{-7} I

[G VII$_{d5}^{-7}$ I]

    In the following examples, we see other transient leading tone chords (each marked with an *) leading to other chords in a fashion typical of progressions involving leading tone chords.

B♭   I   IV   V   (aV^{d7})   VI⁻ IV   V   G   V^{-7} I   I^{-6} (aI^6)   II⁻ V^{-7} I

[g VII^{d7} I⁻]   [a VII$_-^6$ I⁻]

There are two types of lessons in this series: figured bass dictation and chord identification in a key; both involving series of chords. Instructions appear with each lesson. When you have done this series, take Test D10. The test does not include figured bass dictation. While your achievement in this skill is not tested, it will help you with chord identification in a key, which is tested.

Lesson D10-1a

Figured bass symbols are used to identify foreign chords just as they are used to identify regular chords in the key. It is essential that the figured bass symbols for foreign chords in figured bass dictation exercises be completely accurate, since there is no special symbol to indicate that the chords are indeed foreign. The only indication in these exercises that a foreign chord is present is that the figured bass symbol associated with a particular bass note is not the symbol for a regular chord in the key.

This is a lesson in figured bass dictation of foreign chords. The following instructions apply to all lessons of this type in this series and in series D11.

The purpose of these lessons is to develop your ability to write the bass notes and figured bass symbols for progressions involving foreign chords. A printed worksheet and a tape recording are provided for each lesson. The frames on the worksheet are separated by double bar lines. Each frame involves a series of five chords. At the beginning of the frame you will find as a starting reference the bass notes and figured bass symbols for the first two chords, followed by a blank space on the staff for your response. The answer appears at the end of the frame and consists of the bass notes and figured bass symbols for the last three chords. To do each frame, start by shielding the answer. When you have heard the series of chords, stop the tape and write the bass notes on the staff and the figured bass symbols below the staff for the last three chords. Then slide the shield to the right and compare your response to the printed answer. Circle each frame in which your answer is not entirely correct. Your goal is to complete each lesson with no more than eight incorrect frames. When you have done so, go on to the next lesson. If you have more than eight incorrect frames, repeat the lesson until you reach the goal or until you have done the lesson five times, at which point you should go on to the next lesson regardless of your score.

D10-1a

Figured bass dictation of foreign chords

(Copy 1)

Shield the answer. Listen to the series of five chords and write the bass notes and the figured bass symbols for the last three chords; then uncover the answer and compare your response. Goal: No more than eight incorrect frames.

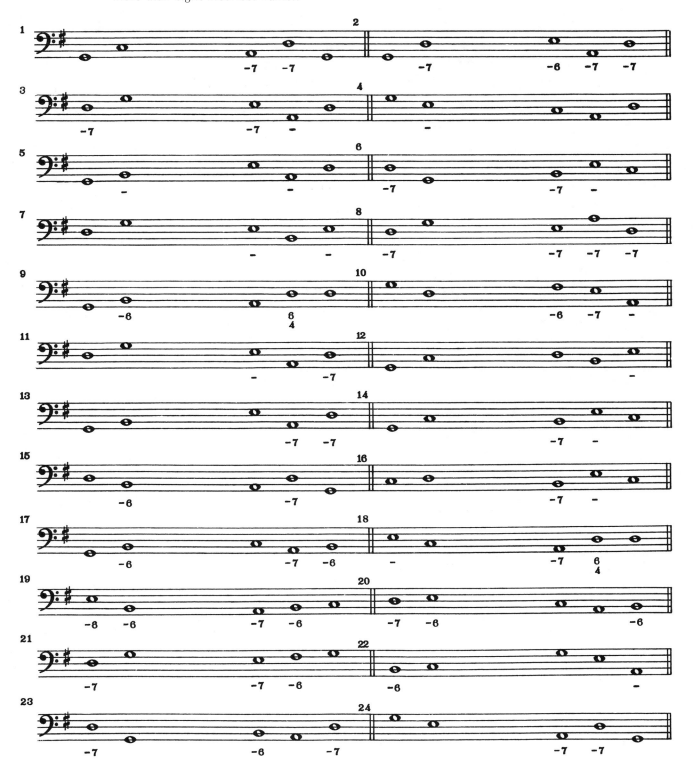

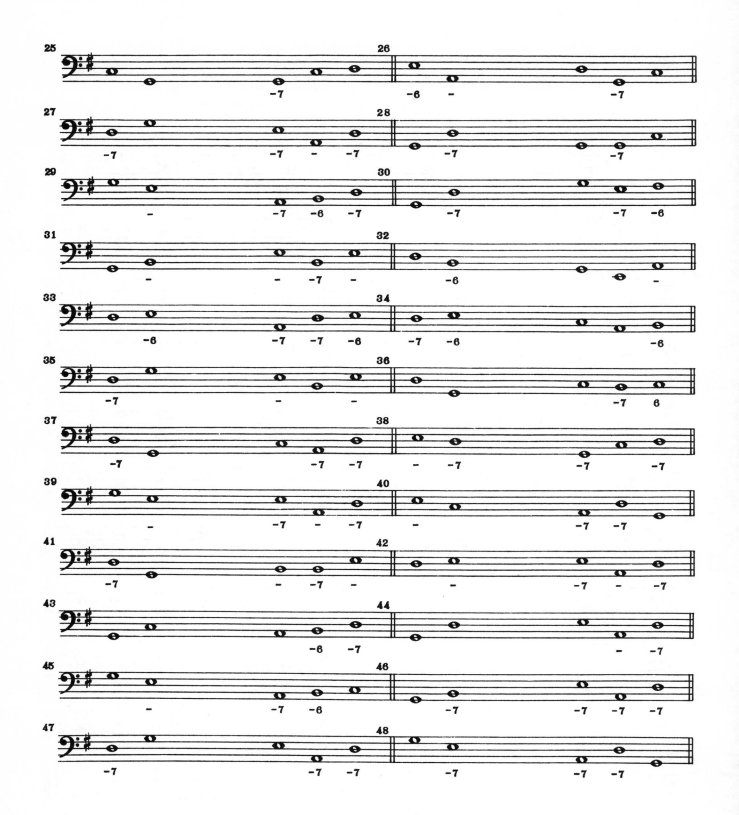

D10-1a

(Copy 2)

Figured bass dictation of foreign chords

Shield the answer. Listen to the series of five chords and write the bass notes and the figured bass symbols for the last three chords; then uncover the answer and compare your response. Goal: No more than eight incorrect frames.

231

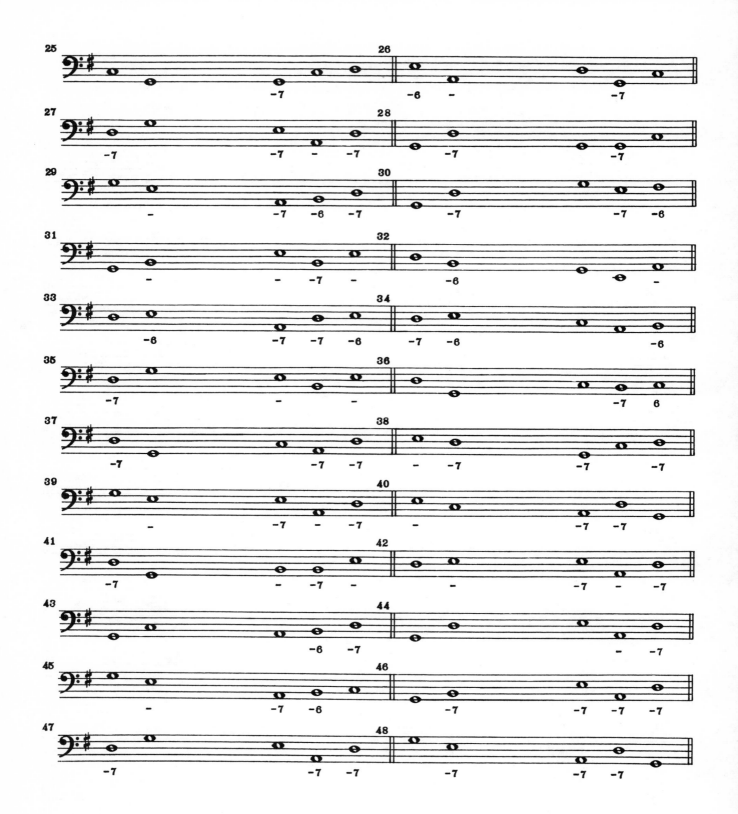

232

D10-1a

(Copy 3)

Figured bass dictation of foreign chords

Shield the answer. Listen to the series of five chords and write the bass notes and the figured bass symbols for the last three chords; then uncover the answer and compare your response. Goal: No more than eight incorrect frames.

233

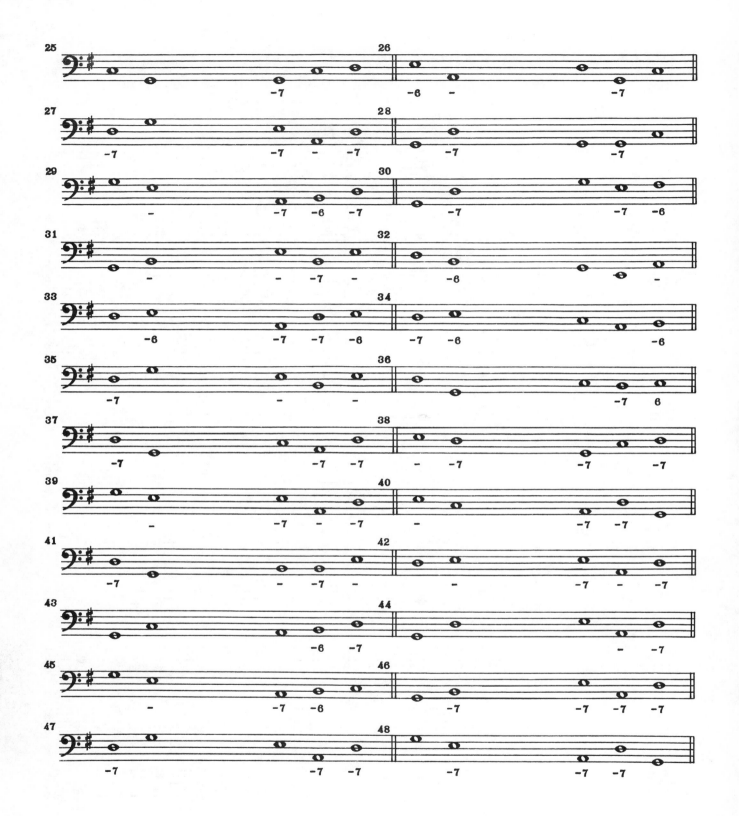

D10-1a
(Copy 4)

Figured bass dictation of foreign chords

Shield the answer. Listen to the series of five chords and write the bass notes and the figured bass symbols for the last three chords; then uncover the answer and compare your response. Goal: No more than eight incorrect frames.

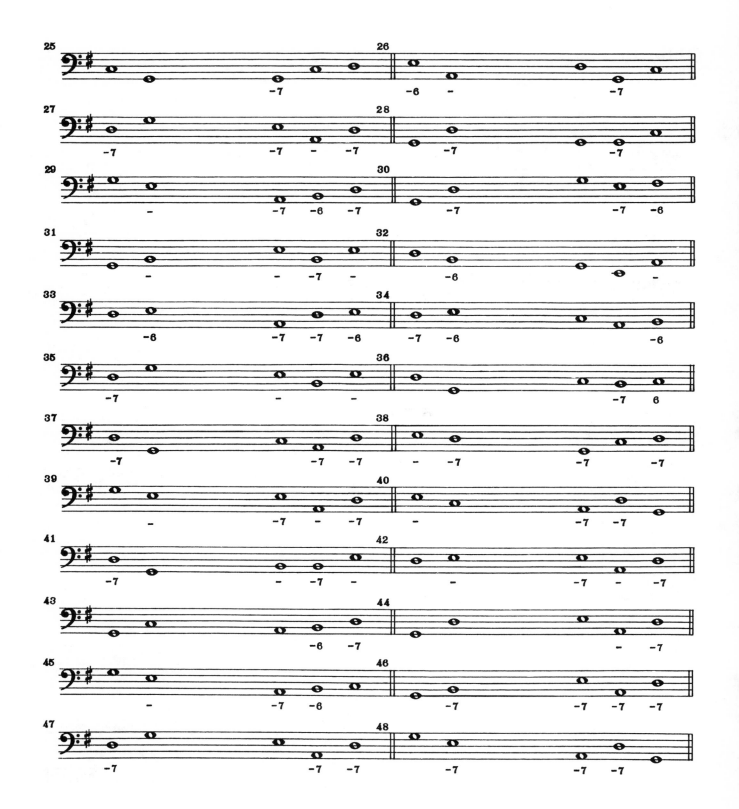

D10-1a

(Copy 5)

Figured bass dictation of foreign chords

Shield the answer. Listen to the series of five chords and write the bass notes and the figured bass symbols for the last three chords; then uncover the answer and compare your response. Goal: No more than eight incorrect frames.

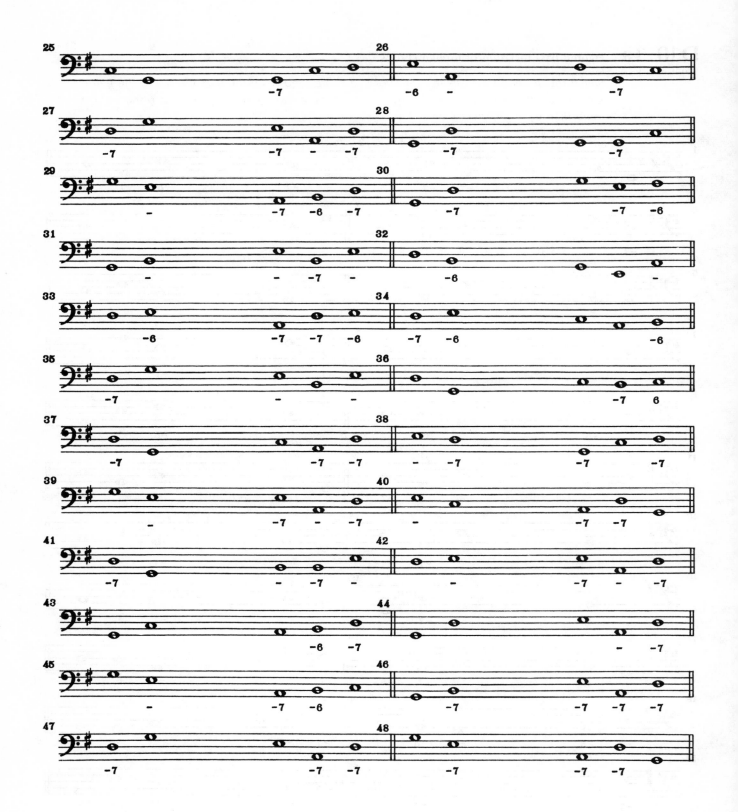

Lesson **D10–1b**

This lesson introduces the composite chord symbols for transient dominant chords in root position in a major key.

The composite chord symbol for all types of foreign chords includes parentheses. The symbols within the parentheses—the key location symbol and figured bass symbol—are treated in the same manner as for a regular chord in a key. The parentheses indicate that the symbol stands for a foreign chord.

Since the transient dominant chord and the transient leading tone chord are special kinds of foreign chords, it is useful to distinguish them from other kinds of foreign chords. We do this by adding an underline to the symbol, for example, $(\underline{\text{II}^{-7}})$.

The following composite chord symbols are introduced in this lesson: $(\underline{\text{II}})$, $(\underline{\text{III}})$, $(\underline{\text{VI}})$, $(\underline{\text{I}^{-7}})$, $(\underline{\text{II}^{-7}})$, $(\underline{\text{III}^{-7}})$, and $(\underline{\text{VI}^{-7}})$. These are symbols for transient dominant chords in root position. Of these chords, those with the blank figured bass symbol are major triads in root position, and those with the figured bass symbol of $^{-7}$ are dominant seventh chords in root position. Since the root is in the bass for these chords, the second degree of the key will be in the bass for the $(\underline{\text{II}})$ chord, the third degree of the key will be in the bass for the $(\underline{\text{III}})$, and so forth.

This is a lesson in identification of foreign chords. The following instructions apply to all lessons of this type in this series and in series D11.

The purpose of these lessons is to develop your ability to identify chords in progressions involving foreign chords. A printed worksheet and a tape recording are provided for each lesson. Each frame involves a series of five chords. On the worksheet, the frame contains the composite chord symbols for the first two chords, three blanks for your response, and then the correct answer. To do each frame, start by shielding the answer at the end of the frame. When you have heard the group of five chords, stop the tape and write the composite chord symbols for the last three chords in the answer blanks. Then slide the shield to the right and compare your response with the printed answer. Circle each frame in which you have identified one or more chords incorrectly. Your goal is to complete each lesson with no more than eight incorrect frames. When you have done so, go on to the next lesson. If you have more than eight incorrect frames, repeat the lesson until you reach the goal or until you have done the lesson five times, at which point you should go on to the next lesson regardless of your score.

Identification of foreign chords

Shield the answer. Listen to the group of five chords and write the composite chord symbols for the last three chords; then uncover the answer and compare your response. Goal: No more than eight incorrect frames.

1 I IV ____ ____ ____ $(\underline{\text{II}}^{-7})$ V^{-7} I

2 I V^{-7} ____ ____ ____ IV^{-6} $(\underline{\text{II}}^{-7})$ V^{-7}

3 V^{-7} I ____ ____ ____ $(\underline{\text{VI}}^{-7})$ II^{-} V

4 I VI^{-} ____ ____ ____ IV $(\underline{\text{II}})$ V

5 I III^{-} ____ ____ ____ $(\underline{\text{VI}})$ II^{-} V

6 V^{-7} I ____ ____ ____ $(\underline{\text{III}}^{-7})$ VI^{-} IV

7 V I ____ ____ ____ VI^{-} $(\underline{\text{III}})$ VI^{-}

8 V^{-7} I ____ ____ ____ $(\underline{\text{VI}}^{-7})$ $(\underline{\text{II}}^{-7})$ V^{-7}

9 I I^{-6} ____ ____ ____ $(\underline{\text{II}})$ I$_4^6$ V

10 I V ____ ____ ____ V^{-6} $(\underline{\text{VI}}^{-7})$ II^{-}

11 V I ____ ____ ____ VI^{-} $(\underline{\text{II}})$ V^{-7}

12 I IV ____ ____ ____ V $(\underline{\text{III}})$ VI^{-}

13 I $(\underline{\text{III}})$ ____ ____ ____ $(\underline{\text{VI}})$ $(\underline{\text{II}}^{-7})$ V^{-7}

14 I IV ____ ____ ____ $(\underline{\text{III}}^{-7})$ VI^{-} IV

15 V I^{-6} ____ ____ ____ $(\underline{\text{II}})$ V^{-7} I

16 IV V ____ ____ ____ $(\underline{\text{III}}^{-7})$ VI^{-} IV

17 I I^{-6} ____ ____ ____ IV $(\underline{\text{II}}^{-7})$ I^{-6}

18 VI^{-} IV ____ ____ ____ $(\underline{\text{II}}^{-7})$ I$_4^6$ V

19 IV^{-6} I^{-6} ____ ____ ____ $(\underline{\text{II}}^{-7})$ I^{-6} IV

20 V^{-7} IV^{-6} ____ ____ ____ IV $(\underline{\text{II}})$ I^{-6}

21 V^{-7} I ____ ____ ____ $(\underline{\text{VI}}^{-7})$ V^{-6} I

22 I^{-6} IV ____ ____ ____ I $(\underline{\text{VI}})$ II^{-}

23 V^{-7} I ____ ____ ____ I^{-6} $(\underline{\text{II}})$ V^{-7}

24 I $(\underline{\text{VI}})$ ____ ____ ____ $(\underline{\text{II}}^{-7})$ V^{-7} I

25 IV I ____ ____ ____ $(\underline{\text{I}}^{-7})$ IV V

26 IV^{-6} II^{-} ____ ____ ____ V $(\underline{\text{I}}^{-7})$ IV

27 V^{-7} I ____ ____ ____ $(\underline{\text{VI}}^{-7})$ II^{-} V^{-7}

28 I V^{-7} ____ ____ ____ I $(\underline{\text{I}}^{-7})$ IV

29 I VI^{-} ____ ____ ____ $(\underline{\text{II}}^{-7})$ I^{-6} V^{-7}

30 I V^{-7} ____ ____ ____ I $(\underline{\text{VI}}^{-7})$ V^{-6}

31 I III^{-} ____ ____ ____ VI^{-} $(\underline{\text{III}}^{-7})$ VI^{-}

32 V I^{-6} ____ ____ ____ I $(\underline{\text{VI}})$ II^{-}

33 V IV^{-6} ____ ____ ____ $(\underline{\text{II}}^{-7})$ V^{-7} IV^{-6}

34 V^{-7} IV^{-6} ____ ____ ____ IV $(\underline{\text{II}})$ I^{-6}

35 V^{-7} I ____ ____ ____ VI^{-} $(\underline{\text{III}})$ VI^{-}

36 V I ____ ____ ____ IV $(\underline{\text{III}}^{-7})$ II^6

37 V^{-7} I ____ ____ ____ IV $(\underline{\text{II}}^{-7})$ V^{-7}

38 VI^{-} V^{-7} ____ ____ ____ $(\underline{\text{I}}^{-7})$ IV V^{-7}

39 I VI^{-} ____ ____ ____ $(\underline{\text{VI}}^{-7})$ II^{-} V^{-7}

40 VI^{-} IV ____ ____ ____ $(\underline{\text{II}}^{-7})$ V^{-7} I

41 V^{-7} I ____ ____ ____ III^{-} $(\underline{\text{III}}^{-7})$ VI^{-}

42 V VI^{-} ____ ____ ____ $(\underline{\text{VI}}^{-7})$ II^{-} V^{-7}

43 I IV ____ ____ ____ $(\underline{\text{II}})$ I^{-6} V^{-7}

44 I V ____ ____ ____ $(\underline{\text{VI}})$ II^{-} V^{-7}

45 I VI^{-} ____ ____ ____ $(\underline{\text{II}}^{-7})$ I^{-6} IV

46 I $(\underline{\text{III}}^{-7})$ ____ ____ ____ $(\underline{\text{VI}}^{-7})$ $(\underline{\text{II}}^{-7})$ V^{-7}

47 V^{-7} I ____ ____ ____ $(\underline{\text{VI}})$ $(\underline{\text{II}}^{-7})$ V^{-7}

48 I $(\underline{\text{VI}}^{-7})$ ____ ____ ____ $(\underline{\text{II}}^{-7})$ V^{-7} I

D10-1b Identification of foreign chords

Shield the answer. Listen to the group of five chords and write the composite chord symbols for the last three chords; then uncover the answer and compare your response. Goal: No more than eight incorrect frames.

1 I IV _____ _____ _____ ($\underline{II}^{-7}$) V^{-7} I

2 I V^{-7} _____ _____ _____ IV^{-6} ($\underline{II}^{-7}$) V^{-7}

3 V^{-7} I _____ _____ _____ ($\underline{VI}^{-7}$) II^- V

4 I VI^- _____ _____ _____ IV ($\underline{II}$) V

5 I III^- _____ _____ _____ ($\underline{VI}$) II^- V

6 V^{-7} I _____ _____ _____ ($\underline{III}^{-7}$) VI^- IV

7 V I _____ _____ _____ VI^- ($\underline{III}$) VI^-

8 V^{-7} I _____ _____ _____ ($\underline{VI}^{-7}$) ($\underline{II}^{-7}$) V^{-7}

9 I I^{-6} _____ _____ _____ ($\underline{II}$) I_4^6 V

10 I V _____ _____ _____ V^{-6} ($\underline{VI}^{-7}$) II^-

11 V I _____ _____ _____ VI^- ($\underline{II}$) V^{-7}

12 I IV _____ _____ _____ V ($\underline{III}$) VI^-

13 I ($\underline{III}$) _____ _____ _____ ($\underline{VI}$) ($\underline{II}^{-7}$) V^{-7}

14 I IV _____ _____ _____ ($\underline{III}^{-7}$) VI^- IV

15 V I^{-6} _____ _____ _____ ($\underline{II}$) V^{-7} I

16 IV V _____ _____ _____ ($\underline{III}^{-7}$) VI^- IV

17 I I^{-6} _____ _____ _____ IV ($\underline{II}^{-7}$) I^{-6}

18 VI^- IV _____ _____ _____ ($\underline{II}^{-7}$) I_4^6 V

19 IV^{-6} I^{-6} _____ _____ _____ ($\underline{II}^{-7}$) I^{-6} IV

20 V^{-7} IV^{-6} _____ _____ _____ IV ($\underline{II}$) I^{-6}

21 V^{-7} I _____ _____ _____ ($\underline{VI}^{-7}$) V^{-6} I

22 I^{-6} IV _____ _____ _____ I ($\underline{VI}$) II^-

23 V^{-7} I _____ _____ _____ I^{-6} ($\underline{II}$) V^{-7}

24 I ($\underline{VI}$) _____ _____ _____ ($\underline{II}^{-7}$) V^{-7} I

25 IV I _____ _____ _____ ($\underline{I}^{-7}$) IV V

26 IV^{-6} II^- _____ _____ _____ V ($\underline{I}^{-7}$) IV

27 V^{-7} I _____ _____ _____ ($\underline{VI}^{-7}$) II^- V^{-7}

28 I V^{-7} _____ _____ _____ I ($\underline{I}^{-7}$) IV

29 I VI^- _____ _____ _____ ($\underline{II}^{-7}$) I^{-6} V^{-7}

30 I V^{-7} _____ _____ _____ I ($\underline{VI}^{-7}$) V^{-6}

31 I III^- _____ _____ _____ VI^- ($\underline{III}^{-7}$) VI^-

32 V I^{-6} _____ _____ _____ I ($\underline{VI}$) II^-

33 V IV^{-6} _____ _____ _____ ($\underline{II}^{-7}$) V^{-7} IV^{-6}

34 V^{-7} IV^{-6} _____ _____ _____ IV ($\underline{II}$) I^{-6}

35 V^{-7} I _____ _____ _____ VI^- ($\underline{III}$) VI^-

36 V I _____ _____ _____ IV ($\underline{III}^{-7}$) II^6

37 V^{-7} I _____ _____ _____ IV ($\underline{II}^{-7}$) V^{-7}

38 VI^- V^{-7} _____ _____ _____ ($\underline{I}^{-7}$) IV V^{-7}

39 I VI^- _____ _____ _____ ($\underline{VI}^{-7}$) II^- V^{-7}

40 VI^- IV _____ _____ _____ ($\underline{II}^{-7}$) V^{-7} I

41 V^{-7} I _____ _____ _____ III^- ($\underline{III}^{-7}$) VI^-

42 V VI^- _____ _____ _____ ($\underline{VI}^{-7}$) II^- V^{-7}

43 I IV _____ _____ _____ ($\underline{II}$) I^{-6} V^{-7}

44 I V _____ _____ _____ ($\underline{VI}$) II^- V^{-7}

45 I VI^- _____ _____ _____ ($\underline{II}^{-7}$) I^{-6} IV

46 I ($\underline{III}^{-7}$) _____ _____ _____ ($\underline{VI}^{-7}$) ($\underline{II}^{-7}$) V^{-7}

47 V^{-7} I ____ ____ ____ ($\underline{VI}$) ($\underline{II}^{-7}$) V^{-7}

48 I ($\underline{VI}^{-7}$) _____ _____ _____ ($\underline{II}^{-7}$) V^{-7} I

D10-1b
(Copy 3)   **Identification of foreign chords**

Shield the answer. Listen to the group of five chords and write the composite chord symbols for the last three chords; then uncover the answer and compare your response. Goal: No more than eight incorrect frames.

1 I IV ___ ___ ___ (II⁻⁷) V⁻⁷ I   25 IV I ___ ___ ___ (I⁻⁷) IV V

2 I V⁻⁷ ___ ___ ___ IV⁻⁶ (II⁻⁷) V⁻⁷   26 IV⁻⁶ II⁻ ___ ___ ___ V (I⁻⁷) IV

3 V⁻⁷ I ___ ___ ___ (VI⁻⁷) II⁻ V   27 V⁻⁷ I ___ ___ ___ (VI⁻⁷) II⁻ V⁻⁷

4 I VI⁻ ___ ___ ___ IV (II) V   28 I V⁻⁷ ___ ___ ___ I (I⁻⁷) IV

5 I III⁻ ___ ___ ___ (VI) II⁻ V   29 I VI⁻ ___ ___ ___ (II⁻⁷) I⁻⁶ V⁻⁷

6 V⁻⁷ I ___ ___ ___ (III⁻⁷) VI⁻ IV   30 I V⁻⁷ ___ ___ ___ I (VI⁻⁷) V⁻⁶

7 V I ___ ___ ___ VI⁻ (III) VI⁻   31 I III⁻ ___ ___ ___ VI⁻ (III⁻⁷) VI⁻

8 V⁻⁷ I ___ ___ ___ (VI⁻⁷) (II⁻⁷) V⁻⁷   32 V I⁻⁶ ___ ___ ___ I (VI) II⁻

9 I I⁻⁶ ___ ___ ___ (II) I⁶₄ V   33 V IV⁻⁶ ___ ___ ___ (II⁻⁷) V⁻⁷ IV⁻⁶

10 I V ___ ___ ___ V⁻⁶ (VI⁻⁷) II⁻   34 V⁻⁷ IV⁻⁶ ___ ___ ___ IV (II) I⁻⁶

11 V I ___ ___ ___ VI⁻ (II) V⁻⁷   35 V⁻⁷ I ___ ___ ___ VI⁻ (III) VI⁻

12 I IV ___ ___ ___ V (III) VI⁻   36 V I ___ ___ ___ IV (III⁻⁷) II⁶

13 I (III) ___ ___ ___ (VI) (II⁻⁷) V⁻⁷   37 V⁻⁷ I ___ ___ ___ IV (II⁻⁷) V⁻⁷

14 I IV ___ ___ ___ (III⁻⁷) VI⁻ IV   38 VI⁻ V⁻⁷ ___ ___ ___ (I⁻⁷) IV V⁻⁷

15 V I⁻⁶ ___ ___ ___ (II) V⁻⁷ I   39 I VI⁻ ___ ___ ___ (VI⁻⁷) II⁻ V⁻⁷

16 IV V ___ ___ ___ (III⁻⁷) VI⁻ IV   40 VI⁻ IV ___ ___ ___ (II⁻⁷) V⁻⁷ I

17 I I⁻⁶ ___ ___ ___ IV (II⁻⁷) I⁻⁶   41 V⁻⁷ I ___ ___ ___ III⁻ (III⁻⁷) VI⁻

18 VI⁻ IV ___ ___ ___ (II⁻⁷) I⁶₄ V   42 V VI⁻ ___ ___ ___ (VI⁻⁷) II⁻ V⁻⁷

19 IV⁻⁶ I⁻⁶ ___ ___ ___ (II⁻⁷) I⁻⁶ IV   43 I IV ___ ___ ___ (II) I⁻⁶ V⁻⁷

20 V⁻⁷ IV⁻⁶ ___ ___ ___ IV (II) I⁻⁶   44 I V ___ ___ ___ (VI) II⁻ V⁻⁷

21 V⁻⁷ I ___ ___ ___ (VI⁻⁷) V⁻⁶ I   45 I VI⁻ ___ ___ ___ (II⁻⁷) I⁻⁶ IV

22 I⁻⁶ IV ___ ___ ___ I (VI) II⁻   46 I (III⁻⁷) ___ ___ ___ (VI⁻⁷) (II⁻⁷) V⁻⁷

23 V⁻⁷ I ___ ___ ___ I⁻⁶ (II) V⁻⁷   47 V⁻⁷ I ___ ___ ___ (VI) (II⁻⁷) V⁻⁷

24 I (VI) ___ ___ ___ (II⁻⁷) V⁻⁷ I   48 I (VI⁻⁷) ___ ___ ___ (II⁻⁷) V⁻⁷ I

D10-1b (Copy 4) Identification of foreign chords

Shield the answer. Listen to the group of five chords and write the composite chord symbols for the last three chords; then uncover the answer and compare your response. Goal: No more than eight incorrect frames.

1 I IV _____ _____ _____ ($\underline{\text{II}^{-7}}$) V^{-7} I

2 I V^{-7} _____ _____ _____ IV^{-6} ($\underline{\text{II}^{-7}}$) V^{-7}

3 V^{-7} I _____ _____ _____ ($\underline{\text{VI}^{-7}}$) II$^-$ V

4 I VI$^-$ _____ _____ _____ IV ($\underline{\text{II}}$) V

5 I III$^-$ _____ _____ _____ ($\underline{\text{VI}}$) II$^-$ V

6 V^{-7} I _____ _____ _____ ($\underline{\text{III}^{-7}}$) VI$^-$ IV

7 V I _____ _____ _____ VI$^-$ ($\underline{\text{III}}$) VI$^-$

8 V^{-7} I _____ _____ _____ ($\underline{\text{VI}^{-7}}$) ($\underline{\text{II}^{-7}}$) V^{-7}

9 I I^{-6} _____ _____ _____ ($\underline{\text{II}}$) I$^6_4$ V

10 I V _____ _____ _____ V^{-6} ($\underline{\text{VI}^{-7}}$) II$^-$

11 V I _____ _____ _____ VI$^-$ ($\underline{\text{II}}$) V^{-7}

12 I IV _____ _____ _____ V ($\underline{\text{III}}$) VI$^-$

13 I ($\underline{\text{III}}$) _____ _____ _____ ($\underline{\text{VI}}$) ($\underline{\text{II}^{-7}}$) V^{-7}

14 I IV _____ _____ _____ ($\underline{\text{III}^{-7}}$) VI$^-$ IV

15 V I^{-6} _____ _____ _____ ($\underline{\text{II}}$) V^{-7} I

16 IV V _____ _____ _____ ($\underline{\text{III}^{-7}}$) VI$^-$ IV

17 I I^{-6} _____ _____ _____ IV ($\underline{\text{II}^{-7}}$) I^{-6}

18 VI$^-$ IV _____ _____ _____ ($\underline{\text{II}^{-7}}$) I$^6_4$ V

19 IV^{-6} I^{-6} _____ _____ _____ ($\underline{\text{II}^{-7}}$) I^{-6} IV

20 V^{-7} IV^{-6} _____ _____ _____ IV ($\underline{\text{II}}$) I^{-6}

21 V^{-7} I _____ _____ _____ ($\underline{\text{VI}^{-7}}$) V^{-6} I

22 I^{-6} IV _____ _____ _____ I ($\underline{\text{VI}}$) II$^-$

23 V^{-7} I _____ _____ _____ I^{-6} ($\underline{\text{II}}$) V^{-7}

24 I ($\underline{\text{VI}}$) _____ _____ _____ ($\underline{\text{II}^{-7}}$) V^{-7} I

25 IV I _____ _____ _____ ($\underline{\text{I}^{-7}}$) IV V

26 IV^{-6} II$^-$ _____ _____ _____ V ($\underline{\text{I}^{-7}}$) IV

27 V^{-7} I _____ _____ _____ ($\underline{\text{VI}^{-7}}$) II$^-$ V^{-7}

28 I V^{-7} _____ _____ _____ I ($\underline{\text{I}^{-7}}$) IV

29 I VI$^-$ _____ _____ _____ ($\underline{\text{II}^{-7}}$) I^{-6} V^{-7}

30 I V^{-7} _____ _____ _____ I ($\underline{\text{VI}^{-7}}$) V^{-6}

31 I III$^-$ _____ _____ _____ VI$^-$ ($\underline{\text{III}^{-7}}$) VI$^-$

32 V I^{-6} _____ _____ _____ I ($\underline{\text{VI}}$) II$^-$

33 V IV^{-6} _____ _____ _____ ($\underline{\text{II}^{-7}}$) V^{-7} IV^{-6}

34 V^{-7} IV^{-6} _____ _____ _____ IV ($\underline{\text{II}}$) I^{-6}

35 V^{-7} I _____ _____ _____ VI$^-$ ($\underline{\text{III}}$) VI$^-$

36 V I _____ _____ _____ IV ($\underline{\text{III}^{-7}}$) II^6

37 V^{-7} I _____ _____ _____ IV ($\underline{\text{II}^{-7}}$) V^{-7}

38 VI$^-$ V^{-7} _____ _____ _____ ($\underline{\text{I}^{-7}}$) IV V^{-7}

39 I VI$^-$ _____ _____ _____ ($\underline{\text{VI}^{-7}}$) II$^-$ V^{-7}

40 VI$^-$ IV _____ _____ _____ ($\underline{\text{II}^{-7}}$) V^{-7} I

41 V^{-7} I _____ _____ _____ III$^-$ ($\underline{\text{III}^{-7}}$) VI$^-$

42 V VI$^-$ _____ _____ _____ ($\underline{\text{VI}^{-7}}$) II$^-$ V^{-7}

43 I IV _____ _____ _____ ($\underline{\text{II}}$) I^{-6} V^{-7}

44 I V _____ _____ _____ ($\underline{\text{VI}}$) II$^-$ V^{-7}

45 I VI$^-$ _____ _____ _____ ($\underline{\text{II}^{-7}}$) I^{-6} IV

46 I ($\underline{\text{III}^{-7}}$) _____ _____ _____ ($\underline{\text{VI}^{-7}}$) ($\underline{\text{II}^{-7}}$) V^{-7}

47 V^{-7} I _____ _____ _____ ($\underline{\text{VI}}$) ($\underline{\text{II}^{-7}}$) V^{-7}

48 I ($\underline{\text{VI}^{-7}}$) _____ _____ _____ ($\underline{\text{II}^{-7}}$) V^{-7} I

D10-1b   Identification of foreign chords
(Copy 5)

Shield the answer. Listen to the group of five chords and write the composite chord symbols for the last three chords; then uncover the answer and compare your response. Goal: No more than eight incorrect frames.

1   I IV _____ _____ _____ ($\underline{II}^{-7}$) V^{-7} I

2   I V^{-7} _____ _____ _____ IV^{-6} ($\underline{II}^{-7}$) V^{-7}

3   V^{-7} I _____ _____ _____ ($\underline{VI}^{-7}$) II^- V

4   I VI^- _____ _____ _____ IV ($\underline{II}$) V

5   I III^- _____ _____ _____ ($\underline{VI}$) II^- V

6   V^{-7} I _____ _____ _____ ($\underline{III}^{-7}$) VI^- IV

7   V I _____ _____ _____ VI^- ($\underline{III}$) VI^-

8   V^{-7} I _____ _____ _____ ($\underline{VI}^{-7}$) ($\underline{II}^{-7}$) V^{-7}

9   I I^{-6} _____ _____ _____ ($\underline{II}$) I_4^6 V

10   I V _____ _____ _____ V^{-6} ($\underline{VI}^{-7}$) II^-

11   V I _____ _____ _____ VI^- ($\underline{II}$) V^{-7}

12   I IV _____ _____ _____ V ($\underline{III}$) VI^-

13   I ($\underline{III}$) _____ _____ _____ ($\underline{VI}$) ($\underline{II}^{-7}$) V^{-7}

14   I IV _____ _____ _____ ($\underline{III}^{-7}$) VI^- IV

15   V I^{-6} _____ _____ _____ ($\underline{II}$) V^{-7} I

16   IV V _____ _____ _____ ($\underline{III}^{-7}$) VI^- IV

17   I I^{-6} _____ _____ _____ IV ($\underline{II}^{-7}$) I^{-6}

18   VI^- IV _____ _____ _____ ($\underline{II}^{-7}$) I_4^6 V

19   IV^{-6} I^{-6} _____ _____ _____ ($\underline{II}^{-7}$) I^{-6} IV

20   V^{-7} IV^{-6} _____ _____ _____ IV ($\underline{II}$) I^{-6}

21   V^{-7} I _____ _____ _____ ($\underline{VI}^{-7}$) V^{-6} I

22   I^{-6} IV _____ _____ _____ I ($\underline{VI}$) II^-

23   V^{-7} I _____ _____ _____ I^{-6} ($\underline{II}$) V^{-7}

24   I ($\underline{VI}$) _____ _____ _____ ($\underline{II}^{-7}$) V^{-7} I

25   IV I _____ _____ _____ ($\underline{I}^{-7}$) IV V

26   IV^{-6} II^- _____ _____ _____ V ($\underline{I}^{-7}$) IV

27   V^{-7} I _____ _____ _____ ($\underline{VI}^{-7}$) II^- V^{-7}

28   I V^{-7} _____ _____ _____ I ($\underline{I}^{-7}$) IV

29   I VI^- _____ _____ _____ ($\underline{II}^{-7}$) I^{-6} V^{-7}

30   I V^{-7} _____ _____ _____ I ($\underline{VI}^{-7}$) V^{-6}

31   I III^- _____ _____ _____ VI^- ($\underline{III}^{-7}$) VI^-

32   V I^{-6} _____ _____ _____ I ($\underline{VI}$) II^-

33   V IV^{-6} _____ _____ _____ ($\underline{II}^{-7}$) V^{-7} IV^{-6}

34   V^{-7} IV^{-6} _____ _____ _____ IV ($\underline{II}$) I^{-6}

35   V^{-7} I _____ _____ _____ VI^- ($\underline{III}$) VI^-

36   V I _____ _____ _____ IV ($\underline{III}^{-7}$) II^6

37   V^{-7} I _____ _____ _____ IV ($\underline{II}^{-7}$) V^{-7}

38   VI^- V^{-7} _____ _____ _____ ($\underline{I}^{-7}$) IV V^{-7}

39   I VI^- _____ _____ _____ ($\underline{VI}^{-7}$) II^- V^{-7}

40   VI^- IV _____ _____ _____ ($\underline{II}^{-7}$) V^{-7} I

41   V^{-7} I _____ _____ _____ III^- ($\underline{III}^{-7}$) VI^-

42   V VI^- _____ _____ _____ ($\underline{VI}^{-7}$) II^- V^{-7}

43   I IV _____ _____ _____ ($\underline{II}$) I^{-6} V^{-7}

44   I V _____ _____ _____ ($\underline{VI}$) II^- V^{-7}

45   I VI^- _____ _____ _____ ($\underline{II}^{-7}$) I^{-6} IV

46   I ($\underline{III}^{-7}$) _____ _____ _____ ($\underline{VI}^{-7}$) ($\underline{II}^{-7}$) V^{-7}

47   V^{-7} I _____ _____ _____ ($\underline{VI}$) ($\underline{II}^{-7}$) V^{-7}

48   I ($\underline{VI}^{-7}$) _____ _____ _____ ($\underline{II}^{-7}$) V^{-7} I

D10-2a
(Copy 1)

Figured bass dictation of foreign chords

Shield the answer. Listen to the series of five chords and write the bass notes and the figured bass symbols for the last three chords; then uncover the answer and compare your response. Goal: No more than eight incorrect frames.

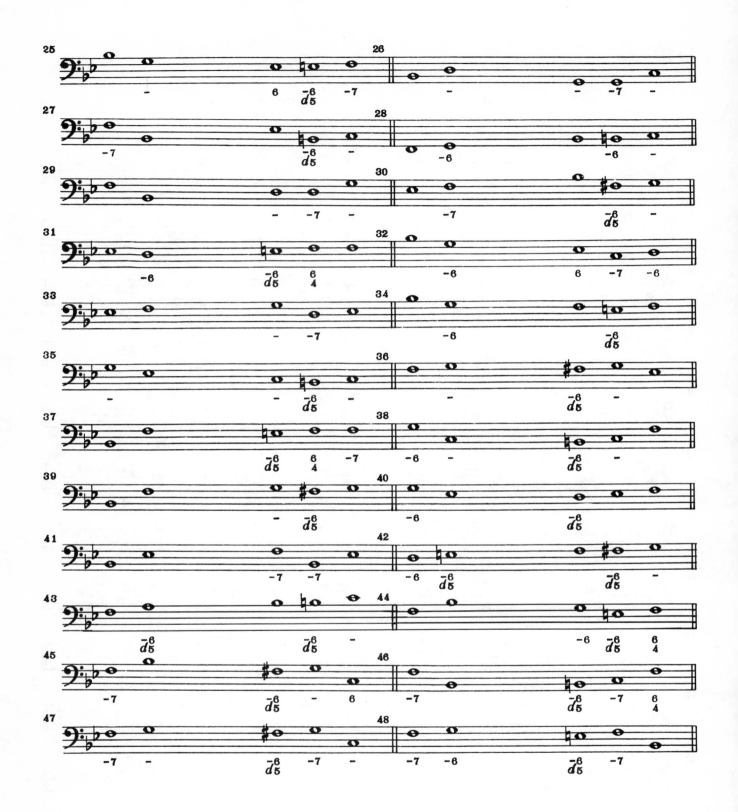

D10-2a
(Copy 2)

Figured bass dictation of foreign chords

Shield the answer. Listen to the series of five chords and write the bass notes and the figured bass symbols for the last three chords; then uncover the answer and compare your response. Goal: No more than eight incorrect frames.

247

D10-2a

(Copy 3)

Figured bass dictation of foreign chords

Shield the answer. Listen to the series of five chords and write the bass notes and the figured bass symbols for the last three chords; then uncover the answer and compare your response. Goal: No more than eight incorrect frames.

249

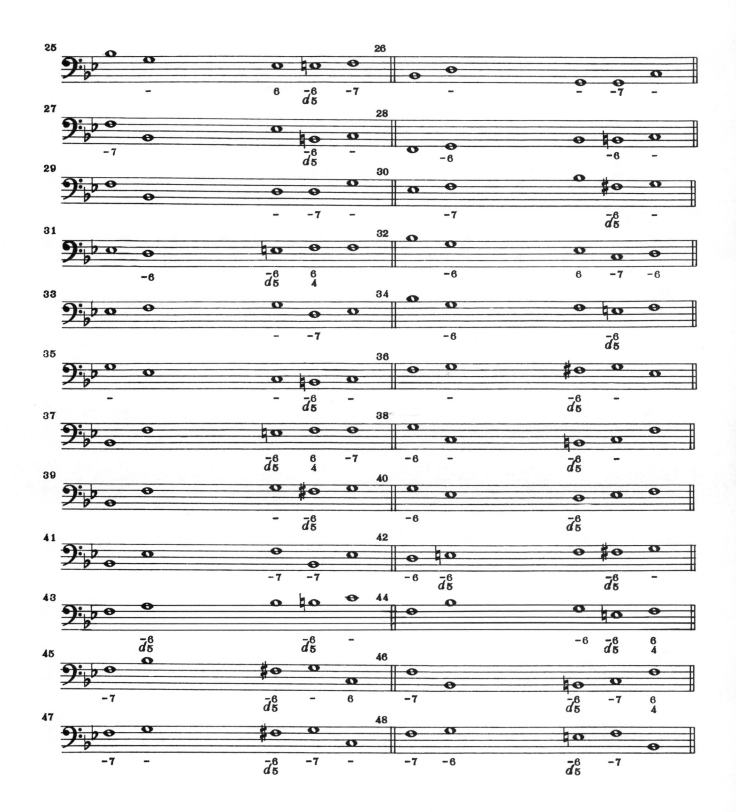

D10-2a

Figured bass dictation of foreign chords

(Copy 4)

Shield the answer. Listen to the series of five chords and write the bass notes and the figured bass symbols for the last three chords; then uncover the answer and compare your response. Goal: No more than eight incorrect frames.

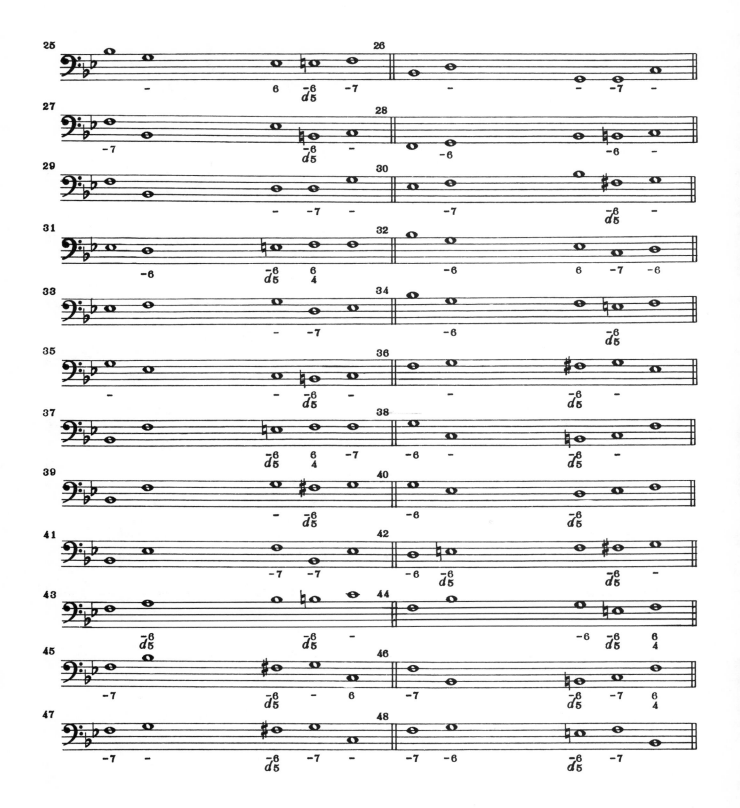

D10-2a Figured bass dictation of foreign chords
(Copy 5)

Shield the answer. Listen to the series of five chords and write the bass notes and the figured bass symbols for the last three chords; then uncover the answer and compare your response. Goal: No more than eight incorrect frames.

253

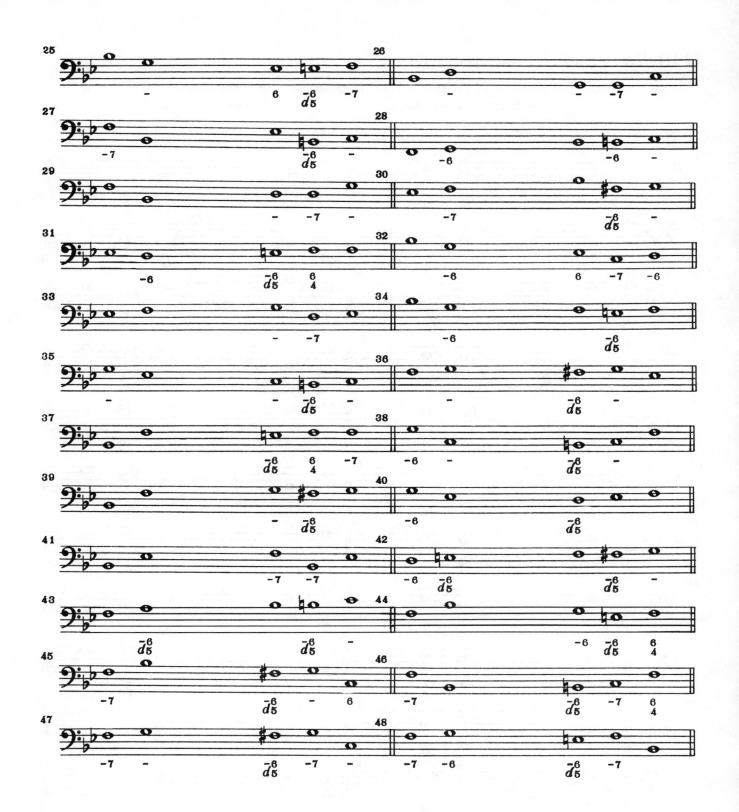

Lesson D10-2b

This lesson introduces the composite chord symbols for transient dominant chords in first inversion in a major key. The symbols for these chords are $(\underline{II^{-6}})$, $(\underline{III^{-6}})$, $(\underline{VI^{-6}})$, $(\underline{I_{d5}^{-6}})$, $(\underline{II_{d5}^{-6}})$, $(\underline{III_{d5}^{-6}})$, and $(\underline{VI_{d5}^{-6}})$. Since these are first inversions, the third of the chord appears in the bass.

The bass of the $(\underline{II^{-6}})$ and $(\underline{II_{d5}^{-6}})$ chords is an augmented fourth above the tonic, that is, the raised fourth degree of the key.

The bass of the $(\underline{III^{-6}})$ and $(\underline{III_{d5}^{-6}})$ chords is an augmented fifth above the tonic, that is, the raised fifth degree of the key.

The bass of the $(\underline{VI^{-6}})$ and $(\underline{VI_{d5}^{-6}})$ chords is an augmented prime above the tonic, that is, the raised first degree of the key.

The bass of the $(\underline{I_{d5}^{-6}})$ chord is a major third above the tonic, that is, the third degree of the key.

D10-2b
Identification of foreign chords

Shield the answer. Listen to the group of five chords and write the composite chord symbols for the last three chords; then uncover the answer and compare your response. Goal: No more than eight incorrect frames.

1 I IV ___ ___ ___ ($\underline{\text{II}^{-6}_{d5}}$) V I

2 I IV ___ ___ ___ ($\underline{\text{II}^{-7}}$) ($\underline{\text{II}^{-6}_{d5}}$) V^{-7}

3 I VI$^-$ ___ ___ ___ ($\underline{\text{II}^{-7}}$) I$^6_4$ V

4 V^{-7} I ___ ___ ___ ($\underline{\text{VI}^{-6}_{d5}}$) II$^-$ V

5 IV^{-6} V ___ ___ ___ I ($\underline{\text{VI}^{-6}_{d5}}$) II$^-$

6 V^{-7} I ___ ___ ___ VI$^-$ ($\underline{\text{II}^{-6}_{d5}}$) V^{-7}

7 I VI$^-$ ___ ___ ___ IV ($\underline{\text{II}^{-6}}$) I$^6_4$

8 V I ___ ___ ___ V ($\underline{\text{III}^{-6}_{d5}}$) VI$^-$

9 V I ___ ___ ___ ($\underline{\text{III}^{-6}_{d5}}$) VI$^-$ IV

10 I VI$^-$ ___ ___ ___ ($\underline{\text{II}^{-6}_{d5}}$) I$^6_4$ V

11 I V$^6_4$ ___ ___ ___ I^{-6} ($\underline{\text{VI}^{-6}_{d5}}$) II$^-$

12 V^{-7} I ___ ___ ___ I^{-6} ($\underline{\text{III}^{-6}_{d5}}$) VI$^-$

13 I IV ___ ___ ___ ($\underline{\text{I}^{-6}_{d5}}$) IV V^{-7}

14 V^{-7} I ___ ___ ___ VI$^-$ ($\underline{\text{I}^{-6}_{d5}}$) IV

15 I IV ___ ___ ___ ($\underline{\text{II}}$) ($\underline{\text{II}^{-6}}$) V^{-7}

16 VI$^-$ IV ___ ___ ___ ($\underline{\text{II}^{-6}_{d5}}$) ($\underline{\text{II}^{-7}}$) V^{-7}

17 I II^6 ___ ___ ___ ($\underline{\text{II}^{-6}}$) I$^6_4$ V

18 I II^6 ___ ___ ___ V ($\underline{\text{III}^{-6}_{d5}}$) VI$^-$

19 II$^-$ V ___ ___ ___ I^{-6} ($\underline{\text{I}^{-6}_{d5}}$) IV

20 I V^{-7} ___ ___ ___ ($\underline{\text{I}^{-7}}$) IV V

21 IV^{-6} V^{-7} ___ ___ ___ I ($\underline{\text{III}^{-6}_{d5}}$) VI$^-$

22 IV V ___ ___ ___ ($\underline{\text{III}^{-6}}$) VI$^-$ IV

23 V^{-7} I ___ ___ ___ IV ($\underline{\text{VI}^{-6}}$) II$^-$

24 V^{-7} I ___ ___ ___ ($\underline{\text{VI}^{-7}}$) II$^-$ V^{-7}

25 I VI$^-$ ___ ___ ___ II^6 ($\underline{\text{II}^{-6}_{d5}}$) V^{-7}

26 I III$^-$ ___ ___ ___ VI$^-$ ($\underline{\text{VI}^{-7}}$) II$^-$

27 V^{-7} I ___ ___ ___ IV ($\underline{\text{VI}^{-6}_{d5}}$) II$^-$

28 V IV^{-6} ___ ___ ___ I ($\underline{\text{VI}^{-6}}$) II$^-$

29 V I ___ ___ ___ III$^-$ ($\underline{\text{III}^{-7}}$) VI$^-$

30 IV V^{-7} ___ ___ ___ I ($\underline{\text{III}^{-6}_{d5}}$) VI$^-$

31 IV I^{-6} ___ ___ ___ ($\underline{\text{II}^{-6}_{d5}}$) I$^6_4$ V

32 I IV^{-6} ___ ___ ___ II^6 ($\underline{\text{II}^{-7}}$) I^{-6}

33 IV V ___ ___ ___ VI$^-$ ($\underline{\text{III}^{-7}}$) IV

34 I IV^{-6} ___ ___ ___ V ($\underline{\text{II}^{-6}_{d5}}$) V

35 VI$^-$ IV ___ ___ ___ II$^-$ ($\underline{\text{VI}^{-6}_{d5}}$) II$^-$

36 V VI$^-$ ___ ___ ___ ($\underline{\text{III}^{-6}_{d5}}$) VI$^-$ IV

37 I V ___ ___ ___ ($\underline{\text{II}^{-6}_{d5}}$) I$^6_4$ V^{-7}

38 IV^{-6} II$^-$ ___ ___ ___ ($\underline{\text{VI}^{-6}_{d5}}$) II$^-$ V

39 I V ___ ___ ___ VI$^-$ ($\underline{\text{III}^{-6}_{d5}}$) VI$^-$

40 IV^{-6} IV ___ ___ ___ ($\underline{\text{I}^{-6}_{d5}}$) IV V

41 I IV ___ ___ ___ V^{-7} ($\underline{\text{I}^{-7}}$) IV

42 I^{-6} ($\underline{\text{II}^{-6}_{d5}}$) ___ ___ ___ V ($\underline{\text{III}^{-6}_{d5}}$) VI$^-$

43 V V$^{-6}_{d5}$ ___ ___ ___ I ($\underline{\text{VI}^{-6}_{d5}}$) II$^-$

44 V I ___ ___ ___ IV^{-6} ($\underline{\text{II}^{-6}_{d5}}$) I$^6_4$

45 V^{-7} I ___ ___ ___ ($\underline{\text{III}^{-6}_{d5}}$) VI$^-$ II^6

46 V^{-7} I ___ ___ ___ ($\underline{\text{VI}^{-6}_{d5}}$) ($\underline{\text{II}^{-7}}$) I$^6_4$

47 V^{-7} VI$^-$ ___ ___ ___ ($\underline{\text{III}^{-6}_{d5}}$) ($\underline{\text{VI}^{-7}}$) II$^-$

48 V^{-7} IV^{-6} ___ ___ ___ ($\underline{\text{II}^{-6}_{d5}}$) V^{-7} I

Shield the answer. Listen to the group of five chords and write the composite chord symbols for the last three chords; then uncover the answer and compare your response. Goal: No more than eight incorrect frames.

1. I IV ___ ___ ___ $(\underline{\text{II}^{-6}_{d5}})$ V I
2. I IV ___ ___ ___ $(\underline{\text{II}^{-7}})$ $(\underline{\text{II}^{-6}_{d5}})$ V^{-7}
3. I VI$^-$ ___ ___ ___ $(\underline{\text{II}^{-7}})$ I$^6_4$ V
4. V^{-7} I ___ ___ ___ $(\underline{\text{VI}^{-6}_{d5}})$ II$^-$ V
5. IV^{-6} V ___ ___ ___ I $(\underline{\text{VI}^{-6}_{d5}})$ II$^-$
6. V^{-7} I ___ ___ ___ VI$^-$ $(\underline{\text{II}^{-6}_{d5}})$ V^{-7}
7. I VI$^-$ ___ ___ ___ IV $(\underline{\text{II}^{-6}})$ I$^6_4$
8. V I ___ ___ ___ V $(\underline{\text{III}^{-6}_{d5}})$ VI$^-$
9. V I ___ ___ ___ $(\underline{\text{III}^{-6}_{d5}})$ VI$^-$ IV
10. I VI$^-$ ___ ___ ___ $(\underline{\text{II}^{-6}_{d5}})$ I$^6_4$ V
11. I V$^6_4$ ___ ___ ___ I^{-6} $(\underline{\text{VI}^{-6}_{d5}})$ II$^-$
12. V^{-7} I ___ ___ ___ I^{-6} $(\underline{\text{III}^{-6}_{d5}})$ VI$^-$
13. I IV ___ ___ ___ $(\underline{\text{I}^{-6}_{d5}})$ IV V^{-7}
14. V^{-7} I ___ ___ ___ VI$^-$ $(\underline{\text{I}^{-6}_{d5}})$ IV
15. I IV ___ ___ ___ $(\underline{\text{II}})$ $(\underline{\text{II}^{-6}})$ V^{-7}
16. VI$^-$ IV ___ ___ ___ $(\underline{\text{II}^{-6}_{d5}})$ $(\underline{\text{II}^{-7}})$ V^{-7}
17. I II^6 ___ ___ ___ $(\underline{\text{II}^{-6}})$ I$^6_4$ V
18. I II^6 ___ ___ ___ V $(\underline{\text{III}^{-6}_{d5}})$ VI$^-$
19. II$^-$ V ___ ___ ___ I^{-6} $(\underline{\text{I}^{-6}_{d5}})$ IV
20. I V^{-7} ___ ___ ___ $(\underline{\text{I}^{-7}})$ IV V
21. IV^{-6} V^{-7} ___ ___ ___ I $(\underline{\text{III}^{-6}_{d5}})$ VI$^-$
22. IV V ___ ___ ___ $(\underline{\text{III}^{-6}})$ VI$^-$ IV
23. V^{-7} I ___ ___ ___ IV $(\underline{\text{VI}^{-6}})$ II$^-$
24. V^{-7} I ___ ___ ___ $(\underline{\text{VI}^{-7}})$ II$^-$ V^{-7}

25. I VI$^-$ ___ ___ ___ II^6 $(\underline{\text{II}^{-6}_{d5}})$ V^{-7}
26. I III$^-$ ___ ___ ___ VI$^-$ $(\underline{\text{VI}^{-7}})$ II$^-$
27. V^{-7} I ___ ___ ___ IV $(\underline{\text{VI}^{-6}_{d5}})$ II$^-$
28. V IV^{-6} ___ ___ ___ I $(\underline{\text{VI}^{-6}})$ II$^-$
29. V I ___ ___ ___ III$^-$ $(\underline{\text{III}^{-7}})$ VI$^-$
30. IV V^{-7} ___ ___ ___ I $(\underline{\text{III}^{-6}_{d5}})$ VI$^-$
31. IV I^{-6} ___ ___ ___ $(\underline{\text{II}^{-6}_{d5}})$ I$^6_4$ V
32. I IV^{-6} ___ ___ ___ II^6 $(\underline{\text{II}^{-7}})$ I^{-6}
33. IV V ___ ___ ___ VI$^-$ $(\underline{\text{III}^{-7}})$ IV
34. I IV^{-6} ___ ___ ___ V $(\underline{\text{II}^{-6}_{d5}})$ V
35. VI$^-$ IV ___ ___ ___ II$^-$ $(\underline{\text{VI}^{-6}_{d5}})$ II$^-$
36. V VI$^-$ ___ ___ ___ $(\underline{\text{III}^{-6}_{d5}})$ VI$^-$ IV
37. I V ___ ___ ___ $(\underline{\text{II}^{-6}_{d5}})$ I$^6_4$ V^{-7}
38. IV^{-6} II$^-$ ___ ___ ___ $(\underline{\text{VI}^{-6}_{d5}})$ II$^-$ V
39. I V ___ ___ ___ VI$^-$ $(\underline{\text{III}^{-6}_{d5}})$ VI$^-$
40. IV^{-6} IV ___ ___ ___ $(\underline{\text{I}^{-6}_{d5}})$ IV V
41. I IV ___ ___ ___ V^{-7} $(\underline{\text{I}^{-7}})$ IV
42. I^{-6} $(\underline{\text{II}^{-6}_{d5}})$ ___ ___ ___ V $(\underline{\text{III}^{-6}_{d5}})$ VI$^-$
43. V V$^{-6}_{d5}$ ___ ___ ___ I $(\underline{\text{VI}^{-6}_{d5}})$ II$^-$
44. V I ___ ___ ___ IV^{-6} $(\underline{\text{II}^{-6}_{d5}})$ I$^6_4$
45. V^{-7} I ___ ___ ___ $(\underline{\text{III}^{-6}_{d5}})$ VI$^-$ II^6
46. V^{-7} I ___ ___ ___ $(\underline{\text{VI}^{-6}_{d5}})$ $(\underline{\text{II}^{-7}})$ I$^6_4$
47. V^{-7} VI$^-$ ___ ___ ___ $(\underline{\text{III}^{-6}_{d5}})$ $(\underline{\text{VI}^{-7}})$ II$^-$
48. V^{-7} IV^{-6} ___ ___ ___ $(\underline{\text{II}^{-6}_{d5}})$ V^{-7} I

D10-2b
(Copy 3)   **Identification of foreign chords**

Shield the answer. Listen to the group of five chords and write the composite chord symbols for the last three chords; then uncover the answer and compare your response. Goal: No more than eight incorrect frames.

1 I IV _____ _____ _____ $(\underline{II}^{-6}_{d5})$ V I

2 I IV _____ _____ _____ $(\underline{II}^{-7})$ $(\underline{II}^{-6}_{d5})$ V^{-7}

3 I VI^- _____ _____ _____ $(\underline{II}^{-7})$ I^6_4 V

4 V^{-7} I _____ _____ _____ $(\underline{VI}^{-6}_{d5})$ II^- V

5 IV^{-6} V _____ _____ _____ I $(\underline{VI}^{-6}_{d5})$ II^-

6 V^{-7} I _____ _____ _____ VI^- $(\underline{II}^{-6}_{d5})$ V^{-7}

7 I VI^- _____ _____ _____ IV $(\underline{II}^{-6})$ I^6_4

8 V I _____ _____ _____ V $(\underline{III}^{-6}_{d5})$ VI^-

9 V I _____ _____ _____ $(\underline{III}^{-6}_{d5})$ VI^- IV

10 I VI^- _____ _____ _____ $(\underline{II}^{-6}_{d5})$ I^6_4 V

11 I V^6_4 _____ _____ _____ I^{-6} $(\underline{VI}^{-6}_{d5})$ II^-

12 V^{-7} I _____ _____ _____ I^{-6} $(\underline{III}^{-6}_{d5})$ VI^-

13 I IV _____ _____ _____ $(\underline{I}^{-6}_{d5})$ IV V^{-7}

14 V^{-7} I _____ _____ _____ VI^- $(\underline{I}^{-6}_{d5})$ IV

15 I IV _____ _____ _____ $(\underline{II})$ $(\underline{II}^{-6})$ V^{-7}

16 VI^- IV _____ _____ _____ $(\underline{II}^{-6}_{d5})$ $(\underline{II}^{-7})$ V^{-7}

17 I II^6 _____ _____ _____ $(\underline{II}^{-6})$ I^6_4 V

18 I II^6 _____ _____ _____ V $(\underline{III}^{-6}_{d5})$ VI^-

19 II^- V _____ _____ _____ I^{-6} $(\underline{I}^{-6}_{d5})$ IV

20 I V^{-7} _____ _____ _____ $(\underline{I}^{-7})$ IV V

21 IV^{-6} V^{-7} _____ _____ _____ I $(\underline{III}^{-6}_{d5})$ VI^-

22 IV V _____ _____ _____ $(\underline{III}^{-6})$ VI^- IV

23 V^{-7} I _____ _____ _____ IV $(\underline{VI}^{-6})$ II^-

24 V^{-7} I _____ _____ _____ $(\underline{VI}^{-7})$ II^- V^{-7}

25 I VI^- _____ _____ _____ II^6 $(\underline{II}^{-6}_{d5})$ V^{-7}

26 I III^- _____ _____ _____ VI^- $(\underline{VI}^{-7})$ II^-

27 V^{-7} I _____ _____ _____ IV $(\underline{VI}^{-6}_{d5})$ II^-

28 V IV^{-6} _____ _____ _____ I $(\underline{VI}^{-6})$ II^-

29 V I _____ _____ _____ III^- $(\underline{III}^{-7})$ VI^-

30 IV V^{-7} _____ _____ _____ I $(\underline{III}^{-6}_{d5})$ VI^-

31 IV I^{-6} _____ _____ _____ $(\underline{II}^{-6}_{d5})$ I^6_4 V

32 I IV^{-6} _____ _____ _____ II^6 $(\underline{II}^{-7})$ I^{-6}

33 IV V _____ _____ _____ VI^- $(\underline{III}^{-7})$ IV

34 I IV^{-6} _____ _____ _____ V $(\underline{II}^{-6}_{d5})$ V

35 VI^- IV _____ _____ _____ II^- $(\underline{VI}^{-6}_{d5})$ II^-

36 V VI^- _____ _____ _____ $(\underline{III}^{-6}_{d5})$ VI^- IV

37 I V _____ _____ _____ $(\underline{II}^{-6}_{d5})$ I^6_4 V^{-7}

38 IV^{-6} II^- _____ _____ _____ $(\underline{VI}^{-6}_{d5})$ II^- V

39 I V _____ _____ _____ VI^- $(\underline{III}^{-6}_{d5})$ VI^-

40 IV^{-6} IV _____ _____ _____ $(\underline{I}^{-6}_{d5})$ IV V

41 I IV _____ _____ _____ V^{-7} $(\underline{I}^{-7})$ IV

42 I^{-6} $(\underline{II}^{-6}_{d5})$ _____ _____ _____ V $(\underline{III}^{-6}_{d5})$ VI^-

43 V V^{-6}_{d5} _____ _____ _____ I $(\underline{VI}^{-6}_{d5})$ II^-

44 V I _____ _____ _____ IV^{-6} $(\underline{II}^{-6}_{d5})$ I^6_4

45 V^{-7} I _____ _____ _____ $(\underline{III}^{-6}_{d5})$ VI^- II^6

46 V^{-7} I _____ _____ _____ $(\underline{VI}^{-6}_{d5})$ $(\underline{II}^{-7})$ I^6_4

47 V^{-7} VI^- _____ _____ _____ $(\underline{III}^{-6}_{d5})$ $(\underline{VI}^{-7})$ II^-

48 V^{-7} IV^{-6} _____ _____ _____ $(\underline{II}^{-6}_{d5})$ V^{-7} I

D10–2b   Identification of foreign chords

(Copy 4)

Shield the answer. Listen to the group of five chords and write the composite chord symbols for the last three chords; then uncover the answer and compare your response. Goal: No more than eight incorrect frames.

1 I IV _____ _____ _____ $(\underline{\text{II}_{d5}^{-6}})$ V I

2 I IV _____ _____ _____ $(\underline{\text{II}^{-7}})$ $(\underline{\text{II}_{d5}^{-6}})$ V^{-7}

3 I VI^- _____ _____ _____ $(\underline{\text{II}^{-7}})$ I_4^6 V

4 V^{-7} I _____ _____ _____ $(\underline{\text{VI}_{d5}^{-6}})$ II^- V

5 IV^{-6} V _____ _____ _____ I $(\underline{\text{VI}_{d5}^{-6}})$ II^-

6 V^{-7} I _____ _____ _____ VI^- $(\underline{\text{II}_{d5}^{-6}})$ V^{-7}

7 I VI^- _____ _____ _____ IV $(\underline{\text{II}^{-6}})$ I_4^6

8 V I _____ _____ _____ V $(\underline{\text{III}_{d5}^{-6}})$ VI^-

9 V I _____ _____ _____ $(\underline{\text{III}_{d5}^{-6}})$ VI^- IV

10 I VI^- _____ _____ _____ $(\underline{\text{II}_{d5}^{-6}})$ I_4^6 V

11 I V_4^6 _____ _____ _____ I^{-6} $(\underline{\text{VI}_{d5}^{-6}})$ II^-

12 V^{-7} I _____ _____ _____ I^{-6} $(\underline{\text{III}_{d5}^{-6}})$ VI^-

13 I IV _____ _____ _____ $(\underline{\text{I}_{d5}^{-6}})$ IV V^{-7}

14 V^{-7} I _____ _____ _____ VI^- $(\underline{\text{I}_{d5}^{-6}})$ IV

15 I IV _____ _____ _____ $(\underline{\text{II}})$ $(\underline{\text{II}^{-6}})$ V^{-7}

16 VI^- IV _____ _____ _____ $(\underline{\text{II}_{d5}^{-6}})$ $(\underline{\text{II}^{-7}})$ V^{-7}

17 I II^6 _____ _____ _____ $(\underline{\text{II}^{-6}})$ I_4^6 V

18 I II^6 _____ _____ _____ V $(\underline{\text{III}_{d5}^{-6}})$ VI^-

19 II^- V _____ _____ _____ I^{-6} $(\underline{\text{I}_{d5}^{-6}})$ IV

20 I V^{-7} _____ _____ _____ $(\underline{\text{I}^{-7}})$ IV V

21 IV^{-6} V^{-7} _____ _____ _____ I $(\underline{\text{III}_{d5}^{-6}})$ VI^-

22 IV V _____ _____ _____ $(\underline{\text{III}^{-6}})$ VI^- IV

23 V^{-7} I _____ _____ _____ IV $(\underline{\text{VI}^{-6}})$ II^-

24 V^{-7} I _____ _____ _____ $(\underline{\text{VI}^{-7}})$ II^- V^{-7}

25 I VI^- _____ _____ _____ II^6 $(\underline{\text{II}_{d5}^{-6}})$ V^{-7}

26 I III^- _____ _____ _____ VI^- $(\underline{\text{VI}^{-7}})$ II^-

27 V^{-7} I _____ _____ _____ IV $(\underline{\text{VI}_{d5}^{-6}})$ II^-

28 V IV^{-6} _____ _____ _____ I $(\underline{\text{VI}^{-6}})$ II^-

29 V I _____ _____ _____ III^- $(\underline{\text{III}^{-7}})$ VI^-

30 IV V^{-7} _____ _____ _____ I $(\underline{\text{III}_{d5}^{-6}})$ VI^-

31 IV I^{-6} _____ _____ _____ $(\underline{\text{II}_{d5}^{-6}})$ I_4^6 V

32 I IV^{-6} _____ _____ _____ II^6 $(\underline{\text{II}^{-7}})$ I^{-6}

33 IV V _____ _____ _____ VI^- $(\underline{\text{III}^{-7}})$ IV

34 I IV^{-6} _____ _____ _____ V $(\underline{\text{II}_{d5}^{-6}})$ V

35 VI^- IV _____ _____ _____ II^- $(\underline{\text{VI}_{d5}^{-6}})$ II^-

36 V VI^- _____ _____ _____ $(\underline{\text{III}_{d5}^{-6}})$ VI^- IV

37 I V _____ _____ _____ $(\underline{\text{II}_{d5}^{-6}})$ I_4^6 V^{-7}

38 IV^{-6} II^- _____ _____ _____ $(\underline{\text{VI}_{d5}^{-6}})$ II^- V

39 I V _____ _____ _____ VI^- $(\underline{\text{III}_{d5}^{-6}})$ VI^-

40 IV^{-6} IV _____ _____ _____ $(\underline{\text{I}_{d5}^{-6}})$ IV V

41 I IV _____ _____ _____ V^{-7} $(\underline{\text{I}^{-7}})$ IV

42 I^{-6} $(\underline{\text{II}_{d5}^{-6}})$ _____ _____ _____ V $(\underline{\text{III}_{d5}^{-6}})$ VI^-

43 V V_{d5}^{-6} _____ _____ _____ I $(\underline{\text{VI}_{d5}^{-6}})$ II^-

44 V I _____ _____ _____ IV^{-6} $(\underline{\text{II}_{d5}^{-6}})$ I_4^6

45 V^{-7} I _____ _____ _____ $(\underline{\text{III}_{d5}^{-6}})$ VI^- II^6

46 V^{-7} I _____ _____ _____ $(\underline{\text{VI}_{d5}^{-6}})$ $(\underline{\text{II}^{-7}})$ I_4^6

47 V^{-7} VI^- _____ _____ _____ $(\underline{\text{III}_{d5}^{-6}})$ $(\underline{\text{VI}^{-7}})$ II^-

48 V^{-7} IV^{-6} _____ _____ _____ $(\underline{\text{II}_{d5}^{-6}})$ V^{-7} I

D10-2b Identification of foreign chords
(Copy 5)

Shield the answer. Listen to the group of five chords and write the composite chord symbols for the last three chords; then uncover the answer and compare your response. Goal: No more than eight incorrect frames.

1 I IV _____ _____ _____ ($\underline{\text{II}}_{d5}^{-6}$) V I

2 I IV _____ _____ ($\underline{\text{II}}^{-7}$) ($\underline{\text{II}}_{d5}^{-6}$) V^{-7}

3 I VI$^-$ _____ _____ _____ ($\underline{\text{II}}^{-7}$) I$_4^6$ V

4 V^{-7} I _____ _____ _____ ($\underline{\text{VI}}_{d5}^{-6}$) II$^-$ V

5 IV^{-6} V _____ _____ _____ I ($\underline{\text{VI}}_{d5}^{-6}$) II$^-$

6 V^{-7} I _____ _____ _____ VI$^-$ ($\underline{\text{II}}_{d5}^{-6}$) V^{-7}

7 I VI$^-$ _____ _____ _____ IV ($\underline{\text{II}}^{-6}$) I$_4^6$

8 V I _____ _____ _____ V ($\underline{\text{III}}_{d5}^{-6}$) VI$^-$

9 V I _____ _____ _____ ($\underline{\text{III}}_{d5}^{-6}$) VI$^-$ IV

10 I VI$^-$ _____ _____ _____ ($\underline{\text{II}}_{d5}^{-6}$) I$_4^6$ V

11 I V$_4^6$ _____ _____ _____ I^{-6} ($\underline{\text{VI}}_{d5}^{-6}$) II$^-$

12 V^{-7} I _____ _____ _____ I^{-6} ($\underline{\text{III}}_{d5}^{-6}$) VI$^-$

13 I IV _____ _____ _____ ($\underline{\text{I}}_{d5}^{-6}$) IV V^{-7}

14 V^{-7} I _____ _____ _____ VI$^-$ ($\underline{\text{I}}_{d5}^{-6}$) IV

15 I IV _____ _____ _____ ($\underline{\text{II}}$) ($\underline{\text{II}}^{-6}$) V^{-7}

16 VI$^-$ IV _____ _____ _____ ($\underline{\text{II}}_{d5}^{-6}$) ($\underline{\text{II}}^{-7}$) V^{-7}

17 I II^6 _____ _____ _____ ($\underline{\text{II}}^{-6}$) I$_4^6$ V

18 I II^6 _____ _____ _____ V ($\underline{\text{III}}_{d5}^{-6}$) VI$^-$

19 II$^-$ V _____ _____ _____ I^{-6} ($\underline{\text{I}}_{d5}^{-6}$) IV

20 I V^{-7} _____ _____ _____ ($\underline{\text{I}}^{-7}$) IV V

21 IV^{-6} V^{-7} _____ _____ _____ I ($\underline{\text{III}}_{d5}^{-6}$) VI$^-$

22 IV V _____ _____ _____ ($\underline{\text{III}}^{-6}$) VI$^-$ IV

23 V^{-7} I _____ _____ _____ IV ($\underline{\text{VI}}^{-6}$) II$^-$

24 V^{-7} I _____ _____ _____ ($\underline{\text{VI}}^{-7}$) II$^-$ V^{-7}

25 I VI$^-$ _____ _____ _____ II^6 ($\underline{\text{II}}_{d5}^{-6}$) V^{-7}

26 I III$^-$ _____ _____ _____ VI$^-$ ($\underline{\text{VI}}^{-7}$) II$^-$

27 V^{-7} I _____ _____ _____ IV ($\underline{\text{VI}}_{d5}^{-6}$) II$^-$

28 V IV^{-6} _____ _____ _____ I ($\underline{\text{VI}}^{-6}$) II$^-$

29 V I _____ _____ _____ III$^-$ ($\underline{\text{III}}^{-7}$) VI$^-$

30 IV V^{-7} _____ _____ _____ I ($\underline{\text{III}}_{d5}^{-6}$) VI$^-$

31 IV I^{-6} _____ _____ _____ ($\underline{\text{II}}_{d5}^{-6}$) I$_4^6$ V

32 I IV^{-6} _____ _____ _____ II^6 ($\underline{\text{II}}^{-7}$) I^{-6}

33 IV V _____ _____ _____ VI$^-$ ($\underline{\text{III}}^{-7}$) IV

34 I IV^{-6} _____ _____ _____ V ($\underline{\text{II}}_{d5}^{-6}$) V

35 VI$^-$ IV _____ _____ _____ II$^-$ ($\underline{\text{VI}}_{d5}^{-6}$) II$^-$

36 V VI$^-$ _____ _____ _____ ($\underline{\text{III}}_{d5}^{-6}$) VI$^-$ IV

37 I V _____ _____ _____ ($\underline{\text{II}}_{d5}^{-6}$) I$_4^6$ V^{-7}

38 IV^{-6} II$^-$ _____ _____ _____ ($\underline{\text{VI}}_{d5}^{-6}$) II$^-$ V

39 I V _____ _____ _____ VI$^-$ ($\underline{\text{III}}_{d5}^{-6}$) VI$^-$

40 IV^{-6} IV _____ _____ _____ ($\underline{\text{I}}_{d5}^{-6}$) IV V

41 I IV _____ _____ _____ V^{-7} ($\underline{\text{I}}^{-7}$) IV

42 I^{-6} ($\underline{\text{II}}_{d5}^{-6}$) _____ _____ _____ V ($\underline{\text{III}}_{d5}^{-6}$) VI$^-$

43 V V$_{d5}^{-6}$ _____ _____ _____ I ($\underline{\text{VI}}_{d5}^{-6}$) II$^-$

44 V I _____ _____ _____ IV^{-6} ($\underline{\text{II}}_{d5}^{-6}$) I$_4^6$

45 V^{-7} I _____ _____ _____ ($\underline{\text{III}}_{d5}^{-6}$) VI$^-$ II^6

46 V^{-7} I _____ _____ _____ ($\underline{\text{VI}}_{d5}^{-6}$) ($\underline{\text{II}}^{-7}$) I$_4^6$

47 V^{-7} VI$^-$ _____ _____ _____ ($\underline{\text{III}}_{d5}^{-6}$) ($\underline{\text{VI}}^{-7}$) II$^-$

48 V^{-7} IV^{-6} _____ _____ _____ ($\underline{\text{II}}_{d5}^{-6}$) V^{-7} I

D10-3a (Copy 1) Figured bass dictation of foreign chords

Shield the answer. Listen to the series of five chords and write the bass notes and the figured bass symbols for the last three chords; then uncover the answer and compare your response. Goal: No more than eight incorrect frames.

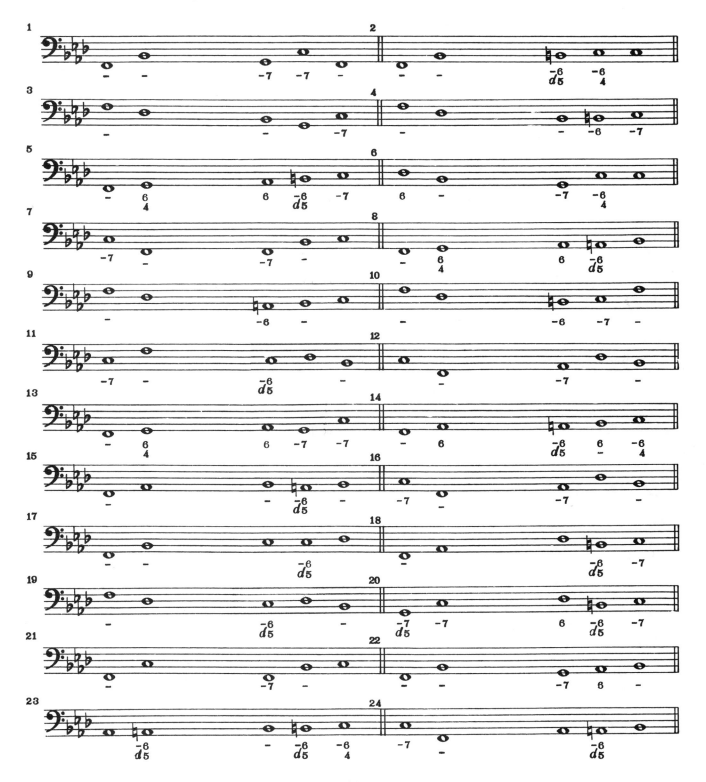

D10-3a Figured bass dictation of foreign chords

(Copy 2)

Shield the answer. Listen to the series of five chords and write the bass notes and the figured bass symbols for the last three chords; then uncover the answer and compare your response. Goal: No more than eight incorrect frames.

263

264

D10-3a

(Copy 3)

Figured bass dictation of foreign chords

Shield the answer. Listen to the series of five chords and write the bass notes and the figured bass symbols for the last three chords; then uncover the answer and compare your response. Goal: No more than eight incorrect frames.

265

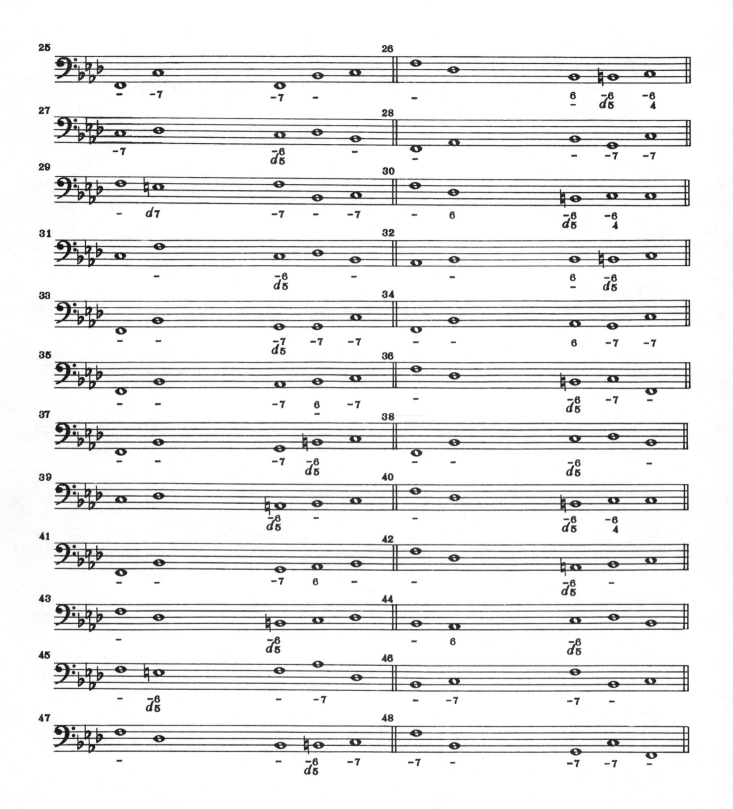

D10-3a Figured bass dictation of foreign chords
(Copy 4)

Shield the answer. Listen to the series of five chords and write the bass notes and the figured bass symbols for the last three chords; then uncover the answer and compare your response. Goal: No more than eight incorrect frames.

D10-3a

Figured bass dictation of foreign chords

Shield the answer. Listen to the series of five chords and write the bass notes and the figured bass symbols for the last three chords; then uncover the answer and compare your response. Goal: No more than eight incorrect frames.

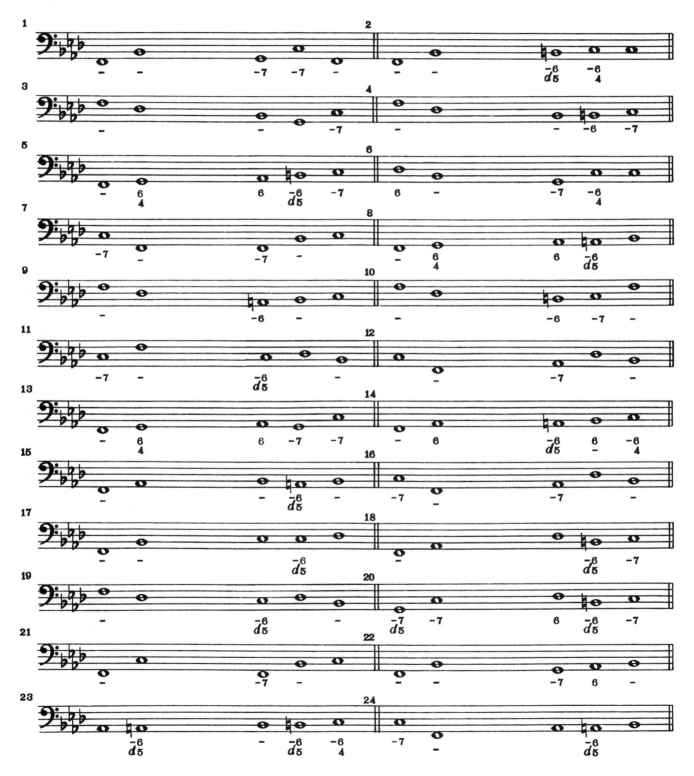

269

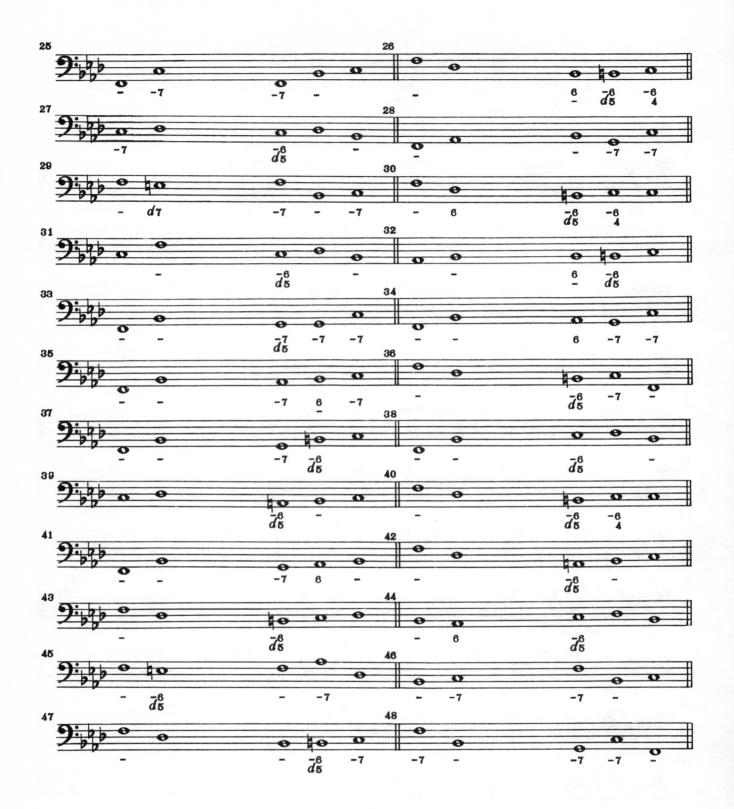

Lesson **D10-3b**

This lesson introduces the composite chord symbols for transient dominant chords in root position and in first inversion in minor keys. Some of these chords are identical with those in a major key and some are not.

The transient dominant chord on the second degree is identical in major and minor keys. Thus we find the $(\underline{II})$, $(\underline{II^{-7}})$, $(\underline{II^{-6}})$, and $(\underline{II^{-6}_{d5}})$ chords in both major and minor keys. The transient dominant seventh chord on the first degree is also identical in both major and minor keys, and we find the $(\underline{I^{-7}})$ and $(\underline{I^{-6}_{d5}})$ chords in both. The transient dominant triad on the first degree occurs as a foreign chord only in minor keys, since it would not be a foreign chord in a major key. Thus the $(\underline{I})$ and $(\underline{I^{-6}})$ chords occur only in minor keys.

The transient dominant chords on the third and sixth degrees will have different composite chord symbols in minor keys because these degrees are not in the same position as in major keys. In minor keys, we find these chords at the key location of ⁻III and ⁻VI, and in major keys at III and VI. It should be noted that the transient dominant chords on the third and sixth degrees in minor keys exist only as seventh chords, and not as triads, since the major triads on these degrees are regular (not foreign) chords. Thus we find the following transient dominant chords on third and sixth degrees in minor keys: $(\underline{^{-}III^{-7}})$, $(\underline{^{-}III^{-6}_{d5}})$, $(\underline{^{-}VI^{-7}})$, and $(\underline{^{-}VI^{-6}_{d5}})$. In major keys, we find the following chords: $(\underline{III})$, $(\underline{III^{-6}})$, $(\underline{III^{-7}})$, $(\underline{III^{-6}_{d5}})$, $(\underline{VI})$, $(\underline{VI^{-6}})$, $(\underline{VI^{-7}})$, and $(\underline{VI^{-6}_{d5}})$.

The bass of transient dominant chords in root position is of course on the degree of the key indicated by the key location symbol, but this is not the case for first inversions. The bass of the $(^{-}III^{-6}_{d5})$ chord is a perfect fifth above the tonic, that is, the fifth degree of the key. The bass of the $(^{-}VI^{-6}_{d5})$ chord is the first degree of the key. These degrees differ from those in a major key, where the bass of the $(\underline{III^{-6}_{d5}})$ chord is on the raised fifth degree and the bass of the $(\underline{VI^{-6}_{d5}})$ chord is the raised first degree.

D10-3b Identification of foreign chords
(Copy 1)

Shield the answer. Listen to the group of five chords and write the composite chord symbols for the last three chords; then uncover the answer and compare your response. Goal: No more than eight incorrect frames.

1   I^- IV^- _____   _____   _____   ($\underline{\text{II}^{-7}}$) V^{-7} I^-

2   I^- IV^- _____   _____   _____   ($\underline{\text{II}^{-6}_{d5}}$) I^{-6}_4 V

3   I^- ^-VI _____   _____   _____ IV^- ($\underline{\text{II}}$) V^{-7}

4   I^- ^-VI _____   _____   _____ IV^- ($\underline{\text{II}^{-6}}$) V^{-7}

5   I^- V^6_4 _____   _____   _____ I^6 ($\underline{\text{II}^{-6}_{d5}}$) V^{-7}

6   IV^6 IV^- _____   _____   _____   ($\underline{\text{II}^{-7}}$) I^{-6}_4 V

7   V^{-7} I^- _____   _____   _____   ($\underline{\text{I}^{-7}}$) IV^- V

8   I^- V^6_4 _____   _____   _____ I^6 ($\underline{\text{I}^{-6}_{d5}}$) IV^-

9   I^- ^-VI _____   _____   _____   ($\underline{\text{I}^{-6}}$) IV^- V

10   I^- ^-VI _____   _____   _____   ($\underline{\text{II}^{-6}}$) V^{-7} I^-

11   V^{-7} I^- _____   _____   _____   ($\underline{^-\text{III}^{-6}_{d5}}$) ^-VI IV^-

12   V I^- _____   _____   _____   ($\underline{^-\text{III}^{-7}}$) ^-VI IV^-

13   I^- V^6_4 _____   _____   _____ I^6 ($\underline{\text{II}^{-7}}$) V^{-7}

14   I^- I^6 _____   _____   _____   ($\underline{\text{I}^{-6}_{d5}}$) II^6_- I^{-6}_4

15   I ^-III _____   _____   _____ IV^- ($\underline{\text{I}^{-6}_{d5}}$) IV^-

16   V^{-7} I^- _____   _____   _____   ($\underline{^-\text{III}^{-7}}$) ^-VI IV^-

17   I^- IV^- _____   _____   _____ V ($\underline{^-\text{III}^{-6}_{d5}}$) ^-VI

18   I^- ^-III _____   _____   _____ ^-VI ($\underline{\text{II}^{-6}_{d5}}$) V^{-7}

19   I^- ^-VI _____   _____   _____   ($\underline{^-\text{III}^{-6}_{d5}}$) ^-VI IV^-

20   II^{-7}_{d5} V^{-7} _____   _____   _____ IV^6 ($\underline{\text{II}^{-6}_{d5}}$) V^{-7}

21   I^- V _____   _____   _____   ($\underline{\text{I}^{-7}}$) IV^- V

22   I^- IV^- _____   _____   _____   ($\underline{\text{II}^{-7}}$) I^6 IV^-

23   I^6 ($\underline{\text{I}^{-6}_{d5}}$)   _____   _____   _____ IV^- ($\underline{\text{II}^{-6}_{d5}}$) I^{-6}_4

24   V^{-7} I^- _____   _____   _____ ^-III ($\underline{\text{I}^{-6}_{d5}}$) IV^-

25   I^- V^{-7} _____   _____   _____   ($\underline{\text{I}^{-7}}$) IV^- V

26   I^- ^-VI _____   _____   _____ II^6_- ($\underline{\text{II}^{-6}_{d5}}$) I^{-6}_4

27   V^{-7} ^-VI _____   _____   _____   ($\underline{^-\text{III}^{-6}_{d5}}$) ^-VI IV^-

28   I^- ^-III _____   _____   _____ IV^- ($\underline{\text{II}^{-7}}$) V^{-7}

29   I^- VII^{d7} _____   _____   _____   ($\underline{\text{I}^{-7}}$) IV^- V^{-7}

30   I^- IV^6 _____   _____   _____   ($\underline{\text{II}^{-6}_{d5}}$) I^{-6}_4 V

31   V I^- _____   _____   _____   ($\underline{^-\text{III}^{-6}_{d5}}$) ^-VI IV^-

32   I^6 IV^- _____   _____   _____ II^6_- ($\underline{\text{II}^{-6}_{d5}}$) V

33   I^- IV^- _____   _____   _____ II^{-7}_{d5} ($\underline{\text{II}^{-7}}$) V^{-7}

34   I^- IV^- _____   _____   _____ I^6 ($\underline{\text{II}^{-7}}$) V^{-7}

35   I^- IV^- _____   _____   _____   ($\underline{^-\text{III}^{-7}}$) II^6_- V^{-7}

36   I^- ^-VI _____   _____   _____   ($\underline{\text{II}^{-6}_{d5}}$) V^{-7} I^-

37   I^- IV^- _____   _____   _____   ($\underline{\text{II}^{-7}}$)   ($\underline{\text{II}^{-6}_{d5}}$) V

38   I^- IV^- _____   _____   _____   ($\underline{^-\text{III}^{-6}_{d5}}$) ^-VI IV^-

39   V ^-VI _____   _____   _____   ($\underline{\text{I}^{-6}_{d5}}$) IV^- V

40   I^- ^-VI _____   _____   _____   ($\underline{\text{II}^{-6}_{d5}}$) I^{-6}_4 V

41   I^- IV^- _____   _____   _____   ($\underline{\text{II}^{-7}}$) I^6 IV^-

42   I^- ^-VI _____   _____   _____   ($\underline{\text{I}^{-6}_{d5}}$) IV^- V

43   I^- ^-VI _____   _____   _____   ($\underline{\text{II}^{-6}_{d5}}$) V ^-VI

44   IV^- I^6 _____   _____   _____   ($\underline{^-\text{III}^{-6}_{d5}}$) ^-VI IV^-

45   I^- V^{-6}_{d5} _____   _____   _____ I^- ($\underline{^-\text{III}^{-7}}$) ^-VI

46   IV^- V^{-7} _____   _____   _____   ($\underline{\text{I}^{-7}}$) IV^- V

47   I^- ^-VI _____   _____   _____ IV^- ($\underline{\text{II}^{-6}_{d5}}$) V^{-7}

48   ($\underline{\text{I}^{-7}}$) IV^- _____   _____   _____   ($\underline{\text{II}^{-7}}$) V^{-7} I^-

D10–3b   Identification of foreign chords

(Copy 2)

Shield the answer. Listen to the group of five chords and write the composite chord symbols for the last three chords; then uncover the answer and compare your response. Goal: No more than eight incorrect frames.

1 I^- IV^- _____ _____ _____ $(\underline{II^{-7}})$ V^{-7} I^-

2 I^- IV^- _____ _____ _____ $(\underline{II^{-6}_{d5}})$ I^{-6}_4 V

3 I^- ^-VI _____ _____ _____ IV^- $(\underline{II})$ V^{-7}

4 I^- ^-VI _____ _____ _____ IV^- $(\underline{II^{-6}})$ V^{-7}

5 I^- V^6_4 _____ _____ _____ I^6 $(\underline{II^{-6}_{d5}})$ V^{-7}

6 IV^6 IV^- _____ _____ _____ $(\underline{II^{-7}})$ I^{-6}_4 V

7 V^{-7} I^- _____ _____ _____ $(\underline{I^{-7}})$ IV^- V

8 I^- V^6_4 _____ _____ _____ I^6 $(\underline{I^{-6}_{d5}})$ IV^-

9 I^- ^-VI _____ _____ _____ $(\underline{I^{-6}})$ IV^- V

10 I^- ^-VI _____ _____ _____ $(\underline{II^{-6}})$ V^{-7} I^-

11 V^{-7} I^- _____ _____ _____ $(\underline{^-III^{-6}_{d5}})$ ^-VI IV^-

12 V I^- _____ _____ _____ $(\underline{^-III^{-7}})$ ^-VI IV^-

13 I^- V^6_4 _____ _____ _____ I^6 $(\underline{II^{-7}})$ V^{-7}

14 I^- I^6 _____ _____ _____ $(\underline{I^{-6}_{d5}})$ II^6_- I^{-6}_4

15 I ^-III _____ _____ _____ IV^- $(\underline{I^{-6}_{d5}})$ IV^-

16 V^{-7} I^- _____ _____ _____ $(\underline{^-III^{-7}})$ ^-VI IV^-

17 I^- IV^- _____ _____ _____ V $(\underline{^-III^{-6}_{d5}})$ ^-VI

18 I^- ^-III _____ _____ _____ ^-VI $(\underline{II^{-6}_{d5}})$ V^{-7}

19 I^- ^-VI _____ _____ _____ $(\underline{^-III^{-6}_{d5}})$ ^-VI IV^-

20 II^{-7}_{d5} V^{-7} _____ _____ _____ IV^6 $(\underline{II^{-6}_{d5}})$ V^{-7}

21 I^- V _____ _____ _____ $(\underline{I^{-7}})$ IV^- V

22 I^- IV^- _____ _____ _____ $(\underline{II^{-7}})$ I^6 IV^-

23 I^6 $(\underline{I^{-6}_{d5}})$ _____ _____ _____ IV^- $(\underline{II^{-6}_{d5}})$ I^{-6}_4

24 V^{-7} I^- _____ _____ _____ ^-III $(\underline{I^{-6}_{d5}})$ IV^-

25 I^- V^{-7} _____ _____ _____ $(\underline{I^{-7}})$ IV^- V

26 I^- ^-VI _____ _____ _____ II^6_- $(\underline{II^{-6}_{d5}})$ I^{-6}_4

27 V^{-7} ^-VI _____ _____ _____ $(\underline{^-III^{-6}_{d5}})$ ^-VI IV^-

28 I^- ^-III _____ _____ _____ IV^- $(\underline{II^{-7}})$ V^{-7}

29 I^- VII^{d7} _____ _____ _____ $(\underline{I^{-7}})$ IV^- V^{-7}

30 I^- IV^6 _____ _____ _____ $(\underline{II^{-6}_{d5}})$ I^{-6}_4 V

31 V I^- _____ _____ _____ $(\underline{^-III^{-6}_{d5}})$ ^-VI IV^-

32 I^6 IV^- _____ _____ _____ II^6_- $(\underline{II^{-6}_{d5}})$ V

33 I^- IV^- _____ _____ _____ II^{-7}_{d5} $(\underline{II^{-7}})$ V^{-7}

34 I^- IV^- _____ _____ _____ I^6 $(\underline{II^{-7}})$ V^{-7}

35 I^- IV^- _____ _____ _____ $(\underline{^-III^{-7}})$ II^6_- V^{-7}

36 I^- ^-VI _____ _____ _____ $(\underline{II^{-6}_{d5}})$ V^{-7} I^-

37 I^- IV^- _____ _____ _____ $(\underline{II^{-7}})$ $(\underline{II^{-6}_{d5}})$ V

38 I^- IV^- _____ _____ _____ $(\underline{^-III^{-6}_{d5}})$ ^-VI IV^-

39 V ^-VI _____ _____ _____ $(\underline{I^{-6}_{d5}})$ IV^- V

40 I^- ^-VI _____ _____ _____ $(\underline{II^{-6}_{d5}})$ I^{-6}_4 V

41 I^- IV^- _____ _____ _____ $(\underline{II^{-7}})$ I^6 IV^-

42 I^- ^-VI _____ _____ _____ $(\underline{I^{-6}_{d5}})$ IV^- V

43 I^- ^-VI _____ _____ _____ $(\underline{II^{-6}_{d5}})$ V ^-VI

44 IV^- I^6 _____ _____ _____ $(\underline{^-III^{-6}_{d5}})$ ^-VI IV^-

45 I^- V^{-6}_{d5} _____ _____ _____ I^- $(\underline{^-III^{-7}})$ ^-VI

46 IV^- V^{-7} _____ _____ _____ $(\underline{I^{-7}})$ IV^- V

47 I^- ^-VI _____ _____ _____ IV^- $(\underline{II^{-6}_{d5}})$ V^{-7}

48 $(\underline{I^{-7}})$ IV^- _____ _____ _____ $(\underline{II^{-7}})$ V^{-7} I^-

D10-3b **Identification of foreign chords**

(Copy 3)

Shield the answer. Listen to the group of five chords and write the composite chord symbols for the last three chords; then uncover the answer and compare your response. Goal: No more than eight incorrect frames.

1 I^- IV^- _____ _____ _____ $(\underline{II}^{-7})$ V^{-7} I^-

2 I^- IV^- _____ _____ _____ $(\underline{II}^{-6}_{d5})$ I^{-6}_4 V

3 I^- ^-VI _____ _____ _____ IV^- $(\underline{II})$ V^{-7}

4 I^- ^-VI _____ _____ _____ IV^- $(\underline{II}^{-6})$ V^{-7}

5 I^- V^6_4 _____ _____ _____ I^6 $(\underline{II}^{-6}_{d5})$ V^{-7}

6 IV^6 IV^- _____ _____ _____ $(\underline{II}^{-7})$ I^{-6}_4 V

7 V^{-7} I^- _____ _____ _____ $(\underline{I}^{-7})$ IV^- V

8 I^- V^6_4 _____ _____ _____ I^6 $(\underline{I}^{-6}_{d5})$ IV^-

9 I^- ^-VI _____ _____ _____ $(\underline{I}^{-6})$ IV^- V

10 I^- ^-VI _____ _____ _____ $(\underline{II}^{-6})$ V^{-7} I^-

11 V^{-7} I^- _____ _____ _____ $(\underline{^-III}^{-6}_{d5})$ ^-VI IV^-

12 V I^- _____ _____ _____ $(\underline{^-III}^{-7})$ ^-VI IV^-

13 I^- V^6_4 _____ _____ _____ I^6 $(\underline{II}^{-7})$ V^{-7}

14 I^- I^6 _____ _____ _____ $(\underline{I}^{-6}_{d5})$ II^6_- I^{-6}_4

15 I ^-III _____ _____ _____ IV^- $(\underline{I}^{-6}_{d5})$ IV^-

16 V^{-7} I^- _____ _____ _____ $(\underline{^-III}^{-7})$ ^-VI IV^-

17 I^- IV^- _____ _____ _____ V $(\underline{^-III}^{-6}_{d5})$ ^-VI

18 I^- ^-III _____ _____ _____ ^-VI $(\underline{II}^{-6}_{d5})$ V^{-7}

19 I^- ^-VI _____ _____ _____ $(\underline{^-III}^{-6}_{d5})$ ^-VI IV^-

20 II^{-7}_{d5} V^{-7} _____ _____ _____ IV^6 $(\underline{II}^{-6}_{d5})$ V^{-7}

21 I^- V _____ _____ _____ $(\underline{I}^{-7})$ IV^- V

22 I^- IV^- _____ _____ _____ $(\underline{II}^{-7})$ I^6 IV^-

23 I^6 $(\underline{I}^{-6}_{d5})$ _____ _____ _____ IV^- $(\underline{II}^{-6}_{d5})$ I^{-6}_4

24 V^{-7} I^- _____ _____ _____ ^-III $(\underline{I}^{-6}_{d5})$ IV^-

25 I^- V^{-7} _____ _____ _____ $(\underline{I}^{-7})$ IV^- V

26 I^- ^-VI _____ _____ _____ II^6_- $(\underline{II}^{-6}_{d5})$ I^{-6}_4

27 V^{-7} ^-VI _____ _____ _____ $(\underline{^-III}^{-6}_{d5})$ ^-VI IV^-

28 I^- ^-III _____ _____ _____ IV^- $(\underline{II}^{-7})$ V^{-7}

29 I^- VII^{d7} _____ _____ _____ $(\underline{I}^{-7})$ IV^- V^{-7}

30 I^- IV^6 _____ _____ _____ $(\underline{II}^{-6}_{d5})$ I^{-6}_4 V

31 V I^- _____ _____ _____ $(\underline{^-III}^{-6}_{d5})$ ^-VI IV^-

32 I^6 IV^- _____ _____ _____ II^6_- $(\underline{II}^{-6}_{d5})$ V

33 I^- IV^- _____ _____ _____ II^{-7}_{d5} $(\underline{II}^{-7})$ V^{-7}

34 I^- IV^- _____ _____ _____ I^6 $(\underline{II}^{-7})$ V^{-7}

35 I^- IV^- _____ _____ _____ $(\underline{^-III}^{-7})$ II^6_- V^{-7}

36 I^- ^-VI _____ _____ _____ $(\underline{II}^{-6}_{d5})$ V^{-7} I^-

37 I^- IV^- _____ _____ _____ $(\underline{II}^{-7})$ $(\underline{II}^{-6}_{d5})$ V

38 I^- IV^- _____ _____ _____ $(\underline{^-III}^{-6}_{d5})$ ^-VI IV^-

39 V ^-VI _____ _____ _____ $(\underline{I}^{-6}_{d5})$ IV^- V

40 I^- ^-VI _____ _____ _____ $(\underline{II}^{-6}_{d5})$ I^{-6}_4 V

41 I^- IV^- _____ _____ _____ $(\underline{II}^{-7})$ I^6 IV^-

42 I^- ^-VI _____ _____ _____ $(\underline{I}^{-6}_{d5})$ IV^- V

43 I^- ^-VI _____ _____ _____ $(\underline{II}^{-6}_{d5})$ V ^-VI

44 IV^- I^6 _____ _____ _____ $(\underline{^-III}^{-6}_{d5})$ ^-VI IV^-

45 I^- V^{-6}_{d5} _____ _____ _____ I^- $(\underline{^-III}^{-7})$ ^-VI

46 IV^- V^{-7} _____ _____ _____ $(\underline{I}^{-7})$ IV^- V

47 I^- ^-VI _____ _____ _____ IV^- $(\underline{II}^{-6}_{d5})$ V^{-7}

48 $(\underline{I}^{-7})$ IV^- _____ _____ _____ $(\underline{II}^{-7})$ V^{-7} I^-

D10–3b Identification of foreign chords

Shield the answer. Listen to the group of five chords and write the composite chord symbols for the last three chords; then uncover the answer and compare your response. Goal: No more than eight incorrect frames.

1 $\text{I}^- \ \text{IV}^-$ ___ ___ ___ $(\underline{\text{II}^{-7}}) \ \text{V}^{-7} \ \text{I}^-$

2 $\text{I}^- \ \text{IV}^-$ ___ ___ ___ $(\underline{\text{II}^{-6}_{d5}}) \ \text{I}^{-6}_{4} \ \text{V}$

3 $\text{I}^- \ {}^-\text{VI}$ ___ ___ ___ $\text{IV}^- \ (\underline{\text{II}}) \ \text{V}^{-7}$

4 $\text{I}^- \ {}^-\text{VI}$ ___ ___ ___ $\text{IV}^- \ (\underline{\text{II}^{-6}}) \ \text{V}^{-7}$

5 $\text{I}^- \ \text{V}^6_4$ ___ ___ ___ $\text{I}^6 \ (\underline{\text{II}^{-6}_{d5}}) \ \text{V}^{-7}$

6 $\text{IV}^6 \ \text{IV}^-$ ___ ___ ___ $(\underline{\text{II}^{-7}}) \ \text{I}^{-6}_{4} \ \text{V}$

7 $\text{V}^{-7} \ \text{I}^-$ ___ ___ ___ $(\underline{\text{I}^{-7}}) \ \text{IV}^- \ \text{V}$

8 $\text{I}^- \ \text{V}^6_4$ ___ ___ ___ $\text{I}^6 \ (\underline{\text{I}^{-6}_{d5}}) \ \text{IV}^-$

9 $\text{I}^- \ {}^-\text{VI}$ ___ ___ ___ $(\underline{\text{I}^{-6}}) \ \text{IV}^- \ \text{V}$

10 $\text{I}^- \ {}^-\text{VI}$ ___ ___ ___ $(\underline{\text{II}^{-6}}) \ \text{V}^{-7} \ \text{I}^-$

11 $\text{V}^{-7} \ \text{I}^-$ ___ ___ ___ $(\underline{{}^-\text{III}^{-6}_{d5}}) \ {}^-\text{VI} \ \text{IV}^-$

12 $\text{V} \ \text{I}^-$ ___ ___ ___ $(\underline{{}^-\text{III}^{-7}}) \ {}^-\text{VI} \ \text{IV}^-$

13 $\text{I}^- \ \text{V}^6_4$ ___ ___ ___ $\text{I}^6 \ (\underline{\text{II}^{-7}}) \ \text{V}^{-7}$

14 $\text{I}^- \ \text{I}^6$ ___ ___ ___ $(\underline{\text{I}^{-6}_{d5}}) \ \text{II}^6_- \ \text{I}^{-6}_{4}$

15 $\text{I} \ {}^-\text{III}$ ___ ___ ___ $\text{IV}^- \ (\underline{\text{I}^{-6}_{d5}}) \ \text{IV}^-$

16 $\text{V}^{-7} \ \text{I}^-$ ___ ___ ___ $(\underline{{}^-\text{III}^{-7}}) \ {}^-\text{VI} \ \text{IV}^-$

17 $\text{I}^- \ \text{IV}^-$ ___ ___ ___ $\text{V} \ (\underline{{}^-\text{III}^{-6}_{d5}}) \ {}^-\text{VI}$

18 $\text{I}^- \ {}^-\text{III}$ ___ ___ ___ ${}^-\text{VI} \ (\underline{\text{II}^{-6}_{d5}}) \ \text{V}^{-7}$

19 $\text{I}^- \ {}^-\text{VI}$ ___ ___ ___ $(\underline{{}^-\text{III}^{-6}_{d5}}) \ {}^-\text{VI} \ \text{IV}^-$

20 $\text{II}^{-7}_{d5} \ \text{V}^{-7}$ ___ ___ ___ $\text{IV}^6 \ (\underline{\text{II}^{-6}_{d5}}) \ \text{V}^{-7}$

21 $\text{I}^- \ \text{V}$ ___ ___ ___ $(\underline{\text{I}^{-7}}) \ \text{IV}^- \ \text{V}$

22 $\text{I}^- \ \text{IV}^-$ ___ ___ ___ $(\underline{\text{II}^{-7}}) \ \text{I}^6 \ \text{IV}^-$

23 $\text{I}^6 \ (\underline{\text{I}^{-6}_{d5}})$ ___ ___ ___ $\text{IV}^- \ (\underline{\text{II}^{-6}_{d5}}) \ \text{I}^{-6}_{4}$

24 $\text{V}^{-7} \ \text{I}^-$ ___ ___ ___ ${}^-\text{III} \ (\underline{\text{I}^{-6}_{d5}}) \ \text{IV}^-$

25 $\text{I}^- \ \text{V}^{-7}$ ___ ___ ___ $(\underline{\text{I}^{-7}}) \ \text{IV}^- \ \text{V}$

26 $\text{I}^- \ {}^-\text{VI}$ ___ ___ ___ $\text{II}^6_- \ (\underline{\text{II}^{-6}_{d5}}) \ \text{I}^{-6}_{4}$

27 $\text{V}^{-7} \ {}^-\text{VI}$ ___ ___ ___ $(\underline{{}^-\text{III}^{-6}_{d5}}) \ {}^-\text{VI} \ \text{IV}^-$

28 $\text{I}^- \ {}^-\text{III}$ ___ ___ ___ $\text{IV}^- \ (\underline{\text{II}^{-7}}) \ \text{V}^{-7}$

29 $\text{I}^- \ \text{VII}^{d7}$ ___ ___ ___ $(\underline{\text{I}^{-7}}) \ \text{IV}^- \ \text{V}^{-7}$

30 $\text{I}^- \ \text{IV}^6$ ___ ___ ___ $(\underline{\text{II}^{-6}_{d5}}) \ \text{I}^{-6}_{4} \ \text{V}$

31 $\text{V} \ \text{I}^-$ ___ ___ ___ $(\underline{{}^-\text{III}^{-6}_{d5}}) \ {}^-\text{VI} \ \text{IV}^-$

32 $\text{I}^6 \ \text{IV}^-$ ___ ___ ___ $\text{II}^6_- \ (\underline{\text{II}^{-6}_{d5}}) \ \text{V}$

33 $\text{I}^- \ \text{IV}^-$ ___ ___ ___ $\text{II}^{-7}_{d5} \ (\underline{\text{II}^{-7}}) \ \text{V}^{-7}$

34 $\text{I}^- \ \text{IV}^-$ ___ ___ ___ $\text{I}^6 \ (\underline{\text{II}^{-7}}) \ \text{V}^{-7}$

35 $\text{I}^- \ \text{IV}^-$ ___ ___ ___ $(\underline{{}^-\text{III}^{-7}}) \ \text{II}^6_- \ \text{V}^{-7}$

36 $\text{I}^- \ {}^-\text{VI}$ ___ ___ ___ $(\underline{\text{II}^{-6}_{d5}}) \ \text{V}^{-7} \ \text{I}^-$

37 $\text{I}^- \ \text{IV}^-$ ___ ___ ___ $(\underline{\text{II}^{-7}}) \ (\underline{\text{II}^{-6}_{d5}}) \ \text{V}$

38 $\text{I}^- \ \text{IV}^-$ ___ ___ ___ $(\underline{{}^-\text{III}^{-6}_{d5}}) \ {}^-\text{VI} \ \text{IV}^-$

39 $\text{V} \ {}^-\text{VI}$ ___ ___ ___ $(\underline{\text{I}^{-6}_{d5}}) \ \text{IV}^- \ \text{V}$

40 $\text{I}^- \ {}^-\text{VI}$ ___ ___ ___ $(\underline{\text{II}^{-6}_{d5}}) \ \text{I}^{-6}_{4} \ \text{V}$

41 $\text{I}^- \ \text{IV}^-$ ___ ___ ___ $(\underline{\text{II}^{-7}}) \ \text{I}^6 \ \text{IV}^-$

42 $\text{I}^- \ {}^-\text{VI}$ ___ ___ ___ $(\underline{\text{I}^{-6}_{d5}}) \ \text{IV}^- \ \text{V}$

43 $\text{I}^- \ {}^-\text{VI}$ ___ ___ ___ $(\underline{\text{II}^{-6}_{d5}}) \ \text{V} \ {}^-\text{VI}$

44 $\text{IV}^- \ \text{I}^6$ ___ ___ ___ $(\underline{{}^-\text{III}^{-6}_{d5}}) \ {}^-\text{VI} \ \text{IV}^-$

45 $\text{I}^- \ \text{V}^{-6}_{d5}$ ___ ___ ___ $\text{I}^- \ (\underline{{}^-\text{III}^{-7}}) \ {}^-\text{VI}$

46 $\text{IV}^- \ \text{V}^{-7}$ ___ ___ ___ $(\underline{\text{I}^{-7}}) \ \text{IV}^- \ \text{V}$

47 $\text{I}^- \ {}^-\text{VI}$ ___ ___ ___ $\text{IV}^- \ (\underline{\text{II}^{-6}_{d5}}) \ \text{V}^{-7}$

48 $(\underline{\text{I}^{-7}}) \ \text{IV}^-$ ___ ___ ___ $(\underline{\text{II}^{-7}}) \ \text{V}^{-7} \ \text{I}^-$

Shield the answer. Listen to the group of five chords and write the composite chord symbols for the last three chords; then uncover the answer and compare your response. Goal: No more than eight incorrect frames.

1   I^- IV^- ____   ____   ____ $(\underline{II^{-7}})$ V^{-7} I^-

2   I^- IV^- ____   ____   ____ $(\underline{II^{-6}_{d5}})$ I^{-6}_{4} V

3   I^- ^-VI ____   ____   ____ IV^- $(\underline{II})$ V^{-7}

4   I^- ^-VI ____   ____   ____ IV^- $(\underline{II^{-6}})$ V^{-7}

5   I^- V^6_4 ____   ____   ____ I^6 $(\underline{II^{-6}_{d5}})$ V^{-7}

6   IV^6 IV^- ____   ____   ____ $(\underline{II^{-7}})$ I^{-6}_4 V

7   V^{-7} I^- ____   ____   ____ $(\underline{I^{-7}})$ IV^- V

8   I^- V^6_4 ____   ____   ____ I^6 $(\underline{I^{-6}_{d5}})$ IV^-

9   I^- ^-VI ____   ____   ____ $(\underline{I^{-6}})$ IV^- V

10   I^- ^-VI ____   ____   ____ $(\underline{II^{-6}})$ V^{-7} I^-

11   V^{-7} I^- ____   ____   ____ $(\underline{^-III^{-6}_{d5}})$ ^-VI IV^-

12   V I^- ____   ____   ____ $(\underline{^-III^{-7}})$ ^-VI IV^-

13   I^- V^6_4 ____   ____   ____ I^6 $(\underline{II^{-7}})$ V^{-7}

14   I^- I^6 ____   ____   ____ $(\underline{I^{-6}_{d5}})$ II_-^6 I^{-6}_4

15   I ^-III ____   ____   ____ IV^- $(\underline{I^{-6}_{d5}})$ IV^-

16   V^{-7} I^- ____   ____   ____ $(\underline{^-III^{-7}})$ ^-VI IV^-

17   I^- IV^- ____   ____   ____ V $(\underline{^-III^{-6}_{d5}})$ ^-VI

18   I^- ^-III ____   ____   ____ ^-VI $(\underline{II^{-6}_{d5}})$ V^{-7}

19   I^- ^-VI ____   ____   ____ $(\underline{^-III^{-6}_{d5}})$ ^-VI IV^-

20   II^{-7}_{d5} V^{-7} ____   ____   ____ IV^6 $(\underline{II^{-6}_{d5}})$ V^{-7}

21   I^- V ____   ____   ____ $(\underline{I^{-7}})$ IV^- V

22   I^- IV^- ____   ____   ____ $(\underline{II^{-7}})$ I^6 IV^-

23   I^6 $(\underline{I^{-6}_{d5}})$ ____   ____   ____ IV^- $(\underline{II^{-6}_{d5}})$ I^{-6}_4

24   V^{-7} I^- ____   ____   ____ ^-III $(\underline{I^{-6}_{d5}})$ IV^-

25   I^- V^{-7} ____   ____   ____ $(\underline{I^{-7}})$ IV^- V

26   I^- ^-VI ____   ____   ____ II_-^6 $(\underline{II^{-6}_{d5}})$ I^{-6}_4

27   V^{-7} ^-VI ____   ____   ____ $(\underline{^-III^{-6}_{d5}})$ ^-VI IV^-

28   I^- ^-III ____   ____   ____ IV^- $(\underline{II^{-7}})$ V^{-7}

29   I^- VII^{d7} ____   ____   ____ $(\underline{I^{-7}})$ IV^- V^{-7}

30   I^- IV^6 ____   ____   ____ $(\underline{II^{-6}_{d5}})$ I^{-6}_4 V

31   V I^- ____   ____   ____ $(\underline{^-III^{-6}_{d5}})$ ^-VI IV^-

32   I^6 IV^- ____   ____   ____ II_-^6 $(\underline{II^{-6}_{d5}})$ V

33   I^- IV^- ____   ____   ____ II^{-7}_{d5} $(\underline{II^{-7}})$ V^{-7}

34   I^- IV^- ____   ____   ____ I^6 $(\underline{II^{-7}})$ V^{-7}

35   I^- IV^- ____   ____   ____ $(\underline{^-III^{-7}})$ II_-^6 V^{-7}

36   I^- ^-VI ____   ____   ____ $(\underline{II^{-6}_{d5}})$ V^{-7} I^-

37   I^- IV^- ____   ____   ____ $(\underline{II^{-7}})$ $(\underline{II^{-6}_{d5}})$ V

38   I^- IV^- ____   ____   ____ $(\underline{^-III^{-6}_{d5}})$ ^-VI IV^-

39   V ^-VI ____   ____   ____ $(\underline{I^{-6}_{d5}})$ IV^- V

40   I^- ^-VI ____   ____   ____ $(\underline{II^{-6}_{d5}})$ I^{-6}_4 V

41   I^- IV^- ____   ____   ____ $(\underline{II^{-7}})$ I^6 IV^-

42   I^- ^-VI ____   ____   ____ $(\underline{I^{-6}_{d5}})$ IV^- V

43   I^- ^-VI ____   ____   ____ $(\underline{II^{-6}_{d5}})$ V ^-VI

44   IV^- I^6 ____   ____   ____ $(\underline{^-III^{-6}_{d5}})$ ^-VI IV^-

45   I^- V^{-6}_{d5} ____   ____   ____ I^- $(\underline{^-III^{-7}})$ ^-VI

46   IV^- V^{-7} ____   ____   ____ $(\underline{I^{-7}})$ IV^- V

47   I^- ^-VI ____   ____   ____ IV^- $(\underline{II^{-6}_{d5}})$ V^{-7}

48   $(\underline{I^{-7}})$ IV^- ____   ____   ____ $(\underline{II^{-7}})$ V^{-7} I^-

D10-4a Figured bass dictation of foreign chords

(Copy 1)

Shield the answer. Listen to the series of five chords and write the bass notes and the figured bass symbols for the last three chords; then uncover the answer and compare your response. Goal: No more than eight incorrect frames.

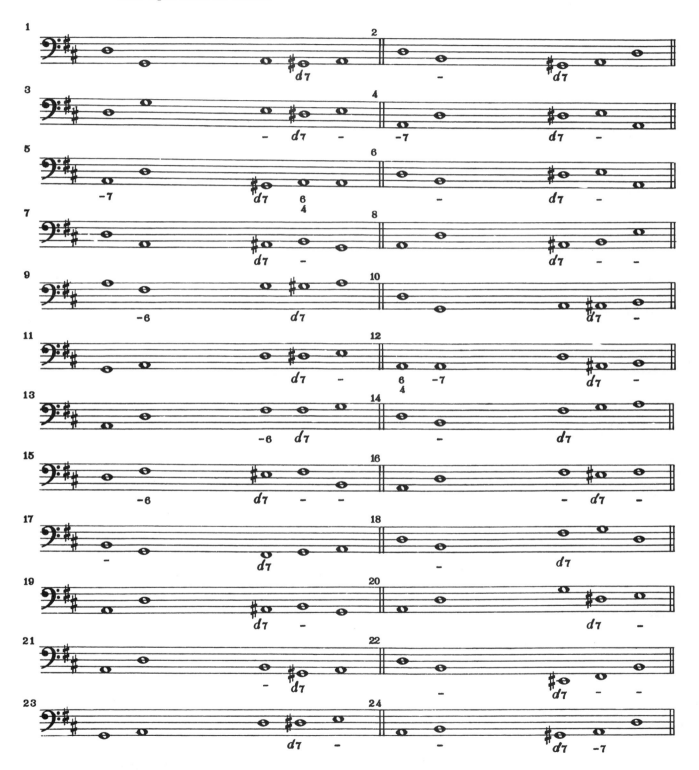

D10-4a Figured bass dictation of foreign chords

(Copy 2)

Shield the answer. Listen to the series of five chords and write the bass notes and the figured bass symbols for the last three chords; then uncover the answer and compare your response. Goal: No more than eight incorrect frames.

279

D10-4a

Figured bass dictation of foreign chords

(Copy 3)

Shield the answer. Listen to the series of five chords and write the bass notes and the figured bass symbols for the last three chords; then uncover the answer and compare your response. Goal: No more than eight incorrect frames.

281

Figured bass dictation of foreign chords

Shield the answer. Listen to the series of five chords and write the bass notes and the figured bass symbols for the last three chords; then uncover the answer and compare your response. Goal: No more than eight incorrect frames.

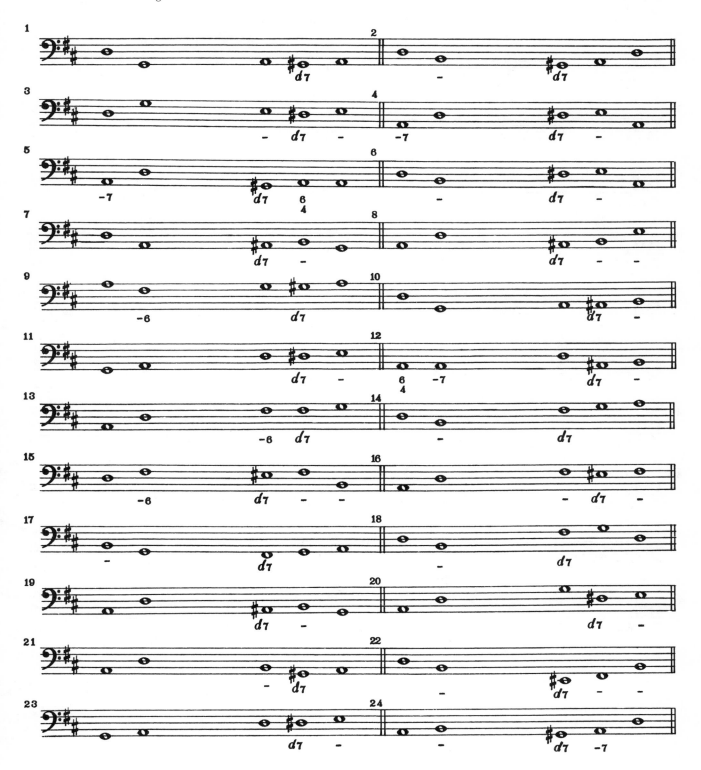

D10-4a

Figured bass dictation of foreign chords

(Copy 5)

Shield the answer. Listen to the series of five chords and write the bass notes and the figured bass symbols for the last three chords; then uncover the answer and compare your response. Goal: No more than eight incorrect frames.

285

286

Lesson **D10-4b**

In this lesson the composite chord symbols are introduced for the following transient leading tone chords in a major key: (aI^{d7}), (aII^{d7}), (III^{d7}), (aIV^{d7}), and (aV^{d7}).

The letter a preceding the Roman numeral indicates an augmented interval above the tonic. Since all these chords are diminished seventh chords, the key location refers to the bass. Therefore the bass of the (aI^{d7}) chord is an augmented prime (a semi-tone) above the tonic, the bass of the (aII^{d7}) chord is an augmented second above the tonic, and so forth.

It is often theoretically possible to indicate the key location of a transient leading tone chord in two ways. For example, a transient leading tone chord that is diminished and has its bass tone a semi-tone above the tonic may theoretically be referred to by the symbol (aI^{d7}) or ($^-II^{d7}$). The proper symbol is (aI^{d7}) since it has a leading tone relation to the chord on the second degree of the key. The principle that guides the choice is that the Roman numeral part of the symbol for a transient leading tone should not be the same as that of the chord to which it has a leading-tone-to-tonic relationship.

D10-4b
Identification of foreign chords

Shield the answer. Listen to the group of five chords and write the composite chord symbols for the last three chords; then uncover the answer and compare your response. Goal: No more than eight incorrect frames.

1 I IV ___ ___ ___ V (a$\underline{\text{IV}}^{d7}$) V

2 I VI⁻ ___ ___ ___ (a$\underline{\text{IV}}^{d7}$) V I

3 I IV ___ ___ ___ II⁻ (a$\underline{\text{I}}^{d7}$) II⁻

4 V⁻⁷ I ___ ___ ___ (a$\underline{\text{I}}^{d7}$) II⁻ V

5 V⁻⁷ I ___ ___ ___ (a$\underline{\text{IV}}^{d7}$) I^6_4 V

6 I VI⁻ ___ ___ ___ (a$\underline{\text{I}}^{d7}$) II⁻ V

7 I V ___ ___ ___ (a$\underline{\text{V}}^{d7}$) VI⁻ IV

8 V I ___ ___ ___ (a$\underline{\text{V}}^{d7}$) VI⁻ II⁻

9 V I⁻⁶ ___ ___ ___ IV (a$\underline{\text{IV}}^{d7}$) V

10 I IV ___ ___ ___ V (a$\underline{\text{V}}^{d7}$) VI⁻

11 IV V ___ ___ ___ I (a$\underline{\text{I}}^{d7}$) II⁻

12 I^6_4 V⁻⁷ ___ ___ ___ I (a$\underline{\text{V}}^{d7}$) VI⁻

13 V I ___ ___ ___ I⁻⁶ ($\underline{\text{III}}^{d7}$) IV

14 I VI⁻ ___ ___ ___ ($\underline{\text{III}}^{d7}$) IV V

15 I I⁻⁶ ___ ___ ___ (a$\underline{\text{II}}^{d7}$) III⁻ VI⁻

16 V I ___ ___ ___ III⁻ (a$\underline{\text{II}}^{d7}$) III⁻

17 VI⁻ IV ___ ___ ___ ($\underline{\text{III}}^{d7}$) IV V

18 I VI⁻ ___ ___ ___ ($\underline{\text{III}}^{d7}$) IV I

19 V I ___ ___ ___ (a$\underline{\text{V}}^{d7}$) VI⁻ IV

20 V I ___ ___ ___ IV (a$\underline{\text{I}}^{d7}$) II⁻

21 V I ___ ___ ___ VI⁻ (a$\underline{\text{IV}}^{d7}$) V

22 I VI⁻ ___ ___ ___ (a$\underline{\text{II}}^{d7}$) III⁻ VI⁻

23 IV V ___ ___ ___ I (a$\underline{\text{I}}^{d7}$) II⁻

24 V VI⁻ ___ ___ ___ (a$\underline{\text{IV}}^{d7}$) V⁻⁷ I

25 I IV ___ ___ ___ ($\underline{\text{II}}^{-6}_{d5}$) I^6_4 V

26 I IV ___ ___ ___ (a$\underline{\text{IV}}^{d7}$) I^6_4 V

27 I IV ___ ___ ___ ($\underline{\text{II}}^{-7}$) I^6_4 V

28 I I⁻⁶ ___ ___ ___ ($\underline{\text{I}}^{-6}_{d5}$) IV V

29 I I⁻⁶ ___ ___ ___ ($\underline{\text{III}}^{d7}$) IV V

30 I IV ___ ___ ___ ($\underline{\text{I}}^{-7}$) IV V

31 V I ___ ___ ___ ($\underline{\text{III}}^{-7}$) VI⁻ IV

32 V I ___ ___ ___ (a$\underline{\text{V}}^{d7}$) VI⁻ IV

33 V^{-6}_{d5} I ___ ___ ___ ($\underline{\text{III}}^{-6}_{d5}$) VI⁻ IV

34 V I ___ ___ ___ ($\underline{\text{VI}}^{-6}_{d5}$) II⁻ V

35 V I ___ ___ ___ (a$\underline{\text{I}}^{d7}$) II⁻ V

36 IV⁻⁶ V ___ ___ ___ I ($\underline{\text{VI}}^{-7}$) II⁻

37 V⁻ V^{-6}_{d5} ___ ___ ___ I⁻ (a$\underline{\text{V}}^{d7}$) VI⁻

38 IV I ___ ___ ___ IV ($\underline{\text{VI}}^{-6}_{d5}$) II⁻

39 V I⁻⁶ ___ ___ ___ (a$\underline{\text{II}}^{d7}$) III⁻ IV

40 V I ___ ___ ___ ($\underline{\text{III}}^{d7}$) IV V

41 I VI⁻ ___ ___ ___ IV ($\underline{\text{II}}^{-6}_{d5}$) V

42 I⁻⁶ IV ___ ___ ___ (a$\underline{\text{IV}}^{d7}$) I^6_4 V

43 V I ___ ___ ___ ($\underline{\text{III}}^{-6}_{d5}$) VI⁻ IV

44 V I ___ ___ ___ (a$\underline{\text{I}}^{d7}$) II⁻ V⁻⁷

45 I VI⁻ ___ ___ ___ ($\underline{\text{I}}^{-6}_{d5}$) IV V

46 V I ___ ___ ___ VI⁻ ($\underline{\text{III}}^{d7}$) IV

47 I V ___ ___ ___ (a$\underline{\text{V}}^{d7}$) VI⁻ IV

48 I VI⁻ ___ ___ ___ (a$\underline{\text{IV}}^{d7}$) V⁻⁷ I

D10-4b   Identification of foreign chords
(Copy 2)

Shield the answer. Listen to the group of five chords and write the composite chord symbols for the last three chords; then uncover the answer and compare your response. Goal: No more than eight incorrect frames.

1   I IV _____ _____ _____ V (aIV^{d7}) V

2   I VI$^-$ _____ _____ _____ (aIV^{d7}) V I

3   I IV _____ _____ _____ II$^-$ (aI^{d7}) II$^-$

4   V^{-7} I _____ _____ _____ (aI^{d7}) II$^-$ V

5   V^{-7} I _____ _____ _____ (aIV^{d7}) I$_4^6$ V

6   I VI$^-$ _____ _____ _____ (aI^{d7}) II$^-$ V

7   I V _____ _____ _____ (aV^{d7}) VI$^-$ IV

8   V I _____ _____ _____ (aV^{d7}) VI$^-$ II$^-$

9   V I^{-6} _____ _____ _____ IV (aIV^{d7}) V

10   I IV _____ _____ _____ V (aV^{d7}) VI$^-$

11   IV V _____ _____ _____ I (aI^{d7}) II$^-$

12   I$_4^6$ V^{-7} _____ _____ _____ I (aV^{d7}) VI$^-$

13   V I _____ _____ _____ I^{-6} (III^{d7}) IV

14   I VI$^-$ _____ _____ _____ (III^{d7}) IV V

15   I I^{-6} _____ _____ _____ (aII^{d7}) III$^-$ VI$^-$

16   V I _____ _____ _____ III$^-$ (aII^{d7}) III$^-$

17   VI$^-$ IV _____ _____ _____ (III^{d7}) IV V

18   I VI$^-$ _____ _____ _____ (III^{d7}) IV I

19   V I _____ _____ _____ (aV^{d7}) VI$^-$ IV

20   V I _____ _____ _____ IV (aI^{d7}) II$^-$

21   V I _____ _____ _____ VI$^-$ (aIV^{d7}) V

22   I VI$^-$ _____ _____ _____ (aII^{d7}) III$^-$ VI$^-$

23   IV V _____ _____ _____ I (aI^{d7}) II$^-$

24   V VI$^-$ _____ _____ _____ (aIV^{d7}) V^{-7} I

25   I IV _____ _____ _____ (II$^{-6}_{d5}$) I$_4^6$ V

26   I IV _____ _____ _____ (aIV^{d7}) I$_4^6$ V

27   I IV _____ _____ _____ (II^{-7}) I$_4^6$ V

28   I I^{-6} _____ _____ _____ (I$^{-6}_{d5}$) IV V

29   I I^{-6} _____ _____ _____ (III^{d7}) IV V

30   I IV _____ _____ _____ (I^{-7}) IV V

31   V I _____ _____ _____ (III^{-7}) VI$^-$ IV

32   V I _____ _____ _____ (aV^{d7}) VI$^-$ IV

33   V$^{-6}_{d5}$ I _____ _____ _____ (III$^{-6}_{d5}$) VI$^-$ IV

34   V I _____ _____ _____ (VI$^{-6}_{d5}$) II$^-$ V

35   V I _____ _____ _____ (aI^{d7}) II$^-$ V

36   IV^{-6} V _____ _____ _____ I (VI^{-7}) II$^-$

37   V$^-$ V$^{-6}_{d5}$ _____ _____ _____ I$^-$ (aV^{d7}) VI$^-$

38   IV I _____ _____ _____ IV (VI$^{-6}_{d5}$) II$^-$

39   V I^{-6} _____ _____ _____ (aII^{d7}) III$^-$ IV

40   V I _____ _____ _____ (III^{d7}) IV V

41   I VI$^-$ _____ _____ _____ IV (II$^{-6}_{d5}$) V

42   I^{-6} IV _____ _____ _____ (aIV^{d7}) I$_4^6$ V

43   V I _____ _____ _____ (III$^{-6}_{d5}$) VI$^-$ IV

44   V I _____ _____ _____ (aI^{d7}) II$^-$ V^{-7}

45   I VI$^-$ _____ _____ _____ (I$^{-6}_{d5}$) IV V

46   V I _____ _____ _____ VI$^-$ (III^{d7}) IV

47   I V _____ _____ _____ (aV^{d7}) VI$^-$ IV

48   I VI$^-$ _____ _____ _____ (aIV^{d7}) V^{-7} I

D10-4b Identification of foreign chords
(Copy 3)

Shield the answer. Listen to the group of five chords and write the composite chord symbols for the last three chords; then uncover the answer and compare your response. Goal: No more than eight incorrect frames.

1 I IV _____ _____ _____ V (a$\underline{IV}^{d7}$) V

2 I VI⁻ _____ _____ _____ (a$\underline{IV}^{d7}$) V I

3 I IV _____ _____ _____ II⁻ (a$\underline{I}^{d7}$) II⁻

4 V⁻⁷ I _____ _____ _____ (a$\underline{I}^{d7}$) II⁻ V

5 V⁻⁷ I _____ _____ _____ (a$\underline{IV}^{d7}$) I$_4^6$ V

6 I VI⁻ _____ _____ _____ (a$\underline{I}^{d7}$) II⁻ V

7 I V _____ _____ _____ (a$\underline{V}^{d7}$) VI⁻ IV

8 V I _____ _____ _____ (a$\underline{V}^{d7}$) VI⁻ II⁻

9 V I⁻⁶ _____ _____ _____ IV (a$\underline{IV}^{d7}$) V

10 I IV _____ _____ _____ V (a$\underline{V}^{d7}$) VI⁻

11 IV V _____ _____ _____ I (a$\underline{I}^{d7}$) II⁻

12 I$_4^6$ V⁻⁷ _____ _____ _____ I (a$\underline{V}^{d7}$) VI⁻

13 V I _____ _____ _____ I⁻⁶ ($\underline{III}^{d7}$) IV

14 I VI⁻ _____ _____ _____ ($\underline{III}^{d7}$) IV V

15 I I⁻⁶ _____ _____ _____ (a$\underline{II}^{d7}$) III⁻ VI⁻

16 V I _____ _____ _____ III⁻ (a$\underline{II}^{d7}$) III⁻

17 VI⁻ IV _____ _____ _____ ($\underline{III}^{d7}$) IV V

18 I VI⁻ _____ _____ _____ ($\underline{III}^{d7}$) IV I

19 V I _____ _____ _____ (a$\underline{V}^{d7}$) VI⁻ IV

20 V I _____ _____ _____ IV (a$\underline{I}^{d7}$) II⁻

21 V I _____ _____ _____ VI⁻ (a$\underline{IV}^{d7}$) V

22 I VI⁻ _____ _____ _____ (a$\underline{II}^{d7}$) III⁻ VI⁻

23 IV V _____ _____ _____ I (a$\underline{I}^{d7}$) II⁻

24 V VI⁻ _____ _____ _____ (a$\underline{IV}^{d7}$) V⁻⁷ I

25 I IV _____ _____ _____ ($\underline{II}_{d5}^{-6}$) I$_4^6$ V

26 I IV _____ _____ _____ (a$\underline{IV}^{d7}$) I$_4^6$ V

27 I IV _____ _____ _____ ($\underline{II}^{-7}$) I$_4^6$ V

28 I I⁻⁶ _____ _____ _____ ($\underline{I}_{d5}^{-6}$) IV V

29 I I⁻⁶ _____ _____ _____ ($\underline{III}^{d7}$) IV V

30 I IV _____ _____ _____ ($\underline{I}^{-7}$) IV V

31 V I _____ _____ _____ ($\underline{III}^{-7}$) VI⁻ IV

32 V I _____ _____ _____ (a$\underline{V}^{d7}$) VI⁻ IV

33 V$_{d5}^{-6}$ I _____ _____ _____ ($\underline{III}_{d5}^{-6}$) VI⁻ IV

34 V I _____ _____ _____ ($\underline{VI}_{d5}^{-6}$) II⁻ V

35 V I _____ _____ _____ (a$\underline{I}^{d7}$) II⁻ V

36 IV⁻⁶ V _____ _____ _____ I ($\underline{VI}^{-7}$) II⁻

37 V⁻ V$_{d5}^{-6}$ _____ _____ _____ I⁻ (a$\underline{V}^{d7}$) VI⁻

38 IV I _____ _____ _____ IV ($\underline{VI}_{d5}^{-6}$) II⁻

39 V I⁻⁶ _____ _____ _____ (a$\underline{II}^{d7}$) III⁻ IV

40 V I _____ _____ _____ ($\underline{III}^{d7}$) IV V

41 I VI⁻ _____ _____ _____ IV ($\underline{II}_{d5}^{-6}$) V

42 I⁻⁶ IV _____ _____ _____ (a$\underline{IV}^{d7}$) I$_4^6$ V

43 V I _____ _____ _____ ($\underline{III}_{d5}^{-6}$) VI⁻ IV

44 V I _____ _____ _____ (a$\underline{I}^{d7}$) II⁻ V⁻⁷

45 I VI⁻ _____ _____ _____ ($\underline{I}_{d5}^{-6}$) IV V

46 V I _____ _____ _____ VI⁻ ($\underline{III}^{d7}$) IV

47 I V _____ _____ _____ (a$\underline{V}^{d7}$) VI⁻ IV

48 I VI⁻ _____ _____ _____ (a$\underline{IV}^{d7}$) V⁻⁷ I

D10-4b Identification of foreign chords
(Copy 4)

Shield the answer. Listen to the group of five chords and write the composite chord symbols for the last three chords; then uncover the answer and compare your response. Goal: No more than eight incorrect frames.

1. I IV _____ _____ _____ V ($a\underline{IV}^{d7}$) V
2. I VI⁻ _____ _____ _____ ($a\underline{IV}^{d7}$) V I
3. I IV _____ _____ _____ II⁻ ($a\underline{I}^{d7}$) II⁻
4. V⁻⁷ I _____ _____ _____ ($a\underline{I}^{d7}$) II⁻ V
5. V⁻⁷ I _____ _____ _____ ($a\underline{IV}^{d7}$) I^6_4 V
6. I VI⁻ _____ _____ _____ ($a\underline{I}^{d7}$) II⁻ V
7. I V _____ _____ _____ ($a\underline{V}^{d7}$) VI⁻ IV
8. V I _____ _____ _____ ($a\underline{V}^{d7}$) VI⁻ II⁻
9. V I⁻⁶ _____ _____ _____ IV ($a\underline{IV}^{d7}$) V
10. I IV _____ _____ _____ V ($a\underline{V}^{d7}$) VI⁻
11. IV V _____ _____ _____ I ($a\underline{I}^{d7}$) II⁻
12. I^6_4 V⁻⁷ _____ _____ _____ I ($a\underline{V}^{d7}$) VI⁻
13. V I _____ _____ _____ I⁻⁶ ($\underline{III}^{d7}$) IV
14. I VI⁻ _____ _____ _____ ($\underline{III}^{d7}$) IV V
15. I I⁻⁶ _____ _____ _____ ($a\underline{II}^{d7}$) III⁻ VI⁻
16. V I _____ _____ _____ III⁻ ($a\underline{II}^{d7}$) III⁻
17. VI⁻ IV _____ _____ _____ ($\underline{III}^{d7}$) IV V
18. I VI⁻ _____ _____ _____ ($\underline{III}^{d7}$) IV I
19. V I _____ _____ _____ ($a\underline{V}^{d7}$) VI⁻ IV
20. V I _____ _____ _____ IV ($a\underline{I}^{d7}$) II⁻
21. V I _____ _____ _____ VI⁻ ($a\underline{IV}^{d7}$) V
22. I VI⁻ _____ _____ _____ ($a\underline{II}^{d7}$) III⁻ VI⁻
23. IV V _____ _____ _____ I ($a\underline{I}^{d7}$) II⁻
24. V VI⁻ _____ _____ _____ ($a\underline{IV}^{d7}$) V⁻⁷ I

25. I IV _____ _____ _____ ($\underline{II}^{-6}_{d5}$) I^6_4 V
26. I IV _____ _____ _____ ($a\underline{IV}^{d7}$) I^6_4 V
27. I IV _____ _____ _____ ($\underline{II}^{-7}$) I^6_4 V
28. I I⁻⁶ _____ _____ _____ ($\underline{I}^{-6}_{d5}$) IV V
29. I I⁻⁶ _____ _____ _____ ($\underline{III}^{d7}$) IV V
30. I IV _____ _____ _____ ($\underline{I}^{-7}$) IV V
31. V I _____ _____ _____ ($\underline{III}^{-7}$) VI⁻ IV
32. V I _____ _____ _____ ($a\underline{V}^{d7}$) VI⁻ IV
33. V^{-6}_{d5} I _____ _____ _____ ($\underline{III}^{-6}_{d5}$) VI⁻ IV
34. V I _____ _____ _____ ($\underline{VI}^{-6}_{d5}$) II⁻ V
35. V I _____ _____ _____ ($a\underline{I}^{d7}$) II⁻ V
36. IV⁻⁶ V _____ _____ _____ I ($\underline{VI}^{-7}$) II⁻
37. V⁻ V^{-6}_{d5} _____ _____ _____ I⁻ ($a\underline{V}^{d7}$) VI⁻
38. IV I _____ _____ _____ IV ($\underline{VI}^{-6}_{d5}$) II⁻
39. V I⁻⁶ _____ _____ _____ ($a\underline{II}^{d7}$) III⁻ IV
40. V I _____ _____ _____ ($\underline{III}^{d7}$) IV V
41. I VI⁻ _____ _____ _____ IV ($\underline{II}^{-6}_{d5}$) V
42. I⁻⁶ IV _____ _____ _____ ($a\underline{IV}^{d7}$) I^6_4 V
43. V I _____ _____ _____ ($\underline{III}^{-6}_{d5}$) VI⁻ IV
44. V I _____ _____ _____ ($a\underline{I}^{d7}$) II⁻ V⁻⁷
45. I VI⁻ _____ _____ _____ ($\underline{I}^{-6}_{d5}$) IV V
46. V I _____ _____ _____ VI⁻ ($\underline{III}^{d7}$) IV
47. I V _____ _____ _____ ($a\underline{V}^{d7}$) VI⁻ IV
48. I VI⁻ _____ _____ _____ ($a\underline{IV}^{d7}$) V⁻⁷ I

D10-4b Identification of foreign chords

(Copy 5)

Shield the answer. Listen to the group of five chords and write the composite chord symbols for the last three chords; then uncover the answer and compare your response. Goal: No more than eight incorrect frames.

1   I   IV ___ ___ ___ V $(\underline{a\text{IV}}^{d7})$ V

2   I   VI⁻ ___ ___ ___ $(\underline{a\text{IV}}^{d7})$ V   I

3   I   IV ___ ___ ___ II⁻ $(\underline{a\text{I}}^{d7})$ II⁻

4   V⁻⁷   I ___ ___ ___ $(\underline{a\text{I}}^{d7})$ II⁻   V

5   V⁻⁷   I ___ ___ ___ $(\underline{a\text{IV}}^{d7})$ I_4^6 V

6   I   VI⁻ ___ ___ ___ $(\underline{a\text{I}}^{d7})$ II⁻   V

7   I   V ___ ___ ___ $(\underline{a\text{V}}^{d7})$ VI⁻   IV

8   V   I ___ ___ ___ $(\underline{a\text{V}}^{d7})$ VI⁻   II⁻

9   V   I⁻⁶ ___ ___ ___ IV $(\underline{a\text{IV}}^{d7})$ V

10   I   IV ___ ___ ___ V $(\underline{a\text{V}}^{d7})$ VI⁻

11   IV   V ___ ___ ___ I $(\underline{a\text{I}}^{d7})$ II⁻

12   I_4^6 V⁻⁷ ___ ___ ___ I $(\underline{a\text{V}}^{d7})$ VI⁻

13   V   I ___ ___ ___ I⁻⁶ $(\underline{\text{III}}^{d7})$ IV

14   I   VI⁻ ___ ___ ___ $(\underline{\text{III}}^{d7})$ IV   V

15   I   I⁻⁶ ___ ___ ___ $(\underline{a\text{II}}^{d7})$ III⁻   VI⁻

16   V   I ___ ___ ___ III⁻ $(\underline{a\text{II}}^{d7})$ III⁻

17   VI⁻   IV ___ ___ ___ $(\underline{\text{III}}^{d7})$ IV   V

18   I   VI⁻ ___ ___ ___ $(\underline{\text{III}}^{d7})$ IV   I

19   V   I ___ ___ ___ $(\underline{a\text{V}}^{d7})$ VI⁻   IV

20   V   I ___ ___ ___ IV $(\underline{a\text{I}}^{d7})$ II⁻

21   V   I ___ ___ ___ VI⁻ $(\underline{a\text{IV}}^{d7})$ V

22   I   VI⁻ ___ ___ ___ $(\underline{a\text{II}}^{d7})$ III⁻   VI⁻

23   IV   V ___ ___ ___ I $(\underline{a\text{I}}^{d7})$ II⁻

24   V   VI⁻ ___ ___ ___ $(\underline{a\text{IV}}^{d7})$ V⁻⁷   I

25   I   IV ___ ___ ___ $(\underline{\text{II}}^{-6}_{d5})$ I_4^6 V

26   I   IV ___ ___ ___ $(\underline{a\text{IV}}^{d7})$ I_4^6 V

27   I   IV ___ ___ ___ $(\underline{\text{II}}^{-7})$ I_4^6 V

28   I   I⁻⁶ ___ ___ ___ $(\underline{\text{I}}^{-6}_{d5})$ IV   V

29   I   I⁻⁶ ___ ___ ___ $(\underline{\text{III}}^{d7})$ IV   V

30   I   IV ___ ___ ___ $(\underline{\text{I}}^{-7})$ IV   V

31   V   I ___ ___ ___ $(\underline{\text{III}}^{-7})$ VI⁻   IV

32   V   I ___ ___ ___ $(\underline{a\text{V}}^{d7})$ VI⁻   IV

33   V^{-6}_{d5} I ___ ___ ___ $(\underline{\text{III}}^{-6}_{d5})$ VI⁻   IV

34   V   I ___ ___ ___ $(\underline{\text{VI}}^{-6}_{d5})$ II⁻   V

35   V   I ___ ___ ___ $(\underline{a\text{I}}^{d7})$ II⁻   V

36   IV⁻⁶   V ___ ___ ___ I $(\underline{\text{VI}}^{-7})$ II⁻

37   V⁻ V^{-6}_{d5} ___ ___ ___ I⁻ $(\underline{a\text{V}}^{d7})$ VI⁻

38   IV   I ___ ___ ___ IV $(\underline{\text{VI}}^{-6}_{d5})$ II⁻

39   V   I⁻⁶ ___ ___ ___ $(\underline{a\text{II}}^{d7})$ III⁻   IV

40   V   I ___ ___ ___ $(\underline{\text{III}}^{d7})$ IV   V

41   I   VI⁻ ___ ___ ___ IV $(\underline{\text{II}}^{-6}_{d5})$ V

42   I⁻⁶   IV ___ ___ ___ $(\underline{a\text{IV}}^{d7})$ I_4^6 V

43   V   I ___ ___ ___ $(\underline{\text{III}}^{-6}_{d5})$ VI⁻   IV

44   V   I ___ ___ ___ $(\underline{a\text{I}}^{d7})$ II⁻   V⁻⁷

45   I   VI⁻ ___ ___ ___ $(\underline{\text{I}}^{-6}_{d5})$ IV   V

46   V   I ___ ___ ___ VI⁻ $(\underline{\text{III}}^{d7})$ IV

47   I   V ___ ___ ___ $(\underline{a\text{V}}^{d7})$ VI⁻   IV

48   I   VI⁻ ___ ___ ___ $(\underline{a\text{IV}}^{d7})$ V⁻⁷   I

D10-5a Figured bass dictation of foreign chords
(Copy 1)

Shield the answer. Listen to the series of five chords and write the bass notes and the figured bass symbols for the last three chords; then uncover the answer and compare your response. Goal: No more than eight incorrect frames.

293

D10-5a

Figured bass dictation of foreign chords

(Copy 2)

Shield the answer. Listen to the series of five chords and write the bass notes and the figured bass symbols for the last three chords; then uncover the answer and compare your response. Goal: No more than eight incorrect frames.

295

D10-5a

Figured bass dictation of foreign chords

(Copy 3)

Shield the answer. Listen to the series of five chords and write the bass notes and the figured bass symbols for the last three chords; then uncover the answer and compare your response. Goal: No more than eight incorrect frames.

297

D10-5a Figured bass dictation of foreign chords
(Copy 4)

Shield the answer. Listen to the series of five chords and write the bass notes and the figured bass symbols for the last three chords; then uncover the answer and compare your response. Goal: No more than eight incorrect frames.

D10-5a Figured bass dictation of foreign chords

(Copy 5)

Shield the answer. Listen to the series of five chords and write the bass notes and the figured bass symbols for the last three chords; then uncover the answer and compare your response. Goal: No more than eight incorrect frames.

Lesson D10-5b

This lesson introduces the following composite chord symbols for transient leading tone chords in minor keys: ($\underline{III}^{d7}$), ($\underline{aIV}^{d7}$), and ($\underline{V}^{d7}$). Of these symbols, the ($\underline{III}^{d7}$) and ($\underline{aIV}^{d7}$) are identical with those for chords in major keys. The symbol ($\underline{V}^{d7}$) is for a chord that appears only in the minor key. The comparable chord in a major key has the symbol ($\underline{aV}^{d7}$).

In this lesson, the figured bass symbol ^{d7} occurs in the composite chord symbol for the regular leading tone seventh chord of the key as well as in the symbols for transient leading tone chords. You will remember that the key location symbol for a diminished seventh chord refers to the bass of the chord rather than the root. Thus we have symbols VII^{d7}, II^{d7}, IV^{d7}, and $^{-}VI^{d7}$, indicating the regular leading tone seventh chord in a minor key with the various members in the bass. The composite chord symbols for these chords do not contain the parentheses and underlining because they are not transient leading tone chords.

D10–5b   Identification of foreign chords
(Copy 1)

Shield the answer. Listen to the group of five chords and write the composite chord symbols for the last three chords; then uncover the answer and compare your response. Goal: No more than eight incorrect frames. When you have done this lesson, take Test D10.

1 I^- IV^- ___ ___ ___ $(\underline{aIV}^{d7})$ V I^-

2 I^- IV^- ___ ___ ___ $(\underline{III}^{d7})$ IV^- V

3 I^- ^-VI ___ ___ ___ $(\underline{V}^{d7})$ ^-VI IV^-

4 V I^- ___ ___ ___ VII^{d7} I^- V

5 I^- ^-VI ___ ___ ___ $(\underline{aIV}^{d7})$ I^{-6}_4 V

6 I^- IV^- ___ ___ ___ I^6 II^{d7} I^-

7 I^- IV^- ___ ___ ___ I^6 $(\underline{II}^{-7})$ V

8 I^- V^6_4 ___ ___ ___ I^6 $(\underline{III}^{d7})$ IV^-

9 V I^- ___ ___ ___ $^-VI^{d7}$ V^{-7} I^-

10 IV^- I^6 ___ ___ ___ $(\underline{III}^{d7})$ IV^- V

11 I^- V ___ ___ ___ IV^{d7} I^6 V

12 I^- IV^- ___ ___ ___ I^6 VII^{d7} I^-

13 I^- IV^- ___ ___ ___ $(\underline{II^{-6}_{d5}})$ I^{-6}_4 V

14 I^- IV^- ___ ___ ___ $(\underline{aIV}^{d7})$ I^{-6}_4 V

15 I^- IV^- ___ ___ ___ $(\underline{II}^{-7})$ I^{-6}_4 V

16 I^- ^-VI ___ ___ ___ IV^- II^{d7} I^-

17 I^- IV^- ___ ___ ___ IV^{d7} I^6 V

18 I^- $\underline{II^6_5}$ ___ ___ ___ IV^{d7} I^6 V

19 I^- IV^{d7} ___ ___ ___ I^6 $(\underline{aIV}^{d7})$ V

20 I^- IV^- ___ ___ ___ I^6 $(\underline{II^{-6}_{d5}})$ V

21 I^- V ___ ___ ___ ^-VI $(\underline{V}^{d7})$ ^-VI

22 IV^- I^- ___ ___ ___ $(\underline{V}^{d7})$ ^-VI IV^-

23 I^- $^-VI^{d7}$ ___ ___ ___ V $(\underline{V}^{d7})$ ^-VI

24 IV^- I^- ___ ___ ___ $(\underline{aIV}^{d7})$ I^{-6}_4 V

25 I^- $(\underline{V}^{d7})$ ___ ___ ___ ^-VI $(\underline{III}^{d7})$ IV^-

26 I^- VII^{d7} ___ ___ ___ I^- $(\underline{V}^{d7})$ ^-VI

27 V I^- ___ ___ ___ $\underline{II^6_5}$ $(\underline{II^{-6}_{d5}})$ I^{-6}_4

28 V I^- ___ ___ ___ $\underline{II^6_5}$ $(\underline{aIV}^{d7})$ I^{-6}_4

29 V I^- ___ ___ ___ IV^{d7} I^6 V

30 I^- V ___ ___ ___ I^6 $(\underline{III}^{d7})$ IV^-

31 I^- IV^- ___ ___ ___ I^6 $(\underline{II}^{-7})$ V

32 I^- IV^- ___ ___ ___ II^{d7} I^- VII^{d7}

33 I^- ^-VI ___ ___ ___ $(\underline{aIV}^{d7})$ V^{-7} $^-VI^{d7}$

34 V V^{a4}_2 ___ ___ ___ I^6 $(\underline{I^{-6}_{d5}})$ IV^-

35 V I^- ___ ___ ___ $(\underline{V}^{d7})$ ^-VI IV^-

36 I^- V ___ ___ ___ $(\underline{^-III^{-6}_{d5}})$ ^-VI V

37 I^- IV^- ___ ___ ___ $^-VI^{d7}$ I^{-6}_4 V^{-7}

38 I^- ^-VI ___ ___ ___ $\underline{II^6_-}$ $(\underline{aIV}^{d7})$ I^{-6}_4

39 V ^-VI ___ ___ ___ $(\underline{I^{-6}_{d5}})$ IV^- I^-

40 VII^{d7} I^- ___ ___ ___ IV^- IV^{d7} I^6

41 I^- ^-VI ___ ___ ___ $(\underline{III}^{d7})$ IV^- V

42 I^- ^-III ___ ___ ___ ^-VI $(\underline{V}^{d7})$ ^-VI

43 ^-IV II^{d7} ___ ___ ___ I^- $(\underline{I}^{-7})$ IV^-

44 V^{-7} I^- ___ ___ ___ $(\underline{^-III}^{-7})$ ^-VI I^{-6}_4

45 V^{-7} I^- ___ ___ ___ I^6 $(\underline{aIV}^{d7})$ V

46 I^- IV^- ___ ___ ___ II^{d7} I^- V^{-6}_{d5}

47 I^- IV^- ___ ___ ___ IV^{d7} I^6 V

48 ^-VI IV^- ___ ___ ___ $(\underline{aIV}^{d7})$ V^{-7} I^-

D10-5b

(Copy 2)

Identification of foreign chords

Shield the answer. Listen to the group of five chords and write the composite chord symbols for the last three chords; then uncover the answer and compare your response. Goal: No more than eight incorrect frames. When you have done this lesson, take Test D10.

1. I^- IV^- ＿＿ ＿＿ ＿＿ $(\underline{aIV}^{d7})$ V I^-

2. I^- IV^- ＿＿ ＿＿ ＿＿ $(\underline{III}^{d7})$ IV^- V

3. I^- ^-VI ＿＿ ＿＿ ＿＿ $(\underline{V}^{d7})$ ^-VI IV^-

4. V I^- ＿＿ ＿＿ ＿＿ VII^{d7} I^- V

5. I^- ^-VI ＿＿ ＿＿ ＿＿ $(\underline{aIV}^{d7})$ I^{-6}_4 V

6. I^- IV^- ＿＿ ＿＿ ＿＿ I^6 II^{d7} I^-

7. I^- IV^- ＿＿ ＿＿ ＿＿ I^6 $(\underline{II}^{-7})$ V

8. I^- V^6_4 ＿＿ ＿＿ ＿＿ I^6 $(\underline{III}^{d7})$ IV^-

9. V I^- ＿＿ ＿＿ ＿＿ $^-VI^{d7}$ V^{-7} I^-

10. IV^- I^6 ＿＿ ＿＿ ＿＿ $(\underline{III}^{d7})$ IV^- V

11. I^- V ＿＿ ＿＿ ＿＿ IV^{d7} I^6 V

12. I^- IV^- ＿＿ ＿＿ ＿＿ I^6 VII^{d7} I^-

13. I^- IV^- ＿＿ ＿＿ ＿＿ $(\underline{II^{-6}_{d5}})$ I^{-6}_4 V

14. I^- IV^- ＿＿ ＿＿ ＿＿ $(\underline{aIV}^{d7})$ I^{-6}_4 V

15. I^- IV^- ＿＿ ＿＿ ＿＿ $(\underline{II}^{-7})$ I^{-6}_4 V

16. I^- ^-VI ＿＿ ＿＿ ＿＿ IV^- II^{d7} I^-

17. I^- IV^- ＿＿ ＿＿ ＿＿ IV^{d7} I^6 V

18. I^- $II^6_{\underline{5}}$ ＿＿ ＿＿ ＿＿ IV^{d7} I^6 V

19. I^- IV^{d7} ＿＿ ＿＿ ＿＿ I^6 $(\underline{aIV}^{d7})$ V

20. I^- IV^- ＿＿ ＿＿ ＿＿ I^6 $(\underline{II^{-6}_{d5}})$ V

21. I^- V ＿＿ ＿＿ ＿＿ ^-VI $(\underline{V}^{d7})$ ^-VI

22. IV^- I^- ＿＿ ＿＿ ＿＿ $(\underline{V}^{d7})$ ^-VI IV^-

23. I^- $^-VI^{d7}$ ＿＿ ＿＿ ＿＿ V $(\underline{V}^{d7})$ ^-VI

24. IV^- I^- ＿＿ ＿＿ ＿＿ $(\underline{aIV}^{d7})$ I^{-6}_4 V

25. I^- $(\underline{V}^{d7})$ ＿＿ ＿＿ ＿＿ ^-VI $(\underline{III}^{d7})$ IV^-

26. I^- VII^{d7} ＿＿ ＿＿ ＿＿ I^- $(\underline{V}^{d7})$ ^-VI

27. V I^- ＿＿ ＿＿ ＿＿ $II^6_{\underline{5}}$ $(\underline{II^{-6}_{d5}})$ I^{-6}_4

28. V I^- ＿＿ ＿＿ ＿＿ $II^6_{\underline{5}}$ $(\underline{aIV}^{d7})$ I^{-6}_4

29. V I^- ＿＿ ＿＿ ＿＿ IV^{d7} I^6 V

30. I^- V ＿＿ ＿＿ ＿＿ I^6 $(\underline{III}^{d7})$ IV^-

31. I^- IV^- ＿＿ ＿＿ ＿＿ I^6 $(\underline{II}^{-7})$ V

32. I^- IV^- ＿＿ ＿＿ ＿＿ II^{d7} I^- VII^{d7}

33. I^- ^-VI ＿＿ ＿＿ ＿＿ $(\underline{aIV}^{d7})$ V^{-7} $^-VI^{d7}$

34. V V^{a4}_2 ＿＿ ＿＿ ＿＿ I^6 $(\underline{I^{-6}_{d5}})$ IV^-

35. V I^- ＿＿ ＿＿ ＿＿ $(\underline{V}^{d7})$ ^-VI IV^-

36. I^- V ＿＿ ＿＿ ＿＿ $(\underline{^-III^{-6}_{d5}})$ ^-VI V

37. I^- IV^- ＿＿ ＿＿ ＿＿ $^-VI^{d7}$ I^{-6}_4 V^{-7}

38. I^- ^-VI ＿＿ ＿＿ ＿＿ $II^6_{\underline{-}}$ $(\underline{aIV}^{d7})$ I^{-6}_4

39. V ^-VI ＿＿ ＿＿ ＿＿ $(\underline{I^{-6}_{d5}})$ IV^- I^-

40. VII^{d7} I^- ＿＿ ＿＿ ＿＿ IV^- IV^{d7} I^6

41. I^- ^-VI ＿＿ ＿＿ ＿＿ $(\underline{III}^{d7})$ IV^- V

42. I^- ^-III ＿＿ ＿＿ ＿＿ ^-VI $(\underline{V}^{d7})$ ^-VI

43. ^-IV II^{d7} ＿＿ ＿＿ ＿＿ I^- $(\underline{I}^{-7})$ IV^-

44. V^{-7} I^- ＿＿ ＿＿ ＿＿ $(\underline{^-III^{-7}})$ ^-VI I^{-6}_4

45. V^{-7} I^- ＿＿ ＿＿ ＿＿ I^6 $(\underline{aIV}^{d7})$ V

46. I^- IV^- ＿＿ ＿＿ ＿＿ II^{d7} I^- V^{-6}_{d5}

47. I^- IV^- ＿＿ ＿＿ ＿＿ IV^{d7} I^6 V

48. ^-VI IV^- ＿＿ ＿＿ ＿＿ $(\underline{aIV}^{d7})$ V^{-7} I^-

D10-5b
Identification of foreign chords

Shield the answer. Listen to the group of five chords and write the composite chord symbols for the last three chords; then uncover the answer and compare your response. Goal: No more than eight incorrect frames. When you have done this lesson, take Test D10.

1   I^- IV^- ___ ___ ___ $(\underline{aIV}^{d7})$ V I^-

2   I^- IV^- ___ ___ ___ $(\underline{III}^{d7})$ IV^- V

3   I^- ^-VI ___ ___ ___ $(\underline{V}^{d7})$ ^-VI IV^-

4   V I^- ___ ___ ___ VII^{d7} I^- V

5   I^- ^-VI ___ ___ ___ $(\underline{aIV}^{d7})$ I^{-6}_4 V

6   I^- IV^- ___ ___ ___ I^6 II^{d7} I^-

7   I^- IV^- ___ ___ ___ I^6 $(\underline{II}^{-7})$ V

8   I^- V^6_4 ___ ___ ___ I^6 $(\underline{III}^{d7})$ IV^-

9   V I^- ___ ___ ___ $^-VI^{d7}$ V^{-7} I^-

10   IV^- I^6 ___ ___ ___ $(\underline{III}^{d7})$ IV^- V

11   I^- V ___ ___ ___ IV^{d7} I^6 V

12   I^- IV^- ___ ___ ___ I^6 VII^{d7} I^-

13   I^- IV^- ___ ___ ___ $(\underline{II}^{-6}_{d5})$ I^{-6}_4 V

14   I^- IV^- ___ ___ ___ $(\underline{aIV}^{d7})$ I^{-6}_4 V

15   I^- IV^- ___ ___ ___ $(\underline{II}^{-7})$ I^{-6}_4 V

16   I^- ^-VI ___ ___ ___ IV^- II^{d7} I^-

17   I^- IV^- ___ ___ ___ IV^{d7} I^6 V

18   I^- II^6_5 ___ ___ ___ IV^{d7} I^6 V

19   I^- IV^{d7} ___ ___ ___ I^6 $(\underline{aIV}^{d7})$ V

20   I^- IV^- ___ ___ ___ I^6 $(\underline{II}^{-6}_{d5})$ V

21   I^- V ___ ___ ___ ^-VI $(\underline{V}^{d7})$ ^-VI

22   IV^- I^- ___ ___ ___ $(\underline{V}^{d7})$ ^-VI IV^-

23   I^- $^-VI^{d7}$ ___ ___ ___ V $(\underline{V}^{d7})$ ^-VI

24   IV^- I^- ___ ___ ___ $(\underline{aIV}^{d7})$ I^{-6}_4 V

25   I^- $(\underline{V}^{d7})$ ___ ___ ___ ^-VI $(\underline{III}^{d7})$ IV^-

26   I^- VII^{d7} ___ ___ ___ I^- $(\underline{V}^{d7})$ ^-VI

27   V I^- ___ ___ ___ II^6_5 $(\underline{II}^{-6}_{d5})$ I^{-6}_4

28   V I^- ___ ___ ___ II^6_5 $(\underline{aIV}^{d7})$ I^{-6}_4

29   V I^- ___ ___ ___ IV^{d7} I^6 V

30   I^- V ___ ___ ___ I^6 $(\underline{III}^{d7})$ IV^-

31   I^- IV^- ___ ___ ___ I^6 $(\underline{II}^{-7})$ V

32   I^- IV^- ___ ___ ___ II^{d7} I^- VII^{d7}

33   I^- ^-VI ___ ___ ___ $(\underline{aIV}^{d7})$ V^{-7} $^-VI^{d7}$

34   V V^{a4}_2 ___ ___ ___ I^6 $(\underline{I}^{-6}_{d5})$ IV^-

35   V I^- ___ ___ ___ $(\underline{V}^{d7})$ ^-VI IV^-

36   I^- V ___ ___ ___ $(\underline{^-III}^{-6}_{d5})$ ^-VI V

37   I^- IV^- ___ ___ ___ $^-VI^{d7}$ I^{-6}_4 V^{-7}

38   I^- ^-VI ___ ___ ___ II^6 $(\underline{aIV}^{d7})$ I^{-6}_4

39   V ^-VI ___ ___ ___ $(\underline{I}^{-6}_{d5})$ IV^- I^-

40   VII^{d7} I^- ___ ___ ___ IV^- IV^{d7} I^6

41   I^- ^-VI ___ ___ ___ $(\underline{III}^{d7})$ IV^- V

42   I^- ^-III ___ ___ ___ ^-VI $(\underline{V}^{d7})$ ^-VI

43   ^-IV II^{d7} ___ ___ ___ I^- $(\underline{I}^{-7})$ IV^-

44   V^{-7} I^- ___ ___ ___ $(\underline{^-III}^{-7})$ ^-VI I^{-6}_4

45   V^{-7} I^- ___ ___ ___ I^6 $(\underline{aIV}^{d7})$ V

46   I^- IV^- ___ ___ ___ II^{d7} I^- V^{-6}_{d5}

47   I^- IV^- ___ ___ ___ IV^{d7} I^6 V

48   ^-VI IV^- ___ ___ ___ $(\underline{aIV}^{d7})$ V^{-7} I^-

Shield the answer. Listen to the group of five chords and write the composite chord symbols for the last three chords; then uncover the answer and compare your response. Goal: No more than eight incorrect frames. When you have done this lesson, take Test D10.

1 I⁻ IV⁻ _____ _____ _____ (aIVᵈ⁷) V I⁻

2 I⁻ IV⁻ _____ _____ _____ (IIIᵈ⁷) IV⁻ V

3 I⁻ ⁻VI _____ _____ _____ (Vᵈ⁷) ⁻VI IV⁻

4 V I⁻ _____ _____ _____ VIIᵈ⁷ I⁻ V

5 I⁻ ⁻VI _____ _____ _____ (aIVᵈ⁷) I⁻⁻⁶₄ V

6 I⁻ IV⁻ _____ _____ _____ I⁶ IIᵈ⁷ I⁻

7 I⁻ IV⁻ _____ _____ _____ I⁶ (II⁻⁷) V

8 I⁻ V⁶₄ _____ _____ _____ I⁶ (IIIᵈ⁷) IV⁻

9 V I⁻ _____ _____ _____ ⁻VIᵈ⁷ V⁻⁷ I⁻

10 IV⁻ I⁶ _____ _____ _____ (IIIᵈ⁷) IV⁻ V

11 I⁻ V _____ _____ _____ IVᵈ⁷ I⁶ V

12 I⁻ IV⁻ _____ _____ _____ I⁶ VIIᵈ⁷ I⁻

13 I⁻ IV⁻ _____ _____ _____ (II⁻⁶𝒹₅) I⁻⁶₄ V

14 I⁻ IV⁻ _____ _____ _____ (aIVᵈ⁷) I⁻⁶₄ V

15 I⁻ IV⁻ _____ _____ _____ (II⁻⁷) I⁻⁶₄ V

16 I⁻ ⁻VI _____ _____ _____ IV⁻ IIᵈ⁷ I⁻

17 I⁻ IV⁻ _____ _____ _____ IVᵈ⁷ I⁶ V

18 I⁻ II⁻⁶₅ _____ _____ _____ IVᵈ⁷ I⁶ V

19 I⁻ IVᵈ⁷ _____ _____ _____ I⁶ (aIVᵈ⁷) V

20 I⁻ IV⁻ _____ _____ _____ I⁶ (II⁻⁶𝒹₅) V

21 I⁻ V _____ _____ _____ ⁻VI (Vᵈ⁷) ⁻VI

22 IV⁻ I⁻ _____ _____ _____ (Vᵈ⁷) ⁻VI IV⁻

23 I⁻ ⁻VIᵈ⁷ _____ _____ _____ V (Vᵈ⁷) ⁻VI

24 IV⁻ I⁻ _____ _____ _____ (aIVᵈ⁷) I⁻⁶₄ V

25 I⁻ (Vᵈ⁷) _____ _____ _____ ⁻VI (IIIᵈ⁷) IV⁻

26 I⁻ VIIᵈ⁷ _____ _____ _____ I⁻ (Vᵈ⁷) ⁻VI

27 V I⁻ _____ _____ _____ II⁻⁶₅ (II⁻⁻⁶𝒹₅) I⁻⁶₄

28 V I⁻ _____ _____ _____ II⁻⁶₅ (aIVᵈ⁷) I⁻⁶₄

29 V I⁻ _____ _____ _____ IVᵈ⁷ I⁶ V

30 I⁻ V _____ _____ _____ I⁶ (IIIᵈ⁷) IV⁻

31 I⁻ IV⁻ _____ _____ _____ I⁶ (II⁻⁷) V

32 I⁻ IV⁻ _____ _____ _____ IIᵈ⁷ I⁻ VIIᵈ⁷

33 I⁻ ⁻VI _____ _____ _____ (aIVᵈ⁷) V⁻⁷ ⁻VIᵈ⁷

34 V Vᵃ⁴₂ _____ _____ _____ I⁶ (I⁻⁶𝒹₅) IV⁻

35 V I⁻ _____ _____ _____ (Vᵈ⁷) ⁻VI IV⁻

36 I⁻ V _____ _____ _____ (⁻III⁻⁶𝒹₅) ⁻VI V

37 I⁻ IV⁻ _____ _____ _____ ⁻VIᵈ⁷ I⁻⁶₄ V⁻⁷

38 I⁻ ⁻VI _____ _____ _____ II⁻⁶ (aIVᵈ⁷) I⁻⁶₄

39 V ⁻VI _____ _____ _____ (I⁻⁶𝒹₅) IV⁻ I⁻

40 VIIᵈ⁷ I⁻ _____ _____ _____ IV⁻ IVᵈ⁷ I⁶

41 I⁻ ⁻VI _____ _____ _____ (IIIᵈ⁷) IV⁻ V

42 I⁻ ⁻III _____ _____ _____ ⁻VI (Vᵈ⁷) ⁻VI

43 ⁻IV IIᵈ⁷ _____ _____ _____ I⁻ (I⁻⁷) IV⁻

44 V⁻⁷ I⁻ _____ _____ _____ (⁻III⁻⁷) ⁻VI I⁻⁶₄

45 V⁻⁷ I⁻ _____ _____ _____ I⁶ (aIVᵈ⁷) V

46 I⁻ IV⁻ _____ _____ _____ IIᵈ⁷ I⁻ V⁻⁶𝒹₅

47 I⁻ IV⁻ _____ _____ _____ IVᵈ⁷ I⁶ V

48 ⁻VI IV⁻ _____ _____ _____ (aIVᵈ⁷) V⁻⁷ I⁻

D10-5b Identification of foreign chords

Shield the answer. Listen to the group of five chords and write the composite chord symbols for the last three chords; then uncover the answer and compare your response. Goal: No more than eight incorrect frames. When you have done this lesson, take Test D10.

1. I^- IV^- ____ ____ ____ ($\underline{\text{aIV}}^{d7}$) V I^-

2. I^- IV^- ____ ____ ____ ($\underline{\text{III}}^{d7}$) IV^- V

3. I^- ^-VI ____ ____ ____ ($\underline{\text{V}}^{d7}$) ^-VI IV^-

4. V I^- ____ ____ ____ VII^{d7} I^- V

5. I^- ^-VI ____ ____ ____ ($\underline{\text{aIV}}^{d7}$) I^{-6}_{4} V

6. I^- IV^- ____ ____ ____ I^6 II^{d7} I^-

7. I^- IV^- ____ ____ ____ I^6 ($\underline{\text{II}}^{-7}$) V

8. I^- V^6_4 ____ ____ ____ I^6 ($\underline{\text{III}}^{d7}$) IV^-

9. V I^- ____ ____ ____ $^-\text{VI}^{d7}$ V^{-7} I^-

10. IV^- I^6 ____ ____ ____ ($\underline{\text{III}}^{d7}$) IV^- V

11. I^- V ____ ____ ____ IV^{d7} I^6 V

12. I^- IV^- ____ ____ ____ I^6 VII^{d7} I^-

13. I^- IV^- ____ ____ ____ ($\underline{\text{II}}^{-6}_{d5}$) I^{-6}_{4} V

14. I^- IV^- ____ ____ ____ ($\underline{\text{aIV}}^{d7}$) I^{-6}_{4} V

15. I^- IV^- ____ ____ ____ ($\underline{\text{II}}^{-7}$) I^{-6}_{4} V

16. I^- ^-VI ____ ____ ____ IV^- II^{d7} I^-

17. I^- IV^- ____ ____ ____ IV^{d7} I^6 V

18. I^- $\underline{\text{II}}^6_5$ ____ ____ ____ IV^{d7} I^6 V

19. I^- IV^{d7} ____ ____ ____ I^6 ($\underline{\text{aIV}}^{d7}$) V

20. I^- IV^- ____ ____ ____ I^6 ($\underline{\text{II}}^{-6}_{d5}$) V

21. I^- V ____ ____ ____ ^-VI ($\underline{\text{V}}^{d7}$) ^-VI

22. IV^- I^- ____ ____ ____ ($\underline{\text{V}}^{d7}$) ^-VI IV^-

23. I^- $^-\text{VI}^{d7}$ ____ ____ ____ V ($\underline{\text{V}}^{d7}$) ^-VI

24. IV^- I^- ____ ____ ____ ($\underline{\text{aIV}}^{d7}$) I^{-6}_{4} V

25. I^- ($\underline{\text{V}}^{d7}$) ____ ____ ____ ^-VI ($\underline{\text{III}}^{d7}$) IV^-

26. I^- VII^{d7} ____ ____ ____ I^- ($\underline{\text{V}}^{d7}$) ^-VI

27. V I^- ____ ____ ____ $\underline{\text{II}}^6_5$ ($\underline{\text{II}}^{-6}_{d5}$) I^{-6}_{4}

28. V I^- ____ ____ ____ $\underline{\text{II}}^6_5$ ($\underline{\text{aIV}}^{d7}$) I^{-6}_{4}

29. V I^- ____ ____ ____ IV^{d7} I^6 V

30. I^- V ____ ____ ____ I^6 ($\underline{\text{III}}^{d7}$) IV^-

31. I^- IV^- ____ ____ ____ I^6 ($\underline{\text{II}}^{-7}$) V

32. I^- IV^- ____ ____ ____ II^{d7} I^- VII^{d7}

33. I^- ^-VI ____ ____ ____ ($\underline{\text{aIV}}^{d7}$) V^{-7} $^-\text{VI}^{d7}$

34. V V^{a4}_{2} ____ ____ ____ I^6 ($\underline{\text{I}}^{-6}_{d5}$) IV^-

35. V I^- ____ ____ ____ ($\underline{\text{V}}^{d7}$) ^-VI IV^-

36. I^- V ____ ____ ____ ($\underline{^-\text{III}}^{-6}_{d5}$) ^-VI V

37. I^- IV^- ____ ____ ____ $^-\text{VI}^{d7}$ I^{-6}_{4} V^{-7}

38. I^- ^-VI ____ ____ ____ $\underline{\text{II}}^6$ ($\underline{\text{aIV}}^{d7}$) I^{-6}_{4}

39. V ^-VI ____ ____ ____ ($\underline{\text{I}}^{-6}_{d5}$) IV^- I^-

40. VII^{d7} I^- ____ ____ ____ IV^- IV^{d7} I^6

41. I^- ^-VI ____ ____ ____ ($\underline{\text{III}}^{d7}$) IV^- V

42. I^- ^-III ____ ____ ____ ^-VI ($\underline{\text{V}}^{d7}$) ^-VI

43. ^-IV II^{d7} ____ ____ ____ I^- ($\underline{\text{I}}^{-7}$) IV^-

44. V^{-7} I^- ____ ____ ____ ($\underline{^-\text{III}}^{-7}$) ^-VI I^{-6}_{4}

45. V^{-7} I^- ____ ____ ____ I^6 ($\underline{\text{aIV}}^{d7}$) V

46. I^- IV^- ____ ____ ____ II^{d7} I^- V^{-6}_{d5}

47. I^- IV^- ____ ____ ____ IV^{d7} I^6 V

48. ^-VI IV^- ____ ____ ____ ($\underline{\text{aIV}}^{d7}$) V^{-7} I^-

Other Foreign Chords and Infrequent Chords in Minor Keys

This series involves the following types of chords: infrequently used regular chords in minor keys, augmented sixth chords, the Neapolitan sixth chord, and foreign chords borrowed from the parallel key. Lessons in this series are similar to those in Series D10, and the instructions for that series apply here. When you have done this series, take Test D11. The test does not include figured bass dictation. While your achievement in this skill is not tested, it will help you with chord identification in a key, which is tested.

Lesson D11–1a

This lesson involves infrequently used regular chords in a minor key, chords that contain either the sixth or seventh degree of the key. One such chord, which will serve as an example, is the major triad on the fourth degree of a minor key. The triad on the fourth degree is usually minor, with the sixth degree of the key at the position called for by the key signature. When the sixth degree is raised, a major triad results. The infrequently used chords in a minor key are not foreign chords, because the sixth and seventh degrees may occur in two positions in a minor key.

The infrequently used chords in minor include one chord of a type we have not previously studied, the *augmented triad*. When an augmented triad is written to appear in root position, the upper tones are at intervals of a major third and an augmented fifth above the bass.

augmented triad
in root position

An augmented triad notated as an inversion is enharmonic with one notated in root position. In the following example, the two inversions of the C augmented triad are compared with enharmonic spellings containing a third and fifth above the lowest tone.

Thus, while the augmented triad can be written in root position and in two inversions, as far as the sound is concerned there is only one form of the chord. In identifying augmented triads by ear, you will not be asked to indicate if they would be written in root position or in inversion. All augmented triads will simply be identified with the abbreviated figured bass symbol a5.

D11-1a
(Copy 1)

Figured bass dictation of infrequent chords in a minor key

Shield the answer. Listen to the series of five chords and write the bass notes and the figured bass symbols for the last three chords; then uncover the answer and compare your response. Goal: No more than eight incorrect frames.

D11-1a

(Copy 2)

Figured bass dictation of infrequent chords in a minor key

Shield the answer. Listen to the series of five chords and write the bass notes and the figured bass symbols for the last three chords; then uncover the answer and compare your response. Goal: No more than eight incorrect frames.

313

D11–1a
(Copy 3)

Figured bass dictation of infrequent chords in a minor key

Shield the answer. Listen to the series of five chords and write the bass notes and the figured bass symbols for the last three chords; then uncover the answer and compare your response. Goal: No more than eight incorrect frames.

315

D11-1a

(Copy 4)

Figured bass dictation of infrequent chords in a minor key

Shield the answer. Listen to the series of five chords and write the bass notes and the figured bass symbols for the last three chords; then uncover the answer and compare your response. Goal: No more than eight incorrect frames.

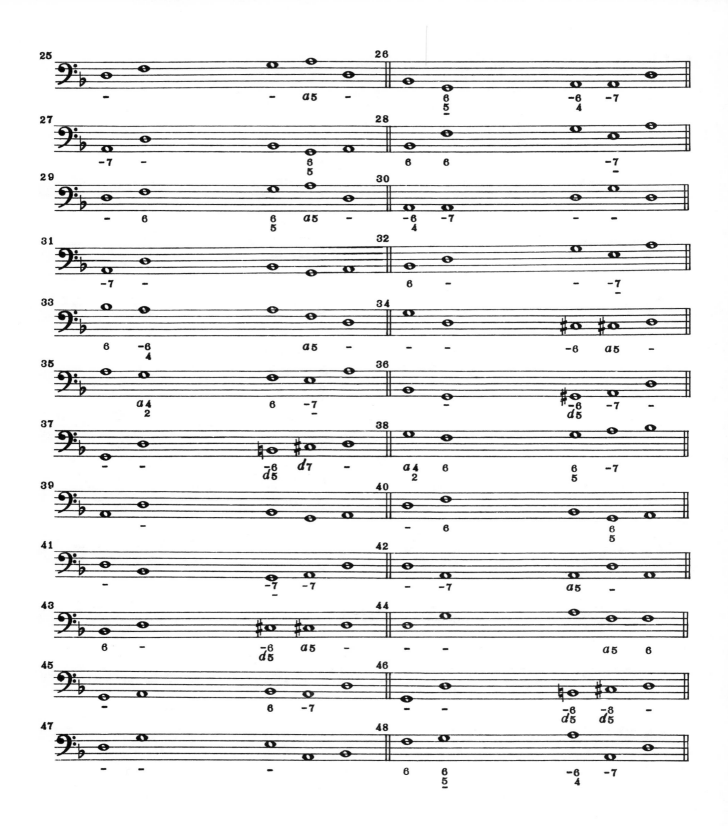

D11-1a Figured bass dictation of infrequent chords in a minor key
(Copy 5)

Shield the answer. Listen to the series of five chords and write the bass notes and the figured bass symbols for the last three chords; then uncover the answer and compare your response. Goal: No more than eight incorrect frames.

319

Lesson **D11-1b**

In this lesson the composite chord symbols are introduced for the following infrequently used regular chords in a minor key: triads and seventh chords in root position and in first inversion on the second and fourth degree of the key with a raised sixth degree, and triads in root position and in inversions on the third degree of the key with a raised seventh degree. Also introduced is the composite chord symbol for the triad on the first degree of a minor key with a Picardy third.

The triad on the second degree of a minor key with a raised sixth degree is a minor triad. The composite chord symbols for this chord in root position and in first inversion are II⁻ and II⁶. (The usual triad on this degree is diminished and is most often found in first inversion, *i.e.*, II⁶₋.)

The seventh chord on the second degree of a minor key with a raised sixth degree is a minor seventh chord. The composite chord symbols for this chord in root position and in first inversion are II⁻⁷ and II⁶₅. (The usual seventh chord on the second degree is half-diminished, *i.e.*, II⁻⁷_{d5} or II⁶₅.)

The triad on the fourth degree of a minor key with raised sixth degree is a major triad. The composite chord symbols for this chord in root position and in first inversion are IV and IV⁻⁶. (The usual triad on the fourth degree is minor, *i.e.*, IV⁻ or IV⁶.)

The seventh chord on the fourth degree of a minor key with raised sixth degree is a dominant seventh chord. The composite chord symbols for this chord in root position and in first inversion are IV⁻⁷ and IV⁻⁶_{d5}. (The usual seventh chord on the fourth degree is minor, *i.e.*, IV⁻⁷ or IV⁶₅.)

The triad on the third degree of a minor key with raised seventh degree is an augmented triad. The composite chord symbol for the inversions of this chord requires a special procedure, the same as the one used for diminished seventh chords. You will remember that because the inversions of the augmented triad sound the same as the root position, all augmented triads regardless of the inversion or spelling with be identified with the abbreviated figured bass symbol ᵃ⁵. The Roman numeral in the composite chord symbol for augmented triads will therefore refer to the *bass* of the chord, as in the composite chord symbol for diminished seventh chords. This is a departure from the usual procedure of referring to the root of the chord, which of course may appear in any part. With this procedure, the various versions of the augmented triad on the third degree of a minor key are identified with different Roman numerals, as shown in the following example.

g   ⁻III^{a5}   V^{a5}   VII^{a5}

Where the triad is in root position, the bass is a minor third above the tonic and the chord symbol is $^{-}III^{a5}$. Where it is in first inversion, the fifth degree is in the bass and the composite chord symbol is V^{a5}. Where it is in second inversion, the seventh degree is in the bass and the chord symbol is VII^{a5}.

A major triad is sometimes used on the first degree of a minor key as a concluding chord in an authentic cadence. The raised third degree of this chord is called a Picardy third. The composite chord symbol for this chord, which is a foreign chord, is (I). A major triad on the first degree of a minor key may also be used in the context of a transient dominant chord, in which case the composite chord symbol should contain an underline. Thus we have the composite chord symbol (I) where a Picardy third occurs and the symbol (I̲) where a transient dominant triad on the first degree of a minor key occurs.

D11-1b Identification of infrequent chords in a minor key

(Copy 1)

Shield the answer. Listen to the group of five chords and write the composite chord symbols for the last three chords; then uncover the answer and compare your response. Goal: No more than eight incorrect frames.

1. V^{-7} I^- _____ _____ _____ IV V I^-
2. V^{-7} I^- _____ _____ _____ IV^{-6} V^{-6} I^-
3. V^{-7} I^- _____ _____ _____ IV^{-6}_{d5} V^{-6}_{d5} I^-
4. I^- IV^- _____ _____ _____ V $^-III^{a5}$ I^-
5. I^- IV^6 _____ _____ _____ V^{-7} V^{a5} I^-
6. ^-VI II^6_5 _____ _____ _____ I^{-6}_4 V^{-7} (I)
7. V^{-6}_{d5} I^- _____ _____ _____ IV^{-6}_{d5} V^{-6}_{d5} I^-
8. IV^6 I^{-6}_4 _____ _____ _____ V V^{a5} I^-
9. IV^- I^6 _____ _____ _____ II^6_5 V^{-7} (I)
10. IV^- I^6 _____ _____ _____ II^6_5 V^{-7} I^-
11. IV^- I^- _____ _____ _____ IV II^{-7} V
12. I^6 IV^- _____ _____ _____ V $^-III^{a5}$ I^-
13. I^- IV^- _____ _____ _____ IV^6 V^{-7} (I)
14. I^- ^-VI _____ _____ _____ II^6_5 V^{-7} I^-
15. I^- ^-VI _____ _____ _____ IV V^{-7} I^-
16. I^6 IV^- _____ _____ _____ II^- V^{-7} IV^6
17. I^- ^-VI _____ _____ _____ IV^{-6} V^{-6}_{d5} I^-
18. I^{-6}_4 V^{-7} _____ _____ _____ (I) IV^- (I)
19. I^- V^6_4 _____ _____ _____ I^6 II^{-7} V
20. I^- II^{d7} _____ _____ _____ I^6 II^6_5 V
21. V^{a4}_2 I^6 _____ _____ _____ II^6_5 (II^{-6}_{d5}) V
22. I^- ^-VI _____ _____ _____ IV^{-7} V^{a5} I^-
23. I^- ^-VI _____ _____ _____ IV II^{-7} V
24. VII^{d7} I^- _____ _____ _____ IV^{-6}_{d5} V^{-6}_{d5} I^-

25. I^- ^-III _____ _____ _____ IV^- V^{a5} I^-
26. ^-VI II^6_5 _____ _____ _____ I^{-6}_4 V^{-7} (I)
27. V^{-7} I^- _____ _____ _____ ^-VI II^6_5 V
28. IV^6 I^6 _____ _____ _____ IV II^{-7} V
29. I^- I^6 _____ _____ _____ II^6_5 V^{a5} I^-
30. I^{-6}_4 V^{-7} _____ _____ _____ I^- IV^- (I)
31. V^{-7} I^- _____ _____ _____ ^-VI IV V
32. IV^6 I^- _____ _____ _____ IV^- II^{-7} V
33. IV^6 I^{-6}_4 _____ _____ _____ V $^-III^{a5}$ I^-
34. IV^- I^- _____ _____ _____ V^{-6} VII^{a5} I^-
35. V V^{a4}_2 _____ _____ _____ I^6 II^{-7} V
36. ^-VI IV^- _____ _____ _____ (II^{-6}_{d5}) V^{-7} I^-
37. IV^- I^- _____ _____ _____ IV^{-6}_{d5} VII^{d7} I^-
38. V^{a4}_2 I^6 _____ _____ _____ II^6_5 V^{-7} ^-VI
39. V I^- _____ _____ _____ ^-VI IV V
40. I^- I^6 _____ _____ _____ ^-VI II^6_5 V
41. I^- ^-VI _____ _____ _____ IV^{-7} V^{-7} (I)
42. I^- V^{-7} _____ _____ _____ V^{a5} I^- V
43. IV^6 I^- _____ _____ _____ V^{-6}_{d5} VII^{a5} I^-
44. I^- IV^- _____ _____ _____ V $^-III^{a5}$ I^6
45. IV^- V _____ _____ _____ IV^6 V^{-7} (I)
46. IV^- I^- _____ _____ _____ IV^{-6}_{d5} V^{-6}_{d5} I^-
47. I^- IV^- _____ _____ _____ II^- V ^-VI
48. I^6 II^6_5 _____ _____ _____ I^{-6}_4 V^{-7} (I)

D11–1b
(Copy 2) **Identification of infrequent chords in a minor key**

Shield the answer. Listen to the group of five chords and write the composite chord symbols for the last three chords; then uncover the answer and compare your response. Goal: No more than eight incorrect frames.

1. V^{-7} I^- _____ _____ _____ IV V I^-

2. V^{-7} I^- _____ _____ _____ IV^{-6} V^{-6} I^-

3. V^{-7} I^- _____ _____ _____ IV^{-6}_{d5} V^{-6}_{d5} I^-

4. I^- IV^- _____ _____ _____ V $^-III^{a5}$ I^-

5. I^- IV^6 _____ _____ _____ V^{-7} V^{a5} I^-

6. ^-VI II^6_5 _____ _____ _____ I^{-6}_4 V^{-7} (I)

7. V^{-6}_{d5} I^- _____ _____ _____ IV^{-6}_{d5} V^{-6}_{d5} I^-

8. IV^6 I^{-6}_4 _____ _____ _____ V V^{a5} I^-

9. IV^- I^6 _____ _____ _____ II^6_5 V^{-7} (I)

10. IV^- I^6 _____ _____ _____ II^6_5 V^{-7} I^-

11. IV^- I^- _____ _____ _____ IV II^{-7} V

12. I^6 IV^- _____ _____ _____ V $^-III^{a5}$ I^-

13. I^- IV^- _____ _____ _____ IV^6 V^{-7} (I)

14. I^- ^-VI _____ _____ _____ II^6_5 V^{-7} I^-

15. I^- ^-VI _____ _____ _____ IV V^{-7} I^-

16. I^6 IV^- _____ _____ _____ II^- V^{-7} IV^6

17. I^- ^-VI _____ _____ _____ IV^{-6} V^{-6}_{d5} I^-

18. I^{-6}_4 V^{-7} _____ _____ _____ (I) IV^- (I)

19. I^- V^6_4 _____ _____ _____ I^6 II^{-7} V

20. I^- II^{d7} _____ _____ _____ I^6 II^6_5 V

21. V^{a4}_2 I^6 _____ _____ _____ II^6_5 (II^{-6}_{d5}) V

22. I^- ^-VI _____ _____ _____ IV^{-7} V^{a5} I^-

23. I^- ^-VI _____ _____ _____ IV II^{-7} V

24. VII^{d7} I^- _____ _____ _____ IV^{-6}_{d5} V^{-6}_{d5} I^-

25. I^- ^-III _____ _____ _____ IV^- V^{a5} I^-

26. ^-VI II^6_5 _____ _____ _____ I^{-6}_4 V^{-7} (I)

27. V^{-7} I^- _____ _____ _____ ^-VI II^6_5 V

28. IV^6 I^6 _____ _____ _____ IV II^{-7} V

29. I^- I^6 _____ _____ _____ II^6_5 V^{a5} I^-

30. I^{-6}_4 V^{-7} _____ _____ _____ I^- IV^- (I)

31. V^{-7} I^- _____ _____ _____ ^-VI IV V

32. IV^6 I^- _____ _____ _____ IV^- II^{-7} V

33. IV^6 I^{-6}_4 _____ _____ _____ V $^-III^{a5}$ I^-

34. IV^- I^- _____ _____ _____ V^{-6} VII^{a5} I^-

35. V V^{a4}_2 _____ _____ _____ I^6 II^{-7} V

36. ^-VI IV^- _____ _____ _____ (II^{-6}_{d5}) V^{-7} I^-

37. IV^- I^- _____ _____ _____ IV^{-6}_{d5} VII^{d7} I^-

38. V^{a4}_2 I^6 _____ _____ _____ II^6_5 V^{-7} ^-VI

39. V I^- _____ _____ _____ ^-VI IV V

40. I^- I^6 _____ _____ _____ ^-VI II^6_5 V

41. I^- ^-VI _____ _____ _____ IV^{-7} V^{-7} (I)

42. I^- V^{-7} _____ _____ _____ V^{a5} I^- V

43. IV^6 I^- _____ _____ _____ V^{-6}_{d5} VII^{a5} I^-

44. I^- IV^- _____ _____ _____ V $^-III^{a5}$ I^6

45. IV^- V _____ _____ _____ IV^6 V^{-7} (I)

46. IV^- I^- _____ _____ _____ IV^{-6}_{d5} V^{-6}_{d5} I^-

47. I^- IV^- _____ _____ _____ II^- V ^-VI

48. I^6 II^6_5 _____ _____ _____ I^{-6}_4 V^{-7} (I)

Shield the answer. Listen to the group of five chords and write the composite chord symbols for the last three chords; then uncover the answer and compare your response. Goal: No more than eight incorrect frames.

1 V^{-7} I^- _____ _____ _____ IV V I^-

2 V^{-7} I^- _____ _____ _____ IV^{-6} V^{-6} I^-

3 V^{-7} I^- _____ _____ _____ IV^{-6}_{d5} V^{-6}_{d5} I^-

4 I^- IV^- _____ _____ _____ V $^-III^{a5}$ I^-

5 I^- IV^6 _____ _____ _____ V^{-7} V^{a5} I^-

6 ^-VI $II^6_{\underline{5}}$ _____ _____ _____ I^{-6}_4 V^{-7} (I)

7 V^{-6}_{d5} I^- _____ _____ _____ IV^{-6}_{d5} V^{-6}_{d5} I^-

8 IV^6 I^{-6}_4 _____ _____ _____ V V^{a5} I^-

9 IV^- I^6 _____ _____ _____ $II^6_{\underline{5}}$ V^{-7} (I)

10 IV^- I^6 _____ _____ _____ $II^6_{\underline{5}}$ V^{-7} I^-

11 IV^- I^- _____ _____ _____ IV $II^{-\underline{7}}$ V

12 I^6 IV^- _____ _____ _____ V $^-III^{a5}$ I^-

13 I^- IV^- _____ _____ _____ IV^6 V^{-7} (I)

14 I^- ^-VI _____ _____ _____ $II^6_{\underline{5}}$ V^{-7} I^-

15 I^- ^-VI _____ _____ _____ IV V^{-7} I^-

16 I^6 IV^- _____ _____ _____ II^- V^{-7} IV^6

17 I^- ^-VI _____ _____ _____ IV^{-6} V^{-6}_{d5} I^-

18 I^{-6}_4 V^{-7} _____ _____ _____ (I) IV^- (I)

19 I^- V^6_4 _____ _____ _____ I^6 $II^{-\underline{7}}$ V

20 I^- II^{d7} _____ _____ _____ I^6 $II^6_{\underline{5}}$ V

21 V^{a4}_2 I^6 _____ _____ _____ $II^6_{\underline{5}}$ $(\underline{II^{-6}_{d5}})$ V

22 I^- ^-VI _____ _____ _____ $IV^{-\underline{7}}$ V^{a5} I^-

23 I^- ^-VI _____ _____ _____ IV $II^{-\underline{7}}$ $V^{\cdot}$

24 VII^{d7} I^- _____ _____ _____ IV^{-6}_{d5} V^{-6}_{d5} I^-

25 I^- ^-III _____ _____ _____ IV^- V^{a5} I^-

26 ^-VI $II^6_{\underline{5}}$ _____ _____ _____ I^{-6}_4 V^{-7} (I)

27 V^{-7} I^- _____ _____ _____ ^-VI $II^6_{\underline{5}}$ V

28 IV^6 I^6 _____ _____ _____ IV $II^{-\underline{7}}$ V

29 I^- I^6 _____ _____ _____ $II^6_{\underline{5}}$ V^{a5} I^-

30 I^{-6}_4 V^{-7} _____ _____ _____ I^- IV^- (I)

31 V^{-7} I^- _____ _____ _____ ^-VI IV V

32 IV^6 I^- _____ _____ _____ IV^- $II^{-\underline{7}}$ V

33 IV^6 I^{-6}_4 _____ _____ _____ V $^-III^{a5}$ I^-

34 IV^- I^- _____ _____ _____ V^{-6} VII^{a5} I^-

35 V V^{a4}_2 _____ _____ _____ I^6 $II^{-\underline{7}}$ V

36 ^-VI IV^- _____ _____ _____ $(\underline{II^{-6}_{d5}})$ V^{-7} I^-

37 IV^- I^- _____ _____ _____ IV^{-6}_{d5} VII^{d7} I^-

38 V^{a4}_2 I^6 _____ _____ _____ $II^6_{\underline{5}}$ V^{-7} ^-VI

39 V I^- _____ _____ _____ ^-VI IV V

40 I^- I^6 _____ _____ _____ ^-VI $II^6_{\underline{5}}$ V

41 I^- ^-VI _____ _____ _____ $IV^{-\underline{7}}$ V^{-7} (I)

42 I^- V^{-7} _____ _____ _____ $_{,}V^{a5}$ I^- V

43 IV^6 I^- _____ _____ _____ V^{-6}_{d5} VII^{a5} I^-

44 I^- IV^- _____ _____ _____ V $^-III^{a5}$ I^6

45 IV^- V _____ _____ _____ IV^6 V^{-7} (I)

46 IV^- I^- _____ _____ _____ IV^{-6}_{d5} V^{-6}_{d5} I^-

47 I^- IV^- _____ _____ _____ II^- V ^-VI

48 I^6 $II^6_{\underline{5}}$ _____ _____ _____ I^{-6}_4 V^{-7} (I)

D11–1b Identification of infrequent chords in a minor key
(Copy 4)

Shield the answer. Listen to the group of five chords and write the composite chord symbols for the last three chords; then uncover the answer and compare your response. Goal: No more than eight incorrect frames.

1. V^{-7} I^- ___ ___ ___ IV V I^-

2. V^{-7} I^- ___ ___ ___ IV^{-6} V^{-6} I^-

3. V^{-7} I^- ___ ___ ___ IV^{-6}_{d5} V^{-6}_{d5} I^-

4. I^- IV^- ___ ___ ___ V $^-III^{a5}$ I^-

5. I^- IV^6 ___ ___ ___ V^{-7} V^{a5} I^-

6. ^-VI II^6_5 ___ ___ ___ I^{-6}_4 V^{-7} (I)

7. V^{-6}_{d5} I^- ___ ___ ___ IV^{-6}_{d5} V^{-6}_{d5} I^-

8. IV^6 I^{-6}_4 ___ ___ ___ V V^{a5} I^-

9. IV^- I^6 ___ ___ ___ II^6_5 V^{-7} (I)

10. IV^- I^6 ___ ___ ___ II^6_5 V^{-7} I^-

11. IV^- I^- ___ ___ ___ IV II^{-7} V

12. I^6 IV^- ___ ___ ___ V $^-III^{a5}$ I^-

13. I^- IV^- ___ ___ ___ IV^6 V^{-7} (I)

14. I^- ^-VI ___ ___ ___ II^6_5 V^{-7} I^-

15. I^- ^-VI ___ ___ ___ IV V^{-7} I^-

16. I^6 IV^- ___ ___ ___ II^- V^{-7} IV^6

17. I^- ^-VI ___ ___ ___ IV^{-6} V^{-6}_{d5} I^-

18. I^{-6}_4 V^{-7} ___ ___ ___ (I) IV^- (I)

19. I^- V^6_4 ___ ___ ___ I^6 II^{-7} V

20. I^- II^{d7} ___ ___ ___ I^6 II^6_5 V

21. V^{a4}_2 I^6 ___ ___ ___ II^6_5 $(\underline{II^{-6}_{d5}})$ V

22. I^- ^-VI ___ ___ ___ IV^{-7} V^{a5} I^-

23. I^- ^-VI ___ ___ ___ IV II^{-7} V

24. VII^{d7} I^- ___ ___ ___ IV^{-6}_{d5} V^{-6}_{d5} I^-

25. I^- ^-III ___ ___ ___ IV^- V^{a5} I^-

26. ^-VI II^6_5 ___ ___ ___ I^{-6}_4 V^{-7} (I)

27. V^{-7} I^- ___ ___ ___ ^-VI II^6_5 V

28. IV^6 I^6 ___ ___ ___ IV II^{-7} V

29. I^- I^6 ___ ___ ___ II^6_5 V^{a5} I^-

30. I^{-6}_4 V^{-7} ___ ___ ___ I^- IV^- (I)

31. V^{-7} I^- ___ ___ ___ ^-VI IV V

32. IV^6 I^- ___ ___ ___ IV^- II^{-7} V

33. IV^6 I^{-6}_4 ___ ___ ___ V $^-III^{a5}$ I^-

34. IV^- I^- ___ ___ ___ V^{-6} VII^{a5} I^-

35. V V^{a4}_2 ___ ___ ___ I^6 II^{-7} V

36. ^-VI IV^- ___ ___ ___ $(\underline{II^{-6}_{d5}})$ V^{-7} I^-

37. IV^- I^- ___ ___ ___ IV^{-6}_{d5} VII^{d7} I^-

38. V^{a4}_2 I^6 ___ ___ ___ II^6_5 V^{-7} ^-VI

39. V I^- ___ ___ ___ ^-VI IV V

40. I^- I^6 ___ ___ ___ ^-VI II^6_5 V

41. I^- ^-VI ___ ___ ___ IV^{-7} V^{-7} (I)

42. I^- V^{-7} ___ ___ ___ V^{a5} I^- V

43. IV^6 I^- ___ ___ ___ V^{-6}_{d5} VII^{a5} I^-

44. I^- IV^- ___ ___ ___ V $^-III^{a5}$ I^6

45. IV^- V ___ ___ ___ IV^6 V^{-7} (I)

46. IV^- I^- ___ ___ ___ IV^{-6}_{d5} V^{-6}_{d5} I^-

47. I^- IV^- ___ ___ ___ II^- V ^-VI

48. I^6 II^6_5 ___ ___ ___ I^{-6}_4 V^{-7} (I)

D11–1b Identification of infrequent chords in a minor key
(Copy 5)

Shield the answer. Listen to the group of five chords and write the composite chord symbols for the last three chords; then uncover the answer and compare your response. Goal: No more than eight incorrect frames.

1. V^{-7} I^- ___ ___ ___ IV V I^-
2. V^{-7} I^- ___ ___ ___ IV^{-6} V^{-6} I^-
3. V^{-7} I^- ___ ___ ___ IV_{d5}^{-6} V_{d5}^{-6} I^-
4. I^- IV^- ___ ___ ___ V $^-III^{a5}$ I^-
5. I^- IV^6 ___ ___ ___ V^{-7} V^{a5} I^-
6. ^-VI $II_{\underline{5}}^{6}$ ___ ___ ___ I_4^{-6} V^{-7} (I)
7. V_{d5}^{-6} I^- ___ ___ ___ IV_{d5}^{-6} V_{d5}^{-6} I^-
8. IV^6 I_4^{-6} ___ ___ ___ V V^{a5} I^-
9. IV^- I^6 ___ ___ ___ $II_{\underline{5}}^{6}$ V^{-7} (I)
10. IV^- I^6 ___ ___ ___ II_5^6 V^{-7} I^-
11. IV^- I^- ___ ___ ___ IV $\underline{II}^{-7}$ V
12. I^6 IV^- ___ ___ ___ V $^-III^{a5}$ I^-
13. I^- IV^- ___ ___ ___ IV^6 V^{-7} (I)
14. I^- ^-VI ___ ___ ___ II_5^6 V^{-7} I^-
15. I^- ^-VI ___ ___ ___ IV V^{-7} I^-
16. I^6 IV^- ___ ___ ___ II^- V^{-7} IV^6
17. I^- ^-VI ___ ___ ___ IV^{-6} V_{d5}^{-6} I^-
18. I_4^{-6} V^{-7} ___ ___ ___ (I) IV^- (I)
19. I^- V_4^6 ___ ___ ___ I^6 $\underline{II}^{-7}$ V
20. I^- II^{d7} ___ ___ ___ I^6 II_5^6 V
21. V_2^{a4} I^6 ___ ___ ___ II_5^6 $(\underline{II_{d5}^{-6}})$ V
22. I^- ^-VI ___ ___ ___ $\underline{IV}^{-7}$ V^{a5} I^-
23. I^- ^-VI ___ ___ ___ IV $\underline{II}^{-7}$ V
24. VII^{d7} I^- ___ ___ ___ IV_{d5}^{-6} V_{d5}^{-6} I^-

25. I^- ^-III ___ ___ ___ IV^- V^{a5} I^-
26. ^-VI $II_{\underline{5}}^{6}$ ___ ___ ___ I_4^{-6} V^{-7} (I)
27. V^{-7} I^- ___ ___ ___ ^-VI II_5^6 V
28. IV^6 I^6 ___ ___ ___ IV $\underline{II}^{-7}$ V
29. I^- I^6 ___ ___ ___ II_5^6 V^{a5} I^-
30. I_4^{-6} V^{-7} ___ ___ ___ I^- IV^- (I)
31. V^{-7} I^- ___ ___ ___ ^-VI IV V
32. IV^6 I^- ___ ___ ___ IV^- $\underline{II}^{-7}$ V
33. IV^6 I_4^{-6} ___ ___ ___ V $^-III^{a5}$ I^-
34. IV^- I^- ___ ___ ___ V^{-6} VII^{a5} I^-
35. V V_2^{a4} ___ ___ ___ I^6 $\underline{II}^{-7}$ V
36. ^-VI IV^- ___ ___ ___ $(\underline{II_{d5}^{-6}})$ V^{-7} I^-
37. IV^- I^- ___ ___ ___ IV_{d5}^{-6} VII^{d7} I^-
38. V_2^{a4} I^6 ___ ___ ___ II_5^6 V^{-7} ^-VI
39. V I^- ___ ___ ___ ^-VI IV V
40. I^- I^6 ___ ___ ___ ^-VI II_5^6 V
41. I^- ^-VI ___ ___ ___ $\underline{IV}^{-7}$ V^{-7} (I)
42. I^- V^{-7} ___ ___ ___ V^{a5} I^- V
43. IV^6 I^- ___ ___ ___ V_{d5}^{-6} VII^{a5} I^-
44. I^- IV^- ___ ___ ___ V $^-III^{a5}$ I^6
45. IV^- V ___ ___ ___ IV^6 V^{-7} (I)
46. IV^- I^- ___ ___ ___ IV_{d5}^{-6} V_{d5}^{-6} I^-
47. I^- IV^- ___ ___ ___ II^- V ^-VI
48. I^6 $II_{\underline{5}}^{6}$ ___ ___ ___ I_4^{-6} V^{-7} (I)

Lesson **D11–2a**

In this lesson, the figured bass symbols for the augmented sixth chords are introduced.

The interval of ten semi-tones may be written as a minor seventh or as an augmented sixth. It is usually written as a minor seventh; the major exception is in augmented sixth chords. In the voice leading of the augmented sixth chord to the following chord, this interval expands to an octave; the upper of the two voices moves up a semi-tone and the lower voice moves down a semi-tone, as in the following example.

There are three common augmented sixth chords. These are the German sixth chord, the Italian sixth chord, and the French sixth chord. The German and Italian sixth chords are enharmonic with the dominant seventh chord, but the French chord has a unique sound. The following example shows each of these chords with the complete figured bass symbols. For comparison, the dominant seventh chords enharmonic with the German and Italian sixth chords are also shown.

The German sixth chord is enharmonic with the complete dominant seventh chord in root position. The Italian sixth chord is enharmonic with the incomplete dominant seventh chord in root position, in which the fifth is omitted. These chords sound very much alike, and you will not be asked to distinguish between them aurally. Hence the abbreviated figured bass symbol ^{a6} will be used to identify both the German and Italian sixth chords in the chord identification lessons in this volume. In the arpeggio singing lessons the complete figured bass symbol for these chords will be given to let you know which to sing. The complete figured bass symbol will be used to identify the French sixth chord. Thus we will use the figured bass symbol $\begin{smallmatrix} a6 \\ a4 \\ 3 \end{smallmatrix}$ to identify the French sixth chord, and the figured bass symbol $a6$ to identify the German and Italian sixth chords.

In order to determine whether a chord should be identified as a dominant seventh chord in root position, -7, or a German or Italian sixth chord, $a6$, it is necessary to listen to the voice leading as the following chord is introduced. If the interval of ten semi-tones expands outward to an octave by semi-tone motion the chord should be identified with the symbol $a6$.

D11–2a
(Copy 1)

Figured bass dictation of foreign chords

Shield the answer. Listen to the series of five chords and write the bass notes and the figured bass symbols for the last three chords; then uncover the answer and compare your response. Goal: No more than eight incorrect frames.

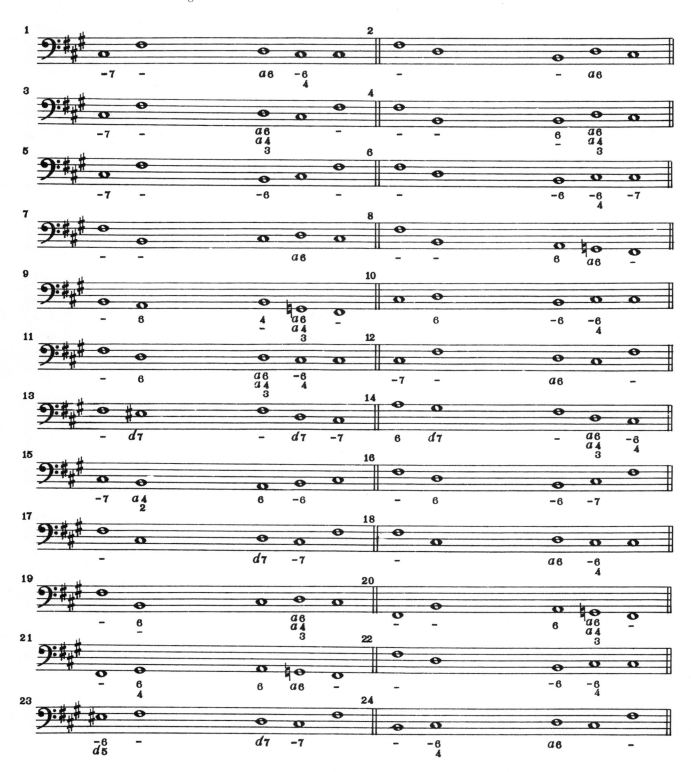

330

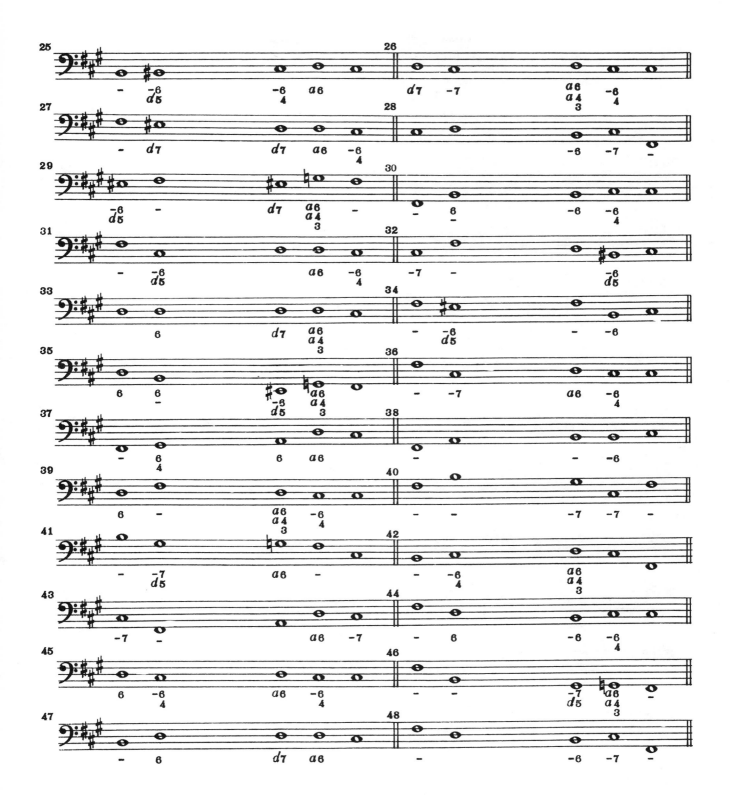

D11-2a

(Copy 2)

Figured bass dictation of foreign chords

Shield the answer. Listen to the series of five chords and write the bass notes and the figured bass symbols for the last three chords; then uncover the answer and compare your response. Goal: No more than eight incorrect frames.

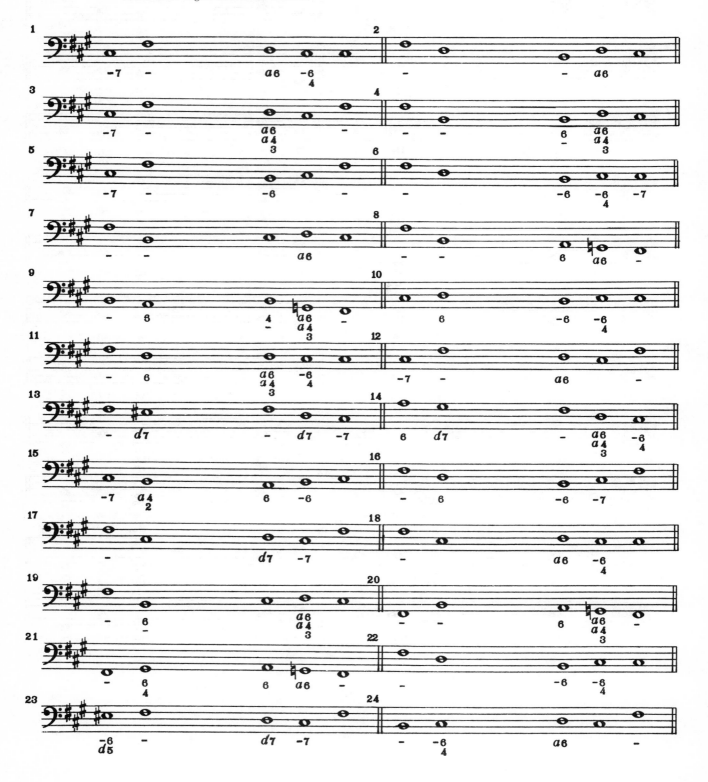

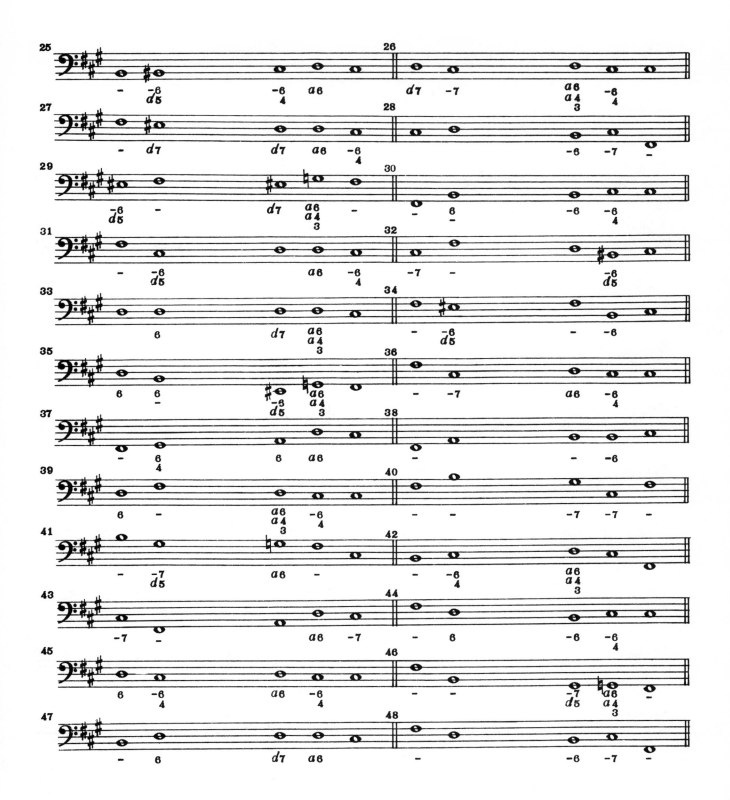

D11-2a

(Copy 3)

Figured bass dictation of foreign chords

Shield the answer. Listen to the series of five chords and write the bass notes and the figured bass symbols for the last three chords; then uncover the answer and compare your response. Goal: No more than eight incorrect frames.

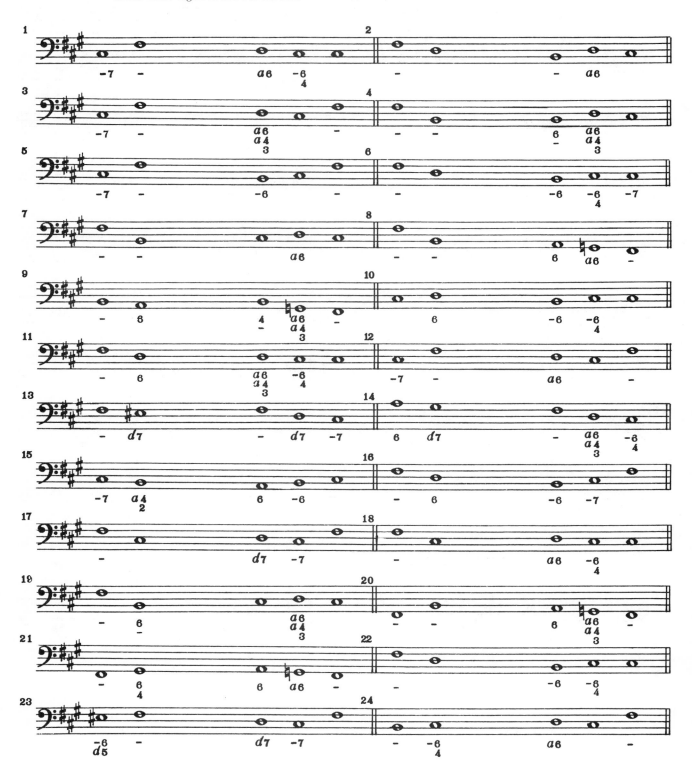

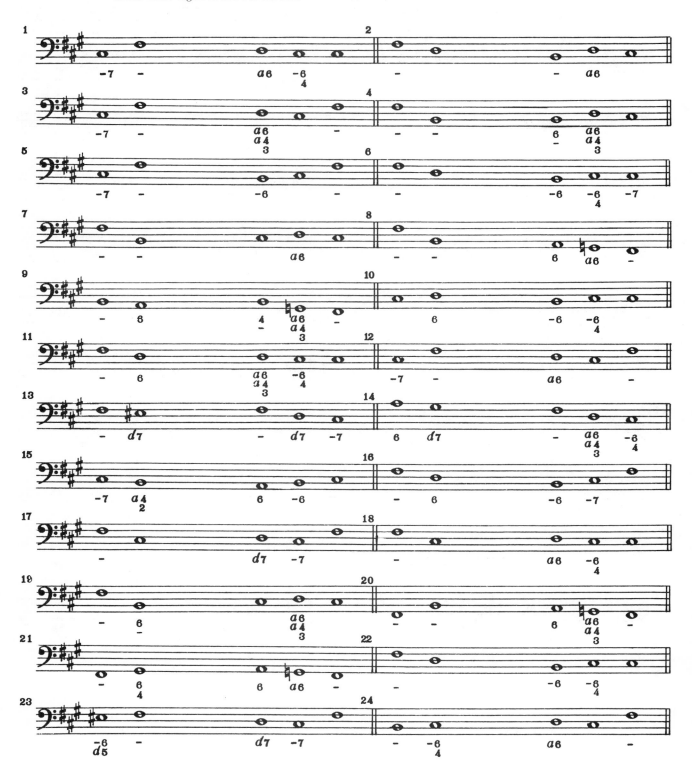

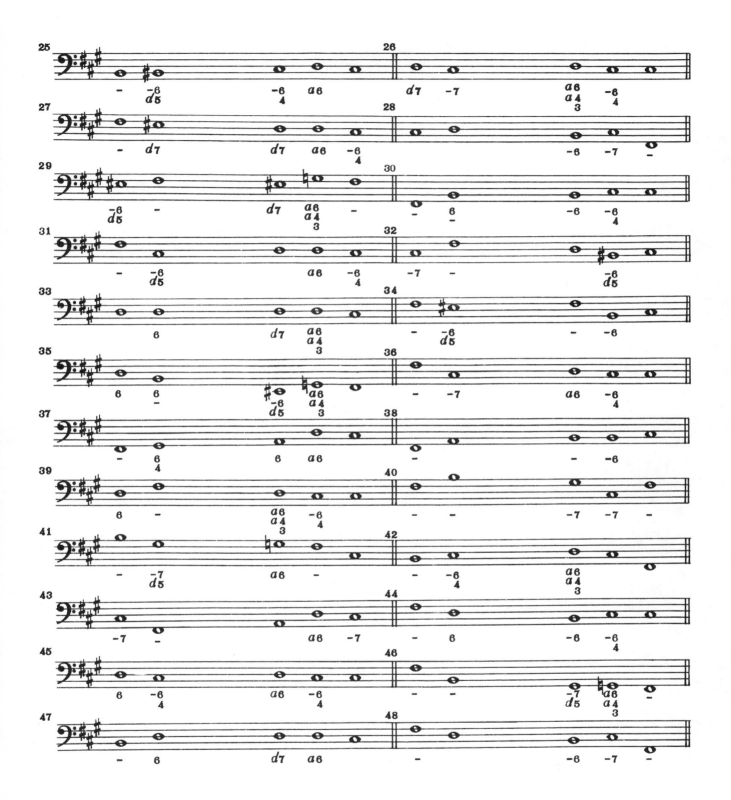

D11-2a Figured bass dictation of foreign chords

(Copy 4)

Shield the answer. Listen to the series of five chords and write the bass notes and the figured bass symbols for the last three chords; then uncover the answer and compare your response. Goal: No more than eight incorrect frames.

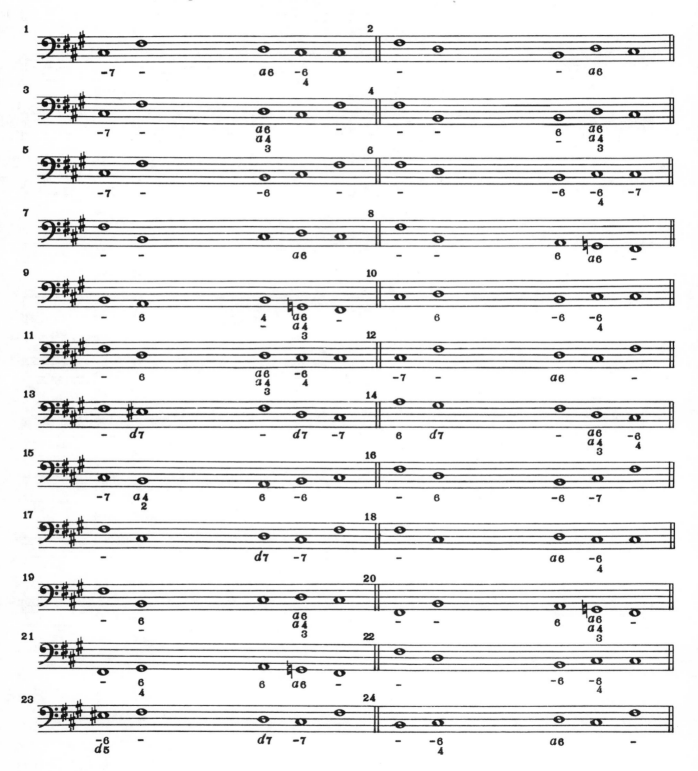

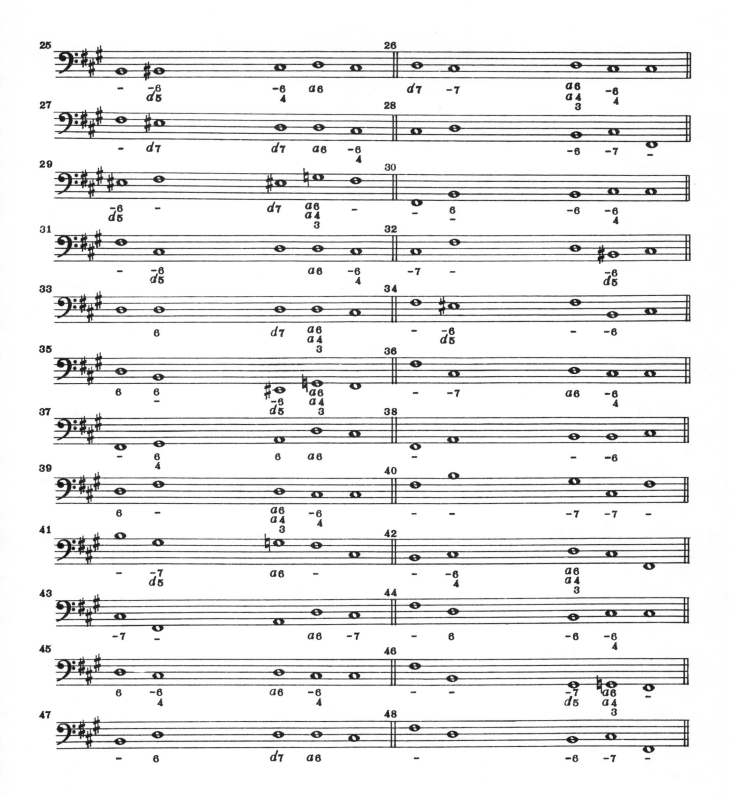

D11-2a

Figured bass dictation of foreign chords

Shield the answer. Listen to the series of five chords and write the bass notes and the figured bass symbols for the last three chords; then uncover the answer and compare your response. Goal: No more than eight incorrect frames.

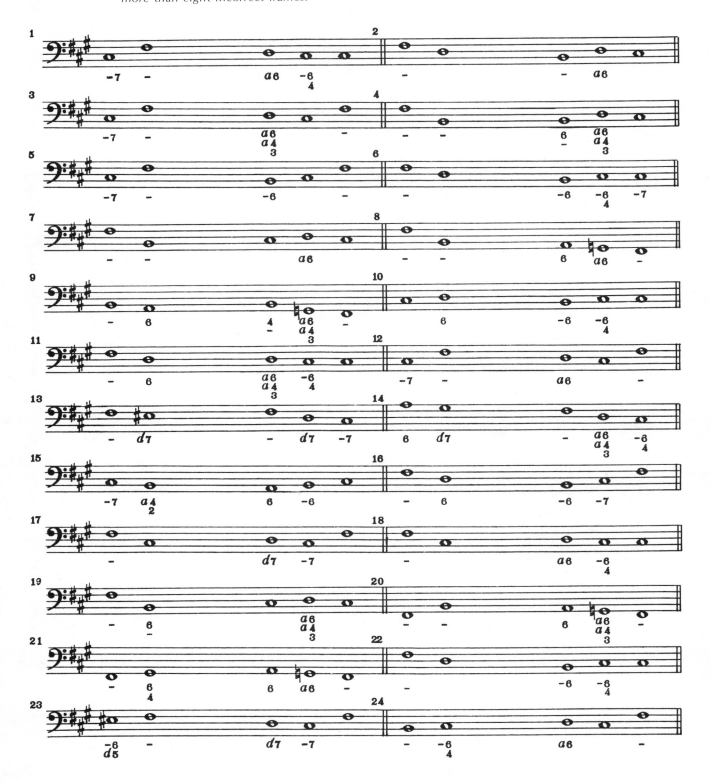

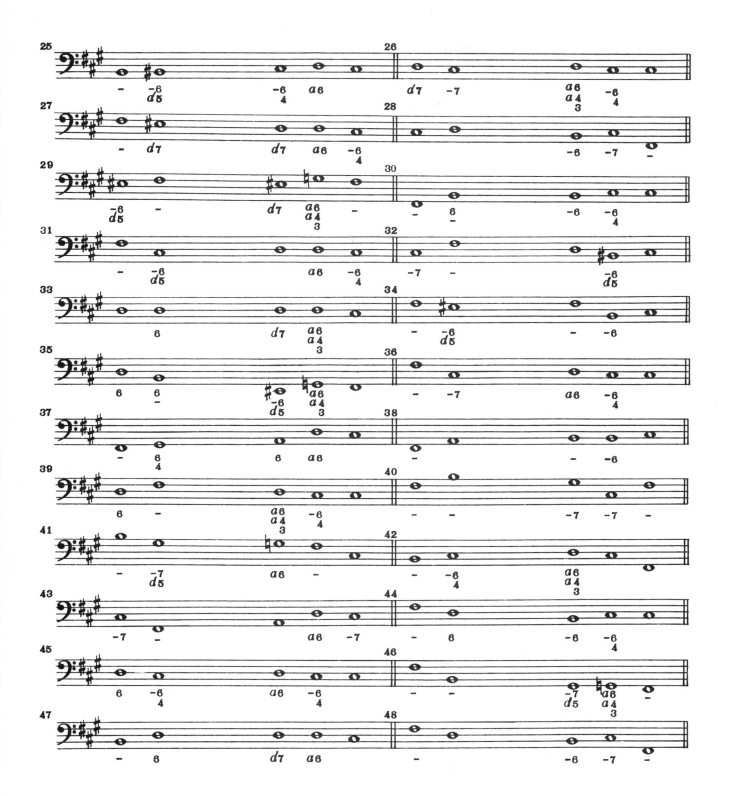

339

Lesson **D11–2b**

In this lesson, the composite chord symbols are introduced for augmented sixth chords on certain degrees of the key and for the Neapolitan sixth chord.

The composite chord symbol for the Neapolitan sixth chord is ($^-$II^{-6}). This is a foreign chord built on the lowered second degree of the key. It is a major triad in first inversion. The fourth degree of the key, which is the third of the chord, appears in the bass.

The key location symbols for augmented sixth chords follow the same procedure used for diminished seventh chords and augmented triads. That is, the key location portion of the composite chord symbol for these chords will refer to the *bass* of the chord. This is a departure from the usual procedure of referring to the root of the chord, which of course may appear in any part. The most common place in both major and minor keys for these chords to appear is at $^-$VI and $^-$II. These will be the only key locations at which you will be asked to identify these chords in this volume. Thus, in this lesson the following composite chord symbols will appear: ($^-$VI^{a6}), ($^-$VI$^{a6}_{a4}$), ($^-$II^{a6}), and ($^-$II$^{a6}_{a4}$).

D11-2b Identification of foreign chords

(Copy 1)

Shield the answer. Listen to the group of five chords and write the composite chord symbols for the last three chords; then uncover the answer and compare your response. Goal: No more than eight incorrect frames.

1. V^{-7} I^- ___ ___ ___ $(^-VI^{a6})$ I^{-6}_{4} V

2. I^- ^-VI ___ ___ ___ IV^- $(^-VI^{a6})$ V

3. V^{-7} I^- ___ ___ ___ $(^-VI^{a6}_{a4}{}_{3})$ V I^-

4. I^- IV^- ___ ___ ___ II^{6}_{-} $(^-VI^{a6}_{a4}{}_{3})$ V

5. V^{-7} I^- ___ ___ ___ $(^-II^{-6})$ V I^-

6. I^- ^-VI ___ ___ ___ $(^-II^{-6})$ I^{-6}_{4} V^{-7}

7. I^- IV^- ___ ___ ___ V $(^-VI^{a6})$ V

8. I^- IV^- ___ ___ ___ I^{6} $(^-II^{a6})$ I^-

9. IV^- I^{6} ___ ___ ___ V^{4}_{-} $(^-II^{a6}_{a4}{}_{3})$ I^-

10. V IV^{6} ___ ___ ___ $(^-II^{-6})$ I^{-6}_{4} V

11. I^- IV^{6} ___ ___ ___ $(^-VI^{a6}_{a4}{}_{3})$ I^{-6}_{4} V

12. V^{-7} I^- ___ ___ ___ $(^-VI^{a6})$ V I^-

13. I^- VII^{d7} ___ ___ ___ I^- $^-VI^{d7}$ V^{-7}

14. I^{6} II^{d7} ___ ___ ___ I^- $(^-VI^{a6}_{a4}{}_{3})$ I^{-6}_{4}

15. V^{-7} V^{a4}_{2} ___ ___ ___ I^{6} $(^-II^{-6})$ V

16. I^- IV^{6} ___ ___ ___ $(^-II^{-6})$ V^{-7} (I)

17. I^- V ___ ___ ___ $^-VI^{d7}$ V^{-7} (I)

18. I^- V ___ ___ ___ $(^-VI^{a6})$ I^{-6}_{4} V

19. I^- II^{6}_{-} ___ ___ ___ V $(^-VI^{a6}_{a4}{}_{3})$ V

20. I^- IV^- ___ ___ ___ I^{6} $(^-II^{a6}_{a4}{}_{3})$ I^-

21. I^- V^{6}_{4} ___ ___ ___ I^{6} $(^-II^{a6})$ I^-

22. I^- ^-VI ___ ___ ___ $(^-II^{-6})$ I^{-6}_{4} V

23. V^{-6}_{d5} I^- ___ ___ ___ $^-VI^{d7}$ V^{-7} (I)

24. IV^- I^{-6}_{4} ___ ___ ___ $(^-VI^{a6})$ V I^-

25. IV^- $(\underline{II^{-6}_{d5}})$ ___ ___ ___ I^{-6}_{4} $(^-VI^{a6})$ V

26. $^-VI^{d7}$ V^{-7} ___ ___ ___ $(^-VI^{a6}_{a4}{}_{3})$ I^{-6}_{4} V

27. I^- VII^{d7} ___ ___ ___ $^-VI^{d7}$ $(^-VI^{a6})$ I^{-6}_{4}

28. V ^-VI ___ ___ ___ $(^-II^{-6})$ V^{-7} I^-

29. V^{-6}_{d5} I^- ___ ___ ___ VII^{d7} $(^-II^{a6}_{a4}{}_{3})$ I^-

30. I^- II^{6}_{-} ___ ___ ___ $(^-II^{-6})$ I^{-6}_{4} V

31. I^- $(\underline{^-III^{-6}_{d5}})$ ___ ___ ___ ^-VI $(\underline{^-VI^{a6}})$ I^{-6}_{4}

32. V^{-7} I^- ___ ___ ___ ^-VI $(\underline{II^{-6}_{d5}})$ V

33. ^-VI IV^{6} ___ ___ ___ $^-VI^{d7}$ $(^-VI^{a6}_{a4}{}_{3})$ V

34. I^- V^{-6}_{d5} ___ ___ ___ I^- $(^-II^{-6})$ V

35. IV^{6} II^{6}_{-} ___ ___ ___ V^{-6}_{d5} $(^-II^{a6}_{a4}{}_{3})$ (I)

36. I^- V^{-7} ___ ___ ___ $(^-VI^{a6})$ I^{-6}_{4} V

37. I^- V^{6}_{4} ___ ___ ___ I^{6} $(\underline{^-VI^{a6}})$ V

38. I^- ^-III ___ ___ ___ IV^- $(^-II^{-6})$ V

39. IV^{6} I^- ___ ___ ___ $(^-VI^{a6}_{a4}{}_{3})$ I^{-6}_{4} V

40. I^- IV^- ___ ___ ___ $(\underline{II^{-7}})$ V^{-7} I^-

41. IV^- II^{-7}_{d5} ___ ___ ___ $(^-II^{a6})$ I^- V

42. IV^- I^{-6}_{4} ___ ___ ___ $(^-VI^{a6}_{a4}{}_{3})$ V (I)

43. V^{-7} I^- ___ ___ ___ ^-III $(^-VI^{a6})$ V^{-7}

44. I^- IV^{6} ___ ___ ___ $(^-II^{-6})$ I^{-6}_{4} V

45. IV^{6} I^{-6}_{4} ___ ___ ___ $(^-VI^{a6})$ I^{-6}_{4} V

46. I^- IV^- ___ ___ ___ II^{-7}_{d5} $(^-II^{a6}_{a4}{}_{3})$ I^-

47. IV^- IV^{6} ___ ___ ___ $^-VI^{d7}$ $(^-VI^{a6})$ V

48. I^- ^-VI ___ ___ ___ $(^-II^{-6})$ V^{-7} I^-

D11-2b Identification of foreign chords
(Copy 2)

Shield the answer. Listen to the group of five chords and write the composite chord symbols for the last three chords; then uncover the answer and compare your response. Goal: No more than eight incorrect frames.

1. V^{-7} I^- ___ ___ ___ $(^-VI^{a6})$ I^{-6}_4 V
2. I^- ^-VI ___ ___ ___ IV^- $(^-VI^{a6})$ V
3. V^{-7} I^- ___ ___ ___ $(^-VI^{a6}_{a4})_{3}$ V I^-
4. I^- IV^- ___ ___ ___ II^6_- $(^-VI^{a6}_{a4})_{3}$ V
5. V^{-7} I^- ___ ___ ___ $(^-II^{-6})$ V I^-
6. I^- ^-VI ___ ___ ___ $(^-II^{-6})$ I^{-6}_4 V^{-7}
7. I^- IV^- ___ ___ ___ V $(^-VI^{a6})$ V
8. I^- IV^- ___ ___ ___ I^6 $(^-II^{a6})$ I^-
9. IV^- I^6 ___ ___ ___ V^4_- $(^-II^{a6}_{a4})_{3}$ I^-
10. V IV^6 ___ ___ ___ $(^-II^{-6})$ I^{-6}_4 V
11. I^- IV^6 ___ ___ ___ $(^-VI^{a6}_{a4})_{3}$ I^{-6}_4 V
12. V^{-7} I^- ___ ___ ___ $(^-VI^{a6})$ V I^-
13. I^- VII^{d7} ___ ___ ___ I^- $^-VI^{d7}$ V^{-7}
14. I^6 II^{d7} ___ ___ ___ I^- $(^-VI^{a6}_{a4})_{3}$ I^{-6}_4
15. V^{-7} V^{a4}_2 ___ ___ ___ I^6 $(^-II^{-6})$ V
16. I^- IV^6 ___ ___ ___ $(^-II^{-6})$ V^{-7} (I)
17. I^- V ___ ___ ___ $^-VI^{d7}$ V^{-7} (I)
18. I^- V ___ ___ ___ $(^-VI^{a6})$ I^{-6}_4 V
19. I^- II^6_- ___ ___ ___ V $(^-VI^{a6}_{a4})_{3}$ V
20. I^- IV^- ___ ___ ___ I^6 $(^-II^{a6}_{a4})_{3}$ I^-
21. I^- V^6_4 ___ ___ ___ I^6 $(^-II^{a6})$ I^-
22. I^- ^-VI ___ ___ ___ $(^-II^{-6})$ I^{-6}_4 V
23. V^{-6}_{d5} I^- ___ ___ ___ $^-VI^{d7}$ V^{-7} (I)
24. IV^- I^{-6}_4 ___ ___ ___ $(^-VI^{a6})$ V I^-

25. IV^- $(\underline{II^{-6}_{d5}})$ ___ ___ ___ I^{-6}_4 $(^-VI^{a6})$ V
26. $^-VI^{d7}$ V^{-7} ___ ___ ___ $(^-VI^{a6}_{a4})_{3}$ I^{-6}_4
27. I^- VII^{d7} ___ ___ ___ $^-VI^{d7}$ $(^-VI^{a6})$ I^{-6}_4
28. V ^-VI ___ ___ ___ $(^-II^{-6})$ V^{-7} I^-
29. V^{-6}_{d5} I^- ___ ___ ___ VII^{d7} $(^-II^{a6}_{a4})_{3}$ I^-
30. I^- II^6_- ___ ___ ___ $(^-II^{-6})$ I^{-6}_4 V
31. I^- $(^-III^{-6}_{d5})$ ___ ___ ___ ^-VI $(\underline{^-VI^{a6}})$ I^{-6}_4
32. V^{-7} I^- ___ ___ ___ ^-VI $(\underline{II^{-6}_{d5}})$ V
33. ^-VI IV^6 ___ ___ ___ $^-VI^{d7}$ $(^-VI^{a6}_{a4})_{3}$ V
34. I^- V^{-6}_{d5} ___ ___ ___ I^- $(^-II^{-6})$ V
35. IV^6 II^6_- ___ ___ ___ V^{-6}_{d5} $(^-II^{a6}_{a4})_{3}$ (I)
36. I^- V^{-7} ___ ___ ___ $(^-VI^{a6})$ I^{-6}_4 V
37. I^- V^6_4 ___ ___ ___ I^6 $(\underline{^-VI^{a6}})$ V
38. I^- ^-III ___ ___ ___ IV^- $(^-II^{-6})$ V
39. IV^6 I^- ___ ___ ___ $(^-VI^{a6}_{a4})_{3}$ I^{-6}_4 V
40. I^- IV^- ___ ___ ___ $(\underline{II^{-7}})$ V^{-7} I^-
41. IV^- II^{-7}_{d5} ___ ___ ___ $(^-II^{a6})$ I^- V
42. IV^- I^{-6}_4 ___ ___ ___ $(^-VI^{a6}_{a4})_{3}$ V (I)
43. V^{-7} I^- ___ ___ ___ ^-III $(^-VI^{a6})$ V^{-7}
44. I^- IV^6 ___ ___ ___ $(^-II^{-6})$ I^{-6}_4 V
45. IV^6 I^{-6}_4 ___ ___ ___ $(^-VI^{a6})$ I^{-6}_4 V
46. I^- IV^- ___ ___ ___ II^{-7}_{d5} $(^-II^{a6}_{a4})_{3}$ I^-
47. IV^- IV^6 ___ ___ ___ $^-VI^{d7}$ $(^-VI^{a6})$ V
48. I^- ^-VI ___ ___ ___ $(^-II^{-6})$ V^{-7} I^-

D11-2b
Identification of foreign chords

Shield the answer. Listen to the group of five chords and write the composite chord symbols for the last three chords; then uncover the answer and compare your response. Goal: No more than eight incorrect frames.

1. V^{-7} I^- _____ _____ _____ $(^-VI^{a6})$ I^{-6}_4 V

2. I^- ^-VI _____ _____ _____ IV^- $(^-VI^{a6})$ V

3. V^{-7} I^- _____ _____ _____ $(^-VI^{a6}_{a4})$ V I^-_3

4. I^- IV^- _____ _____ _____ $II^6_{\_}$ $(^-VI^{a6}_{a4})$ V_3

5. V^{-7} I^- _____ _____ _____ $(^-II^{-6})$ V I^-

6. I^- ^-VI _____ _____ _____ $(^-II^{-6})$ I^{-6}_4 V^{-7}

7. I^- IV^- _____ _____ _____ V $(^-VI^{a6})$ V

8. I^- IV^- _____ _____ _____ I^6 $(^-II^{a6})$ I^-

9. IV^- I^6 _____ _____ _____ $V^4_{\_}$ $(^-II^{a6}_{a4})$ I^-_3

10. V IV^6 _____ _____ _____ $(^-II^{-6})$ I^{-6}_4 V

11. I^- IV^6 _____ _____ _____ $(^-VI^{a6}_{a4})$ I^{-6}_4 V_3

12. V^{-7} I^- _____ _____ _____ $(^-VI^{a6})$ V I^-

13. I^- VII^{d7} _____ _____ _____ I^- $^-VI^{d7}$ V^{-7}

14. I^6 II^{d7} _____ _____ _____ I^- $(^-VI^{a6}_{a4})$ I^{-6}_4 $_3$

15. V^{-7} V^{a4}_2 _____ _____ _____ I^6 $(^-II^{-6})$ V

16. I^- IV^6 _____ _____ _____ $(^-II^{-6})$ V^{-7} (I)

17. I^- V _____ _____ _____ $^-VI^{d7}$ V^{-7} (I)

18. I^- V _____ _____ _____ $(^-VI^{a6})$ I^{-6}_4 V

19. I^- $II^6_{\_}$ _____ _____ _____ V $(^-VI^{a6}_{a4})$ V_3

20. I^- IV^- _____ _____ _____ I^6 $(^-II^{a6}_{a4})$ I^-_3

21. I^- V^6_4 _____ _____ _____ I^6 $(^-II^{a6})$ I^-

22. I^- ^-VI _____ _____ _____ $(^-II^{-6})$ I^{-6}_4 V

23. V^{-6}_{d5} I^- _____ _____ _____ $^-VI^{d7}$ V^{-7} (I)

24. IV^- I^{-6}_4 _____ _____ _____ $(^-VI^{a6})$ V I^-

25. IV^- $(\underline{II^{-6}_{d5}})$ _____ _____ _____ I^{-6}_4 $(^-VI^{a6})$ V

26. $^-VI^{d7}$ V^{-7} _____ _____ _____ $(^-VI^{a6}_{a4})$ I^{-6}_4 V_3

27. I^- VII^{d7} _____ _____ _____ $^-VI^{d7}$ $(^-VI^{a6})$ I^{-6}_4

28. V ^-VI _____ _____ _____ $(^-II^{-6})$ V^{-7} I^-

29. V^{-6}_{d5} I^- _____ _____ _____ VII^{d7} $(^-II^{a6}_{a4})$ I^-_3

30. I^- $II^6_{\_}$ _____ _____ _____ $(^-II^{-6})$ I^{-6}_4 V

31. I^- $(^-III^{-6}_{d5})$ _____ _____ _____ ^-VI $(\underline{^-VI^{a6}})$ I^{-6}_4

32. V^{-7} I^- _____ _____ _____ ^-VI $(\underline{II^{-6}_{d5}})$ V

33. ^-VI IV^6 _____ _____ _____ $^-VI^{d7}$ $(^-VI^{a6}_{a4})$ V_3

34. I^- V^{-6}_{d5} _____ _____ _____ I^- $(^-II^{-6})$ V

35. IV^6 $II^6_{\_}$ _____ _____ _____ V^{-6}_{d5} $(^-II^{a6}_{a4})$ $(I)_3$

36. I^- V^{-7} _____ _____ _____ $(^-VI^{a6})$ I^{-6}_4 V

37. I^- V^6_4 _____ _____ _____ I^6 $(\underline{^-VI^{a6}})$ V

38. I^- ^-III _____ _____ _____ IV^- $(^-II^{-6})$ V

39. IV^6 I^- _____ _____ _____ $(^-VI^{a6}_{a4})$ I^{-6}_4 V_3

40. I^- IV^- _____ _____ _____ $(\underline{II^{-7}})$ V^{-7} I^-

41. IV^- II^{-7}_{d5} _____ _____ _____ $(^-II^{a6})$ I^- V

42. IV^- I^{-6}_4 _____ _____ _____ $(^-VI^{a6}_{a4})$ V $(I)_3$

43. V^{-7} I^- _____ _____ _____ ^-III $(^-VI^{a6})$ V^{-7}

44. I^- IV^6 _____ _____ _____ $(^-II^{-6})$ I^{-6}_4 V

45. IV^6 I^{-6}_4 _____ _____ _____ $(^-VI^{a6})$ I^{-6}_4 V

46. I^- IV^- _____ _____ _____ II^{-7}_{d5} $(^-II^{a6}_{a4})$ I^-_3

47. IV^- IV^6 _____ _____ _____ $^-VI^{d7}$ $(^-VI^{a6})$ V

48. I^- ^-VI _____ _____ _____ $(^-II^{-6})$ V^{-7} I^-

D11-2b Identification of foreign chords
(Copy 4)

Shield the answer. Listen to the group of five chords and write the composite chord symbols for the last three chords; then uncover the answer and compare your response. Goal: No more than eight incorrect frames.

1 V^{-7} I$^-$ _____ _____ _____ ($^-$VI^{a6}) I$^{-6}_4$ V

2 I$^-$ $^-$VI _____ _____ _____ IV$^-$ ($^-$VI^{a6}) V

3 V^{-7} I$^-$ _____ _____ _____ ($^-$VI$^{a6}_{a4}$)$_3$ V I$^-$

4 I$^-$ IV$^-$ _____ _____ _____ II$^6_-$ ($^-$VI$^{a6}_{a4}$)$_3$ V

5 V^{-7} I$^-$ _____ _____ _____ ($^-$II^{-6}) V I$^-$

6 I$^-$ $^-$VI _____ _____ _____ ($^-$II^{-6}) I$^{-6}_4$ V^{-7}

7 I$^-$ IV$^-$ _____ _____ _____ V ($^-$VI^{a6}) V

8 I$^-$ IV$^-$ _____ _____ _____ I^6 ($^-$II^{a6}) I$^-$

9 IV$^-$ I^6 _____ _____ _____ V$^4_-$ ($^-$II$^{a6}_{a4}$)$_3$ I$^-$

10 V IV^6 _____ _____ _____ ($^-$II^{-6}) I$^{-6}_4$ V

11 I$^-$ IV^6 _____ _____ _____ ($^-$VI$^{a6}_{a4}$)$_3$ I$^{-6}_4$ V

12 V^{-7} I$^-$ _____ _____ _____ ($^-$VI^{a6}) V I$^-$

13 I$^-$ VII^{d7} _____ _____ _____ I$^-$ $^-$VI^{d7} V^{-7}

14 I^6 II^{d7} _____ _____ _____ I$^-$ ($^-$VI$^{a6}_{a4}$)$_3$ I$^{-6}_4$

15 V^{-7} V$^{a4}_2$ _____ _____ _____ I^6 ($^-$II^{-6}) V

16 I$^-$ IV^6 _____ _____ _____ ($^-$II^{-6}) V^{-7} (I)

17 I$^-$ V _____ _____ _____ $^-$VI^{d7} V^{-7} (I)

18 I$^-$ V _____ _____ _____ ($^-$VI^{a6}) I$^{-6}_4$ V

19 I$^-$ II$^6_-$ _____ _____ _____ V ($^-$VI$^{a6}_{a4}$)$_3$ V

20 I$^-$ IV$^-$ _____ _____ _____ I^6 ($^-$II$^{a6}_{a4}$)$_3$ I$^-$

21 I$^-$ V$^6_4$ _____ _____ _____ I^6 ($^-$II^{a6}) I$^-$

22 I$^-$ $^-$VI _____ _____ _____ ($^-$II^{-6}) I$^{-6}_4$ V

23 V$^{-6}_{d5}$ I$^-$ _____ _____ _____ $^-$VI^{d7} V^{-7} (I)

24 IV$^-$ I$^{-6}_4$ _____ _____ _____ ($^-$VI^{a6}) V I$^-$

25 IV$^-$ (II$^{-6}_{d5}$) _____ _____ _____ I$^{-6}_4$ ($^-$VI^{a6}) V

26 $^-$VI^{d7} V^{-7} _____ _____ _____ ($^-$VI$^{a6}_{a4}$)$_3$ I$^{-6}_4$ V

27 I$^-$ VII^{d7} _____ _____ _____ $^-$VI^{d7} ($^-$VI^{a6}) I$^{-6}_4$

28 V $^-$VI _____ _____ _____ ($^-$II^{-6}) V^{-7} I$^-$

29 V$^{-6}_{d5}$ I$^-$ _____ _____ _____ VII^{d7} ($^-$II$^{a6}_{a4}$)$_3$ I$^-$

30 I$^-$ II$^6_-$ _____ _____ _____ ($^-$II^{-6}) I$^{-6}_4$ V

31 I$^-$ ($^-$III$^{-6}_{d5}$) _____ _____ _____ $^-$VI ($^-$VI^{a6}) I$^{-6}_4$

32 V^{-7} I$^-$ _____ _____ _____ $^-$VI (II$^{-6}_{d5}$) V

33 $^-$VI IV^6 _____ _____ _____ $^-$VI^{d7} ($^-$VI$^{a6}_{a4}$)$_3$ V

34 I$^-$ V$^{-6}_{d5}$ _____ _____ _____ I$^-$ ($^-$II^{-6}) V

35 IV^6 II$^6_-$ _____ _____ _____ V$^{-6}_{d5}$ ($^-$II$^{a6}_{a4}$)$_3$ (I)

36 I$^-$ V^{-7} _____ _____ _____ ($^-$VI^{a6}) I$^{-6}_4$ V

37 I$^-$ V$^6_4$ _____ _____ _____ I^6 ($^-$VI^{a6}) V

38 I$^-$ $^-$III _____ _____ _____ IV$^-$ ($^-$II^{-6}) V

39 IV^6 I$^-$ _____ _____ _____ ($^-$VI$^{a6}_{a4}$)$_3$ I$^{-6}_4$ V

40 I$^-$ IV$^-$ _____ _____ _____ (II^{-7}) V^{-7} I$^-$

41 IV$^-$ II$^{-7}_{d5}$ _____ _____ _____ ($^-$II^{a6}) I$^-$ V

42 IV$^-$ I$^{-6}_4$ _____ _____ _____ ($^-$VI$^{a6}_{a4}$)$_3$ V (I)

43 V^{-7} I$^-$ _____ _____ _____ $^-$III ($^-$VI^{a6}) V^{-7}

44 I$^-$ IV^6 _____ _____ _____ ($^-$II^{-6}) I$^{-6}_4$ V

45 IV^6 I$^{-6}_4$ _____ _____ _____ ($^-$VI^{a6}) I$^{-6}_4$ V

46 I$^-$ IV$^-$ _____ _____ _____ II$^{-7}_{d5}$ ($^-$II$^{a6}_{a4}$)$_3$ I$^-$

47 IV$^-$ IV^6 _____ _____ _____ $^-$VI^{d7} ($^-$VI^{a6}) V

48 I$^-$ $^-$VI _____ _____ _____ ($^-$II^{-6}) V^{-7} I$^-$

D11-2b Identification of foreign chords
(Copy 5)

Shield the answer. Listen to the group of five chords and write the composite chord symbols for the last three chords; then uncover the answer and compare your response. Goal: No more than eight incorrect frames.

1 V^{-7} I^- ___ ___ ___ $(^-VI^{a6})$ I^{-6}_4 V

2 I^- ^-VI ___ ___ ___ IV^- $(^-VI^{a6})$ V

3 V^{-7} I^- ___ ___ ___ $(^-VI^{a6}_{a4})_3$ V I^-

4 I^- IV^- ___ ___ ___ II^6_- $(^-VI^{a6}_{a4})_3$ V

5 V^{-7} I^- ___ ___ ___ $(^-II^{-6})$ V I^-

6 I^- ^-VI ___ ___ ___ $(^-II^{-6})$ I^{-6}_4 V^{-7}

7 I^- IV^- ___ ___ ___ V $(^-VI^{a6})$ V

8 I^- IV^- ___ ___ ___ I^6 $(^-II^{a6})$ I^-

9 IV^- I^6 ___ ___ ___ V^4_- $(^-II^{a6}_{a4})_3$ I^-

10 V IV^6 ___ ___ ___ $(^-II^{-6})$ I^{-6}_4 V

11 I^- IV^6 ___ ___ ___ $(^-VI^{a6}_{a4})_3$ I^{-6}_4 V

12 V^{-7} I^- ___ ___ ___ $(^-VI^{a6})$ V I^-

13 I^- VII^{d7} ___ ___ ___ I^- $^-VI^{d7}$ V^{-7}

14 I^6 II^{d7} ___ ___ ___ I^- $(^-VI^{a6}_{a4})_3$ I^{-6}_4

15 V^{-7} V^{a4}_2 ___ ___ ___ I^6 $(^-II^{-6})$ V

16 I^- IV^6 ___ ___ ___ $(^-II^{-6})$ V^{-7} (I)

17 I^- V ___ ___ ___ $^-VI^{d7}$ V^{-7} (I)

18 I^- V ___ ___ ___ $(^-VI^{a6})$ I^{-6}_4 V

19 I^- II^6_- ___ ___ ___ V $(^-VI^{a6}_{a4})_3$ V

20 I^- IV^- ___ ___ ___ I^6 $(^-II^{a6}_{a4})_3$ I^-

21 I^- V^6_4 ___ ___ ___ I^6 $(^-II^{a6})$ I^-

22 I^- ^-VI ___ ___ ___ $(^-II^{-6})$ I^{-6}_4 V

23 V^{-6}_{d5} I^- ___ ___ ___ $^-VI^{d7}$ V^{-7} (I)

24 IV^- I^{-6}_4 ___ ___ ___ $(^-VI^{a6})$ V I^-

25 IV^- $(\underline{II^{-6}_{d5}})$ ___ ___ ___ I^{-6}_4 $(^-VI^{a6})$ V

26 $^-VI^{d7}$ V^{-7} ___ ___ ___ $(^-VI^{a6}_{a4})_3$ I^{-6}_4 V

27 I^- VII^{d7} ___ ___ ___ $^-VI^{d7}$ $(^-VI^{a6})$ I^{-6}_4

28 V ^-VI ___ ___ ___ $(^-II^{-6})$ V^{-7} I^-

29 V^{-6}_{d5} I^- ___ ___ ___ VII^{d7} $(^-II^{a6}_{a4})_3$ I^-

30 I^- II^6_- ___ ___ ___ $(^-II^{-6})$ I^{-6}_4 V

31 I^- $(^-III^{-6}_{d5})$ ___ ___ ___ ^-VI $(\underline{^-VI^{a6}})$ I^{-6}_4

32 V^{-7} I^- ___ ___ ___ ^-VI $(\underline{II^{-6}_{d5}})$ V

33 ^-VI IV^6 ___ ___ ___ $^-VI^{d7}$ $(^-VI^{a6}_{a4})_3$ V

34 I^- V^{-6}_{d5} ___ ___ ___ I^- $(^-II^{-6})$ V

35 IV^6 II^6_- ___ ___ ___ V^{-6}_{d5} $(^-II^{a6}_{a4})_3$ (I)

36 I^- V^{-7} ___ ___ ___ $(^-VI^{a6})$ I^{-6}_4 V

37 I^- V^6_4 ___ ___ ___ I^6 $(\underline{^-VI^{a6}})$ V

38 I^- ^-III ___ ___ ___ IV^- $(^-II^{-6})$ V

39 IV^6 I^- ___ ___ ___ $(^-VI^{a6}_{a4})_3$ I^{-6}_4 V

40 I^- IV^- ___ ___ ___ $(\underline{II^{-7}})$ V^{-7} I^-

41 IV^- II^{-7}_{d5} ___ ___ ___ $(^-II^{a6})$ I^- V

42 IV^- I^{-6}_4 ___ ___ ___ $(^-VI^{a6}_{a4})_3$ V (I)

43 V^{-7} I^- ___ ___ ___ ^-III $(^-VI^{a6})$ V^{-7}

44 I^- IV^6 ___ ___ ___ $(^-II^{-6})$ I^{-6}_4 V

45 IV^6 I^{-6}_4 ___ ___ ___ $(^-VI^{a6})$ I^{-6}_4 V

46 I^- IV^- ___ ___ ___ II^{-7}_{d5} $(^-II^{a6}_{a4})_3$ I^-

47 IV^- IV^6 ___ ___ ___ $^-VI^{d7}$ $(^-VI^{a6})$ V

48 I^- ^-VI ___ ___ ___ $(^-II^{-6})$ V^{-7} I^-

D11-3a Figured bass dictation of foreign chords

(Copy 1)

Shield the answer. Listen to the series of five chords and write the bass notes and the figured bass symbols for the last three chords; then uncover the answer and compare your response. Goal: No more than eight incorrect frames.

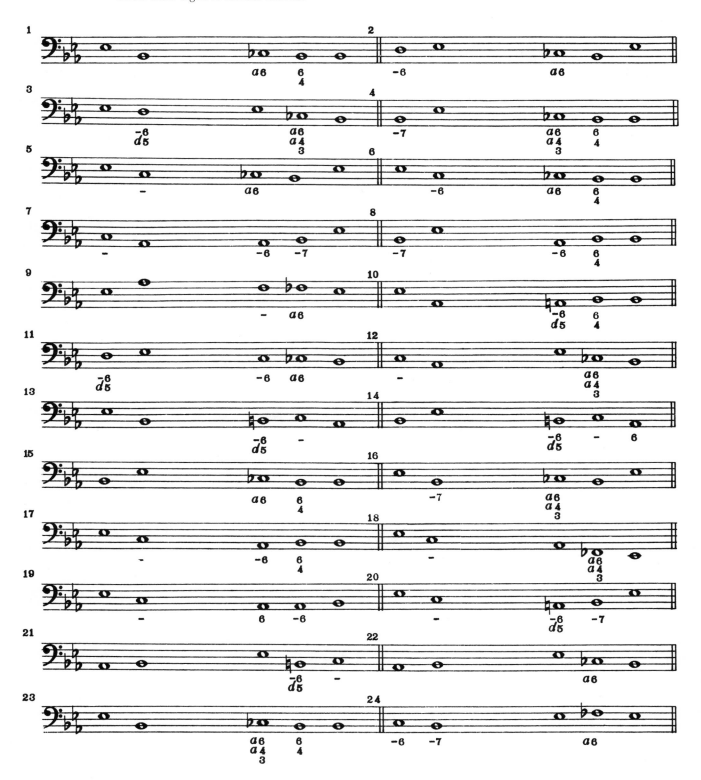

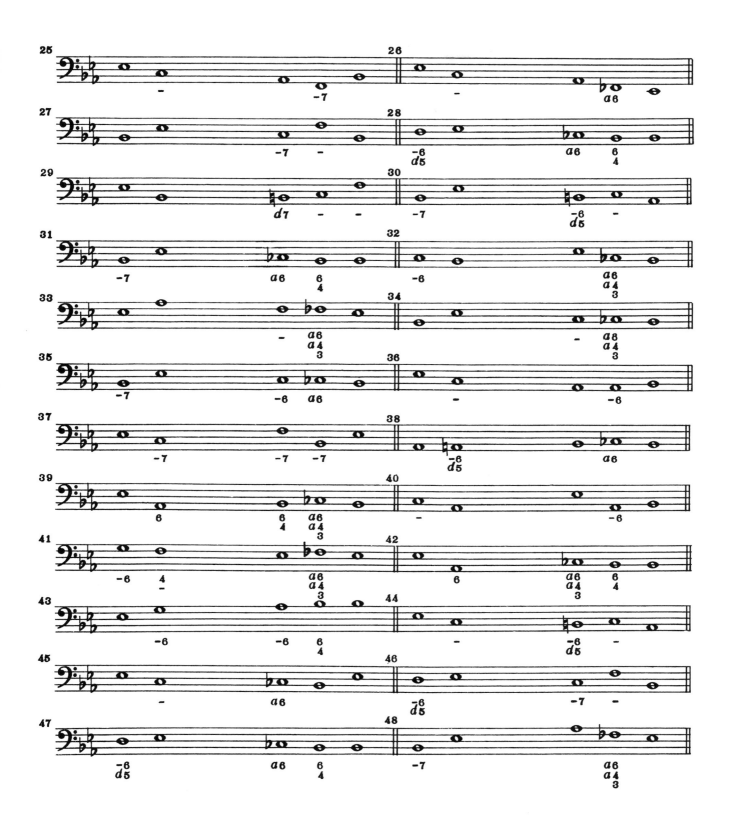

D11-3a Figured bass dictation of foreign chords
(Copy 2)

Shield the answer. Listen to the series of five chords and write the bass notes and the figured bass symbols for the last three chords; then uncover the answer and compare your response. Goal: No more than eight incorrect frames.

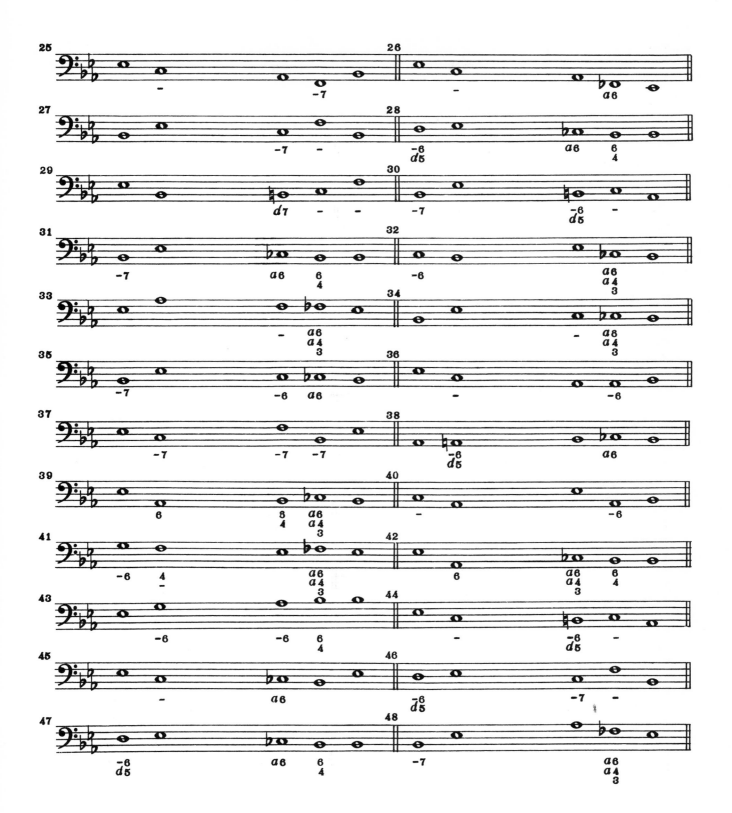

D11-3a Figured bass dictation of foreign chords
(Copy 3)

Shield the answer. Listen to the series of five chords and write the bass notes and the figured bass symbols for the last three chords; then uncover the answer and compare your response. Goal: No more than eight incorrect frames.

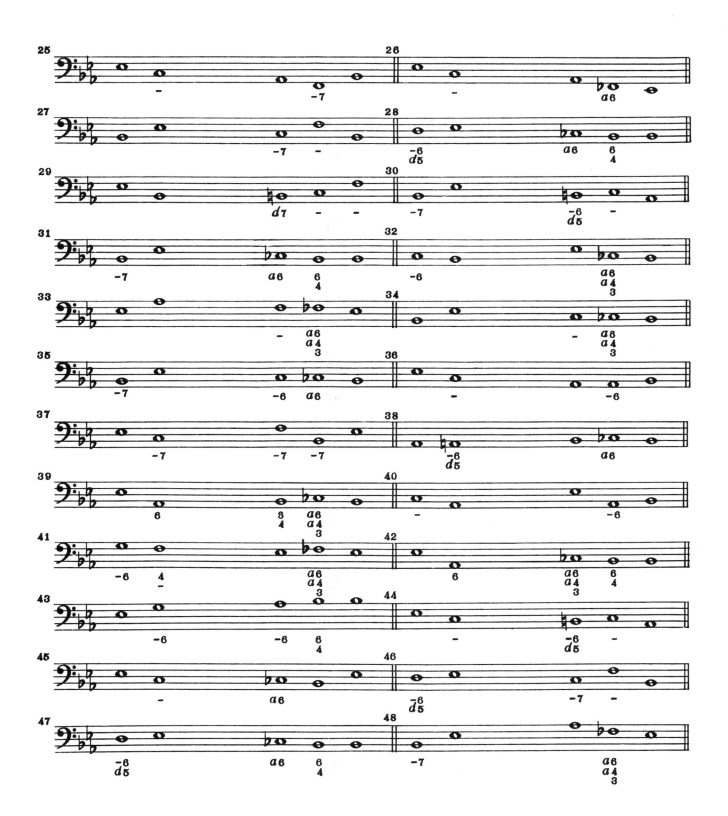

D11-3a Figured bass dictation of foreign chords

Shield the answer. Listen to the series of five chords and write the bass notes and the figured bass symbols for the last three chords; then uncover the answer and compare your response. Goal: No more than eight incorrect frames.

352

D11-3a Figured bass dictation of foreign chords
(Copy 5)

Shield the answer. Listen to the series of five chords and write the bass notes and the figured bass symbols for the last three chords; then uncover the answer and compare your response. Goal: No more than eight incorrect frames.

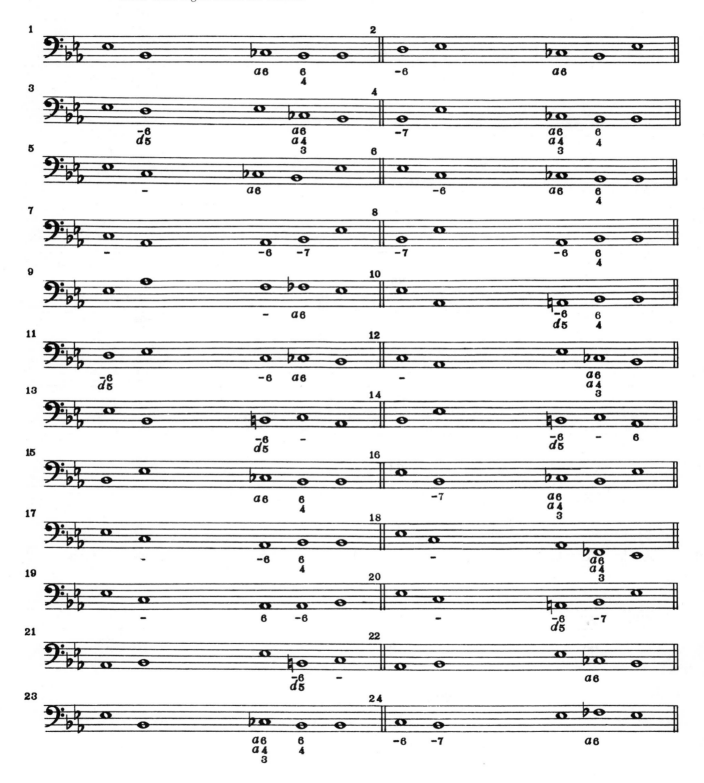

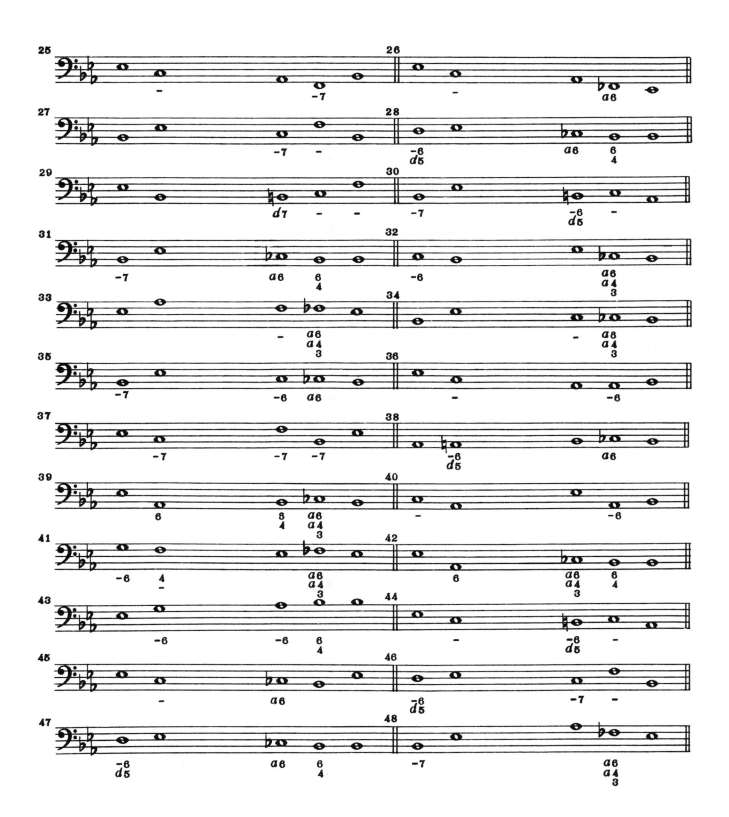

D11–3b Identification of foreign chords
(Copy 1)

Shield the answer. Listen to the group of five chords and write the composite chord symbols for the last three chords; then uncover the answer and compare your response. Goal: No more than eight incorrect frames.

1 I V _____ _____ _____ ($^-$VI^{a6}) I$_4^6$ V

2 V^{-6} I _____ _____ _____ ($^-$VI^{a6}) V I

3 I V$_{d5}^{-6}$ _____ _____ _____ I ($^-$VI$_{a4\;3}^{a6}$) V

4 V^{-7} I _____ _____ _____ ($^-$VI$_{a4\;3}^{a6}$) I$_4^6$ V

5 I VI$^-$ _____ _____ _____ ($^-$VI^{a6}) V I

6 I IV^{-6} _____ _____ _____ ($^-$VI^{a6}) I$_4^6$ V

7 VI$^-$ IV _____ _____ _____ ($^-$II^{-6}) V^{-7} I

8 V^{-7} I _____ _____ _____ ($^-$II^{-6}) I$_4^6$ V

9 I IV _____ _____ _____ II$^-$ ($^-$II^{a6}) I

10 I IV _____ _____ _____ ($\underline{\text{II}_{d5}^{-6}}$) I$_4^6$ V

11 V$_{d5}^{-6}$ I _____ _____ _____ IV^{-6} ($^-$VI^{a6}) V

12 VI$^-$ IV _____ _____ _____ I ($^-$VI$_{a4\;3}^{a6}$) V

13 I V _____ _____ _____ ($\underline{\text{III}_{d5}^{-6}}$) VI$^-$ IV

14 V I _____ _____ _____ ($\underline{\text{III}_{d5}^{-6}}$) VI$^-$ II^6

15 V I _____ _____ _____ ($^-$VI^{a6}) I$_4^6$ V

16 I V^{-7} _____ _____ _____ ($^-$VI$_{a4\;3}^{a6}$) V I

17 I VI$^-$ _____ _____ _____ ($^-$II^{-6}) I$_4^6$ V

18 I VI$^-$ _____ _____ _____ IV ($^-$II$_{a4\;3}^{a6}$) I

19 I VI$^-$ _____ _____ _____ II^6 ($^-$II^{-6}) V

20 I VI$^-$ _____ _____ _____ ($\underline{\text{II}_{d5}^{-6}}$) V^{-7} I

21 IV V _____ _____ _____ I ($\underline{\text{III}_{d5}^{-6}}$) VI$^-$

22 IV V _____ _____ _____ I ($^-$VI^{a6}) V

23 I V _____ _____ _____ ($^-$VI$_{a4\;3}^{a6}$) I$_4^6$ V

24 IV^{-6} V^{-7} _____ _____ _____ I ($^-$II^{a6}) I

25 I VI$^-$ _____ _____ _____ IV ($\underline{\text{II}^{-7}}$) V

26 I VI$^-$ _____ _____ _____ IV ($^-$II^{a6}) I

27 V I _____ _____ _____ ($\underline{\text{VI}^{-7}}$) II$^-$ V

28 V$_{d5}^{-6}$ I _____ _____ _____ ($^-$VI^{a6}) I$_4^6$ V

29 I V _____ _____ _____ (aV^{d7}) VI$^-$ II$^-$

30 V^{-7} I _____ _____ _____ ($\underline{\text{III}_{d5}^{-6}}$) VI$^-$ IV

31 V^{-7} I _____ _____ _____ ($^-$VI^{a6}) I$_4^6$ V

32 IV^{-6} V _____ _____ _____ I $^-$VI$_{a4\;3}^{a6}$ V

33 I IV _____ _____ _____ II$^-$ ($^-$II$_{a4\;3}^{a6}$) I

34 V I _____ _____ _____ VI$^-$ ($^-$VI$_{a4\;3}^{a6}$) V

35 V^{-7} I _____ _____ _____ IV^{-6} ($^-$VI^{a6}) V

36 I VI$^-$ _____ _____ _____ IV ($^-$II^{-6}) V

37 I ($\underline{\text{VI}^{-7}}$) _____ _____ _____ ($\underline{\text{II}^{-7}}$) V^{-7} I

38 IV ($\underline{\text{II}_{d5}^{-6}}$) _____ _____ _____ V ($^-$VI^{a6}) V

39 I II^6 _____ _____ _____ I$_4^6$ ($^-$VI$_{a4\;3}^{a6}$) V

40 VI$^-$ IV _____ _____ _____ I ($^-$II^{-6}) V

41 I^{-6} V$_{\_}^4$ _____ _____ _____ I ($^-$II$_{a4\;3}^{a6}$) I

42 I II^6 _____ _____ _____ ($^-$VI$_{a4\;3}^{a6}$) I$_4^6$ V

43 I I^{-6} _____ _____ _____ ($^-$II^{-6}) I$_4^6$ V

44 I VI$^-$ _____ _____ _____ ($\underline{\text{III}_{d5}^{-6}}$) VI$^-$ IV

45 I VI$^-$ _____ _____ _____ ($^-$VI^{a6}) V I

46 V$_{d5}^{-6}$ I _____ _____ _____ ($\underline{\text{VI}^{-7}}$) II$^-$ V

47 V$_{d5}^{-6}$ I _____ _____ _____ ($^-$VI^{a6}) I$_4^6$ V

48 V^{-7} I _____ _____ _____ IV ($^-$II$_{a4\;3}^{a6}$) I

Shield the answer. Listen to the group of five chords and write the composite chord symbols for the last three chords; then uncover the answer and compare your response. Goal: No more than eight incorrect frames.

1 I V _____ _____ _____ ($^-$VI^{a6}) I$_4^6$ V

2 V^{-6} I _____ _____ _____ ($^-$VI^{a6}) V I

3 I V$_{d5}^{-6}$ _____ _____ _____ I ($^-$VI$_{a4}^{a6}$) V
$\phantom{3 I V_{d5}^{-6} \_\_ \_\_ \_\_ I (^-VI_{a4}^{a6})}$ 3

4 V^{-7} I _____ _____ _____ ($^-$VI$_{a4}^{a6}$) I$_4^6$ V
$\phantom{4 V^{-7} I \_\_ \_\_ \_\_ (^-VI_{a4}^{a6})}$ 3

5 I VI$^-$ _____ _____ _____ ($^-$VI^{a6}) V I

6 I IV^{-6} _____ _____ _____ ($^-$VI^{a6}) I$_4^6$ V

7 VI$^-$ IV _____ _____ _____ ($^-$II^{-6}) V^{-7} I

8 V^{-7} I _____ _____ _____ ($^-$II^{-6}) I$_4^6$ V

9 I IV _____ _____ _____ II$^-$ ($^-$II^{a6}) I

10 I IV _____ _____ _____ (II$_{d5}^{-6}$) I$_4^6$ V

11 V$_{d5}^{-6}$ I _____ _____ _____ IV^{-6} ($^-$VI^{a6}) V

12 VI$^-$ IV _____ _____ _____ I ($^-$VI$_{a4}^{a6}$) V
$\phantom{12 VI^- IV \_\_ \_\_ \_\_ I (^-VI_{a4}^{a6})}$ 3

13 I V _____ _____ _____ (III$_{d5}^{-6}$) VI$^-$ IV

14 V I _____ _____ _____ (III$_{d5}^{-6}$) VI$^-$ II^6

15 V I _____ _____ _____ ($^-$VI^{a6}) I$_4^6$ V

16 I V^{-7} _____ _____ _____ ($^-$VI$_{a4}^{a6}$) V I
$\phantom{16 I V^{-7} \_\_ \_\_ \_\_ (^-VI_{a4}^{a6})}$ 3

17 I VI$^-$ _____ _____ _____ ($^-$II^{-6}) I$_4^6$ V

18 I VI$^-$ _____ _____ _____ IV ($^-$II$_{a4}^{a6}$) I
$\phantom{18 I VI^- \_\_ \_\_ \_\_ IV (^-II_{a4}^{a6})}$ 3

19 I VI$^-$ _____ _____ _____ II^6 ($^-$II^{-6}) V

20 I VI$^-$ _____ _____ _____ (II$_{d5}^{-6}$) V^{-7} I

21 IV V _____ _____ _____ I (III$_{d5}^{-6}$) VI$^-$

22 IV V _____ _____ _____ I ($^-$VI^{a6}) V

23 I V _____ _____ _____ ($^-$VI$_{a4}^{a6}$) I$_4^6$ V
$\phantom{23 I V \_\_ \_\_ \_\_ (^-VI_{a4}^{a6})}$ 3

24 IV^{-6} V^{-7} _____ _____ _____ I ($^-$II^{a6}) I

25 I VI$^-$ _____ _____ _____ IV (II^{-7}) V

26 I VI$^-$ _____ _____ _____ IV ($^-$II^{a6}) I

27 V I _____ _____ _____ (VI^{-7}) II$^-$ V

28 V$_{d5}^{-6}$ I _____ _____ _____ ($^-$VI^{a6}) I$_4^6$ V

29 I V _____ _____ _____ (aV^{d7}) VI$^-$ II$^-$

30 V^{-7} I _____ _____ _____ (III$_{d5}^{-6}$) VI$^-$ IV

31 V^{-7} I _____ _____ _____ ($^-$VI^{a6}) I$_4^6$ V

32 IV^{-6} V _____ _____ _____ I $^-$VI$_{a4}^{a6}$ V
$\phantom{32 IV^{-6} V \_\_ \_\_ \_\_ I ^-VI_{a4}^{a6}}$ 3

33 I IV _____ _____ _____ II$^-$ ($^-$II$_{a4}^{a6}$) I
$\phantom{33 I IV \_\_ \_\_ \_\_ II^- (^-II_{a4}^{a6})}$ 3

34 V I _____ _____ _____ VI$^-$ ($^-$VI$_{a4}^{a6}$) V
$\phantom{34 V I \_\_ \_\_ \_\_ VI^- (^-VI_{a4}^{a6})}$ 3

35 V^{-7} I _____ _____ _____ IV^{-6} ($^-$VI^{a6}) V

36 I VI$^-$ _____ _____ _____ IV ($^-$II^{-6}) V

37 I (VI^{-7}) _____ _____ _____ (II^{-7}) V^{-7} I

38 IV (II$_{d5}^{-6}$) _____ _____ _____ V ($^-$VI^{a6}) V

39 I II^6 _____ _____ _____ I$_4^6$ ($^-$VI$_{a4}^{a6}$) V
$\phantom{39 I II^6 \_\_ \_\_ \_\_ I_4^6 (^-VI_{a4}^{a6})}$ 3

40 VI$^-$ IV _____ _____ _____ I ($^-$II^{-6}) V

41 I^{-6} V$_-^4$ _____ _____ _____ I ($^-$II$_{a4}^{a6}$) I
$\phantom{41 I^{-6} V_-^4 \_\_ \_\_ \_\_ I (^-II_{a4}^{a6})}$ 3

42 I II^6 _____ _____ _____ ($^-$VI$_{a4}^{a6}$) I$_4^6$ V
$\phantom{42 I II^6 \_\_ \_\_ \_\_ (^-VI_{a4}^{a6})}$ 3

43 I I^{-6} _____ _____ _____ ($^-$II^{-6}) I$_4^6$ V

44 I VI$^-$ _____ _____ _____ (III$_{d5}^{-6}$) VI$^-$ IV

45 I VI$^-$ _____ _____ _____ ($^-$VI^{a6}) V I

46 V$_{d5}^{-6}$ I _____ _____ _____ (VI^{-7}) II$^-$ V

47 V$_{d5}^{-6}$ I _____ _____ _____ ($^-$VI^{a6}) I$_4^6$ V

48 V^{-7} I _____ _____ _____ IV ($^-$II$_{a4}^{a6}$) I
$\phantom{48 V^{-7} I \_\_ \_\_ \_\_ IV (^-II_{a4}^{a6})}$ 3

D11-3b Identification of foreign chords
(Copy 3)

Shield the answer. Listen to the group of five chords and write the composite chord symbols for the last three chords; then uncover the answer and compare your response. Goal: No more than eight incorrect frames.

1. I V ___ ___ ___ ($^-$VI^{a6}) I$^6_4$ V
2. V^{-6} I ___ ___ ___ ($^-$VI^{a6}) V I
3. I V$^{-6}_{d5}$ ___ ___ ___ I ($^-$VI$^{a6}_{a4}$)$_3$ V
4. V^{-7} I ___ ___ ___ ($^-$VI$^{a6}_{a4}$)$_3$ I$^6_4$ V
5. I VI$^-$ ___ ___ ___ ($^-$VI^{a6}) V I
6. I IV^{-6} ___ ___ ___ ($^-$VI^{a6}) I$^6_4$ V
7. VI$^-$ IV ___ ___ ___ ($^-$II^{-6}) V^{-7} I
8. V^{-7} I ___ ___ ___ ($^-$II^{-6}) I$^6_4$ V
9. I IV ___ ___ ___ II$^-$ ($^-$II^{a6}) I
10. I IV ___ ___ ___ (II$^{-6}_{d5}$) I$^6_4$ V
11. V$^{-6}_{d5}$ I ___ ___ ___ IV^{-6} ($^-$VI^{a6}) V
12. VI$^-$ IV ___ ___ ___ I ($^-$VI$^{a6}_{a4}$)$_3$ V
13. I V ___ ___ ___ (III$^{-6}_{d5}$) VI$^-$ IV
14. V I ___ ___ ___ (III$^{-6}_{d5}$) VI$^-$ II^6
15. V I ___ ___ ___ ($^-$VI^{a6}) I$^6_4$ V
16. I V^{-7} ___ ___ ___ ($^-$VI$^{a6}_{a4}$)$_3$ V I
17. I VI$^-$ ___ ___ ___ ($^-$II^{-6}) I$^6_4$ V
18. I VI$^-$ ___ ___ ___ IV ($^-$II$^{a6}_{a4}$)$_3$ I
19. I VI$^-$ ___ ___ ___ II^6 ($^-$II^{-6}) V
20. I VI$^-$ ___ ___ ___ (II$^{-6}_{d5}$) V^{-7} I
21. IV V ___ ___ ___ I (III$^{-6}_{d5}$) VI$^-$
22. IV V ___ ___ ___ I ($^-$VI^{a6}) V
23. I V ___ ___ ___ ($^-$VI$^{a6}_{a4}$)$_3$ I$^6_4$ V
24. IV^{-6} V^{-7} ___ ___ ___ I ($^-$II^{a6}) I

25. I VI$^-$ ___ ___ ___ IV (II^{-7}) V
26. I VI$^-$ ___ ___ ___ IV ($^-$II^{a6}) I
27. V I ___ ___ ___ (VI^{-7}) II$^-$ V
28. V$^{-6}_{d5}$ I ___ ___ ___ ($^-$VI^{a6}) I$^6_4$ V
29. I V ___ ___ ___ (aV^{d7}) VI$^-$ II$^-$
30. V^{-7} I ___ ___ ___ (III$^{-6}_{d5}$) VI$^-$ IV
31. V^{-7} I ___ ___ ___ ($^-$VI^{a6}) I$^6_4$ V
32. IV^{-6} V ___ ___ ___ I $^-$VI$^{a6}_{a4}$$_3$ V
33. I IV ___ ___ ___ II$^-$ ($^-$II$^{a6}_{a4}$)$_3$ I
34. V I ___ ___ ___ VI$^-$ ($^-$VI$^{a6}_{a4}$)$_3$ V
35. V^{-7} I ___ ___ ___ IV^{-6} ($^-$VI^{a6}) V
36. I VI$^-$ ___ ___ ___ IV ($^-$II^{-6}) V
37. I (VI^{-7}) ___ ___ ___ (II^{-7}) V^{-7} I
38. IV (II$^{-6}_{d5}$) ___ ___ ___ V ($^-$VI^{a6}) V
39. I II^6 ___ ___ ___ I$^6_4$ ($^-$VI$^{a6}_{a4}$)$_3$ V
40. VI$^-$ IV ___ ___ ___ I ($^-$II^{-6}) V
41. I^{-6} V$^4_-$ ___ ___ ___ I ($^-$II$^{a6}_{a4}$)$_3$ I
42. I II^6 ___ ___ ___ ($^-$VI$^{a6}_{a4}$)$_3$ I$^6_4$ V
43. I I^{-6} ___ ___ ___ ($^-$II^{-6}) I$^6_4$ V
44. I VI$^-$ ___ ___ ___ (III$^{-6}_{d5}$) VI$^-$ IV
45. I VI$^-$ ___ ___ ___ ($^-$VI^{a6}) V I
46. V$^{-6}_{d5}$ I ___ ___ ___ (VI^{-7}) II$^-$ V
47. V$^{-6}_{d5}$ I ___ ___ ___ ($^-$VI^{a6}) I$^6_4$ V
48. V^{-7} I ___ ___ ___ IV ($^-$II$^{a6}_{a4}$)$_3$ I

D11-3b Identification of foreign chords
(Copy 4)

Shield the answer. Listen to the group of five chords and write the composite chord symbols for the last three chords; then uncover the answer and compare your response. Goal: No more than eight incorrect frames.

1. I V _____ _____ _____ $(^-\text{VI}^{a6})$ I^6_4 V

2. V^{-6} I _____ _____ _____ $(^-\text{VI}^{a6})$ V I

3. I V^{-6}_{d5} _____ _____ _____ I $(^-\text{VI}^{a6}_{a4})$ V
$_3$

4. V^{-7} I _____ _____ _____ $(^-\text{VI}^{a6}_{a4})$ I^6_4 V
$_3$

5. I VI^- _____ _____ _____ $(^-\text{VI}^{a6})$ V I

6. I IV^{-6} _____ _____ _____ $(^-\text{VI}^{a6})$ I^6_4 V

7. VI^- IV _____ _____ _____ $(^-\text{II}^{-6})$ V^{-7} I

8. V^{-7} I _____ _____ _____ $(^-\text{II}^{-6})$ I^6_4 V

9. I IV _____ _____ _____ II^- $(^-\text{II}^{a6})$ I

10. I IV _____ _____ _____ $(\underline{\text{II}^{-6}_{d5}})$ I^6_4 V

11. V^{-6}_{d5} I _____ _____ _____ IV^{-6} $(^-\text{VI}^{a6})$ V

12. VI^- IV _____ _____ _____ I $(^-\text{VI}^{a6}_{a4})$ V
$_3$

13. I V _____ _____ _____ $(\underline{\text{III}^{-6}_{d5}})$ VI^- IV

14. V I _____ _____ _____ $(\underline{\text{III}^{-6}_{d5}})$ VI^- II^6

15. V I _____ _____ _____ $(^-\text{VI}^{a6})$ I^6_4 V

16. I V^{-7} _____ _____ _____ $(^-\text{VI}^{a6}_{a4})$ V I
$_3$

17. I VI^- _____ _____ _____ $(^-\text{II}^{-6})$ I^6_4 V

18. I VI^- _____ _____ _____ IV $(^-\text{II}^{a6}_{a4})$ I
$_3$

19. I VI^- _____ _____ _____ II^6 $(^-\text{II}^{-6})$ V

20. I VI^- _____ _____ _____ $(\underline{\text{II}^{-6}_{d5}})$ V^{-7} I

21. IV V _____ _____ _____ I $(\underline{\text{III}^{-6}_{d5}})$ VI^-

22. IV V _____ _____ _____ I $(^-\text{VI}^{a6})$ V

23. I V _____ _____ _____ $(^-\text{VI}^{a6}_{a4})$ I^6_4 V
$_3$

24. IV^{-6} V^{-7} _____ _____ _____ I $(^-\text{II}^{a6})$ I

25. I VI^- _____ _____ _____ IV $(\underline{\text{II}^{-7}})$ V

26. I VI^- _____ _____ _____ IV $(^-\text{II}^{a6})$ I

27. V I _____ _____ _____ $(\underline{\text{VI}^{-7}})$ II^- V

28. V^{-6}_{d5} I _____ _____ _____ $(^-\text{VI}^{a6})$ I^6_4 V

29. I V _____ _____ _____ $(\underline{a\text{V}^{d7}})$ VI^- II^-

30. V^{-7} I _____ _____ _____ $(\underline{\text{III}^{-6}_{d5}})$ VI^- IV

31. V^{-7} I _____ _____ _____ $(^-\text{VI}^{a6})$ I^6_4 V

32. IV^{-6} V _____ _____ _____ I $^-\text{VI}^{a6}_{a4}$ V
$_3$

33. I IV _____ _____ _____ II^- $(^-\text{II}^{a6}_{a4})$ I
$_3$

34. V I _____ _____ _____ VI^- $(^-\text{VI}^{a6}_{a4})$ V
$_3$

35. V^{-7} I _____ _____ _____ IV^{-6} $(^-\text{VI}^{a6})$ V

36. I VI^- _____ _____ _____ IV $(^-\text{II}^{-6})$ V

37. I $(\underline{\text{VI}^{-7}})$ _____ _____ _____ $(\underline{\text{II}^{-7}})$ V^{-7} I

38. IV $(\underline{\text{II}^{-6}_{d5}})$ _____ _____ _____ V $(^-\text{VI}^{a6})$ V

39. I II^6 _____ _____ _____ I^6_4 $(^-\text{VI}^{a6}_{a4})$ V
$_3$

40. VI^- IV _____ _____ _____ I $(^-\text{II}^{-6})$ V

41. I^{-6} V^4_- _____ _____ _____ I $(^-\text{II}^{a6}_{a4})$ I
$_3$

42. I II^6 _____ _____ _____ $(^-\text{VI}^{a6}_{a4})$ I^6_4 V
$_3$

43. I I^{-6} _____ _____ _____ $(^-\text{II}^{-6})$ I^6_4 V

44. I VI^- _____ _____ _____ $(\underline{\text{III}^{-6}_{d5}})$ VI^- IV

45. I VI^- _____ _____ _____ $(^-\text{VI}^{a6})$ V I

46. V^{-6}_{d5} I _____ _____ _____ $(\underline{\text{VI}^{-7}})$ II^- V

47. V^{-6}_{d5} I _____ _____ _____ $(^-\text{VI}^{a6})$ I^6_4 V

48. V^{-7} I _____ _____ _____ IV $(^-\text{II}^{a6}_{a4})$ I
$_3$

D11-3b
(Copy 5)   **Identification of foreign chords**

Shield the answer. Listen to the group of five chords and write the composite chord symbols for the last three chords; then uncover the answer and compare your response. Goal: No more than eight incorrect frames.

1.   I V _____ _____ _____ ($^-$VI^{a6}) I$^6_4$ V

2.   V^{-6} I _____ _____ _____ ($^-$VI^{a6}) V I

3.   I V$^{-6}_{d5}$ _____ _____ _____ I ($^-$VI$^{a6}_{a4}$)$_3$ V

4.   V^{-7} I _____ _____ _____ ($^-$VI$^{a6}_{a4}$)$_3$ I$^6_4$ V

5.   I VI$^-$ _____ _____ _____ ($^-$VI^{a6}) V I

6.   I IV^{-6} _____ _____ _____ ($^-$VI^{a6}) I$^6_4$ V

7.   VI$^-$ IV _____ _____ _____ ($^-$II^{-6}) V^{-7} I

8.   V^{-7} I _____ _____ _____ ($^-$II^{-6}) I$^6_4$ V

9.   I IV _____ _____ _____ II$^-$ ($^-$II^{a6}) I

10.   I IV _____ _____ _____ (II$^{-6}_{d5}$) I$^6_4$ V

11.   V$^{-6}_{d5}$ I _____ _____ _____ IV^{-6} ($^-$VI^{a6}) V

12.   VI$^-$ IV _____ _____ _____ I ($^-$VI$^{a6}_{a4}$)$_3$ V

13.   I V _____ _____ _____ (III$^{-6}_{d5}$) VI$^-$ IV

14.   V I _____ _____ _____ (III$^{-6}_{d5}$) VI$^-$ II^6

15.   V I _____ _____ _____ ($^-$VI^{a6}) I$^6_4$ V

16.   I V^{-7} _____ _____ _____ ($^-$VI$^{a6}_{a4}$)$_3$ V I

17.   I VI$^-$ _____ _____ _____ ($^-$II^{-6}) I$^6_4$ V

18.   I VI$^-$ _____ _____ _____ IV ($^-$II$^{a6}_{a4}$)$_3$ I

19.   I VI$^-$ _____ _____ _____ II^6 ($^-$II^{-6}) V

20.   I VI$^-$ _____ _____ _____ (II$^{-6}_{d5}$) V^{-7} I

21.   IV V _____ _____ _____ I (III$^{-6}_{d5}$) VI$^-$

22.   IV V _____ _____ _____ I ($^-$VI^{a6}) V

23.   I V _____ _____ _____ ($^-$VI$^{a6}_{a4}$)$_3$ I$^6_4$ V

24.   IV^{-6} V^{-7} _____ _____ _____ I ($^-$II^{a6}) I

25.   I VI$^-$ _____ _____ _____ IV (II^{-7}) V

26.   I VI$^-$ _____ _____ _____ IV ($^-$II^{a6}) I

27.   V I _____ _____ _____ (VI^{-7}) II$^-$ V

28.   V$^{-6}_{d5}$ I _____ _____ _____ ($^-$VI^{a6}) I$^6_4$ V

29.   I V _____ _____ _____ (aV^{d7}) VI$^-$ II$^-$

30.   V^{-7} I _____ _____ _____ (III$^{-6}_{d5}$) VI$^-$ IV

31.   V^{-7} I _____ _____ _____ ($^-$VI^{a6}) I$^6_4$ V

32.   IV^{-6} V _____ _____ _____ I $^-$VI$^{a6}_{a4}$$_3$ V

33.   I IV _____ _____ _____ II$^-$ ($^-$II$^{a6}_{a4}$)$_3$ I

34.   V I _____ _____ _____ VI$^-$ ($^-$VI$^{a6}_{a4}$)$_3$ V

35.   V^{-7} I _____ _____ _____ IV^{-6} ($^-$VI^{a6}) V

36.   I VI$^-$ _____ _____ _____ IV ($^-$II^{-6}) V

37.   I (VI^{-7}) _____ _____ _____ (II^{-7}) V^{-7} I

38.   IV (II$^{-6}_{d5}$) _____ _____ _____ V ($^-$VI^{a6}) V

39.   I II^6 _____ _____ _____ I$^6_4$ ($^-$VI$^{a6}_{a4}$)$_3$ V

40.   VI$^-$ IV _____ _____ _____ I ($^-$II^{-6}) V

41.   I^{-6} V$^4_-$ _____ _____ _____ I ($^-$II$^{a6}_{a4}$)$_3$ I

42.   I II^6 _____ _____ _____ ($^-$VI$^{a6}_{a4}$)$_3$ I$^6_4$ V

43.   I I^{-6} _____ _____ _____ ($^-$II^{-6}) I$^6_4$ V

44.   I VI$^-$ _____ _____ _____ (III$^{-6}_{d5}$) VI$^-$ IV

45.   I VI$^-$ _____ _____ _____ ($^-$VI^{a6}) V I

46.   V$^{-6}_{d5}$ I _____ _____ _____ (VI^{-7}) II$^-$ V

47.   V$^{-6}_{d5}$ I _____ _____ _____ ($^-$VI^{a6}) I$^6_4$ V

48.   V^{-7} I _____ _____ _____ IV ($^-$II$^{a6}_{a4}$)$_3$ I

D11-4a Figured bass dictation of foreign chords

(Copy 1)

Shield the answer. Listen to the series of five chords and write the bass notes and figured bass symbols for the last three chords; then uncover the answer and compare your response. Goal: No more than eight incorrect frames.

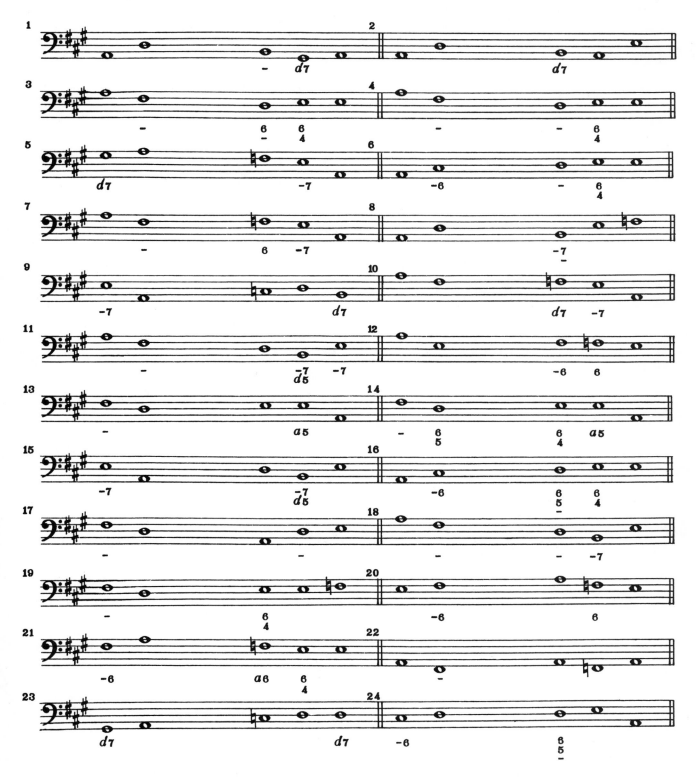

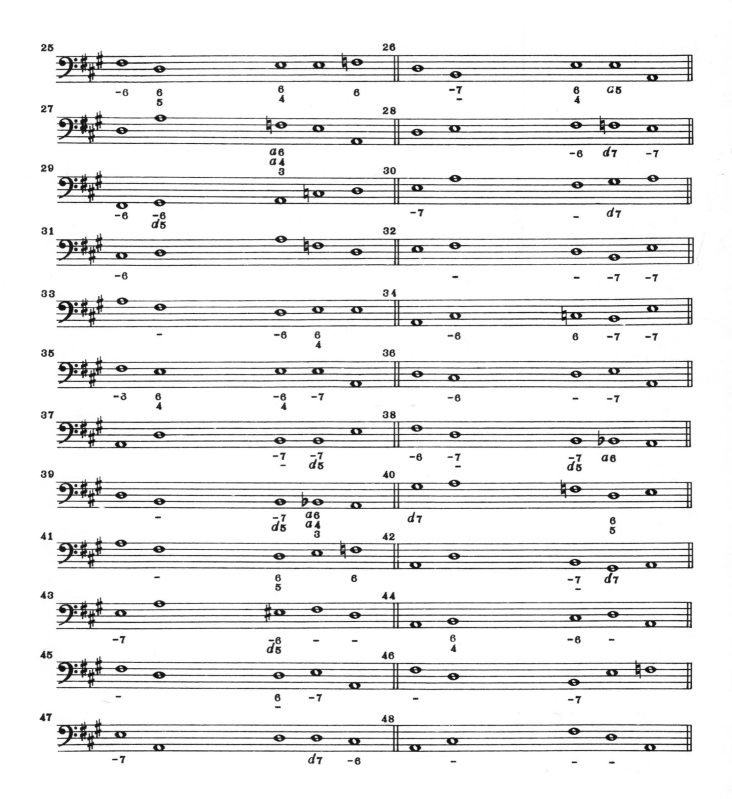

D11-4a Figured bass dictation of foreign chords

(Copy 2)

Shield the answer. Listen to the series of five chords and write the bass notes and figured bass symbols for the last three chords; then uncover the answer and compare your response. Goal: No more than eight incorrect frames.

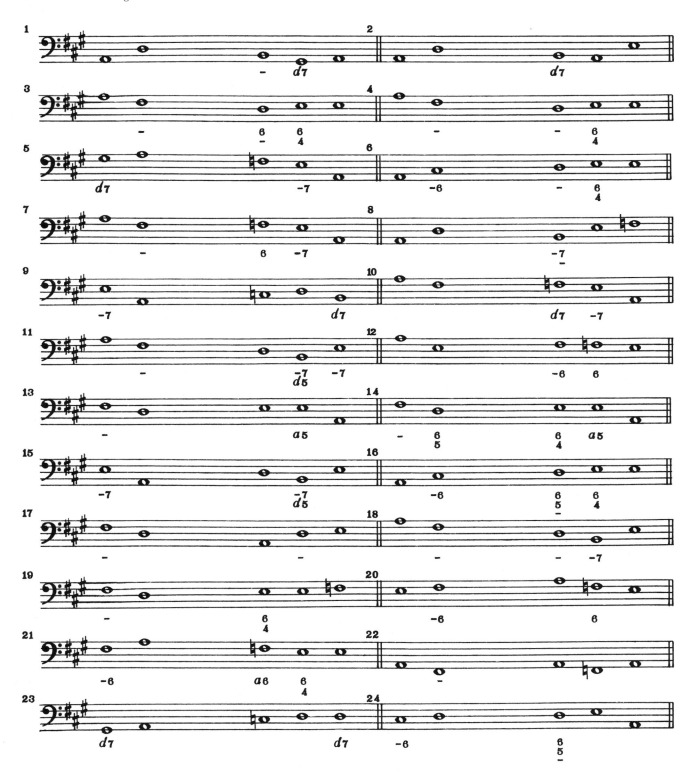

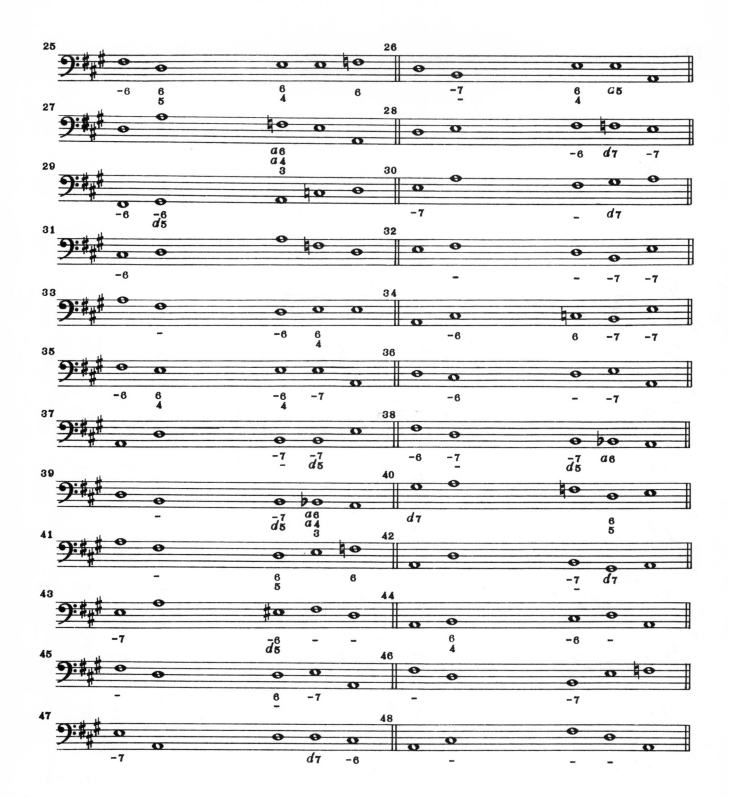

364

D11-4a

(Copy 3)

Figured bass dictation of foreign chords

Shield the answer. Listen to the series of five chords and write the bass notes and figured bass symbols for the last three chords; then uncover the answer and compare your response. Goal: No more than eight incorrect frames.

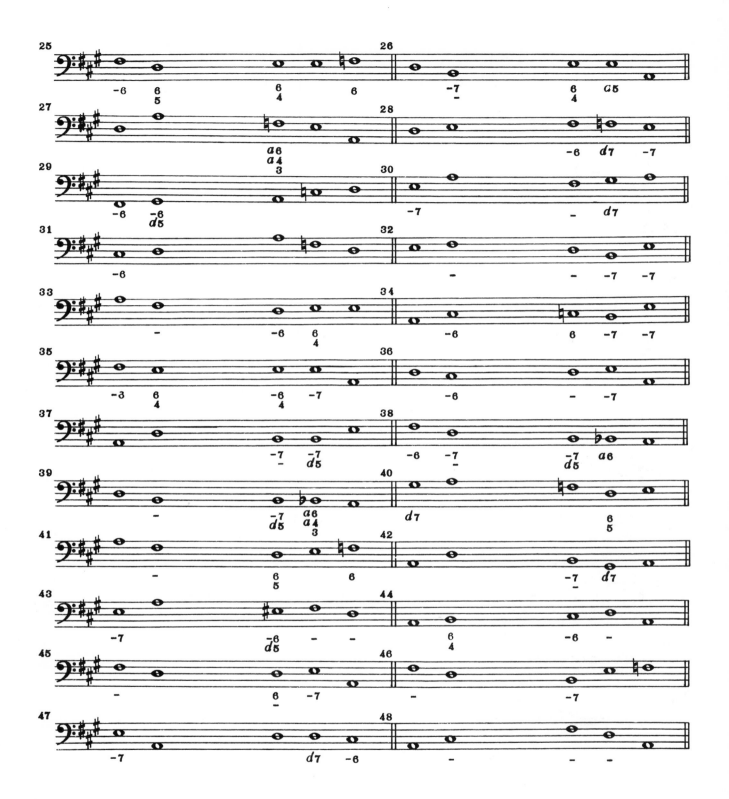

D11-4a Figured bass dictation of foreign chords
(Copy 4)

Shield the answer. Listen to the series of five chords and write the bass notes and figured bass symbols for the last three chords; then uncover the answer and compare your response. Goal: No more than eight incorrect frames.

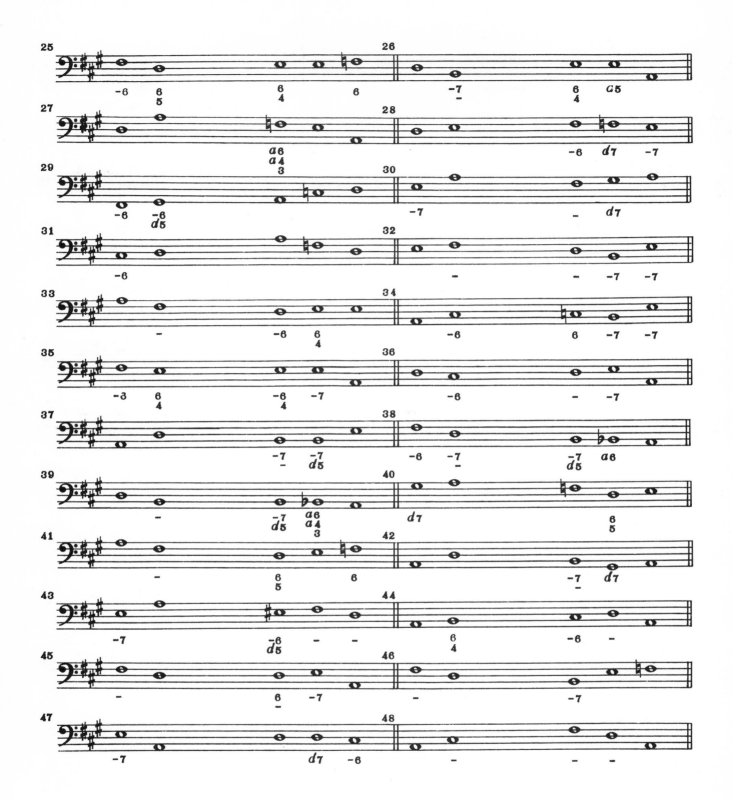

D11-4a

(Copy 5)

Figured bass dictation of foreign chords

Shield the answer. Listen to the series of five chords and write the bass notes and figured bass symbols for the last three chords; then uncover the answer and compare your response. Goal: No more than eight incorrect frames.

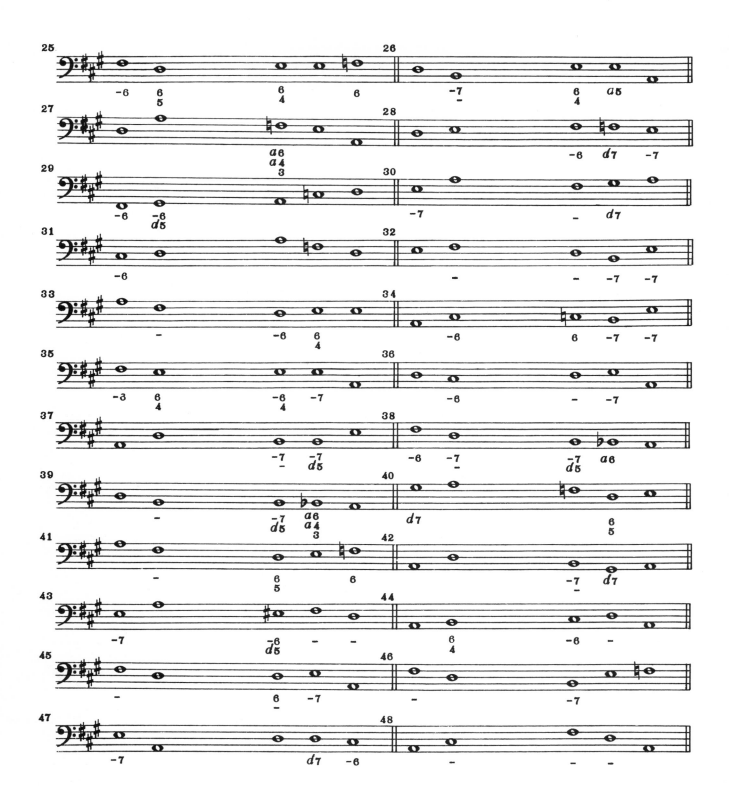

Lesson D11-4b

The major and minor keys with the same tonic are said to be parallel keys: for example, C major and C minor. In this lesson, which is all in one major key, foreign chords appear that are considered to be borrowed from the parallel minor key. When a chord appears that is not a regular member of the key, identify it as a foreign chord. Do not consider any identification that would involve a modulation.

D11-4b Identification of foreign chords

(Copy 1)

Shield the answer. Listen to the group of five chords and write the composite chord symbols for the last three chords; then uncover the answer and compare your response. Goal: No more than eight incorrect frames. When you have done this lesson, take Test D11.

1 I IV _____ _____ _____ II⁻ (VII^{d7}) I

2 I IV _____ _____ _____ (II^{d7}) I V

3 I VI⁻ _____ _____ _____ (II⁻₋) I⁶₄ V

4 I VI⁻ _____ _____ _____ (IV⁻) I⁶₄ V

5 (VII^{d7}) I _____ _____ _____ (⁻VI) V⁻⁷ I

6 I I⁻⁶ _____ _____ _____ (IV⁻) I⁶₄ V

7 I VI⁻ _____ _____ _____ (IV⁶) V⁻⁷ I

8 I IV _____ _____ _____ II⁻⁷₋ V (⁻VI)

9 V⁻⁷ I _____ _____ _____ (⁻III) IV (II^{d7})

10 I VI⁻ _____ _____ _____ (⁻VI^{d7}) V⁻⁷ I

11 I VI⁻ _____ _____ _____ IV (II⁻⁷_{d5}) V⁻⁷

12 I V _____ _____ _____ IV⁻⁶ (IV⁶) V

13 VI⁻ IV _____ _____ _____ V (V^{a5}) I

14 VI⁻ II⁶₅ _____ _____ _____ I⁶₄ (V^{a5}) I

15 V⁻⁷ I _____ _____ _____ IV (II⁻⁷_{d5}) V

16 I I⁻⁶ _____ _____ _____ (II⁶₅₋) I⁶₄ V

17 VI⁻ IV _____ _____ _____ I (IV⁻) V

18 I VI⁻ _____ _____ _____ (IV⁻) (II⁻⁷) V

19 VI⁻ IV _____ _____ _____ I⁶₄ V (⁻VI)

20 V IV⁻⁶ _____ _____ _____ I (IV⁶) V

21 IV⁻⁶ I _____ _____ _____ (⁻VI^{a6}) I⁶₄ V

22 I VI⁻ _____ _____ _____ I (⁻VI) I

23 (VII^{d7}) I _____ _____ _____ (⁻III) IV (IV^{d7})

24 I⁻⁶ IV _____ _____ _____ (II⁶₅₋) V I

25 IV⁻⁶ II⁶₅ _____ _____ _____ I⁶₄ V (IV⁶)

26 IV II⁻⁷₋ _____ _____ _____ I⁶₄ (V^{a5}) I

27 IV I _____ _____ _____ (⁻VI^{a6}_{a4})₃ V I

28 IV V _____ _____ _____ IV⁻⁶ (⁻VI^{d7}) V⁻⁷

29 IV⁻⁶ V⁻⁶_{d5} _____ _____ _____ I (⁻III) IV

30 V⁻⁷ I _____ _____ _____ VI⁻ (VII^{d7}) I

31 I⁻⁶ IV _____ _____ _____ I (⁻VI) IV

32 V VI⁻ _____ _____ _____ (IV⁻) (II⁻⁷) V⁻⁷

33 I VI⁻ _____ _____ _____ (⁻II⁻⁶) I⁶₄ V

34 I I⁻⁶ _____ _____ _____ (I⁶) (II⁻⁷) V⁻⁷

35 IV⁻⁶ I⁶₄ _____ _____ _____ (I⁻⁶₄) V⁻⁷ I

36 IV I⁻⁶ _____ _____ _____ (IV⁻) V⁻⁷ I

37 I IV _____ _____ _____ II⁻⁷₋ (II⁻⁷_{d5}) V

38 IV⁻⁶ II⁻⁷₋ _____ _____ _____ (II⁻⁷_{d5}) (⁻II^{a6}) I

39 IV II⁻ _____ _____ _____ (II⁻⁷_{d5}) (⁻II^{a6}_{a4})₃ I

40 (VII^{d7}) I _____ _____ _____ (⁻VI) II⁶₅ V

41 I VI⁻ _____ _____ _____ II⁶₅ V (IV⁶)

42 I IV _____ _____ _____ II⁻⁷₋ (VII^{d7}) I

43 V⁻⁷ I _____ _____ _____ (III⁻⁶_{d5}) VI⁻ (IV⁻)

44 I V⁶₄ _____ _____ _____ I⁻⁶ (IV⁻) I

45 VI⁻ IV _____ _____ _____ (II⁶₋) V⁻⁷ I

46 VI⁻ IV _____ _____ _____ (II⁻⁷) V (⁻VI)

47 V⁻⁷ I _____ _____ _____ IV (IV^{d7}) I⁻⁶

48 I III⁻ _____ _____ _____ VI⁻ (IV⁻) I

D11-4b
Identification of foreign chords

Shield the answer. Listen to the group of five chords and write the composite chord symbols for the last three chords; then uncover the answer and compare your response. Goal: No more than eight incorrect frames. When you have done this lesson, take Test D11.

1   I   IV _____ _____ _____ II$^-$ (VII^{d7}) I

2   I   IV _____ _____ _____ (II^{d7}) I V

3   I   VI$^-$ _____ _____ _____ (II$_{\underline{-}}^6$) I$_4^6$ V

4   I   VI$^-$ _____ _____ _____ (IV$^-$) I$_4^6$ V

5   (VII^{d7}) I _____ _____ _____ ($^-$VI) V^{-7} I

6   I   I^{-6} _____ _____ _____ (IV$^-$) I$_4^6$ V

7   I   VI$^-$ _____ _____ _____ (IV^6) V^{-7} I

8   I   IV _____ _____ _____ II$_{\underline{-}}^7$ V ($^-$VI)

9   V^{-7} I _____ _____ _____ ($^-$III) IV (II^{d7})

10   I   VI$^-$ _____ _____ _____ ($^-$VI^{d7}) V^{-7} I

11   I   VI$^-$ _____ _____ _____ IV (II$_{d5}^{-7}$) V^{-7}

12   I   V _____ _____ _____ IV^{-6} (IV^6) V

13   VI$^-$ IV _____ _____ _____ V (V^{a5}) I

14   VI$^-$ II$_5^6$ _____ _____ _____ I$_4^6$ (V^{a5}) I

15   V^{-7} I _____ _____ _____ IV (II$_{d5}^{-7}$) V

16   I   I^{-6} _____ _____ _____ (II$_{\underline{5}}^6$) I$_4^6$ V

17   VI$^-$ IV _____ _____ _____ I (IV$^-$) V

18   I   VI$^-$ _____ _____ _____ (IV$^-$) (II^{-7}) V

19   VI$^-$ IV _____ _____ _____ I$_4^6$ V ($^-$VI)

20   V   IV^{-6} _____ _____ _____ I (IV^6) V

21   IV^{-6} I _____ _____ _____ ($^-$VI^{a6}) I$_4^6$ V

22   I   VI$^-$ _____ _____ _____ I ($^-$VI) I

23   (VII^{d7}) I _____ _____ _____ ($^-$III) IV (IV^{d7})

24   I^{-6} IV _____ _____ _____ (II$_{\underline{5}}^6$) V I

25   IV^{-6} II$_5^6$ _____ _____ _____ I$_4^6$ V (IV^6)

26   IV   II$_{\underline{-}}^7$ _____ _____ _____ I$_4^6$ (V^{a5}) I

27   IV   I _____ _____ _____ ($^-$VI$_{a4\atop3}^{a6}$) V I

28   IV   V _____ _____ _____ IV^{-6} ($^-$VI^{d7}) V^{-7}

29   IV^{-6} V$_{d5}^{-6}$ _____ _____ _____ I ($^-$III) IV

30   V^{-7} I _____ _____ _____ VI$^-$ (VII^{d7}) I

31   I^{-6} IV _____ _____ _____ I ($^-$VI) IV

32   V   VI$^-$ _____ _____ _____ (IV$^-$) (II$_{\underline{-}}^7$) V^{-7}

33   I   VI$^-$ _____ _____ _____ ($^-$II^{-6}) I$_4^6$ V

34   I   I^{-6} _____ _____ _____ (I^6) (II$_{\underline{-}}^7$) V^{-7}

35   IV^{-6} I$_4^6$ _____ _____ _____ (I$_4^{-6}$) V^{-7} I

36   IV   I^{-6} _____ _____ _____ (IV$^-$) V^{-7} I

37   I   IV _____ _____ _____ II$_{\underline{-}}^7$ (II$_{d5}^{-7}$) V

38   IV^{-6} II$_{\underline{-}}^7$ _____ _____ _____ (II$_{d5}^{-7}$) ($^-$II^{a6}) I

39   IV   II$^-$ _____ _____ _____ (II$_{d5}^{-7}$) ($^-$II$_{a4\atop3}^{a6}$) I

40   (VII^{d7}) I _____ _____ _____ ($^-$VI) II$_5^6$ V

41   I   VI$^-$ _____ _____ _____ II$_5^6$ V (IV^6)

42   I   IV _____ _____ _____ II$_{\underline{-}}^7$ (VII^{d7}) I

43   V^{-7} I _____ _____ _____ (III$_{d5}^{-6}$) VI$^-$ (IV$^-$)

44   I   V$_4^6$ _____ _____ _____ I^{-6} (IV$^-$) I

45   VI$^-$ IV _____ _____ _____ (II$_{\underline{-}}^6$) V^{-7} I

46   VI$^-$ IV _____ _____ _____ (II^{-7}) V ($^-$VI)

47   V^{-7} I _____ _____ _____ IV (IV^{d7}) I^{-6}

48   I   III$^-$ _____ _____ _____ VI$^-$ (IV$^-$) I

D11-4b Identification of foreign chords
(Copy 3)

Shield the answer. Listen to the group of five chords and write the composite chord symbols for the last three chords; then uncover the answer and compare your response. Goal: No more than eight incorrect frames. When you have done this lesson, take Test D11.

1 I IV _____ _____ _____ II⁻ (VII^{d7}) I

2 I IV _____ _____ _____ (II^{d7}) I V

3 I VI⁻ _____ _____ _____ (II$_-^6$) I$_4^6$ V

4 I VI⁻ _____ _____ _____ (IV⁻) I$_4^6$ V

5 (VII^{d7}) I _____ _____ _____ (⁻VI) V⁻⁷ I

6 I I⁻⁶ _____ _____ _____ (IV⁻) I$_4^6$ V

7 I VI⁻ _____ _____ _____ (IV⁶) V⁻⁷ I

8 I IV _____ _____ _____ II$_-^{-7}$ V (⁻VI)

9 V⁻⁷ I _____ _____ _____ (⁻III) IV (II^{d7})

10 I VI⁻ _____ _____ _____ (⁻VI^{d7}) V⁻⁷ I

11 I VI⁻ _____ _____ _____ IV (II$_{d5}^{-7}$) V⁻⁷

12 I V _____ _____ _____ IV⁻⁶ (IV⁶) V

13 VI⁻ IV _____ _____ _____ V (V^{a5}) I

14 VI⁻ II$_5^6$ _____ _____ _____ I$_4^6$ (V^{a5}) I

15 V⁻⁷ I _____ _____ _____ IV (II$_{d5}^{-7}$) V

16 I I⁻⁶ _____ _____ _____ (II$_{5-}^6$) I$_4^6$ V

17 VI⁻ IV _____ _____ _____ I (IV⁻) V

18 I VI⁻ _____ _____ _____ (IV⁻) (II^{-7}) V

19 VI⁻ IV _____ _____ _____ I$_4^6$ V (⁻VI)

20 V IV⁻⁶ _____ _____ _____ I (IV⁶) V

21 IV⁻⁶ I _____ _____ _____ (⁻VI^{a6}) I$_4^6$ V

22 I VI⁻ _____ _____ _____ I (⁻VI) I

23 (VII^{d7}) I _____ _____ _____ (⁻III) IV (IV^{d7})

24 I⁻⁶ IV _____ _____ _____ (II$_{5-}^6$) V I

25 IV⁻⁶ II$_5^6$ _____ _____ _____ I$_4^6$ V (IV⁶)

26 IV II$_-^{-7}$ _____ _____ _____ I$_4^6$ (V^{a5}) I

27 IV I _____ _____ _____ (⁻VI$_{a4\ 3}^{a6}$) V I

28 IV V _____ _____ _____ IV⁻⁶ (⁻VI^{d7}) V⁻⁷

29 IV⁻⁶ V$_{d5}^{-6}$ _____ _____ _____ I (⁻III) IV

30 V⁻⁷ I _____ _____ _____ VI⁻ (VII^{d7}) I

31 I⁻⁶ IV _____ _____ _____ I (⁻VI) IV

32 V VI⁻ _____ _____ _____ (IV⁻) (II$_-^{-7}$) V⁻⁷

33 I VI⁻ _____ _____ _____ (⁻II⁶) I$_4^6$ V

34 I I⁻⁶ _____ _____ _____ (I⁶) (II$_-^{-7}$) V⁻⁷

35 IV⁻⁶ I$_4^6$ _____ _____ _____ (I$_4^{-6}$) V⁻⁷ I

36 IV I⁻⁶ _____ _____ _____ (IV⁻) V⁻⁷ I

37 I IV _____ _____ _____ II$_-^{-7}$ (II$_{d5}^{-7}$) V

38 IV⁻⁶ II$_-^{-7}$ _____ _____ _____ (II$_{d5}^{-7}$) (⁻II^{a6}) I

39 IV II⁻ _____ _____ _____ (II$_{d5}^{-7}$) (⁻II$_{a4\ 3}^{a6}$) I

40 (VII^{d7}) I _____ _____ _____ (⁻VI) II$_5^6$ V

41 I VI⁻ _____ _____ _____ II$_5^6$ V (IV⁶)

42 I IV _____ _____ _____ II$_-^{-7}$ (VII^{d7}) I

43 V⁻⁷ I _____ _____ _____ (III$_{d5}^{-6}$) VI⁻ (IV⁻)

44 I V$_4^6$ _____ _____ _____ I⁻⁶ (IV⁻) I

45 VI⁻ IV _____ _____ _____ (II$_-^6$) V⁻⁷ I

46 VI⁻ IV _____ _____ _____ (II$_-^{-7}$) V (⁻VI)

47 V⁻⁷ I _____ _____ _____ IV (IV^{d7}) I⁻⁶

48 I III⁻ _____ _____ _____ VI⁻ (IV⁻) I

D11-4b Identification of foreign chords

(Copy 4)

Shield the answer. Listen to the group of five chords and write the composite chord symbols for the last three chords; then uncover the answer and compare your response. Goal: No more than eight incorrect frames. When you have done this lesson, take Test D11.

1 I IV _____ _____ _____ II⁻ (VII^{d7}) I

25 IV⁻⁶ II⁶₅ _____ _____ _____ I⁶₄ V (IV⁶)

2 I IV _____ _____ _____ (II^{d7}) I V

26 IV II⁻⁷̲ _____ _____ _____ I⁶₄ (V^{a5}) I

3 I VI⁻ _____ _____ _____ (II⁶₋) I⁶₄ V

27 IV I _____ _____ _____ (⁻VI^{a6}_{a4}) V I
        ₃

4 I VI⁻ _____ _____ _____ (IV⁻) I⁶₄ V

28 IV V _____ _____ _____ IV⁻⁶ (⁻VI^{d7}) V⁻⁷

5 (VII^{d7}) I _____ _____ _____ (⁻VI) V⁻⁷ I

29 IV⁻⁶ V⁻⁶_{d5} _____ _____ _____ I (⁻III) IV

6 I I⁻⁶ _____ _____ _____ (IV⁻) I⁶₄ V

30 V⁻⁷ I _____ _____ _____ VI⁻ (VII^{d7}) I

7 I VI⁻ _____ _____ _____ (IV⁶) V⁻⁷ I

31 I⁻⁶ IV _____ _____ _____ I (⁻VI) IV

8 I IV _____ _____ _____ II⁻⁷̲ V (⁻VI)

32 V VI⁻ _____ _____ _____ (IV⁻) (II̲⁻⁷) V⁻⁷

9 V⁻⁷ I _____ _____ _____ (⁻III) IV (II^{d7})

33 I VI⁻ _____ _____ _____ (⁻II⁻⁶) I⁶₄ V

10 I VI⁻ _____ _____ _____ (⁻VI^{d7}) V⁻⁷ I

34 I I⁻⁶ _____ _____ _____ (I⁶) (II̲⁻⁷) V⁻⁷

11 I VI⁻ _____ _____ _____ IV (II⁻⁷_{d5}) V⁻⁷

35 IV⁻⁶ I⁶₄ _____ _____ _____ (I⁻⁶₄) V⁻⁷ I

12 I V _____ _____ _____ IV⁻⁶ (IV⁶) V

36 IV I⁻⁶ _____ _____ _____ (IV⁻) V⁻⁷ I

13 VI⁻ IV _____ _____ _____ V (V^{a5}) I

37 I IV _____ _____ _____ II⁻⁷̲ (II⁻⁷_{d5}) V

14 VI⁻ II⁶₅ _____ _____ _____ I⁶₄ (V^{a5}) I

38 IV⁻⁶ II⁻⁷̲ _____ _____ _____ (II⁻⁷_{d5}) (⁻II^{a6}) I

15 V⁻⁷ I _____ _____ _____ IV (II⁻⁷_{d5}) V

39 IV II⁻ _____ _____ _____ (II⁻⁷_{d5}) (⁻II^{a6}_{a4}) I
        ₃

16 I I⁻⁶ _____ _____ _____ (II⁶₅̲) I⁶₄ V

40 (VII^{d7}) I _____ _____ _____ (⁻VI) II⁶₅ V

17 VI⁻ IV _____ _____ _____ I (IV⁻) V

41 I VI⁻ _____ _____ _____ II⁶₅ V (IV⁶)

18 I VI⁻ _____ _____ _____ (IV⁻) (II̲⁻⁷) V

42 I IV _____ _____ _____ II⁻⁷̲ (VII^{d7}) I

19 VI⁻ IV _____ _____ _____ I⁶₄ V (⁻VI)

43 V⁻⁷ I _____ _____ _____ (III̲⁻⁶_{d5}) VI⁻ (IV⁻)

20 V IV⁻⁶ _____ _____ _____ I (IV⁶) V

44 I V⁶₄ _____ _____ _____ I⁻⁶ (IV⁻) I

21 IV⁻⁶ I _____ _____ _____ (⁻VI^{a6}) I⁶₄ V

45 VI⁻ IV _____ _____ _____ (II⁶₋) V⁻⁷ I

22 I VI⁻ _____ _____ _____ I (⁻VI) I

46 VI⁻ IV _____ _____ _____ (II̲⁻⁷) V (⁻VI)

23 (VII^{d7}) I _____ _____ _____ (⁻III) IV (IV^{d7})

47 V⁻⁷ I _____ _____ _____ IV (IV^{d7}) I⁻⁶

24 I⁻⁶ IV _____ _____ _____ (II⁶₅̲) V I

48 I III⁻ _____ _____ _____ VI⁻ (IV⁻) I

Identification of foreign chords

Shield the answer. Listen to the group of five chords and write the composite chord symbols for the last three chords; then uncover the answer and compare your response. Goal: No more than eight incorrect frames. When you have done this lesson, take Test D11.

1 I IV _____ _____ _____ II⁻ (VII^d7) I

2 I IV _____ _____ _____ (II^d7) I V

3 I VI⁻ _____ _____ _____ (II_⁻⁶) I⁶₄ V

4 I VI⁻ _____ _____ _____ (IV⁻) I⁶₄ V

5 (VII^d7) I _____ _____ _____ (⁻VI) V⁻⁷ I

6 I I⁻⁶ _____ _____ _____ (IV⁻) I⁶₄ V

7 I VI⁻ _____ _____ _____ (IV⁶) V⁻⁷ I

8 I IV _____ _____ _____ II_⁻⁷ V (⁻VI)

9 V⁻⁷ I _____ _____ _____ (⁻III) IV (II^d7)

10 I VI⁻ _____ _____ _____ (⁻VI^d7) V⁻⁷ I

11 I VI⁻ _____ _____ _____ IV (II⁻⁷_d5) V⁻⁷

12 I V _____ _____ _____ IV⁻⁶ (IV⁶) V

13 VI⁻ IV _____ _____ _____ V (V^a5) I

14 VI⁻ II⁶₅ _____ _____ _____ I⁶₄ (V^a5) I

15 V⁻⁷ I _____ _____ _____ IV (II⁻⁷_d5) V

16 I I⁻⁶ _____ _____ _____ (II⁶₅⁻) I⁶₄ V

17 VI⁻ IV _____ _____ _____ I (IV⁻) V

18 I VI⁻ _____ _____ _____ (IV⁻) (II_⁻⁷) V

19 VI⁻ IV _____ _____ _____ I⁶₄ V (⁻VI)

20 V IV⁻⁶ _____ _____ _____ I (IV⁶) V

21 IV⁻⁶ I _____ _____ _____ (⁻VI^a6) I⁶₄ V

22 I VI⁻ _____ _____ _____ I (⁻VI) I

23 (VII^d7) I _____ _____ _____ (⁻III) IV (IV^d7)

24 I⁻⁶ IV _____ _____ _____ (II⁶₅⁻) V I

25 IV⁻⁶ II⁶₅ _____ _____ _____ I⁶₄ V (IV⁶)

26 IV II_⁻⁷ _____ _____ _____ I⁶₄ (V^a5) I

27 IV I _____ _____ _____ (⁻VI^a6_a4₃) V I

28 IV V _____ _____ _____ IV⁻⁶ (⁻VI^d7) V⁻⁷

29 IV⁻⁶ V⁻⁶_d5 _____ _____ _____ I (⁻III) IV

30 V⁻⁷ I _____ _____ _____ VI⁻ (VII^d7) I

31 I⁻⁶ IV _____ _____ _____ I (⁻VI) IV

32 V VI⁻ _____ _____ _____ (IV⁻) (II_⁻⁷) V⁻⁷

33 I VI⁻ _____ _____ _____ (⁻II⁻⁶) I⁶₄ V

34 I I⁻⁶ _____ _____ _____ (I⁶) (II_⁻⁷) V⁻⁷

35 IV⁻⁶ I⁶₄ _____ _____ _____ (I⁻⁶₄) V⁻⁷ I

36 IV I⁻⁶ _____ _____ _____ (IV⁻) V⁻⁷ I

37 I IV _____ _____ _____ II_⁻⁷ (II⁻⁷_d5) V

38 IV⁻⁶ II_⁻⁷ _____ _____ _____ (II⁻⁷_d5) (⁻II^a6) I

39 IV II⁻ _____ _____ _____ (II⁻⁷_d5) (⁻II^a6_a4₃) I

40 (VII^d7) I _____ _____ _____ (⁻VI) II⁶₅ V

41 I VI⁻ _____ _____ _____ II⁶₅ V (IV⁶)

42 I IV _____ _____ _____ II_⁻⁷ (VII^d7) I

43 V⁻⁷ I _____ _____ _____ (III⁻⁶_d5) VI⁻ (IV⁻)

44 I V⁶₄ _____ _____ _____ I⁻⁶ (IV⁻) I

45 VI⁻ IV _____ _____ _____ (II⁶_⁻) V⁻⁷ I

46 VI⁻ IV _____ _____ _____ (II_⁻⁷) V (⁻VI)

47 V⁻⁷ I _____ _____ _____ IV (IV^d7) I⁻⁶

48 I III⁻ _____ _____ _____ VI⁻ (IV⁻) I

Arpeggio Singing of Foreign Chords

This series involves the singing of arpeggios from composite chord symbols. When you have done this series, take Test D12.

The procedure for these lessons is the same as for those in Series D8. Each frame on the worksheet contains one composite chord symbol. You will be given the starting pitch for the first frame only. In subsequent frames, you must sing each new arpeggio using the preceding one as a reference. Sing the arpeggios in eighth note patterns for triads and in triplet patterns for seventh chords. Sing with the metronome, which is clicking quarter notes. Then you will hear an arpeggio giving the pitches you should have sung. The composite chord symbols in this lesson are the same as those used in the previous lessons in identification of chords, but with one exception. In the previous lessons the symbol ^{a6} was used to identify both Italian and German sixth chords. In this series the complete figured bass symbols will be used for these chords. Thus we will have $^{a6}_3$ for the Italian sixth chord and $^{a6}_5$ for the German sixth chord.

Whenever you have sung a frame incorrectly, make a tally mark on a piece of paper. Your goal is to complete each lesson with no more than five incorrect frames. When you have done so, go on to the next lesson. If you have more than five incorrect frames, repeat the lesson until you reach the goal or until you have done the lesson five times, at which point you should go on to the next lesson regardless of your score.

D12-1 Arpeggio singing from composite chord symbols

Sing the arpeggio in time with the metronome. Compare your response with the arpeggio you then hear and tally your errors. The starting tone is given for the first frame only. Goal: No more than five incorrect frames.

1   I   IV   (II)   V^{-7} VI$^-$ IV   (II$^{-6}_{d5}$)   V^{-7} I   (VI^{-7})   II$^-$ (II^{-7})

2   V^{-7} (I^{-7})   IV   (II^{-6})   V   VI$^-$ (III$^{-6}_{d5}$)   VI$^-$ (VI)   (II^{-7})   V^{-7} VI$^-$

3   (I$^{-6}_{d5}$)   IV   (VI$^{-6}_{d5}$)   II$^-$ V$^{-6}_{d5}$ I   (VI^{-6})   II$^-$ (II^{-7})   V$^{-6}_{d5}$ I   (III^{-7})

4   VI$^-$ IV   (II^{-6})   V   (III^{-6})   VI$^-$ (II$^{-6}_{d5}$)   V^{-7} I   IV   (I$^{-6}_{d5}$)   IV

5   (II$^{-6}_{d5}$)   V^{-7} (I^{-7})   IV   (II^{-7})   V$^{-6}_{d5}$ I   (VI^{-7})   (II^{-7})   I$^6_4$ V^{-7} I

D12-2 Arpeggio singing from composite chord symbols

Sing the arpeggio in time with the metronome. Compare your response with the arpeggio you then hear and tally your errors. The starting tone is given for the first frame only. Goal: No more than five incorrect frames.

1   I   V   (aIV^{d7})   V   (aV^{d7})   VI$^-$ IV   (aIV^{d7})   V^{-7} I   (aI^{d7})   II$^-$

2   V$^{-6}_{d5}$ I   (aV^{d7})   VI$^-$ (III^{d7})   IV   (aIV^{d7})   V   I   (III$^{-6}_{d5}$)   VI$^-$ (I$^{-6}_{d5}$)

3   IV   (II$^{-6}_{d5}$)   V^{-7} I   (aI^{d7})   (II^{-7})   V   I   (aV^{d7})   VI$^-$ (III^{d7})   IV

4   (I$^{-6}_{d5}$)   IV   (aIV^{d7})   V   (II$^{-6}_{d5}$)   V   (aV^{d7})   VI$^-$ (I$^{-6}_{d5}$)   IV   (aIV^{d7})   V^{-7}

5   I   (III^{d7})   IV   (aI^{d7})   (II^{-7})   V^{-7} (aV^{d7})   VI$^-$ (aIV^{d7})   I$^6_4$ V^{-7} I

D12-3 Arpeggio singing from composite chord symbols

Sing the arpeggio in time with the metronome. Compare your response with the arpeggio you then hear and tally your errors. The starting tone is given for the first frame only. Goal: No more than five incorrect frames.

1 I⁻ IV⁻ (II^{-6}_{d5}) V⁻⁷ ⁻VI (⁻III⁻⁷) ⁻VI IV⁻ (aIVᵈ⁷) V $(^{-}\text{III}^{-6}_{d5})$ ⁻VI

2 IV⁻ (I^{-6}_{d5}) IV⁻ I⁻ VIIᵈ⁷ I⁻ IIᵈ⁷ I⁶ (I^{-6}_{d5}) IV⁻ (IIIᵈ⁷) IV⁻

3 (IVᵈ⁷) I⁶ (I⁻⁷) IV⁻ (II^{-6}_{d5}) V ⁻VIᵈ⁷ V⁻⁷ I⁻ ⁻VI (Vᵈ⁷) ⁻VI

4 (⁻III⁻⁷) ⁻VI V⁻⁷ ⁻VIᵈ⁷ V⁻⁷ I⁻ ⁻VI $(^{-}\text{III}^{-6}_{d5})$ ⁻VI (aIVᵈ⁷) V IVᵈ⁷

5 IIᵈ⁷ I⁻ IV⁻ (II⁻⁷) V I⁶ (IIIᵈ⁷) IV⁻ (aIVᵈ⁷) I^{-6}_{4} V⁻⁷ I⁻

D12-4 Arpeggio singing from composite chord symbols

Sing the arpeggio in time with the metronome. Compare your response with the arpeggio you then hear and tally your errors. The starting tone is given for the first frame only. Goal: No more than five incorrect frames.

1 I⁻ V ⁻VI $(^{-}\text{VI}^{a6}_{5})$₃ I^{-6}_{4} V I⁻ (⁻II⁻⁶) I^{-6}_{4} V $(^{-}\text{VI}^{a6}_{a4})$₃ V

2 Vᵃ⁵ I⁻ $(^{-}\text{II}^{a6}_{5})$₃ I⁻ $(^{-}\text{II}^{a6}_{a4})$₃ I⁻ ⁻VI (⁻II⁻⁶) V ⁻IIIᵃ⁵ I⁶ IV

3 IV⁻⁷ IV^{-6}_{d5} V^{-6}_{d5} I⁻ IV^{-6}_{d5} V^{-6}_{d5} I⁻ $(^{-}\text{VI}^{a6}_{a4})$₃ I^{-6}_{4} V⁻⁷ ⁻VI (⁻II⁻⁶)

4 I^{-6}_{4} V⁻⁷ (I) IV⁻ $(^{-}\text{II}^{a6}_{5})$₃ I⁻ IV^{-6}_{d5} V^{-6}_{d5} I⁻ IV⁻ II⁻ V^{-6}_{d5}

5 I⁻ $(^{-}\text{VI}^{a6}_{a4})$₃ V Vᵃ⁵ I⁻ $(^{-}\text{II}^{a6}_{a4})$₃ I⁻ ⁻VI (⁻II⁻⁶) I^{-6}_{4} V⁻⁷ (I)

D12–5 Arpeggio singing from composite chord symbols

Sing the arpeggio in time with the metronome. Compare your response with the arpeggio you then hear and tally your errors. The starting tone is given for the first frame only. Goal: No more than five errors. When you have done this lesson, take Test D12.

1 I V^{-7} VI$^-$ ($^-$VI$^{a6}_{\substack{5\\3}}$) V^{-7} I ($^-$VI$^{a6}_{\substack{a4\\3}}$) V^{-7} I IV ($^-$II^{-6}) V^{-7}

2 I (VII^{d7}) I (II^{d7}) I^{-6} IV ($^-$II$^{a6}_{\substack{5\\3}}$) I VI$^-$ ($^-$VI^{d7}) V^{-7} ($^-$VI$^{a6}_{\substack{5\\3}}$)

3 I$^6_4$ V^{-7} I ($^-$VI$^{a6}_{\substack{a4\\3}}$) V I ($^-$VI) IV ($\underline{aIV^{d7}}$) V ($^-$VI^{d7}) V^{-7}

4 I ($^-$II^{-6}) V VI$^-$ ($^-$VI$^{a6}_{\substack{5\\3}}$) I$^6_4$ V^{-7} VI$^-$ ($^-$II^{-6}) I$^6_4$ V^{-7} I

5 ($^-$II$^{a6}_{\substack{a4\\3}}$) I (VII^{d7}) (II^{d7}) I VI$^-$ ($^-$VI$^{a6}_{\substack{a4\\3}}$) V VI$^-$ ($^-$II^{-6}) V^{-7} I

Soprano and Bass Dictation with Harmonic Analysis   SERIES D13

This series involves writing the soprano and bass lines and the harmonic analysis of phrases containing foreign chords. Consider each phrase to be entirely in one key. When a chord appears that is not a regular member of the key, identify it as a foreign chord. Do not consider any identifications that would involve a modulation.

The procedure for these lessons is the same as for the lessons in Series D9. Each phrase appears only once on the tape recording, but you may listen to each one as often as necessary by rewinding the tape. On Test D13 you will hear each phrase six times so you should attempt to complete each phrase in no more than six hearings.

For each phrase, you will find initial material followed by the answer, which is the complete phrase. You will need your own manuscript paper for these lessons. To do each frame, start by copying the initial material on your manuscript paper. Then listen to the phrase as many times as you need in order to write the soprano line, the bass line, the key, and the composite chord symbols, and to label the non-harmonic tones. When you have completed your response, compare it with the printed answer. Each lesson in this series should be done only once in preparation for Test D13. The test itself will serve to measure your achievement. Then if you wish to raise your test score, do each of the lessons once more and take the test again.

D13-1 Soprano and bass dictation with harmonic analysis

For each frame, copy the initial material on manuscript paper. Listen to the phrase several times. Write the soprano, the bass, the key, the composite chord symbols, and the non-harmonic tone labels. Do this lesson only once.

1

C   I V^{-7} VI^- IV $(\underline{II^{-6}_{d5}})$ V^{-7} I

2

G   I $(\underline{III^{-7}})$ VI^- $(\underline{I^{-7}})$ IV V^{-7} I

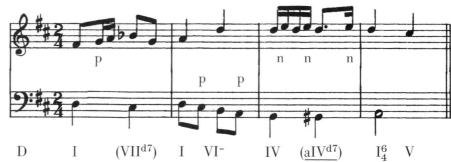

3

D   I (VII^{d7}) I VI^- IV $(\underline{aIV^{d7}})$ I^6_4 V

4

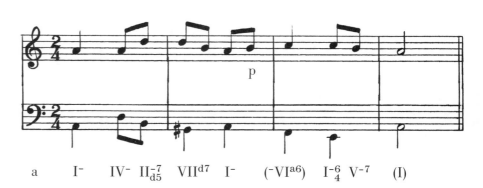

a I^- IV^- II^{-7}_{d5} VII^{d7} I^- $(^-VI^{a6})$ I^{-6}_4 V^{-7} (I)

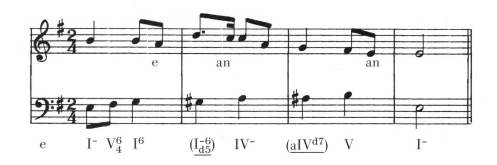

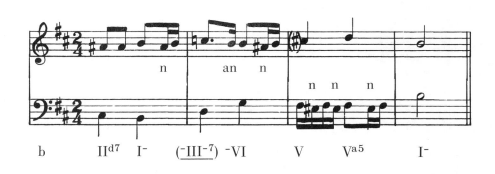

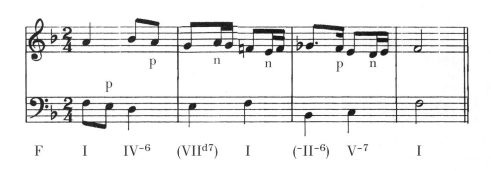

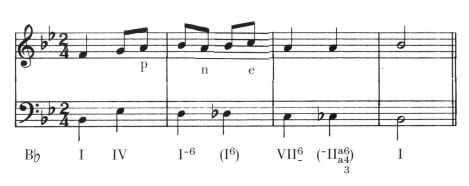

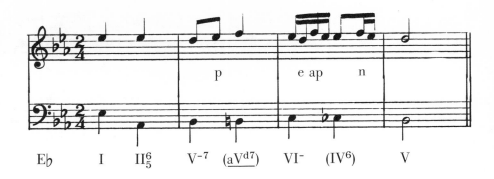

9

p   e ap   n

Eb   I II^6_5 V^{-7} (aV^{d7}) VI^- (IV^6) V

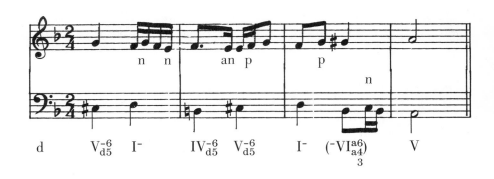

10

n n   an p   p   n

d V^{-6}_{d5} I^- IV^{-6}_{d5} V^{-6}_{d5} I^- $(-VI^{a6}_{a4})$ V
                                                                    3

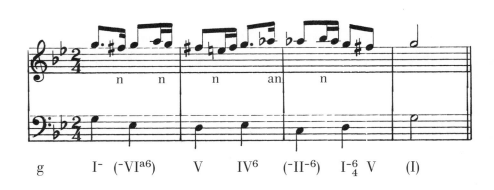

11

n n   n   an   n

g I^- $(-VI^{a6})$ V IV^6 $(-II^{-6})$ I^{-6}_4 V (I)

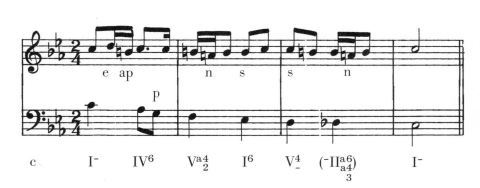

12

e ap   n s s   n

p

c I^- IV^6 V^{a4}_2 I^6 V^4_- $(-II^{a6}_{a4})$ I^-
                                                                    3

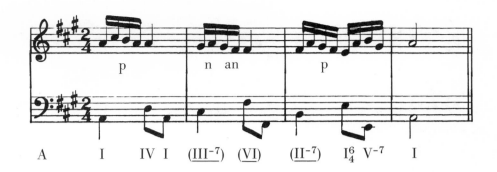

A   I   IV   I   (III^{-7})   (VI)   (II^{-7})   I$^6_4$ V^{-7} I

E   I   V^{-7} (I^{-7})   IV   (II^{d7})   V$^{-6}_{d5}$ V^{-7} I   V   I

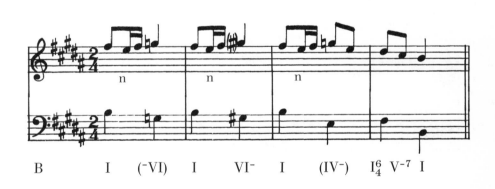

B   I   (−VI)   I   VI$^-$ I   (IV$^-$)   I$^6_4$ V^{-7} I

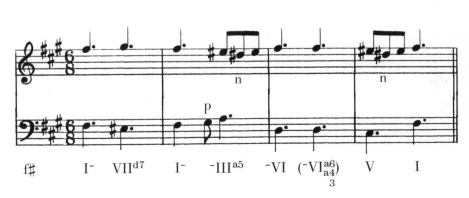

f♯   I$^-$ VII^{d7} I$^-$ −III^{a5} −VI   (−VI$^{a6}_{a4}$)   V   I
                                                                3

c♯   I⁻   ⁻VI   IV⁻⁷ V$^{a4}_2$ I⁶ (⁻VI^{a6}) I$^{-6}_4$ V⁻⁷ I⁻

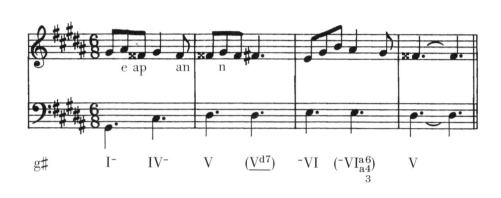

e ap   an   n

g♯   I⁻   IV⁻   V   (V^{d7})   ⁻VI   (⁻VI$^{a6}_{a4}$)   V
                                                                         3

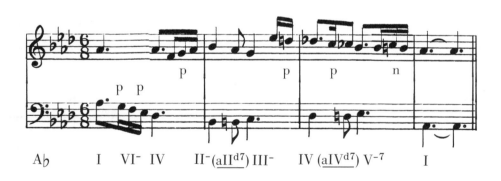

p p   p   p   p   n

p p

A♭   I   VI⁻ IV   II⁻ (aII^{d7}) III⁻   IV (aIV^{d7}) V⁻⁷   I

n   n

f   I⁻ V$^{-6}_{d5}$ I⁻   (aI^{d7}) II$^{-7}_{d5}$ VII^{d7} (⁻II^{a6})   I⁻

D13-2 Soprano and bass dictation with harmonic analysis

For each frame, copy the initial material on manuscript paper. Listen to the phrase several times. Write the soprano, the bass, the key, the composite chord symbols, and the non-harmonic tone labels. When you have done this lesson once, take Test D13.

bb   I⁻ IV⁻ II⁻   V   ⁻VI IV V⁻⁷   I⁻

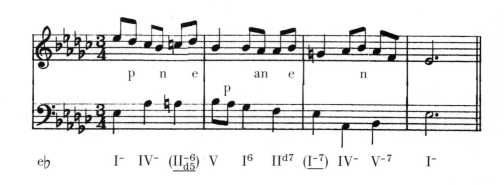

e♭   I⁻ IV⁻ (II⁻⁻⁶_d5) V   I⁶ IIᵈ⁷ (I⁻⁷) IV⁻ V⁻⁷   I⁻

B   I   (VI⁻⁷) (II⁻⁷) V⁻⁷ IV⁻⁶ V⁻⁶_d5 I (IV⁶)   V

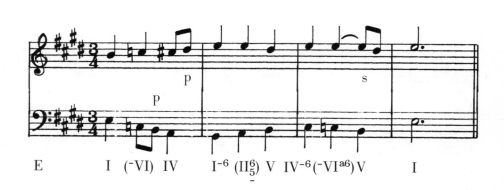

E   I (⁻VI) IV   I⁻⁶ (II⁻⁶_5) V IV⁻⁶(⁻VIᵃ⁶)V   I

388

9

g#   I⁻   IV⁻   V   (⁻III$_{d5}^{-6}$)⁻VI   IV⁻   (II$_{d5}^{-6}$)   I$_4^{-6}$ V⁻⁷   (I)

10

c#   I⁻   I⁶   (III^{d7})   IV⁻   (aIV^{d7})   V   ⁻VI   (⁻II⁻⁶)   V   I⁻

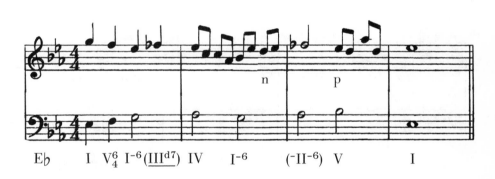

11

E♭   I   V$_4^6$ I^{-6} (III^{d7})   IV   I^{-6} (⁻II⁻⁶)   V   I

12

B♭   I   (⁻VI^{d7})   V⁻⁷   VI⁻   (VI$_{d5}^{-6}$)   II⁻   (⁻II$_{a4}^{a6}$)   I

13

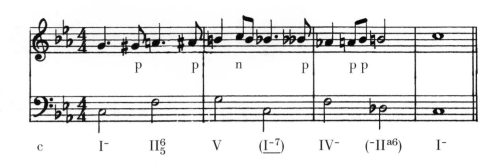

c   I⁻   II$_5^6$ V   (I^{-7})   IV⁻   (⁻II^{a6})   I⁻

14

g   I⁻   V   IV^{-6} V$_{d5}^{-6}$ I⁻   (⁻VI^{a6})   I$_4^{-6}$ V

15

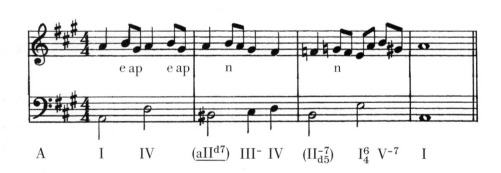

A   I   IV   (aII^{d7}) III⁻ IV   (II$_{d5}^{-7}$)   I$_4^6$ V^{-7} I

16

f♯   I⁻   IV⁻   II$_{-}^{-7}$ V   ⁻VI IV^{-6} VII^{d7} I⁻

17

 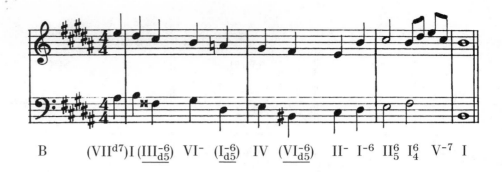

B   (VII^{d7})I (III$^{-6}_{d5}$) VI$^-$ (I$^{-6}_{d5}$) IV (VI$^{-6}_{d5}$) II$^-$ I^{-6} II$^6_5$ I$^6_4$ V^{-7} I

18

 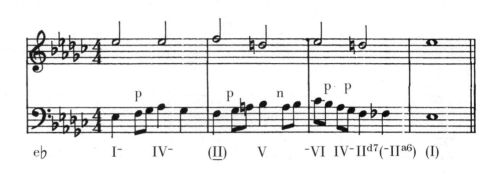

eb   I$^-$ IV$^-$ (II)   V $^-$VI IV$^-$II^{d7}($^-$II^{a6}) (I)

19

F#   I   (III)   (VI)   (II)   V($^-$VI^{a6})I$^6_4$V   I

20

E   I   III$^-$ IV (IV^{d7})I^{-6}(II^{d7})I $^-$VI   IV V^{-7} I

Test Record Sheet

TEST	MAXIMUM	LEVEL 1	LEVEL 2	LEVEL 3	SCORE AND DATE
D1	400	339	278	218	
D2	500	416	333	250	
D3	600	500	400	300	
D4	400	332	271	210	
D5	400	332	271	210	
D6	400	332	271	210	
D7a	300	250	208	166	
D7b	300	250	208	166	
D7c	300	250	212	175	
D7d	300	250	212	175	
D8	300	260	220	180	
D9	900	750	600	450	
D10	600	480	390	300	
D11	600	480	390	300	
D12	400	333	266	200	
D13	900	750	600	450	

All test scores are weighted to compensate for the varying length, difficulty, and importance of the series. The maximum score is the highest attainable score on a test. Level 1 represents high achievement. Level 2 represents moderate or average achievement. Level 3 represents low but significant achievement.

A 0
B 1
C 2
D 3
E 4
F 5
G 6
H 7
I 8
J 9